For my sisters,
Fereshteh
Farangis
Farzaneh
Faezeh

CONTENTS

PREFACE

Bang, bang, bang! A client knocks hard on the door of a lawyer's office. The secretary answers and listens to the client's case and realises that it would be profitable to take it on. With this information, the secretary approaches the lawyer and says that there is someone at the door who is very upset and wishes to see him. The lawyer asks if the secretary told the client how much a simple consultation with him costs. The secretary responded that they did and the client said that it was no problem. The lawyer then allowed the client to enter. The trade of legal rules, provisions, norms, principles, and morality is familiar to lawyers, who can act like real vampires. As it has been stated "lawyers are in the name of their volunteer corps dating from the threat of Napoleonic invasion, The Devil's Own." One should actually "love all lawyers, forgive us ours transgressions … and love all the lawyers, for we know not what they do." [1]

Someone pounds their fists against the law firm's door again, lamenting with pain. This time, it is the client's wife or child. Now, the profitable trade of criminal justice becomes stronger and begins in earnest. The lawyer certainly knows what they are going to talk about. There is a problem that can only be solved by them. The facts and truth of the case do not matter to the lawyer, rather it is the number of meetings and the hours of work they put in because these factors determine the lawyer's

---

[1] David Mellinkoff, *The Conscience of a Lawyer* (1973), p.1 including footnotes.

final paycheck. Here, the notion of conscience has no legal or moral validity for the lawyer. Rather, the lawyer is focused on how they will convince the criminal courts of their arguments.

It is important here to also address the burden of doppelgänger lawyers as it relates to sexual and moral sentiments. For example, at the Siracusa International Institute for Criminal Justice and Human Rights in 1993, almost 110 international lawyers and human rights experts gathered on behalf of the United Nations to speak about war crimes, rape, and crimes against humanity. However, the main subject of the conference was whether the rape of women during wartime constitutes an international crime. The conference was timely, the first meeting for the establishment of a permanent international criminal court or *ad hoc* international criminal tribunal coincided with the mass rape of Muslim women in Srebrenica. The women were tortured and mutilated for the pleasure of the soldiers and to satisfy their sexual urges. On the first day after speaking very enthusiastically about the brutal rape against Muslims in the middle of Europe, the chief *orchestrator* of this significant international meeting (nominated by the United Nations), a well-known international criminal lawyer, began his statements with:

Now, I will give the floor to the intelligent Italian government representative, who is the most beautiful woman in the Italian Parliament. Obviously, this introduction was not only irrelevant, but also humiliating and degrading for the representative because her physical attributes were highlighted in place of her intellectual contributions. She could surely feel the room full of men objectifying her during her brilliant speech. The next day, when I discussed this with one of the other participants – a German woman, her response was to say that such behaviour was the result of the typical *mentality of lawyers at international conferences*.

However, this very well-known international criminal lawyer was infamous among his international colleagues for his inability to control himself among women, despite being a professor of international criminal law and human rights law (a well-known wealthiest Lawyer) who had worked closely with various political authorities over the years. The vast majority of lawyers respected him, but largely only in order to preserve their international positions. The corpus of conscience in the profession of international lawyers does not necessarily rest on knowledge of the law, but rather on who-knows-who. An old Swedish saying tells us to take the right string and not pull it too hard, otherwise you will fall down in the mud. Much can be said about the uncontrollable sexual behaviour of lawyers — who are supposed to have profound ethical conscience and morality.[2] Thus, it is apt to quote here: "Lord love a lawyer? He must you know. Who else does? Lord loves a lawyer indeed. How else explain the mystery of survival, surrounded by so many natural enemies?"[3]

This book deals with the most significant aspects of the duties of lawyers under the system of international criminal jurisdiction and in general. The intention is to address certain notions of morality and codes of ethics which are necessary corollaries of the duties of lawyers. As a result, these notions serve vital roles in ensuring the proper application of international criminal justice and equality and respect for all, especially the victims of international crimes. The purpose is to underscore the fact that the respect of ethical norms is imperative for all lawyers under any criminal jurisdiction and that any falsification, misconduct, or flawed arguments based on unreliable evidence can harm the independence and integrity of justice, and thus create serious problems for the victims of international crimes.

An example of an instance of this was a case brought before the International Court of Justice regarding the acts of genocide carried out by the authorities of Myanmar against the Rohingya minority. In this case, a Canadian lawyer defended the actions of the Myanmar government by

---

[2] For specific examples please see the relevant chapters of this work.

[3] Mellinkoff, *The Conscience of a Lawyer*, note 1, p.1. "There is a vague popular belief that lawyers are necessarily dishonest. I say vague, because when we consider to what extent confidence and honours are reposed in and conferred upon lawyers by the people, it appears improbable that their impression of dishonesty is very distinct and vivid. Yet the impression is common, almost universal. Let no young man choosing the law for a calling for a moment yield to the popular belief -- resolve to be honest at all events; and if in your own judgment you cannot be an honest lawyer, resolve to be honest without being a lawyer. Choose some other occupation, rather than one in the choosing of which you do, in advance, consent to be a knave." Available online at http://www.abrahamlincolnonline.org/lincoln/speeches/lawlect.htm. See also Abraham Lincoln's Advice to Lawyers (abrahamlincolnonline.org). Abraham Lincoln's Advice to Lawyers (abrahamlincolnonline.org).

asserting: “my duty is to protect my client”, without seriously taking the international criminal responsibility of the perpetrators and their accountability for committing a crime of crimes older than the civilisation of mankind into consideration. Recently, the Uighur victims of genocide have been exploited by big powerful states to deliver their own messages through a puppet non-governmental tribunal. There is indeed no limit on big criminals taking advantage of the precarious situations of the victims of international crimes to serve their own political interests in the name of humanity, justice for victims, and ensuring the enforcement of the principles and provisions of international human rights law. All these inhumane actions are orchestrated by our international criminal lawyers.

In this book, I will present many arguments and codes of ethics which must be respected by all those who call themselves lawyers and not two-faced doppelgängers within the systems of national, regional, and international criminal justice. An ancient Japanese idiom also refers to the doppelgänger-nature of lawyers by asserting that “only lawyers and painters can turn white to black”. Additionally, More, in his book *Utopia,* stated that lawyers are "a sort of people, whose profession it is to disguise matters."[4] If we look further back in history, King Louis XII of France expressed that “lawyers use the law as shoemakers use leather; rubbing it, pressing it, and stretching it with their teeth, all to the end of making it fit their purposes."[5] A professional lawyer can consequently avoid the consequences for their own crimes by imprisoning the innocent. According to the American novelist and screenwriter, Mario Puzo, it is not unrealistic to assert that “A lawyer with a briefcase can steal more than a thousand men with guns.” Shakespeare, the great English playwright, went further with his statements against these doppelgängers by declaring that “The first thing we do, let’s kill all the lawyers.”

My purpose with these statements is not to reduce any lawyer in the world to their grave crimes, even those who are sitting in prison. Rather I wish to address the fact that the civilisation of mankind has seen serious

---

[4] T. More, *Utopia* 128 (G. Burnet trans. 1821) (1516).

[5] Tuli Kupferberg, *An Insulting Look at Lawyers Through the Ages*, 8 Juris Doctor (Oct./Nov. 1978), at 62.

problems within the system of criminal justice and the unlawful and immoral protection of those who should not be protected, thereby allowing them to receive impunity. Our intention is to increase the value of the judgments of criminal courts through trust, and not through connections and bribes. The criminal justice of the International Criminal Court (ICC) has been paralysed as a result of the strong powers receiving impunity while the victims of their crimes are left without reparations or justice. The big criminals have become the world leaders, and the weak criminals are the only ones who are prosecuted by the ICC.

All this has to be recognised with open eyes and open minds, without any influence from the doppelgängers of law and justice. We should remember that lawyers should not speak for themselves, but rather for the sake of international rights as guaranteed by the provisions of international human rights laws. As a result, lawyers should act to protect the provisions of human rights law and prevent impunity. A more common understanding of this imperative task of lawyers may relate to a greater understanding of their position in maintaining the balance of justice. The rule that lawyers are appointed to evaluate harm committed against the international community of nations should not be controlled by the personal belief of the counsel or through one-eyed-justice which supports the policies of the strong; as this leads to the kissing of the hands of Western powers and provides impunity for their serious violations of the system of international criminal justice.

There is a story which relates to the friends of justice and begins with a Spanish woman who saw Picasso in a park. She approached Picasso and asked him if he could paint a picture of her. Picasso stated that he did not have time but the woman begged him until he relented and finished the painting in five minutes. As she walked away, Picasso told her she had to pay $100,000. The woman was taken aback and stated that he had only worked on it for five minutes—to which Picasso replied that painting her picture had taken 30 years plus five minutes, as he had devoted his life to the craft at a cost. Similarly, a Chinese emperor asked one of his ministers to draw a dragon as a present for him. Ten years later, the minister asked the emperor if he could draw him a dragon, to which the emperor agreed.

Five minutes later, the minister presented the picture to the emperor who commented that he had asked for the painting 10 years ago and asked the minister why he had not drawn it immediately. The minister responded that it took him ten years to learn how to draw a dragon.

Yes, writing five books during the first half of the 2021 in my particular condition is the culmination of 47 years of reading, writing, and rewriting. *In order to write about impartial justice and the pure truth, one not only needs to experience life, but to also make great personal sacrifices for the victims of the world, for those who are suffering from brutality, and for those who will suffer from the barbarous criminal conducts of any political power. To maintain your independence and not work for profit from the statutes of lady-justice, is the only way to protect the conscience of justice and the essence of human unity from maltreatment.*

A pure international lawyer with a clear conscience of human essence:

- should never think about the victims' cultural, ethnic, or religious backgrounds, but rather about the brutal acts committed against them;
- should not ever implicitly or explicitly support any political agendas, but rather the norm of the united essence of man;
- should under no circumstances work with manipulated titles of human rights, but rather with the joint essence of humankind;
- should never support corruption and injustice, but rather the love for the maintenance of the true conscience of universal justice;
- should never have a bank account based on income, but rather a permanent bank account of humanity;
- should on no occasion evaluate the golden colour of money, but rather the demanding colour of the victims;
- should at no point receive payment for supporting core international crimes, but should rather function as an attorney without borders.

Throughout this work we will discuss the significant principles of the moral attitudes of lawyers.

I hereby would like to thank the rector magnificus (vice-chancellor) of Uppsala University (1989-1997), the Dean of Faculty of Law in Uppsala, the former president of Academia Europaea, and the Professor of Jurisprudence: Stig Strömholm— a man of knowledge who lives by academic codes of ethics and morality, for his continuous support since 1979, his thoughtful and positive encouragement, his honest letters to my non-governmental Institute of International Criminal Law, and for his honest and excellent statements made over the phone and in his office about my work to other professors while serving as Vice Chancellor.

F. Malekian
Uppsala, Sweden
Spring/Autumn 2021
f.malekian.in.crim.l@telia.com
f.malekian.in.crim.l@gmail.com

About the Book

Empowering ethical codes is vital in all branches of law because without these codes, we would be unable to differentiate between right and wrong in our personal judgments. Lawyers can either be the most precious or the most precarious parties in a criminal case—depending on the state of their conscience. In such cases, immorality replaces morality, and legal norms become pawns in a game, the goal of which is to serve the economic interests of lawyers. Lawyers become a greater threat to the truth when they support the establishment of special tribunals meant to hide the truth, such as was seen in Iraq, or when they receive payment in order to cover up genocide in places such as Myanmar and in the territories of the super powers. Such lawyers then turn around and condemn the same crimes in places such as China. They speak out against crimes against humanity carried out by the Iranian government, but do not say a single word about the crimes against humanity, war crimes, and genocide committed by the Saudi Arabian, Israeli, American, French, and British governments. Here, doppelgänger puppet attorneys do not present the true image of justice, but rather work to convince the international public that their brutal clients are innocent. The situation becomes even more complicated when we are dealing with very sensitive questions of international criminal justice under various criminal procedures directed by lawyers in the ICJ, the ICC, or in *ad hoc* tribunals. What is the nature of integrity, impartiality, conscience, truth, and payments, and why are lawyers increasingly being sponsored and directed by outsiders? This book reveals the forbidden truth— an embarrassment and moral weakness of conscience.

Chapter 1

The Basic Principles of the Profession of Lawyers

1.1. Rebuilding the Conscience of Lawyers

The notion of conscience is a very thoughtful question of ethics, which becomes even more sensitive when we argue about the moral and ethical duties of prosecutors, judges, and lawyers.[6] These three groups deal with the primary questions of justice, and should be conscious of the fact that their opinions can decide the fate of the parties involved in the cases that they work on. As we will examine, there are very significant differences between these three groups, based on the fact that the third group, lawyers,

---

[6] For the notion of morality and its development consult Kant Immanuel, *Answering the Question: What is Enlightenment?* (1784); Kant Immanuel, *Critique of Judgment* (1790); Immanuel Kant, *Critique of Pure Reason* (1781); Immanuel Kant, *Groundwork of the Metaphysic of Morals* (1785); Immanuel Kant, *Metaphysical Foundations of Natural Science* (1786); Immanuel Kant, *Opus Postumum* (1995); Immanuel Kant, *Perpetual Peace, and Other Essays on Politics, History, and Morals* (1784); Immanuel Kant, *Perpetual Peace: A Philosophical Sketch* (1795); Immanuel Kant, Practical Philosophy (editor: Mary J. Gregor, 1999); Immanuel Kant, *Prolegomena to Any Future Metaphysics* (1783); Immanuel Kant, *Religion within the Bounds of Bare Reason* (1793); Immanuel Kant, *The Critique of Practical Reason* (1788); Immanuel Kant, *The Metaphysics of Morals* (1797); Immanuel Kant, *The Only Possible Argument in Support of a Demonstration of the Existence of God* (1763); Immanuel Kant, *The Science of Right* (1790). For further literature on Kant see bibliography.

are usually paid by private individuals, unless a court has appointed the lawyer to represent the defendant due to the defendant's inability to pay for one themselves. However, even in such cases the lawyer is still paid. Thus, while most would view the first group (prosecutors) as being honest, lawyers are known to be swayed by money.

A professional lawyer can achieve impunity for their client and send innocent individuals to prison in their place. This implies the fact that prosecutors and judges have much greater responsibility than lawyers do because they must ensure that lawyers do not present false evidence or attain impunity for criminals.[7] "We should remember that law is a box of nonsense without the existence of the notion of morality and not violate the law of international morality."[8] As Martin Luther King stated, "the richer we have become materially, the poorer we become morally and spiritually. We have learned to fly in the air like birds and swim in the sea like fish, but we have not learned the simple art of living together as brothers."

Although the theory of the conscience of lawyers should have a framework consisting of similar ethical principles and codes, the reality is that the freedom of lawyers in the presentation of evidence is quite wide-ranging and its interpretation, application, and use varies depending on the person. Therefore, speaking about the ethical morality of lawyers is more a reference to the personal character of the lawyer as compared to those of judges and prosecutors.[9] The latter two are bound by the principle of impartiality, while the former cannot limit themselves to the code of the principle of impartiality based on the very fact that they have to represent the interests of their clients, and thus cannot remain impartial. *As a result, even if a lawyer realises that their client is guilty or that their rights were not harmed, that lawyer may still act in accordance with the wishes of their clients, thereby violating the code of ethics—simply because they are being*

---

[7] L Cummings Scott, 'Introduction: What Good are Lawyers?' in Scott L. Cummings (ed.), Paradox of Professionalism Lawyers and the Possibility of Justice (2011); William H. Simon, *The Practice of Justice: A Theory of Lawyers' Ethics* (1998).

[8] Farhad Malekian, *Classical Morality in International Peremptory Criminal Law* (Cambridge Scholars Publishing, 2018, 2021), p.2. For further examination of the notion of morality in national and international criminal law consult the bibliography of the book.

[9] *Id.*, pp.239-240.

paid to do so. That is why the image of a lawyer as a lawless individual is quite common across all cultures.

It may therefore be necessary to recover and rebuild the broken pillars of criminal jurisdiction and rebuild them upon the appropriate ethical conscience. However, the existence of such rules and principles of ethics is not by itself sufficient, as law must be comprehensive in order to be sufficient. Thus, there must be several ways to reach and enforce the system of law and its defence by lawyers that are not influenced by fees, politics, and culture. This ideal may be difficult to achieve, however it is not impossible as long as individual lawyers are prepared to serve with love for the implementation of justice and are not seeking to advance their economic interests. This is one of the most difficult tasks of the system of international human rights law— to find educated and capable lawyers who are fighting for the rights of victims and not solely seeking a big paycheck. Here, my arrow is pointed to the principle of morality.[10]

1.2. Dedication to Justice by Good Lawyers

The issue of the conscience of lawyers and the requirement of high morality cannot be resolved because even in ordinary situations, lawyers seek out competition and deny the rights of others in order to serve their interests and the interests of their clients. The situation becomes even more sensitive when the gate of justice is left open for everyone, regardless of their moral standards. However, this morality cannot be measured and stems from personal understanding, and all legal and moral rules of ethics can be denied and explained away by lawyers.[11]

---

[10] Farhad Malekian, *Conscience of Judges in International Criminal Law, The Heart of Judgments* (New York: Nova Science Publishers, 2021); see *also* Alasdair MacIntyre, *After Virtue: A Study in Moral Theory* (Notre Dame: University of Notre Dame Press, 1982).

[11] On morality principle consult Malekian, *Classical Morality in International Peremptory Criminal Law*, note 8; K. Robert Vischer, *Martin Luther King Jr. and the Morality of Legal Practice: Lessons in Love and Justice* (2014); David Lyons, 'Moral Aspects of Legal Theory' in Kenneth Himma and Brian Bix (eds) *Law and Morality* (2005); A. R. C. Duncan, *Practical Reason and Morality* (Nelson, 1957); Luvios Lon Fuller, *The Morality of Law* (Yale Law University, 2nd ed., 1969); Joseph Raz, *Ethics in the Public Domain: Essays in*

An international criminal lawyer will often take the time to re-educate themselves and study the law. The legal profession actually requires practicing lawyers to have deep knowledge of various legal disciplines, particularly for specialists such as international criminal lawyers. The duty of an international criminal lawyer is to counsel, advise, and represent different agencies, in particular government agencies. This means that politics cannot be avoided and can impact the lawyer's actions and decisions. As a result, the lawyer is unable to remain independent and has to comply with the orders of government authorities or risk losing their job. It is very rare for lawyers, especially international criminal lawyers, to dismiss themselves from a case that they had to compete for with others in order to take it on. This is where the system of international criminal law and the body and principles of international human rights law lose their independence because of the actions of the lawyers involved.[12] As a result, the slogan of freedom and equality for all becomes meaningless.

Therefore, an international lawyer needs to prepare themselves for the compromising of rights, and that they may be forced to follow powerful criminal requirements in certain sensitive situations. The result is often catastrophic because lawyers become the enemies of the victims in order to serve their personal interests. These enemies i.e., lawyers, do not necessarily need to be involved in the commission of international crimes, barbarous acts of crimes against humanity, war crimes, genocide, or the torture and rape of individuals. However, by supporting and defending the criminal conducts of criminals, lawyers aid and assist directly or indirectly in putting salt in the wounds of the victims and deny them justice.[13]

---

the Morality of Law and Politics (Oxford: Oxford University Press, 1994); K. Robert Vischer, *Martin Luther King Jr. and the Morality of Legal Practice: Lessons in Love and Justice* (2014).

[12] Examine Farhad Malekian, *Documents on the Principles of International Human Rights* (Stockholm: Norstedts Juridik, 2007); Frederik Harhoff, 'It's All in the Process: Reflections on the Relation Between International Criminal Trials and International Humanitarian Law', 78 *NORDIC J. INT'L L.* (2010); R. Nieto-Navia, *International Peremptory Norms (Jus cogens) and International Humanitarian Law* (2011); Javaid Rehman, *International Human Rights Law* (London and New York: Longman Pub Group, 2nd ed., 2010).

[13] William Schabas, in his remorseless, sponsored statement against the victims of Myanmar in the International Court of Justice stated that "22. Myanmar submits that the information in the Application and in the materials invoked in its support essentially the reports of the Fact-Finding Mission, provide ample evidence to indicate alternative inferences alternative

Lawyers do not actually need to directly participate in the military attacks against occupied countries or other regions. It is sufficient that these lawyers are working for injustice and argue to the international public that the acts of big political parties against certain nations were justified. Accepting inhuman acts and defending them through various legal arguments equates to the commission of crimes against humanity, and anyone who presents such arguments can be identified as an enemy of mankind. A good lawyer, an honest citizen of the earth, or a good individual would prefer to go to jail or lose money than to sell justice.

A few examples of such good individuals include Mahatma Gandhi, Patrice Lumumba, Martin Luther King Jr., Malcolm X, Rosa Parks, Mohammed Ali, Mohammad Mosaddegh, Bertrand Russell, and Mother Teresa. Some of these individuals were also great lawyers with a strong quality of universal conscience, fighting for the sake of men and their united essence. A lawyer who loses their independence is actually in the stage of *nobodiness,* as their *somebodiness* has been sacrificed in exchange for money and to protect the oppressors. This was seen with the establishment of the fake special tribunal for Saddam Hussein, as well as with the case of the Myanmar genocide against the Rohingya minority brought before the ICJ. A further example of such lawyers includes those who protect and justify the brutal, uncivilised conducts of the Chinese government against the Muslim Uighurs.[14]

---

explanations for the alleged conduct, other than that it is the product of genocidal intent. Should the Court agree that there is ample support for an alternative explanation, then it cannot but conclude that the Application has no reasonable chance of success on the merits. Not a 50 per cent chance. Not a 25 per cent chance. No chance. If there is a reasonable alternative explanation for the intent behind the alleged acts then the Application simply cannot succeed. And if it cannot succeed, it is not "plausible" for the purposes of a request for provisional measures." See 'Professor William Schabas's Full Transcript in Myanmar's defense in genocide trial', https://elevenmyanmar.com/news/professor-william-schabass-full-transcript-in-myanmars-defense-in-genocide-trial. How a lawyer can rely on evidence presented by criminal powerful authorities relates to the moral and conscious capacity of the lawyer to make lies into the truth and the truth into lies.

[14] "A clear example of this is the British puppet, Nice, and his opus of injustice against the Uighur victims, which he presented as justice." Farhad Malekian, *Orchestrating Diversity in International Criminal Justice* (New York: Nova Science Publishers, 2021), p.113. Consult also Farhad Malekian, *Conscience of Prosecutors in International Criminal Law, the Heart of the Heart of the Matter* (New York: Nova Science Publishers, 2021); Malekian, *Conscience of Judges in International Criminal Law, the Heart of Judgements*, note 10.

1.3. Rates Affecting the Conscience of Lawyers

It would be naive to assert that lawyers should not accept responsibility for the duties that they take on under the supervision and control of their clients. Certainly, when a lawyer accepts a case, they are happy to receive additional payment, and the payment is important to the lawyer and their firm. There are however different ways for lawyers to be paid. The nature of payment is usually discussed in the first meeting between lawyers and clients and the agreement on compensation has a large impact on how much one will ultimately pay for the firm's services. The agreement may also be modified as the investigation progresses, since the case may go on for longer or require more work than anticipated. Generally, legal fees vary and depend on several case-dependent factors.

The fee may therefore not be fixed, and the final payment amount may depend on the amount of time the lawyer ends up devoting to the case. Additionally, many other factors also have direct connections to the case, and may therefore affect the fee amount. Thus, the scope of the case, the reputation of the lawyer, the reputation of the case, and the lawyer's professional ability – including their past experiences, may also impact how much money the lawyer receives in the end. All this means that the serious engagement of a lawyer in a case demands increased compensation for their work. Therefore, unique cases may require even greater compensation. All these factors are measured against one another not only by the lawyer or attorney, but also by the client.

A lawyer who agrees to take on a case also takes on the responsibility for the case and for their client, the public, and the system of criminal justice. It is however difficult to prove that a lawyer has indirectly participated in the criminal conduct of the accused by hiding the truth and taking responsibility for their actions or being held responsible for their criminal conspiracy.[15] Although it may be impossible to say that a lawyer

---

[15] In addition, the "argument concerning the supposed existence of pluralism as claimed by international criminal lawyers is seriously weakened by the enforcement of Chapter VII of the UN Charter. Our point here is not to diminish the strengths of the UN Charter and the value of the organisation, but to highlight the fact that the most sensitive international issues

became involved in the criminal conduct of their client, it is also true that under the provisions of criminal law of all states in the world, complicity is also considered criminal conduct. This does not necessarily mean that the lawyer directly participated in criminal conduct, but they may have presented false evidence or concealed the truth in order to assist the criminal. This is especially clear in cases where the lawyer has received a large payment in exchange for remaining silent and hiding the truth. Some may even maintain that moral categories in the office of the lawyer and how they explain their conduct under the procedures of the relevant criminal case are natural aspects of the duties of a lawyer, since they are compelled to remain silent.

1.4. Abstaining Due to Financial Reasons

Refraining from holding certain individuals criminally responsible due to the competing financial interests of the lawyer violates the ethics of criminal justice. In other words, there are certain ethical duties which require lawyers to speak the truth and not violate the judicial conscience of criminal justice or its impartiality. One may argue that lawyers cannot be impartial and are ethically and legally responsible for protecting their clients. However, this does not extend to cases where lawyers conceal or destroy evidence in order to protect their clients. However, lawyers, as we will examine, have the right to protect the accused from criminal accusations and to work to mitigate their punishment.

The situation may seem very complicated if a lawyer knows that their client has committed a crime but still plans to clear them of all criminal accusations and avoid punishment. Nonetheless, according to the philosophy of criminal justice and criminal procedures, all those who are deeply engaged in the system of criminal provisions are required to uphold

---

are exclusively being decided upon by the five permanent members who are guided by their interests." Malekian, *Orchestrating Diversity in International Criminal Justice*, note 14, p.113.

the basic principles of criminal ethics and moral codes.[16] Protection of an accused individual does not necessarily equate to the denial of their criminality and the disrespect of the rights of the victims. *Therefore, to assert that lawyers either should or should not be held accountable for their conduct and for hiding the true evidence about the guilt of the accused means believing that the system of criminal justice officially protects financially strong individuals.*

Although we do not deny that criminal justice must treat all its subjects equally, the fact is that the rich are able to receive impunity while their victims do not receive justice. Thus, any suggestion that lawyers should not be held criminally responsible for their complicity does not consequently imply their exemption from ethical or moral judgment if they seriously violate the system of judicial conscience. It may rather be that a superseding moral judgment must be taken into consideration when lawyers examine the ethical considerations of a case and the immoral treatment of the victims. A lawyer should realise that criminal jurisdiction is not a bazaar where arguments can be sold, although in practice, it is, and that is one of the main reasons why we look for a good person and a good lawyer. A good lawyer is one that is able to convince the judge and jury that their arguments are correct and that the guilty are innocent and cannot be punished. This not only occurs in all cases of national criminal justice, but also in international cases where financial interests are at play.

Thus, in reality, money buys innocence. The question is: how can the philosophy or the notion of justice be open to all individuals, if good counsel is not made available to the accused? In other words, guilt is usually a question of the lawyer's ability to convince the judge and jury of innocence, not the actual facts of a case. Moreover, someone may be paid to confess to a crime in order to protect someone else. They may accept guilt, even if money is not involved, due to personal circumstances and the desire to protect loved ones. Judges, prosecutors, or lawyers may take

---

[16] Consult L. M. Baum, 'Pursuing Justice in a Climate of Moral Outrage: An Evaluation of the Rights of the Accused in the Rome Statute of the International Criminal Court,' 19 *Wisconsin International Law Journal* (2001); P.M. Bekker, 'The undefended accused/defendant: a brief overview of the development of the American, American Indian and South African Positions' *XXIV CILSA* (1991), pp.151-188.

advantage of such situations and relationships in order to protect wealthier and more powerful clients. This implies that our judgments, and those of lawyers, may be made prior to criminal jurisdiction being established, therefore banishing the love for true justice.[17] Thus, *lawyers extract the words from law books and manipulate them in the courtroom.*

A great part of the study of law is the study of rules and how to interpret them, which is why most counsels or defence lawyers play with the words of the law and manipulate them to serve their needs. Although a lawyer is bound by legal rules, the moral conscience of a lawyer plays the most significant role in a case. Additionally, since the morality of the lawyer is strongly connected with the compensation they receive, they may sometimes come to conclusions which others would not in order to receive their payment. Thus, one may be able to escape the law by employing certain debate strategies in the courtroom. This can only be performed by a professional lawyer and someone who is willing to pay them a hefty price for their services. The law of reason or the law of the statute may be guided by the law of the moral conscience of the lawyer— however, this is not always the case.[18]

The interpretation of certain legal questions and definitions in order to create loopholes in the law can be achieved by skilled lawyers who then receive large payments in return. Although a powerful government may be guilty of committing intentional crimes, their superior position should not be a reason for granting government officials impunity and allowing them

---

[17] Moreover, "Impartial sympathy judgement is the major implication of the principle of love. It requires the judges to take the moral perspective of all the parties to legal process. A judge has to use all her or his ability of imagination and intuition to penetrate the inner world of these who will be affected by judicial decision. A judge must endeavour to understand their motives and emotions. Sympathy does not require the judge to deny or disregard their own moral beliefs and convictions. What it does require is that a judge should not accept his on moral convictions as the only true and correct ones, but be ready to engage into dialogue with the moral world of another. The essence of sympathy judgement lies in genius willingness to do good to the persons affected by judicial decisions through understanding and critical acceptance of the moral perspective of those persons. Only though having such understanding and acceptance is a judge able to give a proper evaluation of the facts and interpretation of the relevant legal rules." Alexander Nikolaevich Shytov, Conscience and Love in Making Judicial Decisions (2001), p.xiv.

[18] Read Alasdair MacIntyre, *After Virtue: A Study in Moral Theory* (Notre Dame: University of Notre Dame Press, 1982). Consult also Alasdair MacIntyre, *A Short History of Ethics: a History of Moral Philosophy from the Homeric Age to the Twentieth Century* (1965).

to escape from international criminal justice. If the rules of international criminal justice are not respected, and a lawyer helps officials escape accountability, the lawyer also becomes an accomplice to the crimes. A lawyer who helps a guilty person go free after committing international crimes is therefore complicit in the commission of the relevant crimes. This is because the most important duty of lawyers in the systems of national and international criminal justice is not to establish or disprove guilt, but to present a case and allow the processes of criminal justice to be carried out appropriately.[19] We should not forget the fact that a lawyer is not a judge, and their judgements should thus play no role in court proceedings. A lawyer should serve as an advocate and not pass judgements about the provisions of international crimes, as they should be determined by the court.

1.5. Ethical Stages of the Conscience of Lawyers

The ethical conscience of lawyers is based on the moral standard of the lawyer and how they see and evaluate the systems of criminal justice and international criminal justice. Ethics and morality speak about righteousness and direct our actions to ensure that we do not violate moral principles.[20] We must then ask: what are moral principles really? How can we identify that such moral principles are correct? Is it legally and practically permissible for us to determine the difference between right and wrong? These questions are particularly relevant when it comes to financial matters and people's motivations for becoming lawyers. Certainly, law firms are established to make money, and this money comes from those who find themselves at conflict with other parties. The clients

---

[19] Farhad Malekian, *Trading Virginity of International Criminal Justice* (New York: Nova Science Publishers, 2020), pp.8-9.

[20] Examine Rosalyn Higgins, 'Ethics and International Law', 23 *Leiden Journal of International Law* (2010), pp.283-287; Elena Cima, 'Ethical Conduct in International Criminal Courts: Whose Ethics?', *American Journal of International Law*(2019), pp.296-301. Available online at https://www.researchgate.net/; H. Jefferson Powell., *Constitutional Conscience: The Moral Dimension of Judicial Decision* (.(University of Chicago Press, 2008

must negotiate the criminal components of the state or the system of criminal mechanism which requires the prosecution and punishment of certain individuals. Here, the lawyer or counsel or attorney serves as the representative of their client and has to defend them and work to clear their name.

Thus, what one lawyer regards as fair and exemplary, is to take their defence and act according to a standard of criminal justice. This means that they must not only respect the local standard of ethics, but must also have the capacity to act correctly. Some of the common ethical principles which guide lawyers and relate to their level of conscience include:

a) Lawyers should always fulfil their professional obligations in order to respect the dignity of the legal profession,
b) Lawyers should not violate their oath to uphold the truth, and the dignity and independence of criminal justice,
c) A lawyer should always act conscientiously and with full moral responsibility,
d) Professional dignity always has to be taken into account in the public and private lives of lawyers,
e) The legal activities of a lawyer must be carried out in accordance with the provisions of the relevant country,
f) Any psychological pressure on the part of the client should not be a reason to issue more charges against them and exacerbate the situation,
g) The previous legal position of an attorney in the administration of justice should not be used to strengthen their present office,
h) The impartiality of lawyers and attorneys constitutes one of the significant ethical principles of the profession,
i) The belief and conscience of lawyers in the truth plays a dominant role in the presentation of criminal cases,
j) An attorney is the protector of the rights of citizens and legal entities, thus their relationships with their clients and the opposing party/attorney must be conducted in compliance with the rights of citizens,

k) A lawyer should think before they speak in order to not offend anyone,
l) Lawyers must uphold moral and ethical codes and not discriminate against anyone in private or in public,
m) A lawyer has to foster trust not only with their clients, but also with the public,
n) The respect of the principles of international human rights law must be a guiding light for a lawyer,
o) All endeavours which are undertaken by attorneys should be compatible with the legal profession,
p) An attorney should not choose their clients based on their background or based on cultural, religious, or other social considerations,
q) An attorney should be very cautious and not disclose information about a case to the opposing parties,
r) All fees issued by a lawyer should align with regulations,
s) No under-the-table payments should be accepted,
t) A lawyer is responsible for keeping up to date with new laws,
u) All advice given by lawyers should align with the law,
v) A lawyer should avoid advertising to attract new clients,
w) A lawyer should not attract new clients based on the dissemination of misinformation,
x) Any advertising done by a lawyer should follow domestic regulations and not mislead the public,
y) A lawyer should respect the regulations of the Bar Association and relevant codes of ethical conduct,
z) A lawyer should respect any warnings or disciplinary decisions issued by the Bar,
aa) These warnings may also be applicable to other people working in the firm of the lawyer,
bb) Any expression made by a lawyer which questions the legislation must respect the rules of professional ethics,
cc) A lawyer is responsible for the conduct of all members of their office.

1.6. Basic Principles on the Role of Lawyers

In order to regulate the ethical rules which establish the scope of the duties of lawyers and their moral, ethical, and legal responsibilities, many nations have passed laws to regulate the duties of lawyers and their obligations towards the judicial system, victims, and clients.[21] One of the most well-known international agreements on the function and duties of lawyers is the *Basic Principles on the Role of Lawyers* (BPRL) adopted by the United Nations Congress on the Prevention of Crime and the Treatment of Offenders.[22] The intention of this document is clarified in its preamble as it compels UN members to undertake certain measures in order to protect the rights of those who find themselves the subjects of criminal jurisdiction.

The BPRL refers to the UN Charter and its significant function in establishing and promoting conditions under which justice can be maintained, and the respect for human rights and fundamental freedoms without any distinction as to race, sex, language, or religion can be encouraged. It also compels members of the United Nations to uphold the important role of the Universal Declaration of Human Rights and the International Covenant on Civil and Political Rights in enshrining the principles of equality before the law, including the presumption of innocence and the right to a fair and public hearing by an independent and impartial court. Accordingly, these are some of the basic principles which protect individuals who have been accused of crimes.

Among other documents that are referred to in the BPRL are those which work to prevent violations of human rights under specific circumstances. Such documents include the International Covenant on Economic, Social, and Cultural Rights, which protects the rights of

---

[21] See also appendix. Examine Michael Asimow, 'When the Lawyer Knows the Client is Guilty: David Mellinkoff's 'The Conscience of a Lawyer'', Legal Ethics, Literature, and Popular Culture, SSRN Electronic Journal DOI:10.2139/ssrn.948291; Mellinkoff, *The Conscience of a Lawyer*, note 1.

[22] The Basic Principles on the Role of Lawyers, Adopted by the *Eighth United Nations Congress on the Prevention of Crime and the Treatment of Offenders*, Havana, Cuba 27 August to 7 September 1990. https://www.ohchr.org/en/professionalinterest/pages/roleoflawyers.aspx.

individuals in certain circumstances, and the Body of the Principles for the Protection of All Persons under Any Form of Detention or Imprisonment (1988), which protects the rights of detained individuals, including their right to counsel. The BPRL also refers to the merit of documents relating to the Standard Minimum Rules for the Treatment of Prisoners and the fact that safeguards guaranteeing the protection of those facing the death penalty reaffirm the rights of everyone suspected of, or charged with, a crime to which capital punishment may be applicable. The Declaration of the Basic Principles of Justice for Victims of Crime and Abuse of Power, which concerns access to justice, fair treatment, restitution, and compensation and assistance for victims of crimes, is another document which is referenced by the BPRL. All these references in the BPRL are strengthened by reference to the merit of the professional associations of lawyers and the need for such associations to cooperate with governmental and other institutions in order to support justice and the public interest.

1.7. Major Recommended Professional Principles

The intention of the Basic Principles on the Role of Lawyers is generally to assist Member States in promoting and ensuring the proper conduct of lawyers. A further goal is also to protect lawyers and those acting as lawyers without having the formal status thereof.

The BPRL encourages the existence of professional associations of lawyers and encourages lawyers to form and join self-governing professional associations which represent the interests of lawyers, promote education and training, and protect their professional integrity. There should be an executive body in every professional association which should be elected by its members without external interference. The professional associations of lawyers should work together with governments in order to ensure that everyone has effective and equal access to legal services. It should also be ensured that lawyers are able to, without inappropriate intervention, assist and counsel their clients with due regard for the requirements of law and in accordance with recognised professional standards and ethics.

A further obligation for governments is to provide development programs, such as educational training programs, which qualify and train professional lawyers and instruct them about their ethical duties as per international human rights law and fundamental freedoms. Moreover, governments, professional associations of lawyers, and educational institutions should ensure that they do not discriminate against potential lawyers based on their race, colour, sex, ethnic origin, religion, political or other opinion, national or social origin, property status, birth, economic, or any other status. The only exception to this principle is if a nation requires its lawyers to be citizens of said nation. If certain groups which have been the victims of past discrimination exist within the territory of a state, governments, professional associations of lawyers, and educational institutions should create opportunities for candidates from these groups to enter into the legal profession and be trained as lawyers.

The Basic Principles also consider access to lawyers and legal services to be significant for the protection of accused parties.[23] This means that all individuals are entitled to request the help, service, or support of a lawyer chosen to protect the rights of individuals during criminal proceedings. Accordingly, it is also the duty of governments to ensure that efficient procedures and responsive equal access mechanisms are provided for all individuals within their territory who are subject to their jurisdiction. Services should be provided to all individuals without discrimination on the basis of race, colour, ethnic origin, sex, language, religion, political or other opinion, national or social origin, property status, birth, economic, or other status. Governments are also obliged to ensure that lower income individuals receive the necessary financial support for the aforementioned services. Accordingly, it is also a duty of governments and professional associations of lawyers to promote programmes which inform the public of their rights and the important role of lawyers in protecting their fundamental freedoms.

---

[23] For the text of Basic Principles on the Role of Lawyers see appendix.

The BPRL also requires that special safeguards be set in place by governments concerning criminal justice matters. This means that they should ensure that all individuals within their criminal jurisdiction are aware of their right to be assisted by a lawyer of their own choosing upon arrest or detention, including when charged with a criminal offence during ongoing trial procedures. Anyone who does not have a lawyer should receive one, such that the lawyer can provide them with their experience and knowledge during criminal proceedings. The intention here is to provide effective legal assistance to those who have been arrested or detained. If the accused is unable to afford the services of a lawyer, then financial assistance must be provided. It is also a duty of governments to ensure that anyone who is arrested or detained has prompt access to a lawyer. This access should not be dependent on the type of criminal charges faced by the accused. A lawyer should be provided to the accused no more than 48 hours after their initial arrest or detention. The accused should also be provided with adequate opportunity to visit and consult with a lawyer without delay. In particular, governments should not impede or censor the meetings between the accused and their lawyer, and all matters should be handled with complete confidentiality.

1.8. Basic Principal Obligations of Lawyers

The Basic Principles on the Role of Lawyers (BPRL) adopted by the United Nations Congress on the Prevention of Crime and the Treatment of Offenders includes a number of duties and responsibilities for lawyers to follow in order to ensure that the mechanism of criminal justice is respected and not violated during legal proceedings of criminal justice. These duties and responsibilities are connected with other parts of the BPRL and are thus integral parts of the document and work to prevent any discrimination based on race, colour, ethnic origin, sex, language, religion, political or other opinion, national or social origin, property status, birth, economic, or other status.

All basic principles which guide the conduct of lawyers should be based on certain codes of professional conduct which are necessary and essential for the performance of the duties and responsibilities of lawyers. This means that the BPRL requires the establishment of legal professional codes through appropriate channels or the legislation of a country. Accordingly, the Code should respect and not contradict national law, custom, or the international standards and norms for codes of professional ethics. The BPRL also protects lawyers who may face charges or complaints against them while performing their duties. Lawyers, like other accused individuals, should have the right to their own lawyer, fair and appropriate procedures, and a fair hearing. Any disciplinary proceedings against lawyers should be carried out by an impartial disciplinary committee established by legal professionals or an independent statutory authority. These hearings should be held before a court and be subject to an independent judicial review and to the code of professional conduct. With these elementary provisions, the Basic Principles on the Role of Lawyers outlines the duties and responsibilities of lawyers in the following list:

> 12. Lawyers shall at all times maintain the honour and dignity of their profession as essential agents of the administration of justice.
> 13. The duties of lawyers towards their clients shall include:
> (a) Advising clients as to their legal rights and obligations, and as to the working of the legal system in so far as it is relevant to the legal rights and obligations of the clients;
> (b) Assisting clients in every appropriate way, and taking legal action to protect their interests;
> (c) Assisting clients before courts, tribunals or administrative authorities, where appropriate.
> 14. Lawyers, in protecting the rights of their clients and in promoting the cause of justice, shall seek to uphold human rights and fundamental freedoms recognized by national and international law and shall at all times act freely and diligently in accordance with the law and recognized standards and ethics of the legal profession.
> 15. Lawyers shall always loyally respect the interests of their clients.

Guarantees for the functioning of lawyers

16. Governments shall ensure that lawyers (a) are able to perform all of their professional functions without intimidation, hindrance, harassment or improper interference; (b) are able to travel and to consult with their clients freely both within their own country and abroad; and (c) shall not suffer, or be threatened with, prosecution or administrative, economic or other sanctions for any action taken in accordance with recognized professional duties, standards and ethics.

17. Where the security of lawyers is threatened as a result of discharging their functions, they shall be adequately safeguarded by the authorities.

18. Lawyers shall not be identified with their clients or their clients' causes as a result of discharging their functions.

19. No court or administrative authority before whom the right to counsel is recognized shall refuse to recognize the right of a lawyer to appear before it for his or her client unless that lawyer has been disqualified in accordance with national law and practice and in conformity with these principles.

20. Lawyers shall enjoy civil and penal immunity for relevant statements made in good faith in written or oral pleadings or in their professional appearances before a court, tribunal or other legal or administrative authority.

21. It is the duty of the competent authorities to ensure lawyers access to appropriate information, files and documents in their possession or control in sufficient time to enable lawyers to provide effective legal assistance to their clients. Such access should be provided at the earliest appropriate time.

22. Governments shall recognize and respect that all communications and consultations between lawyers and their clients within their professional relationship are confidential.

1.9. Ethical Conscience not to Raise Charges

There are certain norms in the code of ethics and in the customs of nations which imply that works and goods have certain values, and those values should not be overestimated or exploited in emergency situations, such as during a pandemic. Although this example is far removed from the work done by lawyers, and in particular trial attorneys, the fact is that there are always certain limits for the costs and for the evaluation of the work of the attorney. In other words, a crisis in the heart of the client must not be exploited for financial gain by attorneys. Therefore, every matter must be handled logically in the office of the attorney and in accordance with the prevailing code of ethical fees in the relevant country. This is particularly significant when an attorney chooses their clients and agrees to take on their cases and work with clear ethical conscience.[24]

Thus, in all circumstances, the attorney is responsible for not increasing or creating unnecessary procedural costs for their client. Moreover, a trial attorney whose failure to succeed creates more problems and costs for the client should accept responsibility and consider a reduction of the final fee. A failure here refers to any misunderstanding on the part of the attorney, a lack of certain knowledge, the use of other facilities which were not necessary, or any cost incurred during proceedings which resulted from delinquency on the part of the attorney. An attorney should represent and defend their clients conscientiously and with the intention of defending their rights and winning the case. This implies that they should use all the necessary legal means to do so, as long as they remain within the realm of the procedures of justice as is considered necessary for the protection of the attorney and their defence. There must therefore be a balance between the means and the end, which should be fairly compensated. However, an attorney should not identify themselves with the client but rather with the domain of the integrity of a counsel and a defence attorney.

In any unconventional situation that an attorney may face before or during a trail, they have to consult with the client and inform them that they may have to pay more in order to win the case. This situation still varies upon the calculations and the examination and evaluation of the situation by the attorney, especially when the client is detained and is

---

[24] Cima, 'Ethical Conduct in International Criminal Courts: Whose Ethics?, note 20, pp.296-301. https://www.researchgate.net/publication/335848353_Ethical_Conduct_in_International_Criminal_Courts_Whose_Ethics.

unable to help with the case and has to blindly follow the instructions given by their attorney. That is why we speak about the code of ethics which must be upheld in all procedures of justice. Thus, we must protect the framework of jurisdiction, judgements, and justice, which cannot be criticised by the public or by the sphere of judicial conscience.

1.10. Woe unto Lawyers

The only function of the system of justice is to find the truth. If the truth is revealed, then all other matters will become clear as well. Sometimes it takes time to uncover the truth because it is in our nature to bury it. That is why lawyers can be used as scapegoats if a problem cannot be solved. This means in cases where we have begged for the implementation of justice, asked for the manifestation of our rights, required that our violated rights be compensated, or have cried out against large injustices— the lawyers have been employed as scapegoats.[25]

A lawyer generally knows that their duty is to prevent the accused from being found guilty and to escape punishment. This is not a theory, but rather the way in which lawyers have to work and pursue their own interests. Historically, this intention of lawyers has also been proven by many factors and it is not without reason that it has been correctly stated "Woe unto you, lawyers! for ye have taken away the key of knowledge: ye entered not in yourselves, and them that were entering in ye hindered." This expression solemnly means that *even Jesus believed "Woe unto you, lawyers..." and that human beings seeking justice seek an honest man*

---

[25] This can be seen in the concluding words of William Schabas in the Myanmar genocide case under the procedures of the International Court of Justice. "To conclude, Mr. President, Your Excellencies, the Application fails utterly to address the essential issue of the specific intent to perpetrate genocide. As the Court has said repeatedly in its recent case law, where proof of genocidal intent depends upon inferences drawn from a pattern of conduct, other explanations for the mental element of the crime must be excluded. The Application, and the oral submissions by counsel, do not even speak to this essential point. *For that reason alone, the request for provisional measures should be rejected*. Mr. President, Your Excellencies, *that concludes my observations*." Professor William Schabas's Full Transcript in Myanmar's defense in genocide trial', https://elevenmyanmar.com/news/professor-william-schabass-full-transcript-in-myanmars-defense-in-genocide-trial.

rather than a knowledgeable lawyer. This statement of Jesus is over 2,000 years old, yet is still valid today. This is how the profession of lawyer was described by a man who represented the spiritual essence of humanity.

According to pure humanity in the name of the service of the nature of man, natural law states that a lawyer should be lawyer of conscience, a lawyer of legislation, a lawyer of humanity, a lawyer of criminal law, a lawyer of truth, and a lawyer of love. There is a story in which a lawyer asked Jesus:

> What I shall do to inherit eternal life. He said to him, what is written in the law? How do you read it? He answered, you shall love the Lord your God with all your heart, with all your soul, with all your strength, with your entire mind, and your neighbour as yourself. He said to him, you have answered correctly. Do this and you will live. But he, desiring to justify himself, asked Jesus, Who is my neighbour? And Jesus answering said, A certain man went down from Jerusalem to Jericho, and fell among thieves, which stripped him of his raiment, and wounded him, and departed, leaving him half dead. And by chance there came down a certain priest that way: and when he saw him, he passed by on the other side. And likewise a Levite, when he was at the place, came and looked on him, and passed by on the other side. But a certain Samaritan, as he journeyed, came where he was: and when he saw him, he had compassion on him, and went to him, and bound up his wounds, pouring in oil and wine, and set him on his own beast, and brought him to an inn, and took care of him. And on the morrow when he departed, he took out two pence, and gave them to the host, and said unto him, Take care of him; and when I return, I will reimburse you for any extra expense you may have. Which one of these three, do you think was a neighbour unto him that fell among the thieves? The lawyer said, He who showed mercy on him. Then said Jesus unto him, Go, and do likewise.[26]

The notion of a lawyer is therefore a very sensible notion which cannot be described with words and ethical norms. In other words, a lawyer may lose their human essence in many situations although they remain human.

---

[26] Luke 10:25-37 NIV.

Therefore, when we speak about lawyers, we are speaking about a profession which encompasses the art of argumentation and the art of lies, and also, sometimes, the art of finding the truth. A lawyer and the truth are really two different matters since the lawyer is the one who works with law and has the knowledge of the law, and lawyers are humans with human nature. Thirdly, their character is composed of the truth, lies, half-truths, and falsehoods. Although these three points speak about the same thing, the difference is that the third is the consequence of the first two points, and therefore there is some interdependency between all three characterisations of lawyers. However, the third description is decisive and demonstrates the nature of the lawyer and the separation of lawyers from the truth or lies.

The profession of lawyer may therefore create contradiction between different matters and the truth may disappear because of the circumstances established by a lawyer in order to convince the jury, judges, and courts of their arguments. Finding the truth is always difficult and may take a great amount of time due to its complex nature.[27] This complexity becomes even more complicated when the conscience of a lawyer is based on fees, although everyone must realise that there is just one truth and there cannot be several truths because even if there are several variations of the truth,

[27] When we think of lawyers, we think of games. In most games, one must follow the rules and play against an opponent who is following the same rules. Likewise, a lawyer may not even second guess the fairness and justice of the rules being evoked against the victims. This is without considering the possible consequences for other parties in general. Then the lawyer may question, while in the middle of playing chess or baseball, whether the rules are fair and just, and try to modify their strategy in the interest of equality and justice. This does not occur often. The pitcher who wishes to serve their own interests and not help their team win is playing a different game. A moral judgment about fairness is only achieved when the rules of combat are expressed and not when the rules take effect mid-game. However, there are a considerable number of difficulties with this judgment between lawyers and games. The rules of battle in the opposition system persist and are uncertain and most often provocative. What seems to be fair to one lawyer concerning protecting their client from ongoing criminal activities, may not be the same for another lawyer and may even seem unfair to them. By way of comparison, the rules of baseball or chess have already been settled and are therefore clear, but there are no set rules in law that can stop greedy lawyers. Moral conundrums do not taint every distinct optimal policy and the interpretation of every choice is controversial. In all games, the rules are fixed and the opposing parties agree to put aside their interests and play morally. However, lawyers fail to do this. Thomas Morawetz, 'Lawyers and Conscience', *Faculty Articles and Papers* 114 (1989), pp.383-396, at 384-385.

the central core of the truth remains the same.[28] Any other truth around the core truth is a sub-truth that still embodies the initial seed of the truth. That is what a system of justice or criminal justice is about, and what the requirements of justice demand. However, we are also aware of the fact that in criminal cases, all of the accused parties and all of the victims and witnesses speak the truth they believe in. At the same time, we all believe that we speak the truth and that the truth is in the justification of our own conduct— but that it is absent in the conduct of our friends, neighbours, and all those with whom we have come into contact.[29]

---

[28] Abbe Smith, 'The Lawyer's "Conscience" and the Limits of Persuasion', 36 *Hofstra Law Review* (2007), pp.479-496.

[29] M. Cherif Bassiouni, 'International Recognition of Victims' Rights,' in Bassiouni (ed.), III *International Criminal Law* (2008), pp.655-701.

Chapter 2

Burden of Reasonableness in the Office of Lawyers

2.1. Versus the Burden of Proof

In criminal law, it is the burden of proof which decides whether or not the accused is found guilty of the commission of a crime. The burden of proof in the common law system lies with the jury, i.e., it is the jury (or judge) who decides whether the accused is guilty or not. The burden of proof therefore constitutes a major element of criminal jurisdiction. It actually plays the most crucial role in the success of the system of criminal justice, including in civil cases. This means that meeting the burden of proof and convincing a jury that the accused has committed the crime beyond any reasonable doubt is one of the most important elements of criminal proceedings. However, there can also be reasonable doubt present. In this case, the term "reasonable doubt" refers to the belief that there is a real possibility that a defendant is not guilty. If the notion or the criteria of burden of proof is not fully met and doubt about the guilt of the accused remains, then the accused is entitled to appeal the decision based on the failure of the prosecution to prove beyond a reasonable doubt that they have committed the given crime.[30]

The term "burden of proof" generally refers to acts, conducts, or evidence which provide sufficient reasonable proof that the accused is guilty of the relevant crime or crimes. The process of meeting the burden of proof is normally completed by the plaintiff and prosecutor in a criminal case. Victims and the prosecutor may work together against the accused. However, the burden of proof may be partially or completely rejected by the attorney, and the lawyer may argue against every piece of evidence against their client. The defendant often has the burden of verifying any defence. The trier of fact, i.e., the judge or jury, decides whether a party has met the burden of proof during a trial. However, in countries with civil law systems, juries are not present in criminal trials and it is the judges who decide about the value of the burden of proof presented by the prosecutor. The trial is an official hearing at which the jury or judge hears evidence and decides whether a defendant is guilty of the crimes as charged.

In common law systems, such as that of the United States, jurors are not legal experts and do not have legal knowledge. Here, it is the judge who explains the burden of proof to jury members in a common appeal. We must also mention that the members of the jury must pass *voir dire* before being accepted as jurors. *Voir dire* refers to the pretrial questioning of individuals who have been selected as potential jurors. Therefore, *voir dire* is the process by which attorneys select or reject certain jurors to hear a case.

---

[30] "The 'beyond a reasonable doubt' standard is the highest standard of proof that may be imposed upon a party at trial, and it is usually the standard used in criminal cases. This standard requires the prosecution to show that the only logical explanation that can be derived from the facts is that the defendant committed the alleged crime, and that no other logical explanation can be inferred or deduced from the evidence. The United States Supreme Court in *Victor v. Nebraska*, 511 U.S. 1 (1994), described this standard as 'such doubt as would give rise to a grave uncertainty, raised in your mind by reasons of the unsatisfactory character of the evidence or lack thereof . . . . What is required is not an absolute or mathematical certainty, but a moral certainty.' Evidentiary Standards and Burdens of Proof in Legal Proceedings, available online at https://www.justia.com/trials-litigation/lawsuits-and-the-court-process/evidentiary-standards-and-burdens-of-proof/

2.2. Duty of Lawyers in Disputed Charges

The burden of proof is the responsibility of a party to a case to prove that a disputed charge, allegation, or defence is true. During court proceedings, said party presents evidence to the judge or jury. The burden of persuasion refers to the obligation to convince the judges or the members of the jury of the defendant's innocence beyond a reasonable doubt.[31] This means that the value and legitimacy of the evidence presented, and the quality and amount thereof, is carefully considered by the judges or jury during criminal proceedings. Thus, it is essential for a party to present enough compelling evidence i.e., to meet the necessary requirements for the burden of proof in order for the accused to be found guilty. However, the lawyer of the accused may argue against this burden of proof and deny its legal validity. These are some of the imperative duties of a lawyer who works to protect their clients from all types of accusations, although once this is accomplished, the accused cannot be seen as innocent in the eyes of the jury or public.

Interpreting evidence is another duty for lawyers who have professional experience, knowledge of the provisions of criminal law, and who are able to use additional evidence to craft counterarguments. One of the ways to argue against the validity of the "burden of proof" is to establish certain facts and theories which demonstrate that the burden of proof as presented is incomplete and certain evidence has been suppressed or hidden.

Within the criminal statutes of most criminal jurisdictions in the world, the burden of proof always lays with the prosecutor's office, which must thus endeavour to prove that the accused is guilty of the crime as charged. This means that the district attorney or a similar prosecutor carries the burden of proof. In certain rare cases, the attorney general (the high prosecutor) may present the case. The district attorney or state attorney, who has the burden of proof, may arrest a person charged with a crime and

---

[31] Consult Kimberley Brownlee, 'Responsibilities of Criminal Justice Officials', *Journal of Applied Philosophy* (2010), pp.1-17.

then has to prove their guilt beyond a reasonable doubt. The burden of proof is the most difficult part of criminal justice, not only for the prosecutor or the district attorney but also for the lawyer or the attorney, defence counsel, and defence attorney. However, concerning the duties of defence attorneys and law enforcement officers, it has been asserted that:

> Law enforcement officers have the obligation to convict the guilty and to make sure they do not convict the innocent. They must be dedicated to making the criminal trial a procedure for the ascertainment of the true facts surrounding the com-mission of the crime. To this extent, our so-called adversary system is not adversary at all; nor should it be. But defence counsel has no comparable obligation to ascertain or present the truth. Our system assigns him a different mission. He must be and is interested in not convicting the innocent, but, absent a voluntary plea of guilty, we also insist that he defend his client whether he is innocent or guilty. The State has the obligation to present the evidence. Defence counsel need present nothing, even if he knows what the truth is. He need furnish no witnesses to the police, reveal any confidences of his client, nor furnish any other information to help the prosecution's case. If he can confuse a witness, even a truthful one, or make him appear at a disadvantage, unsure or indecisive, that will be his normal course. Our interest in not convicting the innocent permits counsel to put the State to its proof is to put the State's case in the worst possible light, regardless of what he thinks or knows to be the truth. Undoubtedly there are some limits which defence counsel must observe but more often than not, defence counsel will cross-examine a prosecution witness, and impeach him if he can, even if he thinks the witness is telling the truth, just as he will attempt to destroy a witness who he thinks is lying. In this respect, as part of our modified adversary system and as part of the duty imposed on the most honourable defence counsel, we countenance or require conduct which in many instances has little, if any, relation to the search for truth.[32]

[32] Monroe H. Freedman, 'The Professional Responsibility of the Prosecuting Attorney', Maurice A. Deane School of Law at Hofstra University, Scholarly Commons at Hofstra Law (1967), p.1047.

The accused must answer questions before the jury or judge with the assistance of their lawyer, who is supposed to work to defend the accused. This means that the lawyer assists the accused and believes that they are innocent. It is also the duty of the judges, prosecutors, and the jury to assume that the accused is innocent until guilt has been proven beyond a reasonable doubt. Therefore, *it is not the duty of the accused to prove that they have not committed the crime they were accused of, but rather the prosecutor or the district attorney has to prove that the accused committed the crime by presenting witnesses and evidence in order to convince the judge and jury.* It is here that the client or their attorney has to provide counterarguments for the given evidence and demonstrate that the burden of proof is flawed and insufficient to convict the accused of the relevant crime. This implies that the lawyer presents proof which contradicts the prosecutor's proof.

2.3. The Burden of Proof Contradicting the Requirements of Justice

Fulfilling the burden of proof is the central task of the prosecution and the reason why accused parities need to have a skilled lawyer to defend them against the presented evidence.[33] There are two types of burden of proof with which lawyers must be familiar: the burden of proof in civil cases and the burden of proof in criminal cases. Thus, the burden of proof varies from case-to-case depending on the nature of the case being tried in a court. The fulfilment of the burden of proof by the plaintiff in a civil case is known as a "preponderance of evidence". This demands that the plaintiff present more convincing evidence than the defence. This means that where the evidence provided by the plaintiff and defence is equal, the case becomes more complicated. When the preponderance of evidence

---

[33] The Latin term for "burden of proof" is phrased *semper necessitas probandi incumbit ei qui agit*, which means the necessity of proof always lies with the person who makes a claim. See also *Cargile, James 'On the burden of proof', Philosophy Cambridge University Press* (1997), pp. 59–83.

constitutes the burden of proof, the judge or jury must acknowledge that it is more likely than not that the defendant is not guilty.

However, if the plaintiff's evidence is not clear, the judge or jury may assert that the burden of proof has not been fulfilled, and the plaintiff would then lose the case. During these procedures, arguments, and the presentation of evidence, the defence lawyer and the prosecutor must provide convincing arguments to the judge or jury in order to protect their clients. Here, the more skilled lawyer will win the case. A skilled lawyer has good knowledge of the law, vast experience, respectable argumentation, speaks competently, and is respectful and polite.

We must also state that there is a major difference between the burden of proof in civil law and in criminal law. That is why a majority of lawyers specialise in one of these fields. The burden of proof in a criminal case is a complicated process through which one seeks to prove the validity of the presented evidence. That is the reason why proving guilt "beyond a reasonable doubt" plays an essential role in criminal cases.

> What is reasonable doubt? It is a term often used, probably pretty well understood, but not easily defined. It is not mere possible doubt; because everything relating to human affairs, and depending on moral evidence, is open to some possible or imaginary doubt. It is that state of the case, which, after the entire comparison and consideration of all the evidence, leaves the minds of the jurors in that condition that they cannot say they feel an abiding conviction, to a moral certainty, of the truth of the charge. The burden of proof is upon the prosecutor. All the presumptions of the law independent of evidence are in favour of innocence; and every person is presumed to be innocent until he is proven guilty. If upon such proof there is reasonable doubt remaining, the accused is entitled to the benefit of it by an acquittal. For it is not sufficient to establish a probability, though a strong one arising from the doctrine of chances, that the fact charged is more likely to be true than the contrary; but the evidence must establish the truth of the fact to a reasonable and moral certainty; a certainty that convinces and directs the understanding, and satisfies the

reason and judgment, of those who are bound to act conscientiously upon it. This we take to be proof beyond a reasonable doubt.[34]

The requirements for fulfilling the burden of proof of the defendant differ from country-to-country since the methods for evaluating evidence also differ. In some countries, such as Islamic states, the defendant is responsible for meeting the burden of proof, as well as for proving their innocence by disproving the presented evidence.[35] The defence lawyer therefore must match the presented evidence as well as provide additional, contradictory evidence which proves that the accused is innocent or that the evidence presented by the prosecution is insufficient. Thus, although presenting counterevidence is necessary, the judge may reach the conclusion that the presented evidence is insufficient for proving guilt beyond a reasonable doubt and close the case. As a result, the court may release the accused and could even charge the accuser with falsification of evidence and accusation without proof. In this case, the defendant would not have to meet any requirements for the fulfilment of the burden of production or persuasion.

---

[34] Commonwealth v. Webster (2010).

[35] For the principles of Islamic international human rights consult Mashood A. Baderin, 'Effective Legal Representation in '*Shariah*' Courts as a Means of Addressing Human Rights Concerns in the Islamic Criminal Justice System of Muslim States.' 11 *Yearbook of Islamic and Middle Eastern Law* (2006), pp.135-167; A. Mashood Baderin, *International Human Rights and Islamic Law* (New York, NY: Oxford University Press, 2005); A. Mashood Baderin, *International Law and Islamic Law* (Ashgate, 2008); A Mashood Baderin, 'A Comparative Analysis of the Right to a Fair Trial and due Process under International Human Rights Law and Saudi Arabian Domestic Law', 10 (3) *The International Journal of Human Rights* (2006); M. Cherif Bassiouni, 'Protection of Diplomats under Islamic Law', 74 *American Journal of International Law* (1980), pp.609-655; M. Cherif Bassiouni, 'Islam: Concept, Law and Word *Habeas Corpus'*, 2 *Rutgers Camden Law Journal* (1970); M. Cherif Bassiouni, *Studies in Early Hadith Literature* (Indianapolis, 1978); M. Cherif Bassiouni, 'Sources of Islamic Law and the Protection of Human Rights' in Bassiouni, the *Islamic Criminal Justice System* (1982); M. Cherif Bassiouni, *The Shariah and Islamic Criminal Justice in the Time of War and Peace* (Cambridge University Press, Cambridge, 2014); Mashood A. Baderin, 'Islamic Socio-Legal Norms and International Criminal Justice in Context: Advancing an 'Object and Purpose'cum 'Maqáṣid' Approach' in T. Gray, *Islam and International Criminal Law and Justice* (Torkel Opsahl Academic EPublisher, 2018).

2.4. Irrebuttable Arguments

Parties to a criminal case can help meet the burden of proof. However, this varies from country-to-county, based on the way in which the criminal jurisdiction is applied in a given court. A judge is permitted to get involved in the case in order to clarify certain matters. The judge or jury may also make presumptions. An interference means the judge or jury (in common law systems) may come to certain conclusions based on case law. This means that presumption is the policy of the judge, and thus all criminal defendants are presumed innocent until proven guilty. The defence lawyer's duty is also to help judges and juries to respect the presumed innocence of the accused throughout proceedings. Presumptions can be rebuttable or conclusive (irrebuttable). The difference between irrebuttable and irrefutable is that the former cannot be argued against, while irrefutable implies that it is impossible to disprove something.

A party can disprove a rebuttable presumption. This implies that the prosecution can deny or rebut the presumption that the accused is innocent according to the evidence, thus proving beyond a reasonable doubt that the defendant is guilty. The conclusive presumption is indisputable and *cannot* be disproved, such is the case with young children accused of crimes. In such cases, it is the duty of the defence lawyer or the defence attorney to prevent the case from going to trial. However, in the United Kingdom young children continue to be prosecuted because the age of criminal responsibility in England and Wales is ten years old, which violates international conventions on the rights of children.[36]

---

[36] Consult Farhad Malekian, *International Criminal Law of Children* (Nova Science Publishers, 2021); Farhad Malekian, Kerstin Nordlöf, *Confessing the International Rights of Children: The Basic documents with Analysis* (Cambridge: Cambridge Scholars Publishing, 2012). Farhad Malekian, Kerstin Nordlöf, *Prohibition of Sexual Exploitation of Children Constituting Obligation Erga Omnes* (Cambridge: Cambridge Scholars Publishing, 2013). Farhad Malekian, Kerstin Nordlöf, *The Sovereignty of Children in Law* (Cambridge: Cambridge Scholars Publishing, 2012). Farhad Malekian, 'The Child as an Autonomous Subject of Justice' in Farhad Malekian, Kerstin Nordlöf, *Sovereignty of Children in Law* (Cambridge: Cambridge Scholars Publishing, 2012), pp. 2-55. Farhad Malekian, 'Consolidating the International Criminal Law of Children', 26, (3) *Criminal Law Forum* (2015), pp. 569-593.

2.5. Lawyer versus Reasonable Suspicion

The burden of proof can be evaluated in different ways. It generally requires authentic evidence, reasonable suspicion, significant substantive evidence, strong, rich, and convincing evidence, rational indications, motive to believe the cause, probable cause, the existence of credible evidence, and sufficient evidence in order to prove guilt beyond a reasonable doubt.[37] Nonetheless, we must emphasise that the evidence may not be strong enough to prove the wrongful conduct outright, but some pieces of evidence may be strong enough to create doubt. Furthermore, evidence may create problems and cause suspicion when the term "reasonable suspicion", which implies a relatively low level of proof of criminality of the accused, is employed. This may then lead to the accused being found innocent and to "probable cause" having to be proven, which requires a much higher standard of proof. Probable cause denotes a reasonable ground for the belief that the defendant committed a crime or that a certain piece of evidence can be definitively connected to the relevant crime.

It is here that the lawyer of the accused works to prove that the evidence supporting reasonable suspicion and probable cause is insufficient or false, and as such, the accused cannot be found guilty. A criminal defence attorney or lawyer may build reasonable doubt in the minds of a judge or a jury. While the burden of accusation rests on the prosecution, who has to prove that the accused has committed the crime and is therefore guilty, this may be challenged by the criminal defence lawyer and be questioned intensively. It is consequently the obligation and

---

[37] Jack B. Weinstein, Ian Dewsbury, 'Comment on the meaning of 'proof beyond a reasonable doubt' ', 5 (2) *Law, Probability and Risk* (2006), pp.167–173. The term is differently defined in the United States criminal procedures. According to the United States Judicial Center, "Proof beyond a reasonable doubt is proof that leaves you firmly convinced of the defendant's guilt. There are very few things in this world that we know with absolute certainty, and in criminal cases the law does not require proof that overcomes every possible doubt. If, based on your consideration of the evidence, you are firmly convinced that the defendant is guilty of the crime charged, you must find him guilty. If on the other hand, you think there is a real possibility that he is not guilty, you must give him the benefit of the doubt and find him not guilty." *Id.* Available online at https://academic.oup.com/lpr/article/5/2/167/927735.

responsibility of the defence lawyer to diligently and persuasively prove the inability of the prosecution to meet its burden. This means that a criminal defence lawyer should have the ability to put forward good arguments to be accepted by the judges and/or jury. A skilled lawyer may therefore direct the court to agree that the prosecution has not met its burden of establishing guilt beyond a reasonable doubt.

Generally, one may assert that reasonable doubt refers to any doubt that would cause a wise person to hesitate before taking any decision or action which is highly sensitive and significant for their judgments. The presence of reasonable doubt therefore implies that there is a strong possibility that the accused has not committed the crime, and is therefore not guilty of the criminal conduct. Thus, despite the evidence and arguments presented, the fact-finders, including judges or juries, are unable to conclude that the accused is guilty of the relevant crime. For these reasons, it is vital and reasonable that during criminal proceedings, the criminal defence attorney must systematically and carefully examine each prospective juror to detect any prejudices, biases, or any other potential factors that may affect the impartiality of the juror.

Although the prosecution has the burden of proof, it may not be essential to prove their case beyond a reasonable doubt. A judge may inform a jury that reasonable doubt does not mean the elimination of any possible doubt.[38] Therefore, the prosecution's duty to prove guilt beyond a reasonable doubt is very difficult and needs to be handled with care, honesty, morality, and impartiality in order to preserve the independence of the court.[39]

---

[38] According to the Federal Courts of the United States, "It is not required that the government prove guilt beyond all possible doubt. The test is one of reasonable doubt. A reasonable doubt is a doubt based upon reason and common sense—the kind of doubt that would make a reasonable person hesitate to act. Proof beyond a reasonable doubt must, therefore, be *proof of such a convincing character that a reasonable person would not hesitate to rely and act upon it in the most important of his own affairs*. The jury will remember that a defendant is never to be convicted on mere suspicion or conjecture." *Id*. Available online at https://academic.oup.com/lpr/article/5/2/167/927735.

[39] Examine Code of Conduct for the Office of the Prosecutor entered into force (5 September 2013), https://www.icc-cpi.int/iccdocs/oj/otp-coc-Eng.pdf; see *also* Prosecutor v Katanga and Ngudjolo, ICC - 01 - /04 - 01/07, *Judgment on Unlawful Detention and Stay of Proceedings* (12 July 2010); examine also Statement of the Prosecutor of the International Criminal Court, Fatou Bensouda, following the surrender and transfer of alleged militia

2.6. Attorney Scrutinizing the Burden of Proof

A defence attorney who represents the defendant during criminal prosecution (or a lawsuit) should always be aware that they are responsible for evaluating the evidence presented by the prosecution. Since any defence attorney should have regularly represented criminal defendants, they must have a lot of experience with evaluating evidence and the way in which judges or juries interpret the burden of proof. We must also remember that the burden of proof is the obligation of a party to prove a charge, allegation, or defence. At the same time, the defence attorney must prepare sufficient documentation in order to contradict the criminal burden of proof for the prosecution, which must be proven beyond a reasonable doubt.

The duty of the defence lawyer becomes more complicated if circumstantial evidence indirectly implicates the defendant in the crime. This means that circumstantial evidence can indirectly imply the fact that the defendant was present at the time of the commission of the crime. Such evidence can include a fingerprint found at the scene of the crime. In such situations, the defence lawyer must change their strategy and now seek to prove that the defendant did not intend to commit a crime, or was forced to do so by a third party. Furthermore, the difference between circumstantial evidence and direct evidence is that the latter directly proves that the accused was engaged in the relevant criminal conduct. An example of such evidence would be a confession.

The role of circumstantial evidence is most important when the prosecution cannot prove beyond a reasonable doubt that the defendant was engaged in the commission of criminal conduct. Some of the most common forms of circumstantial evidence include traces of blood, DNA, and fingerprints.[40] A fingerprint of the defendant at the crime scene thus constitutes direct evidence, and when direct evidence is presented, the

---

leader, Ali Muhammad Ali Abd-Al-Rahman, also known as Ali Kushayb, to the Court (9 June 2020), available online at https://www.icc-cpi.int/Pages/item.aspx?name=200609-otp-statement-ali-kushayb.

40 Consult 'The Use of DNA in Criminal Investigations,' available online at https://www.lawcom.govt.nz/our-projects/use-dna-criminal-investigations.

duties of the defence attorney become more about the presentation of new arguments, rather than the prevention of accusation and condemnation. Generally speaking, criminal cases built upon circumstantial evidence can complicate final judgment; although in some cases circumstantial evidence, such as DNA evidence, can be very compelling and useful from a practical point of view.[41] Prosecution teams have often succeeded in fulfilling the burden of proof by using circumstantial evidence alone. That is why the duty of the defence attorney is to reduce the punishment faced by the accused through the presentation of facts.

Under all these conditions, the defence attorney has to scrutinise all of the evidence which has been presented in criminal cases by the prosecutor, including by questioning witnesses on both sides of the case. This is because direct evidence such as eyewitness testimony can directly prove the involvement of the defendant in the commission of the crime. As a result, defence lawyers have to be vigilant and skilled in evaluating the quality of evidence. One of the most common examples of direct evidence includes eyewitness testimony, which is considered to be reliable in certain cases.

Direct evidence can also include the confession of a defendant or a picture or video of the defendant at the time of the commission of a crime. Although direct evidence is useful, it cannot compete with circumstantial evidence since direct evidence may be fabricated and eyewitnesses can be unreliable. That is why defence lawyers have to be careful when examining evidence and determining its reliability. However, in the case of certain serious crimes in which government authorities are involved, even circumstantial evidence such as DNA evidence may be falsified or not reliable.

---

[41] *Id.*

2.7. Conscience of a Trial Lawyer

It has been correctly stated that "*few literary lawyers manage to be both skilled advocates and decent human beings*."[42] The term 'conscience' plays a significant role within all aspects of criminal jurisdiction. Where there is no particular conscience, lies and intrigues take over, and the innocent are painted as guilty and the guilty as innocent, and this guides the final judgement. That is why we always need to establish ethical codes in all branches of law, without which we may be unable to see what is really right and what is wrong. However, ethical conscience cannot help a lawyer, particularly a trial lawyer, if the lawyer has completely lost the intention of all types of judicial conscience and places immorality before morality, and if legal norms have become bargaining chips with which economic interests can be achieved. In such cases, we are not facing true justice but rather participating in a competition. This becomes particularly dangerous when we are dealing with the very sensible question of international criminal justice jurisdiction under various criminal procedures by trial lawyers in the Chambers of International Criminal Court.

The question then becomes, what is a trial lawyer really? And why do the majority of lawyers take on this job without seriously considering that a trial lawyer should acknowledge the limits of ethical conscience and its very significant role in impartial trials? A trial lawyer's principal duty is to defend the accused in order to demonstrate their lack of guilt by presenting evidence of the contrary. The trial lawyer thus has a very serious duty before criminal courts and juries in order to provide balance between various matters in the courtroom. The duty of the trial lawyer is thus to prepare the case, meet judges, and if relevant, to select jurors/*voir dire*, and thereafter to work the case up through the end of criminal proceedings.

---

[42] Asimow, When the Lawyer Knows the Client is Guilty: Mellinkoff's 'The Conscience of a Lawyer', note 21.

Therefore, the trial lawyer must act upon certain ethical codes of contact and be aware of the fact that any mistake they make may seriously mislead the judges and jury. That is why trial lawyers have specific tasks and responsibilities, including examining the case carefully and authentically without bias. This is done so that the trial lawyer does not modify the evidence or jeopardise its objectivity. The trial lawyer also represents their client in the criminal trial and defends them before the court. In order to accomplish this, the trial lawyer may meet with their clients to receive further clarification about matters. Additionally, the trial lawyer must inform their clients about court dates. Furthermore, the trial lawyer is responsible for cross-examining witnesses and any argument against or in favour of the accused. During these cross-examinations, other matters may be revealed, which may require the immediate attention of the trial lawyer. Therefore, the trial lawyer's conduct and investigations should be based on moral, legal, and ethical conscience and should not violate the principle of impartiality.[43]

As a result, the trial lawyer must have certain competences and skills relating to matters of criminal jurisdiction and with presenting cases to judges/juries. A considerable number of requirements may need to be met in order to assert that a trial lawyer is capable enough to fulfil their duties. Additionally, a trial lawyer must be able to analyse cases and keep track of all significant facts and details. As a result, trial lawyers must update their knowledge in time with the revision of criminal laws and regulations. In particular, trial lawyers must always be aware of their ethical duties and should not sell the judicial independence of criminal jurisdiction, nor should they make any arrangements or deals with other parties which either help or hurt their clients.

---

[43] In general, "the preliminary examination process is conducted on the basis of the facts and information available, and in the context of the overarching principles of independence, impartiality and objectivity." OTP, *Policy Paper on Preliminary Examinations*, 1 November 2013, para.25, available online at https://www.icc-cpi.int/iccdocs/otp/OTP-Policy_Paper_Preliminary_Examinations_2013-ENG.pdf.

2.8. ETHICAL CONFIDENTIALITY FOR THE CLIENT

Any lawyer who presents a case has certain ethical duties towards their clients that must be respected at all times. We must also emphasise that in most civil law systems, the synonyms lawyer and attorney are not at all interchangeable, although both professions require an education in law. However, attorneys must meet the requirements of the Bar. This means that an attorney-at-law is a lawyer who has been specifically educated to defend the rights of their clients as an official lawyer. Attorneys have to follow certain ethical codes and are supposed to be more professional than plain lawyers.

Lawyers must speak and act with full ethical purity with their clients and should not mislead them or give them false information. If a lawyer has misunderstood a law or misinterpreted it, they have an ethical duty to inform their client and admit fault. These are some of the necessary requirements of purity. Ethical purity means that one should act in accordance with the code of legal ethics. In simple terms, they must tell their client the entire truth in simple language. Therefore, lawyers are responsible for presenting the entire case in clear, plain language such that their clients can understand.

Moreover, if a client is unable to understand the language of the relevant law, their lawyer must be patient, tolerant, and keep an open mind in order to realise that the majority of clients will not be familiar with legal vocabulary and terms. The lawyer must therefore not stress their client in any way and recognise that it takes time to understand the complexities of the law and its rules, since the language of the law is complicated and can even be misinterpreted by lawyers themselves. That is why the use of certain Latin words is less popular in certain regions such as Canada or Australia and more popular in Europe.[44] All this also implies the capacity and skill of the lawyer in relation to their client.

---

[44] Examine also, J. N. Adams *Bilingualism and the Latin language* (Cambridge: Cambridge University Press, (2003); V. G. Curran, *Comparative law: An introduction* (Durham: Carolina Academic Press, 2002); Peter R. Macleod, 'Latin in Legal Writing: An Inquiry into the Use of Latin in the Modern Legal World', 39 (1) *Boston College Law Review* (1997), pp. 235-251, available online at

2.9. Conscientious Representation of Clients

A lawyer has to be faithful to their clients, and this is one of the basic and fundamental duties of the lawyer in connection with the continuation of court procedures. Therefore, lawyers should not take on more clients than they can handle in order to ensure that they can dedicate enough time to each case and thereby not harm the clients or the reputation of their office. Lawyers should always prioritise the quality of each case over the quantity of cases they take on. Thus, faithfulness of the lawyer implies their personal dignity and that of their firm, and preserves their good reputation. However, as we will see, many lawyers are neither faithful towards their clients nor toward the greater society as a whole. It is imperative for lawyers to maintain their loyalty toward their clients and colleagues in the firm and in the courts. According to one view:

> At the same time, there is a narrower dimension within which a lawyer has choices. Notwithstanding the difficulties of enforcement and the necessary vagueness of its provisions, a code of professional ethics can do more than formulate rules for minimally acceptable conduct. A code can also express aspirations. Similarly, legal training can do much more than merely arm lawyers with technical skills. Legal education can acquaint law students with moral reasoning, can show them that lawyers are not exempt from moral judgment, and can make them thoughtful about the consequences of their actions. If in fact legal training gives rise to amorality and moral cynicism, the problem is only partially remediable. Understanding and accepting the inevitable reasons why lawyers will be "hated"'" is the first step in acting to counter and discredit that hatred.[45]

---

https://lawdigitalcommons.bc.edu/cgi/viewcontent.cgi?referer=&httpsredir=1&article=2089&context=bclr. "The Latin phrases that show an increase in usage are not crucial to the understanding of a person's argument. They are a rhetorical tool. A person using Latin may intend a certain nuance, may intend to affect a reader a certain way. He or she cannot be sure that the reader will take it that way. This malleability of meaning can make it a useful and flexible tool for a member of the legal profession to use." *Id.* See also Duhaime's International Law Dictionary, available online at http://www.duhaime.org/LegalDictionary/Category/InternationalLawDictionary.aspx.

[45] Morawetz, 'Lawyers and Conscience', note 27, pp. 395-396.

Attorneys have the legal obligation to, and are ethically responsible for, working at their full capacity when representing a client and to support all their clients without prioritising one over the other based on their social positions. Consequently, an attorney must exercise appropriate caution in order to maintain the circumstances of the case and not worsen the position of their clients. It is actually the capacity of the conscience of the lawyer or their diligence, as well as their carefulness, which call upon their ethical duty toward their client and their case. For instance, if a lawyer believes that their client must be set free on bail in order for the investigation to be carried out properly and for evidence to be found, they must seek permission from the prosecutor or other relevant court authorities for this. An attorney is thus responsible for not jeopardising the position of their client in any way.

An attorney's duty is to reach the heart of the matter with full confidence. Therefore, they have to be faithful, particularly in criminal cases in which the safety of the accused outweighs the attorney's profit. The attorney should render all legal assistance with full conscience and use their legal knowledge and unmatched familiarity with the case to help their client. All questions asked by the client must be answered with reference to relevant legislation and with consideration for all ethical norms of the Bar. This means that the attorney should not refuse to directly answer the questions of the client and should also be aware of the fact that they should avoid confusing their client.

2.10. Falsified Subjective Measurement

A lawyer should be aware of the fact that they should not take on cases from people who find themselves at conflict with their current clients. When a lawyer simultaneously pursues different cases with the intention of proving that both parties are entitled to reparations, questions about the fairness and content of the lawyer's arguments may arise. Ethically, one should not argue similar cases with different contradictory reasonings.

This duality also leaves the window open to the risk that individual lawyers may have confidence in that they are proceeding for the cause of justice and that their engagement with opposite ethical norms contains correct codes. A wise man may argue that they are in fact obstructing the development of ethical morality as a result of taking on another case. In other words, this situation implies the existence of false consciousness and cognizance on the part of relevant lawyers who intend to pursue justice but instead misrepresent their cases. Hence,

> These hostile characterizations of the lawyer put her at a distance, as though her performances were something especially devious and different from the rest of us. If our acceptance of the acting profession demonstrates that we have come to acknowledge that role-playing is an integral aspect of modem experience, our excoriation of lawyers illustrates that this acceptance has definite limits. The performances of the lawyer are hidden, and hence they obliterate the distinction between the performing self and the true or innate self. But in this the lawyer is merely representative of the concealed performances we must all undertake every day. We would like to believe that we are the master of our many roles, rather than the reverse, but the persistent and unsettling example of the lawyer will not let us rest easy in this belief.[46]

Falsification by lawyers is not new and has even been observed in cases where power is prioritised over the interests of the victims. However, these cases are not necessarily the result of lawyers pursuing economic interests. The fact is that many resolutions of the Security Council have led to thousands of people being killed and created millions of refugees.[47] However, lawyers ignore these events because they pretend and believe that the Security Council is doing good and making the right decisions. International political laundering needs an invisible judicial horse with tailor-made riding boots. We would never dare answer simple questions,

---

[46] Robert C. Post, 'On the Popular Image of the Lawyer: Reflections in a Dark Glass', 75 California Law Review (1987), 379-389, at 389.

[47] Malekian, *Trading Virginity of International Criminal Justice*, note 19, pp.73-74.

since they would impact the income, international or academic position, and the future of certain lawyers.

Many of those who work for international judicial entities, such as the permanent International Criminal Court, attempt to reach their goals without giving the necessary ethical and moral thought to their statements, and without realising the fact that moral deliberation has to be free from personal interests.[48] However, the recent development in the Court and the partial statement of the dissenting lawyer against Palestine in support of the criminal conduct of the Israeli government demonstrates the clear personal nature of some international criminal lawyers and judges, whose positions and words are based on cultural or economic self-interest. These are two factors which should not interfere in judicial judgments or in the judicial conscience. Justice should not be bound by cultural norms and financial interests. Such justice is no longer justice, but rather the presentation of one-eyed-justice.

These are the peculiar parts of our criminal law, justice, investigations, and jurisdiction, with our tiny judges and lawyers with their special uniforms. We are blind and accustomed to calling certain acts legal and certain other acts illegal based on the opinions of lawyers concerning the imperative order and their direct interactions with big criminals. One should not draw lines in the recognition of criminals, all criminals are the same, however certain criminals are bigger, superior criminals. Lawyers, professors of law, and judges come from across the globe in order to assist these criminals in gaining impunity and to fill their deep pockets. However, they also help the *victims*. Such lawyers who help criminals are not only found at the University of Tehran, Allameh Tabatabai University, Tel Aviv University, Peking University, Tsinghua University School of Law, Pierre

---

[48] *Id.*, p.74; Farhad Malekian, *Allegations by Political Laundering* (Newcastle: Cambridge Scholars Publishing, 2019); Farhad Malekian, 'Emasculating the Philosophy of International Criminal Justice in the Iraqi Special Tribunal,' Vol. 38: 3, *Cornell International Law Journal* (2005). Available online at: http://scholarship.law.cornell.edu/cilj/vol38/iss3/2; Farhad Malekian, 'The Canon of Love against the Use of Force in Islamic and Public International Law: Part II: The Anatomy of Love Against Violations,' 15 *International Criminal Law Review*, 2015), pp.861-895; Farhad Malekian, 'The Canon of Love against the Use of Force in Islamic and Public International Law: Part I: The Chamber of Love within Legal Discipline,' 15 *International Criminal Law Review*, 2015), pp.591-628.

Mendès-France University (Grenoble Tsinghua University), University of Jordan Faculty of Law, King Saud University but also at Harvard University, the University of Oxford, Lomonosov Moscow State University, University of London, McGill University, Middlesex University, Case Western Reserve University School of Law, the Raoul Wallenberg Institute of Human Rights and Humanitarian Law, and Stockholm University—to name just a few examples. The arrow of this writing is pointed at academics who know that their position is under serious question. It is indeed shameful that in the history of international criminal law, international criminal justice, international human rights law, and Islamic international criminal law and justice, that these systems have claimed to be fair, just, and actively protecting human rights, although they do not even attempt to truly protect universal justice.[49]

The notion of non-criminality in international criminal justice is very narrow, but lawyers know how to make a criminal appear innocent and the innocent, criminal. *There are no criteria which specifically highlight how criminality and non-criminality are presented in the arguments of a sold lawyer. All criteria come from human rights-based law, misunderstandings between legality and illegality and from misinterpretations of the law. An act, which in many cases would not be called criminal, is designated as such, and an act which is criminal, is deemed legal. Defending occupied land with military force is called terroristic by lawyers, while the criminal acts of the occupier government are deemed legal. This is the true story of criminal law, justice, and criminal lawyers. The same is true concerning criminal legislation— it steers the car of criminal justice with its eyes closed. With all this, I am not saying that our criminal machinery is wrong and that our lawyers assist criminals, nor am I trying to say that criminal law is not independent. My goal is rather to say that we are forced by the hands of time to understand that our criminal law permits the commission of serious crimes at an international level during armed conflicts.*

---

[49] Farhad Malekian, 'Comparative Substantive International Criminal Justice', in Ronald Slye (ed.), *The Nuremberg Principles in Non-western Societies: A Reflection on their Universality, Legitimacy and Application* (2017), pp.10-44.

2.11. Adopting a Case with Ethical Standards

There are certain acts which should not be carried out by an attorney as they violate national and/or international norms. As a generally accepted and consolidated rule of law, acts and decisions of an attorney should conform to the principles of human rights law and should not ignore the rights of those who have asked the attorney for help, especially since they are willing to pay for their services. Therefore, attorneys ought to respect certain norms and standards of ethics which are central to human rights and essential to criminal procedures in which the attorney plays an important role for their client and their family members or relatives.

For example, attorneys are not allowed to come into contact with the opposing party to a case. This is regardless of whether or not their client is present, absent, or in jail. However, contact may potentially be permitted if the client consents to it, and, if after consultation between attorney and client, they reach the conclusion that attorney should contact the opposing party. However, the client's approval for the conduct must also be clear and they should also set boundaries concerning what exactly the attorney is allowed to discuss with the opposing party. Moreover, an attorney should not accept the representation of a co-plaintiff or a co-defendant if their interests are in conflict with those of their client. Therefore, an attorney is supposed to refuse legal assistance in certain cases which could give rise to ethical issues, such as if the attorney works for the same firm as the attorney of the opposing party. Similarly, attorneys must avoid taking on cases which they have worked on in the past or have a personal interest in. Additionally, if the attorney has worked on the same legal matter as a law trainee with the attorney who will represent the opposing party, they should not accept the case.

These are some of the ethical questions that an attorney should raise and discuss with their client before accepting a case. Still, if a case is presented to a firm and the lawyer believes that it is in the best interest of the client that the case not be presented in court because it could be solved without a trial, they should do all they can to avoid trial. Even if a case has been submitted to the court and the lay judges have been chosen, the lawyer should attempt to encourage the parties to the case to resolve the dispute through friendly discussions and by evaluating all potential consequences in court.

If an attorney is unable to further represent their client for one reason or another, they must inform their client as soon as possible and provide the reason for why they are unable to continue to represent them. Such reasons could include illness, personal circumstances, and the identification of a conflict of interest. In such cases, after informing the client, the attorney should, under no circumstances, provide any information about the case to other parties. This means that the attorney has the ethical, moral, and legal responsibility to keep information about their client confidential. This is imperative, and any wrongful behaviour, conduct, or written statement represents the serious violation of the ethical norms of judicial conscience.

This means that the attorney should preserve their objectivity regarding their former client if the opposing party comes to them with another case. In such cases, the attorney should not take on the case because it would violate the ethical code of professional conduct. Moreover, an attorney who has personal connections with the opposing party should inform their client and potentially refuse to represent that client due to their inability to remain impartial. Thus, it would be up to the discretion of the client to accept the attorney or to look for another one.

2.12. Ethical Conscience Concerning the Opposing Party

Attorneys are responsible for not reopening closed cases in order to represent the opposing party. Obviously, if an attorney is still working with their former client, they should not accept to take on the case of the opposing party. These are some of the basic conditions of the ethical conscience of the attorney and their legal duty to not take on cases from opposing parties. Furthermore, attorneys have a great ethical responsibility to never disclose information about opposing parties even years after a case has been closed. This is not only for the purpose of protecting the integrity and independence of the parties involved, but also to prevent any information disclosed by the attorney from leading to the reopening of a case.

Despite all this, attorneys do have the responsibility to reopen an old case if they feel as though the condemned person was wrongly found guilty or that the procedures were flawed. In such cases, an attorney should immediately take action and consult with legal authorities about reopening the case. Certainly, and without any hesitation, a lawyer is responsible for reporting their own misconduct or misunderstandings to legal authorities. This is imperative for the maintenance of the dignity and integrity of criminal justice.

This ethical conscience or ethical norm in the case of the false condemnation of a person constitutes an imperative duty of the procedures of justice. Even if an attorney is offered a large amount of money in order to remain silent and not report the case, they ought to reject the offer and pursue justice through the proper channels. Any shortcomings on the part of the attorney imply their assistance in hiding the truth and promoting misinterpretation. This is regardless of whether the trial lawyer was misled along with the attorney or if attorneys intentionally misled the court in order to win the case. Here, the ethical codes of righteousness and conscientiousness compel the lawyer, attorney, and the trial attorney to respect the integrity of justice and to not mislead the justice through false arguments.[50]

---

[50] "Our actions are surely condemned along with the wise men, our actions are certainly wrong, our conclusions are surely irrational, and our commitments obviously reflect our personal interests and social priorities. We are all criminals in the eyes of the law and justice as long as we do not see the truth, do not fight for the truth, continue to hide the truth, and fail to promote the truth. Judicial conscience, ethical conscience, and moral conscience are nonsensical principles if there are millions of law books speaking about the ethical codes of justice for judges. Furthermore, if we are pure judges of our own actions and demands ourselves, it will be very difficult to request practical conscience from judges. These concluding words do not reflect the emotions of the author, nor do they seek to simply fill a page. Duties within criminal justice, criminal politics, and international politics must be based on the truth and on seeking the truth in order to prevent widespread suffering among victims, who thus represent the consequences of our personal, public, and judicial

2.13. Lawyers' Ethical Duties towards Opposing Parties

Lawyers and attorneys have to be capable people who not only treat all individuals equally, politely, and respectfully, but who also treat the opposing party in the same way. This is based on the basic standards of social relations with those they are protecting and those who are not represented by the lawyer but are a part of their social relations. However, a lawyer does not know which one of the opposing parties is wrong, and even if they knew, it would not give the lawyer permission to treat the opposing parties as inferior. With the word polite, we do not mean that the attorney should make friends with the opposing party or reveal information about their client or strategy. However, there may be conversations between the lawyers of both sides in order to find a solution to the case without having to bring it to trial.

Lawyers must treat the opposing party in a thoughtful and impartial manner with the hope of reaching a satisfactory conclusion for both sides. During all these procedures, lawyers are to refrain from allowing any unjustifiable personal interferences and from increasing tension between the parties in order to prolong proceedings and receive a larger payment. In addition, it is possible that the opposing party is unable to afford a lawyer, and in such cases the lawyer for the other side should not degrade the opposing party or abuse them based on their social standing. Additionally, if the opposing party or their lawyers do not conduct themselves properly, this does not mean that the other party should lose their temper as well.

Therefore, it is the duty of all lawyers to treat the opposing party civilly at all times in order not to increase tensions or aggravate the situation and make matters more difficult. This requires the lawyer to remain objective and to control their feelings, as misconduct on the part of the lawyer can lead to their reputation being damaged or even to disciplinary actions being

---

intrigues." Malekian, *Conscience of Judges in International Criminal Law,* note 10, pp.210-211.

taken by the Bar. Ruthlessness and dishonesty may lead to even greater unsubstantiated confrontation in the legal system. One way to reduce tensions between parties is for a lawyer not to come into contact with the opposing party without the consent of the party's counsel or without the expressed consent of their client. Another possibility is that the lawyers of both sides may agree to a reasonable and a suitable deadline for both sides of the case in order to avoid any delay in closing the case. However, any criminal conduct by any of the parties must be rejected by the lawyers and should strictly be avoided. Moreover, objectivity and morality should be guidelines for all parties and the lawyers, even if one of the parties does not have a lawyer themselves.[51]

2.14. Rejection of a Case by Attorneys

As a general rule of ethical norms, attorneys are responsible for accepting a case when it comes into their office and should not reject it without good reason. However, many factors play essential roles in an attorney accepting or rejecting a case. Any rejection ought to be based on legitimate reasons and should not be based on the social standing of the client or on which crime they are accused of. Thus, if an attorney rejects a case because they have too many cases at the moment, they have not violated the ethical rules of the administration of justice. However, if they reject a case based on the race, religion, cultural background, or ethnicity of the potential client, then the attorney has violated human rights principles.

Therefore, any case submitted to the attorney's office must be properly evaluated and not outright rejected without consideration. Thus, if a case is presented to an attorney by a client of a different nationality, their case should not be rejected in favour of the case of a client who shares the attorney's nationality, as this would constitute discrimination. However,

---

[51] Joseph Hoover, 'Moral Practices: Assigning Responsibility in the International Criminal Court', 76 *Law and Contemporary Problems* (2014), pp.263-86;

this situation is almost impossible to control. This may even occur in the case of nationals of the same country who have different cultural or religious backgrounds, as was seen with the Milosevic case in the International Criminal Tribunal for the former Yugoslavia.

However, an attorney may refuse the request of a client for other reasons such as insufficient knowledge in a particular legal field or the inability of the client to pay their fees. This is permitted as long as the attorney speaks the truth, and the truth may never be revealed if the attorney does not want it to be but continues to maintain a valid argument. This is why we refer to ethical codes of conduct in the office of the attorney and their moral responsibility to speak the truth. The ethical norms, in particular the ethical codes of criminal justice, require all those who are engaged in criminal cases to be noble and honest and to respect the integrity of the system of criminal justice. A personal decision of an attorney may not be seen clearly in criminal justice, but when it is systematic and seen in the conduct of a large number of lawyers then it is an epidemic, and trust in the components of criminal justice disappears and law firms become forums for trading criminal justice.[52]

[52] For further discussions see Farhad Malekian, *Judgments of Love in Criminal Justice* (Switzerland: Springer: 2017, republished 2018), p. 101.

Chapter 3

International Frame of Justice within the Profession of Lawyers

3.1. Towards International Rules for Ethical Conducts

There are certain rules of conduct in the system of law that are, or should be, the same for all lawyers, and these rules should not be falsely evaluated by any lawyer or attorney. This is based on the fact that lawyers deal with the system of justice, and the system of justice must have more or less the same standard of recognition all over the world. In other words, the ethical standards of the legal profession must be the same and demand righteousness of lawyers and their sincerity to the principle of (criminal) justice. The basic principles of this ethical code have not necessarily been written down by all states of the world, but it is clear that members of the legal profession should act honestly, fairly, justly, decently, in good conscience, reliably, politely, friendly, and courteously. These are a few examples of the expectations of the international population concerning attorneys, lawyers, and legal advisers. It is also the way in which we understand legal jurisdiction and the honesty of criminal jurisdiction as a whole. The same expectations exist concerning prosecutors, judges, and all those involved in one way or another with criminal jurisdictions, procedures, proceedings, and the application of judgments.

Therefore, lawyers throughout all states are specialised professionals who work only in the best interest of their clients, with the sole intention of protecting their rights. Furthermore, lawyers have a certain understanding that they should work for the interests of justice. The intention is to strive to attain a positive opinion of the rules of justice and all questions surrounding the system of justice which relate to trust and justice. This implies that fairness and truth are the two main pillars of the legal profession. Lawyers must also remain impartial, not conceal or destroy evidence, and must fulfil the burden of proof for their cases. They are obliged to uphold the law through the development of legislation and to stay up-to-date on judicial progress in order to form their arguments.

The services which lawyers provide for their clients should be equal and based on ethical standards. Lawyers should not only respect their clients, but should also respect the court and the independence of criminal jurisdiction as a whole. This means they have received the power of judgment in their field in order to represent their clients and therefore have legitimate power to maintain a reasonable standard of argumentation for all cases brought to their office. However, we do not deny the fact that there are certainly different understandings of certain principles of justice and criminal justice among lawyers, prosecutors, and judges, which is why argumentation is used to decide the final application of the rule of law. This means that tension is unavoidable. The theory of judicial conscience in the legal profession intends to establish a common conventional framework in order to provide a source for the appropriate codes of conduct for lawyers in any nation. Therefore, as a general rule of ethics, lawyers should respect all rules which are necessary corollaries for the administration of justice.

3.2. Independence of Lawyers

The legal profession requires the independence of advisers. This is because without the principle of independence, one cannot properly establish justice. It is independence which reveals the truth and establishes justice for all parties. With independence, we do not mean the satisfaction of all parties, since if all parties were satisfied, there would be no dispute and no case. It is in this case that we seek to establish true justice with the presentation of independent truth. However, the truth may cause pain for some of the parties to the case, and may not be appreciated. Despite this, the truth implies that the objectivity of justice has been preserved during the procedures. This independence is particularly essential in criminal cases where the innocent are condemned and the guilty are set free. That is why we demand the impartiality of prosecutors, judges, and the trial attorney during all procedures of criminal justice.[53]

The principle of independence means that lawyers ought to exercise independence without any interference during criminal procedures and should not tamper with the evidence or witnesses in order to win the case and receive a larger payment. Furthermore, the independence of lawyers is particularly significant regarding systematic crimes that have been committed over many years by their clients and caused immeasurable harm to the victims. Here, our reference is not only to the national criminal system, but also the international criminal system, where lawyers know that their services have been employed to help the accused. A clear example of this, as we will discuss later, occurred in Myanmar concerning the crimes of the government against the Rohingya minority. In this case, the lawyer for the Myanmar government, William Schabas, supported the genocide, crimes against humanity, and war crimes committed by the Myanmar authorities against the Rohingya minority and denied the genocide with one-eyed-justice in order to receive his payment. He rejected the 444-page report of the UN Independent International Fact-

---

[53] Vladimir Tochilovsky, 'Objectivity of the ICC Preliminary Examinations', in Morten Bergsmo and Carsten Stahn (editors), *Quality Control in Preliminary Examination*, Vol. 2 (Torkel Opsahl Academic EPublisher, Bruss, 2018).

Finding Mission on Myanmar's brutal crimes against the Rohingya civilians submitted to the Human Rights Council in September 2018. The report clarifies that:

> documented how Myanmar's military brutally and systemically violated the human rights of ethnic minorities throughout the country. It focused on the military's 'clearance operations' against the Rohingya minority in Rakhine State in 2017, when security forces killed thousands of Rohingya civilians, raped and sexually abused women and girls and burned their villages in an explosion of violence that forced the exodus of more than 700,000 people in two months. Both military and civilian sides of Myanmar's government persistently deny the facts and disclaim any responsibility for crimes under international law. Following this violence, Myanmar authorities have levelled empty Rohingya villages with bulldozers, effectively destroying criminal evidence, while making no substantive progress in resolving the ethnic animosities that have helped fuel the crisis.[54]

Maintaining unbiased, professional judgment while advising a client is thus not only a duty of lawyers, but is also essential for maintaining their independence. The intention of a lawyer must be to protect their client during legal or criminal procedures. Lawyers must also be aware of the fact that they should not modify the case at the expense of the victims in favour of their clients. But what is really meant with independence is indeed complicated, since a lawyer carries out two functions: one is to protect their clients with full independence through offering unbiased advice and representation, and the other is to uphold the principles of criminal justice, respect the judicial conscience, and maintain the basic principles of justice.[55]

---

[54] UN Independent International Fact-Finding Mission on Myanmar urges financial isolation of Myanmar military, available online at https://www.ohchr.org/EN/HRBodies/HRC/Pages/NewsDetail.aspx?NewsID=24608&LangID=E.

[55] Kevin Boyle, *Arc of Justice: A Saga of Race, Civil Rights, and Murder in the Jazz Age* (2002); B. E. Harcourt, *Beccaria's on crimes and Punishments*: *A Mirror on the History of the Foundations of Modern Criminal Law* (2013); Matthew Lippman., *Contemporary Criminal Law: Concepts, Cases, and Controversies* (5th ed., 2021); Richard G. Singer., *Examples & Explanations for Criminal Law* (7th ed., 2018); Farhad Malekian, *The Monopolization of*

Thus, murder is murder and cannot have another definition. However, murder can be carried out under many different circumstances. For example, murdering a person with full consideration of the principle of proportionality may be interpreted as self-defence based on the given evidence and the conditions under which the murder was carried out. This means that although a court may use the term "murder", they may reduce the sentence of the accused or allow for acquittal based on the evidence. The result is a soft concept of the criminal responsibility of the accused. Additionally, the client may argue that the accused committed the crimes in self-defence in order to save lives. Here again, the case depends on the evidence presented by the trial lawyer, their presentation, and how convincing their arguments are.

3.3. Professional Independence of Lawyers

The independence of the administration of criminal justice is so essential and vital that it is imperative and indispensable to the components of criminal justice and the appropriate operation of the law. A lawyer should not act without first properly examining the evidence and basing their judgements and conclusions thereon for the sake of their clients. At the same time, the independence of lawyers also plays a significant role in the administration of criminal justice. This means that a lawyer should not be given orders by others and their independence should not be hindered in an attempt to hide the truth. In many countries, the independence of lawyers is artificial and dependent upon the involvement of political authorities who take interest in finding certain people guilty of crimes. This is especially common in non-democratic countries which lack political independence.

International Criminal Law in the United Nations, A Jurisprudential Approach (Almqvist Wiksell International, 1st ed., 1993), (2nd ed., 1995); Farhad Malekian, *The Mirage of International Criminal Law: Kant's Metaphysics of Mens Rea* (Cambridge Scholars Publishing, 2018); Malekian, *Conscience of Prosecutors in International Criminal Law, the Heart of the Heart of the Matter*, note 14.

Thus, even if a lawyer agrees to defend a client in court, they may be prevented from doing so by authorities who wish to conceal evidence which could exonerate the client. Therefore, the independence of a lawyer is not guaranteed and their efforts can be interfered with or hindered, especially by those in power. It would be difficult for a lawyer fully to protect their clients. The guarantee that lawyers keep their independence is a basic requirement for the protection of the rights of citizens in any democratic society. The requirement of independence demands that lawyers not provide information to government officials or anyone else who may be interested in the case. It is therefore imperative for all internal bodies of a country to respect the legal profession of lawyers.

However, the independence of lawyers is often interfered with and violated. This is also regardless of the fact that the clients of a lawyer are entitled to independent, impartial, unbiased, dispassionate, unprejudiced, and candid advice from their lawyers. Although the requirements of clients are logical and based on the human rights of the accused, the lawyer may or may not maintain their independence if interfered with. In such circumstances, the lawyer should inform their clients and not attempt to conceal the pressure being placed on them by authorities. Maintaining independence necessitates that lawyers act for their clients in the absence of improper conflicting self-interest, excessive external influences, or any other matter that may interfere in the case and impact the best interests of the client with due regard to their professional judgment.[56]

There may also be other factors which impact the independence of a lawyer. Such factors include the involvement of the lawyer in business transactions with the client, improper disclosure of information, and a lack

[56] However, with this we do not mean that a lawyer should manipulate justice and modify the basic definitions of law and ethics. The principle of morality, i.e. the truth, should be the guiding principle in all national and international cases. However, this morality also depends upon love. If love for the morality of justice and for the morality of the truth and conscience does not prevail in the heart of the lawyer, the corpus juris of justice will be seriously damaged. A clear example of this is the Myanmar case in the International Court of Justice and William Schabas' denial of genocide. See *infra*. A further example is the Chinese genocide against the Uighur population and the interference by the United States and the United Kingdom through their puppet Geoffrey Nice, a British lawyer, in order to protect the superpowers' interests in place of the fundamental principles of human rights. See also *infra*.

of expressed consent for their actions from their client. Therefore, it may be that a lawyer becomes involved in an occupation or activity whilst working for a client which creates a conflict of interest on the part of the lawyer.

3.4. Honesty in the Profession of Lawyers

Honesty in the legal profession, although rarely seen, constitutes the basic ethical foundation of the profession. It is assumed that lawyers maintain the highest standards of honesty in their profession at all times, and do not violate the integrity of justice in any way. Lawyers should always serve and protect their clients with honesty and integrity. Honesty, integrity, and fairness should also be respected in the court and by judges, prosecutors, and their colleagues. A lawyer is supposed to work independently and honestly advise their clients.

Therefore, lawyers should act in a manner which demonstrates that their words can be trusted and such that their actions are visible. In particular, it is imperative that every member of the legal profession maintains their honesty, integrity, personal morality, and fairness in all situations.[57] That is why the term judicial conscience not only relates to judges or prosecutors of a court, but also to lawyers who are supposed to respect the integrity of judicial conscience at all times and not violate its code of ethics. It is generally presumed that even lay people who act as witnesses are honest in their statements.

That is why lawyers and trial attorneys have a moral duty to not present false documentation or make false accusations against any party in the case. This is particularly evident in criminal cases where the lawyer is responsible for simultaneously protecting their clients and the integrity of the criminal jurisdiction. Thus, a lawyer who knowingly presents a false statement of the principles of law or the rule of law is actually violating

[57] L. M. Baum, 'Pursuing Justice in a Climate of Moral Outrage: An Evaluation of the Rights of the Accused in the Rome Statute of the International Criminal Court,' 19 *Wisconsin International Law Journal* (2001).

the essence of justice and the integrity of criminal jurisdiction in order to serve their economic interests. Thus, in the course of representing a client, a lawyer must be cautious in giving advice. As a result, lawyers have an obligation to be professional towards their clients, the opposing parties, and other members of the legal profession. This also includes the courts, its judges, and the office of the prosecutor, as well as court personnel and the public. Accordingly, the obligations include acting with courtesy, respect, politeness, candour, diligence, professional integrity, personal dignity, and also impartial cooperation regarding all matters which arise during a case.

It is also imperative for all lawyers in the world to formulate their arguments in a polite manner and to speak respectfully and calmly. This is because the duty of lawyers is to be peaceful and tranquil in order to offer balance and time for others to understand the case. This implies the fact that lawyers should not threaten any of the parties to the case in the court or anyone outside of the court. All this denotes the skill of lawyers and their ability to uphold the standards of integrity and dignity as required by the administration of criminal justice. That is why we list courtesy, respect, civility, frankness, thoroughness, expert capacity, personal dignity, and impartial professional talent as some of the necessary requirements to be met by a lawyer in order to ensure that criminal justice is being protected. All these qualities are seen as being essential to the fair administration of justice and conflict resolution between parties.

Nonetheless, it is also a fact that there are various standards foreseen for the clients, the court, and professional colleagues, since lawyers and the trial attorneys have different obligations to the members of different professions. When we talk about the obligations of lawyers, we are talking about different criminal legal systems which have various classifications of criminal legal professions. This means that the appearance of these duties or obligations of lawyers varies from one jurisdiction to another. Although national and international ethical rules may be similar, a lawyer is obliged to follow the particular ethical rules of international criminal tribunals or courts if their client's case requires it. This is the same in the case of a lawyer working in the International Court of Justice in The

Hague. Moreover, if there is cross-border teamwork and cooperation between lawyers from different criminal jurisdictions or regions at play, the ethical norms require that the lawyers be adaptable and flexible regarding the differences between legal systems, and are therefore presumed to follow the rules and regulations of the legal profession of certain regions as well. This also means that lawyers are required to understand and follow the host state's standards of ethical norms, and at the same time not violate the international standard of norms.

3.5. DOPPELGÄNGER SMOKESCREEN OF THE CONSCIENCE OF LAWYERS

With the term "doppelgänger" we refer *inter alia* to the duality of human nature and to individuals who act differently depending on the situation they are in and who pretend to be a certain type of person, when they are not so in reality.[58] A doppelgänger may knowingly or unknowingly murder or harm the victims of crimes against humanity, war crimes, and genocide in order to pursue their own interests. With the term the "burden of doppelgänger", we refer to the duty of a lawyer who has a split personality when it comes to their duties. Normally, it is presumed that a lawyer works in the pursuit of justice and the truth. The "burden of doppelgänger" of a lawyer therefore shows the two-faced nature of lawyers, with the second face following the money.

Additionally, within the majority of cultures, lawyers are seen as having doppelgänger traits, which means they have different personalities depending on the circumstances of a case. Furthermore, the doppelgänger double can be described as an equivalent to the self. Thus, the image of a doppelgänger lawyer is commonplace and the doppelgänger's

[58] Donald Nicolson, 'Making Lawyers Moral? Ethical Codes and Moral Character', 25 (4) Legal Studies (2005), pp.601-626. DOI: https://doi.org/10.1111/j.1748-121X.2005.tb00686.x; K. Economides (ed) *Ethical Challenges to Legal Education and Conduct* (Oxford: Hart Publishing, 1998); S. Parker and C Sampford (eds) *Legal Ethics and Legal Practice* (Oxford: Clarendon Press, 1995); R. Cranston (ed) *Legal Ethics and Professional Responsibility* (Oxford: Clarendon Press, 1995).

interpretation of the law changes based on who is writing them the bigger check at the time. The lawyer is often a protagonist in a criminal court and is often opposed to by an antagonist who may be the opposing lawyer, a member of the jury, the prosecutor, or a judge of the court. The use of the doppelgänger motif is not employed in order to degrade national or international lawyers, but to highlight the fact that lawyers can have a doppelgänger-esque character. This character may mislead the jury and judges as well as the international public. As a result of this, struggles for the peaceful settlement of international disputes or struggles to bring criminals under criminal jurisdiction for appropriate prosecution and punishment may fail. This nature of lawyers could be seen during and after the establishment of the Saddam Hussein tribunal where certain American lawyers were the puppets of the ventriloquist politicians of the US government and the CIA. One lawyer involved in the tribunal was a professor of criminal law who followed the orders of the United States government and worked very closely with the CIA and other international criminal law lawyers.[59]

Therefore, lawyers have multi-faced moralities which change depending on who is paying them. It has been said that such lawyers can run with you like the best running dogs but then kill you like wolves. In order to be sure that they have different characters, they may have more than their fair share of common moral shortcomings. Criticisms of lawyers' mentality therefore have a long history in the system of jurisdiction. As stated in the New Testament: "Woe to you lawyers also! For you load people with burdens hard to bear, and you yourselves do not touch the burdens with one of your fingers."

A lawyer in a conflict needs to know what the law is, not what the values behind the law might be. As a result, they rarely pose questions of reason, but rather pose themselves the question of how they can win the case and succeed in the relevant proceedings. This means we have lost sight of the ultimate objective because of one-eyed justice. If an attorney does the work required of them then the client pays the attorney's hourly

[59] Malekian, 'Emasculating the Philosophy of International Criminal Justice in the Iraqi Special Tribunal', note 48.

charges. Consequently, the attorney has to follow the conditions set by the client. Normally, for the lawyer, it is not the norm of judicial conscience or justice which plays the most important role, but rather the norm of cash which brings them more clients and improves their reputation.[60] For most lawyers, winning a case is their main goal, while the morality, legality, or ethics implicated in the case are hardly addressed. One example of this was when William Schabas, a Canadian lawyer who represented the Government of Myanmar, defended their acts of genocide against the Rohingya minority by stating that these acts did not in fact constitute acts of genocide.[61] Therefore, the relevant lawyer is two-faced, with one face supporting the system of international law, while the other follows the money and rejects the system when necessary in the ICJ. Thus, he can be referred to as a doppelgänger lawyer. Two and a half centuries earlier, King Louis XII of France made a statement which fits the situation in The Hague: "Lawyers use the law as shoemakers use leather; rubbing it, pressing it, and stretching it with their teeth, all to the end of making it fit their purposes."[62] However, we fully understand that a person is not trained with the conscience of a lawyer to destroy, but they learn it throughout their life. Boswell long ago asked: "but what do you think of supporting a cause which you know to be bad or you know that has already committed?" How can a lawyer strongly condemn capital punishment by declaring its abolition but then support the criminal acts of certain governments based on a different interpretation of the same principle? It is not therefore irrelevant here to quote the song by ABBA - -"Money Money Money"

I work all night, I work all day
To pay the bills I have to pay

---

60 Quoted with modification from Malekian, *Judgments of Love in Criminal Justice,* note *52*, pp.158-159.

61 Here, we are referring to an author "who is supposed to know" and not "is he supposed to know". For instance consult his work on William A. Schabas, 'O Brave New World': The Role of the Prosecutor of the International Criminal Court,' 83 (4) *Die Friedens-Warte*, -(2008), pp.11-31. The fact is that Schabas orchestrates a *one-eyed-justice*.. For Schabas see also Malekian, *Judgments of Love in Criminal Justice*, note 52, pp.290, 294, 298, 299, 304, 309 and 310.

62 Tuli Kupferberg, *An Insulting Look at Lawyers Through the Ages*, 8 Juris Doctor (Oct./Nov. 1978), at 62.

Ain't it sad?
And still there never seems to be
A single penny left for me
That's too bad

In my dreams I have a plan
If I got me a wealthy man
I wouldn't have to work at all
I'd fool around and have a ball

Money, money, money
Must be funny
In the rich man's world
Money, money, money
Always sunny
In the rich man's world
(*In the Lawyer world*)[63]

3.6. Conscientious Duties of Defence Attorneys

The defence attorney of the defendant has to remain loyal to their client, treat them as innocent, and respect their human rights. Therefore, there are certain principles that must be fulfilled by the defence attorney and which act as guidelines under the procedures of criminal justice. These principles also have an ethical nature and demonstrate the high moral and professional understanding of the defence attorney concerning their profession including the judicial conscience of the defence lawyer. Some of these principles include:

a) All defence attorneys are prohibited from exploiting the circumstances faced by prisoners in order to gain more work for their offices,
b) Defence attorneys should not compete with one another in order to take the work of one office into their own office and therefore treat the accused as pawns in their game,

[63] The modification of term is mine.

c) Defence attorneys should be faithful to defendants as prescribed by their duties and profession,
d) Defence attorneys should also be faithful to all those who provide assistance to the defendant,
e) It is a recognised duty of defence attorneys to take all necessary measures in order to protect their clients. This includes not only utilising their knowledge and skills, but all also doing everything within their power to protect a defendant,
f) It is incumbent on defence lawyers to offer their experience in criminal cases without delay,
g) The defence attorney must not jeopardise the rights of the defendant under any circumstance,
h) All presentations made during the procedures of criminal jurisdiction must be done in consultation with the defendants,
i) Any document presented by the defendant to the defence attorney must be evaluated carefully in order to determine its legitimacy,
j) The defence attorney must be conscientious when exercising their professional obligations regarding the attorney,
k) The defence lawyer should not hesitate in providing any assistance to the defendant,
l) Once the defence attorney has accepted the case, they should fully protect the defendant,
m) The defence attorney should provide assistance through the end of proceedings and should not cease providing support to their clients in favour of taking on other cases,
n) In certain circumstances in which the defence may no longer be useful to the defendant, the defence attorney must inform the defendant and withdraw themselves from the case,
o) All assistance provided to the defendants must be equal and should not be based on the social positions of the defendants,
p) When there exists irrefutable evidence that the defendant has committed the prescribed crime, the defence attorney must take all measures to ensure that the defendant is not put in danger by the opposition,

q) If the client has admitted guilt, the defence lawyer must work to protect the defendant, their future, and their reputation,

r) The defence attorney should not exploit the position of the defendant in order to get more cases,

s) Any public statement about the defendant must be made cautiously, and if possible, be avoided, in order to avoid jeopardising the position of the defendant,

t) The defence attorney must respect the human rights of the defendant for the duration of proceedings as well as after the final judgement,

u) The attorney is responsible for putting the truth on the desk of the court and not hiding the truth,

v) The defence attorney should not create false evidence in exchange for payment,

w) The defence attorney should not ignore the rights of other parties if they know the defendant to be guilty,

x) An attorney shall not defend or free the defendant from guilt in such a way as to shift the blame to other co-defendants, or increase their responsibility in order to decrease the level of involvement of their client,

y) If there are several people accused of a collaborative crime, the defence attorney should not allow race to impact their treatment of the co-defendants,

z) All presentations made under the procedures of criminal jurisdiction must be made in consultation with defendants,

aa) The defence attorney must not only show their loyalty to the defendant, but also towards the judicial conscience and its independence.

3.7. Cover-up or Discovery of the Root of Truth

The question facing lawyers is normally: how would you like to cover-up the basic hidden facts of a case? Most lawyers pay attention to the arguments presented by their client but ignore the opposing party's side of the story. Examples of this include the South African lawyers who were complicit in the criminal conducts of the Apartheid regime against the native population.[64] Attorneys do not properly see the practical effects, the practical loss, or the real nature of the relations they are carrying out and what harm they are causing, rather they look at their bank accounts. One cannot deny the fact that there may be other situations in which lawyers truly work for the love of justice with full conscience and ethical responsibility. However, this rarely occurs and the first instance is more common.

An example of lawyers representing politics instead of justice are the lawyers who participated in the criminal tribunal for Saddam Hussein.[65] In 2004, the United States government, with the assistance of its intelligence agencies, drafted a plan to bring Saddam Hussein under national prosecution and to punish him with the assistance of an American international criminal lawyer, Swedish human rights lawyers, and judges who participated in the fake tribunal in London. Given the large number of lawyers and teachers in the United States, the question is why the United States needed a Swedish lawyer. Was there a shortage of lawyers in the United States? Definitely not. The reason was simply to have different names involved, and to demonstrate that there were also other countries

---

64 Gracia-Amador, 'The Crime of Apartheid: Responsibility and Reparations', *Review of Contemporary Law* (1981), pp. 31-38; J.K. Feimpong & S. Azadon Tiewel, 'Can Apartheid Successfully Defy the International Legal System?' 5 *The Black Law Journal* (1977), pp. 287-311; Garry Seltzer, 'The Rule of the South Africa Criminal Code in Implementing Apartheid', 8 *Georgia Journal of International and Comparative Law* (1978), pp.176-194; Roger. S. Clark, 'The Crime of Apartheid', in M. Cherif Bassiouni (ed.), *International Criminal Law*, vol. I (1986), pp. 299-323; *Paris Declaration, International Conference on Sanctions Against South Africa (And Special Declaration on Namibia),* 27 May1981, Published by the United Nations Center Against Apartheid; Enuga S. Reddy, *Apartheid: The United Nations and the International Community* (1986); Enuga S. Reddy, 'India and the Struggle Against Apartheid', 26 *Indian Journal of International Law* (1986), pp. 551-567; Farhad Malekian, *International Criminal Law*, vol. I, (Almqvist Wiksell International, 1991), pp. 324-375.

65 Malekian, 'Emasculating the philosophy of international criminal justice in the Iraqi special tribunal', note 48, 673–723; see also Jordan Engelhardt, *The Pre-eminent State: National Dominance in the Effort to Try Saddam Hussein, Cornell Journal of International Law*, (2009); Jeremy Peterson, 'Unpacking Show Trials: Situating the Trial of Saddam Hussein,' 48 *Harvard International Law Journal* (2007).

that agreed with the United States' involvement in the punishment of Saddam Hussein.

The aim was for the president of Iraq not to be prosecuted by an international court, based on the fact that Saddam Hussein could release confidential information about his prolonged complicity with the United States concerning certain international matters, which would not have had a good impact on US foreign policy.[66] Consequently, the United States came up with the idea of establishing a national criminal court in order to prosecute Saddam Hussein and other relevant authorities, which became a show tribunal. President Bush decided to have the prosecutors and judges for the Tribunal trained in London. This was because the judges and the prosecutors of the Special Tribunal for Hussein did not have the requisite knowledge of national or international crimes. It was hence necessary for the United States to demonstrate to the world that the Tribunal was a real Tribunal similar to the International Criminal Tribunal for the former Yugoslavia. This meant they decided to invite and hire lawyers to come give lectures to the judges of the new tribunal.

In practice, this meant that the Tribunal was using certain internationally-known lawyers in order to give the impression that the procedures were legitimate and supported by those who were delivering the lectures. The search began among international lawyers to find those suitable for the job. Personally, I was in Beijing, China, attending the meetings of the International Penal Association, where a number of international criminal lawyers were discussing questions relating to juvenile justice, trafficking, and the principle of *ne bis in idem*. It was at this time that the Secretary General of the United Nations, Kofi Annan, asked international lawyers to reject the request of the United States government to teach in the tribunal. This was because the Secretary General considered the tribunal to be monopolised by superpower diplomacy.

Sometime later, a well-known Swedish international lawyer, Hans Axel Valdemar Corell, who had agreed to teach in London, appeared on a

---

[66] Adopted from Malekian, 'Emasculating the Philosophy of International Criminal Justice in the Iraqi Special Tribunal,' note 48.

TV program. The reporter, who disagreed with the position taken by the lawyer, raised the question: 'are you aware of the fact that the Secretary General of the United Nations has required international lawyers not to give a positive response to the request of the United States government?' The lawyer responded to the question without any shame by stating: "I couldn't turn my back to the request." Here, obviously the lawyer was not only ignoring the very respectful official statement of the Secretary General of the United Nations concerning the illegality of the Special Criminal Tribunal for Saddam Hussein, but was also strongly engaged against the principle of ethical conscience for justice, rules of law, humanity, the respect of the principles of international criminal courts, and the basic principles of international human rights law according to European law. This was a lawyer who had been engaged in the identification and protection of the principles of international human rights law and had protected and supported human rights conventions, declarations, and agreements. These agreements were codified under the United Nations Security Council's immeasurable legal power, where all problems of inequality in the international system originate. Corell could not see this problem, and could not understand the fact that international criminal justice was being monopolised by the big members including by the UK and the US. Alternatively, he understood this, but still chose to ignore this fact for as long as those governments supported him.

Corell apparently did not have true respect for the independence of justice from politics and the integrity of the impartiality of the judges and lawyers and the court to any extent. Although he was working on drafting a convention governing crimes against humanity in Nuremberg, this did not guide him to reject the payment. Additionally, before agreeing to the lecture, the lawyer should have known about the opinion of Hans Blix, a Swedish international lawyer known for his strong statements against the propaganda promoted by the United States government against Iraq in an attempt to access oil by claiming that Saddam Hussein had weapons of mass destruction in his possession.[67]

---

[67] On earlier works of Blix consult Hans Blix, Sovereignty, Aggression and Neutrality (Dag Hammarskjöld Foundation1970).

Since Corell was also an official diplomat of the Swedish government, he should have known about the CIA's decades-long alliance with Saddam Hussein's regime. He should also have been aware of the fact that the US sanctions against Saddam Hussein were based on political conspiracies and were issued with the goal of obtaining access to oil. These sanctions led to the suffering of over 550,000 children during the Gulf Crisis.[68] Obviously, Corell knew all these facts. One may raise the question regarding what the real reason was for ignoring all these factors and giving in to lecture lawyers who only had experience with traffic law. It is here that Hans Axel Valdemar Corell, who claimed to be a supporter of human rights law, should have known that the Tribunal had already decided in advance to apply capital punishment, which violated international standards.

"What is wrong with lawyers' ethics?"[69] Alternatively, what is the real strength: to love justice or to be a hard-hearted person who lacks the capacity for genuine compassion for true justice? However, lawyers may yearn to access justice by identifying its legal merits. Nonetheless in the aforementioned case, the lawyer ignored the real face of justice by viewing "clients as walking boundless of legal rights and interests rather than as whole persons whose legal issues come deeply intertwined with other concerns relationships, loyalties, hopes, uncertainties, fears, doubts, and values – which shape the objectives they bring to legal representation."[70] In addition, a lawyer is morally responsible both for the advice they give, as well as for the advice they fail to give.[71] This is particularly significant

---

[68] Consult Farhad Malekian, *Prohibition Governing Child Soldiers Constituting an Integral Part of Jus cogens and Obligatio Erga Omnes*, XVII *World Congress of the International Association of Youth and Family Judges and Magistrates*, Belfast, Northern Ireland, 27 August – 2 September (2006); Malekian Farhad and Kerstin Nordlöf, - - 'International Legal Status of Children' in the *Encyclopaedia of Criminology & Criminal Justice* (United States: Wiley-Blackwell (5 volumes, 2013), vol.III, pp.1173-1178; Malekian, 'The Child as an Autonomous Subject of Justice' note 36, pp.2-55; Farhad Malekian, Kerstin Nordlöf, *Confessing the International Rights of Children: The Basic documents with Analysis* (Cambridge Scholars Publishing, 2012); Farhad Malekian, Kerstin Nordlöf, *Prohibition of Sexual Exploitation of Children Constituting Obligation Erga Omnes* (Cambridge Scholars Publishing, 2013).

[69] B. Wendel, *Lawyers and fidelity to law. New Jersey* (Princeton University Press, 2012).

[70] K. R. Kruse, Lawyers in Character and Lawyers in Role, 10 *Nevada Law Review*, 10, 393. (2010), p. 393.

[71] R. Pearce, 'Model Rule 1.0: Lawyers are Morally – Accountable', 70 *Fordham Law Review* (2002), p. 1807.

in the case of international crimes committed by the Iraqi president with the support of the United States.[72] Did Corell provide advice to the ill-equipped judges of the Tribunal that they should not follow government orders or that they should not violate the prohibition on capital punishment? Without any hesitation, Corell seriously violated the system of international criminal law, the provisions of international criminal justice, and basic international human rights norms.

3.8. Defence Attorneys in International Criminal Courts

A defendant within the system of international criminal justice can stand trial *pro se,* which means that they represent themselves without an attorney during a hearing or trial. This however is not advisable with reference to the fact that defending oneself in an international court without the assistance of a defence team/defence counsel is not only difficult, but an act of self-sabotage. The procedures of criminal justice are very demanding in the preliminary hearing, which is held in order to determine if there is enough evidence i.e., probable cause, to proceed with a prosecution. Therefore, it is advisable for defendants to engage lawyers to represent them.

In the system of international criminal law, we have ratified a number of international treaties dealing with the notion of international crimes. Still, the system not only relies on the merit of international conventions but also the value of certain customary norms of international criminal law which prohibit the commission of certain international crimes by individuals, organisations, groups, governments, and states. All these recognitions under the system of international criminal law are still not automatically empowered; their enforcement is based on several factors and the policies of a given criminal jurisdiction. Generally, violations of

---

72 Presented by modification from Malekian, *Judgments of Love in Criminal Justice*, note 52, 158-161.

the system of international criminal law are treated in several ways. If violators of international law are arrested, they are brought under the power of criminal jurisdiction, whether under the authority of the International Criminal Court (ICC), an *ad hoc* international criminal tribunal, or, in certain situations, they will be prosecuted according to the principle of complementarity.[73]

According to the Statute of the ICC, all national criminal jurisdictions in the world are empowered to punish those who have committed international criminal crimes, and if they cannot perform this international obligation for any reason, they should submit the suspects to the jurisdiction of the ICC or an *ad hoc* international criminal tribunal, which is a mixed tribunal with both national and international characters. There is also another alternative for the prosecution of violators of international criminal conventions or *jus cogens* international criminal law. Through this alternative, individuals are prosecuted using the principle of universality which permits all states to bring the perpetrators of international crimes under their jurisdiction to be prosecuted and punished.[74]

---

[73] Consult Jann K. Kleffner, *Complementarity in the Rome Statute and National Criminal Jurisdictions* (Oxford, 2008); Ondřej Svaček, 'The Human Rights Dimension of the ICC's Complementarity Regime', Czech Yearbook of Public and Private International Law, 2015, Vol. 6, pp. 273-288; *Mohamed El Zeidy, The Principle of Complementarity in International Criminal Law: Origin, Development and Practice* (Brill, 2008); *Sarah* M Nouwen, *Complementarity in the Line of Fire: The Catalysing Effect of the International Criminal Court in Uganda and Sudan* (2013); S. Fouladvand, Complementarity and cultural sensitivity: Decision-making by the International Criminal Court (ICC) Prosecutor in Relation to the Situations in the Darfur Region of the Sudan and the Democratic Republic of Congo (DRC) (2012); William W. Burke-White, 'Implementing a Policy of Positive Complementarity in the Rome System of Justice', 19 *Criminal Law Forum* (2008). See also Malekian, *Orchestrating Diversity in International Criminal Justice*, note 14, pp.35-37, 125-128, 140-143, 173-176, 221-224.

[74] Farhad Malekian, 'Conundrums of *Jus cogens:* In Case Law' (Part II), No.13 *Вісник Південного регіонального центру Національної академії правових наук України, No.13 Journal of the South regional Center of National Academy of Legal Sciences of Ukraine (*2017), pp.12-21; Farhad Malekian, 'Conundrums of *Jus cogens*: in International Criminal Law' (Part I), *Вісник Південного регіонального центру Національної академії правових наук України No.12 Journal of the South regional Center of National Academy of Legal Sciences of Ukraine (*2017), pp.8-16; A Cassese, 'For an Enhanced Role of *Jus cogens*' in A Cassese, (ed.), *Realizing Utopia* (2012); Antônio Augusto *Cançado Trindade* '*Jus cogens* in Contemporary International Law', UN Audiovisual Library, (http://www.un.org/law/avl); M. Byers 'Conceptualising the Relationship Between *Jus cogens* and *Erga Omnes Rules*' 66 *Nordic Journal of International Law* (1997); J. Brunnée,

3.9. Specific Rights of Defendants in the ICC

As a whole, and despite the aforementioned ignorance of the system of international human rights by powerful states and slave lawyers, the system of international criminal jurisdiction intends to be fair and just because all those who have committed international crimes should be prosecuted fairly and justly. That is why the system of international criminal law officially empowers all courts dealing with the violators of international criminal conventions to ensure that the accused have official defence attorneys to assist them throughout proceedings. This assistance is given from the initiation of criminal procedures up until the judgment is read. Therefore, within the system of international criminal courts and tribunals, every defendant is entitled to public and fair international proceedings. This entitlement extends to plea hearings where the defendant gives their formal plea of guilty or not guilty to the charges they are facing. In addition, a *nolo contendere* plea is similar to a guilty plea— it carries the same fundamental consequences, but does not constitute an official admission of guilt. A plea of 'not guilty' implies that the defendant is denying that they committed the crime with which they were charged. In sum, all procedures should be conducted impartially and all parties should be treated equally. The Rome Statute of the ICC grants defendants specific rights including:

a) The right to be informed of the charges against them or the reason why they are accused of committing international crimes,

---

'The Prohibition on Torture: Driving *Jus cogens* Home?' 104 *Proceedings of the Annual Meeting of the American Society of International Law* (2010); A. Bianchi, 'Human Rights and the Magic of *Jus cogens*', 19 *European Journal of International Law* (2008), pp.491-508; C. Chinkin, '*Jus cogens*, Article 103 of the UN Charter and other Hierarchical Techniques of Conflict Solution' *Finnish Yearbook of International Law* (2006); C. Chinkin, '*Jus Cogens*, Article 103 of the UN Charter and Other Hierarchical Techniques of Conflict Solution', 17 *Finnish Yearbook of International Law* (2008), pp.63-90;, A. D. Amato, 'It's a Bird, It's a Plane, It's *Jus Cogens*' 6 *Connecticut Journal of International Law* (1990); C Bassiouni, 'International Crimes: *Jus cogens* and *Obligatio Erga Omnes*' 59 *Law and Contemporary Problems* (1996).

b) The accused person should receive sufficient time to prepare their defence for the Court,
c) The accused has the right to ask for criminal procedures to begin immediately,
d) The accused should not be forced to work with any specific defence attorney, rather they should have the right to freely choose their attorney themselves,
e) The accused's defence attorney has the right to examine all witnesses and present necessary evidence, and no one can be forced to testify or confess guilt. This denotes the free expression of consent to any matter and the prohibition of psychological or any other immoral pressure placed upon the accused,
f) Anyone being investigated by the prosecutor's office is permitted to remain silent and cannot be forced to disclose information,
g) The accused should be informed of any evidence uncovered by the prosecutor which speaks for their innocence,
h) It is also the right of the accused to obtain evidence in the possession of the prosecutor which may mitigate the guilt of the accused,
i) The accused is also entitled to be able follow the proceedings in a language which they understand. Interpreters and translations must be provided if necessary.

3.10. Assistance of the Office of the Public Counsel

It is imperative that the procedures of defence be independent since a powerful defence is a dynamic component of a fair criminal trial. A defence team's duty is to represent and safeguard the rights of the defendant at all times. As an element of criminal jurisdiction, all defendants are presumed innocent until proven guilty *beyond a reasonable doubt* following the proceedings of an international criminal court.[75]

According to ICC requirements, the counsel for the defence is independent and is not considered part of ICC staff. Therefore, any defence team must be qualified to protect the rights of the accused before the Court. The Court has also set-up facilities which are necessary for the defence team in order to be able to prepare for cases brought before its jurisdiction. The ICC may also arrange reasonable compensation for the legal representation of anyone unable to pay for their defence. Moreover, the defence team may also receive assistance from the Office of Public Counsel for the Defence (OPCD), which was established according to the Regulation 77 of the Court. The OPCD is an independent office and also falls within the Registry's sphere, however solely for administrative purposes. This entire means that the defence team is independent, which allows the Office to work without being subjected to pressure of any kind and helps preserve attorney-client privilege.

The tasks of the OPCD include protecting the rights of the defence during the initial stages of an investigation, providing support and assistance to the defence counsel— such as by providing legal advice and appearing before a Chamber, and acting as *ad hoc* counsel if appointed by a Chamber to secure permanent legal representation for the accused. The OPCD is not an office of public defender per se because the accused are guaranteed a free choice of counsel under the Rome Statute. The OPCD does not interfere with, nor regulate the policy of the individual defence team. The Office helps the defence team offer quality representation to their clients in an efficient and speedy manner.

[75] On international criminal court consult See Vespesian V. Pella, Plan d'un Code Répressif Mondial, 6 Rewe International de Droit Pénal 1948 (1935); United Nations War Crimes Commission, History of the United Nations War Commission and the Development of the Laws of War. 443-50 (1949); Vespesian V. Pella, Towards an International Criminal Court, 44 American Journal of International Law 37 (1950); A. Sowilet, Sowilet A., The Problem of the Creation of a Permanent International Criminal Court (1951).

Chapter 4

DUTY OF THE DEFENCE TEAM TO PRESENT THE BARE TRUTH

4.1. PROFESSIONAL DEFENCE TEAM IN THE ICC

The ICC has a mandate to try cases using reasonable, independent, and objective methods. This means that the ICC seeks to establish justice which is impartial from all aspects and which does not create unfair and immoral reasonings.[76] Therefore, in cases where guilt is established beyond a reasonable doubt, the condemned will be held responsible for the serious crimes that they have committed against the established rules of the international legal community. The intention of the Court is to serve as a practical, good model of the judicial administration of criminal justice and to ensure that the proceedings of the Court conform with the highest legal values and with the due process rights of suspects, the accused, and the condemned. In order to present impartial justice, the defence must be represented correctly in order to ensure that the procedures of the Court run smoothly. Both are integral parts of one another and should not be presented in isolation. Criminal justice which does not have a good

[76] Alasdair MacIntyre, *After Virtue: A Study in Moral Theory* (Notre Dame: University of Notre Dame Press, 1982).

administration of defence cannot be just since the suspect or the accused cannot defend themselves appropriately, nor can their case be properly heard.

The key element of good criminal justice is a professional "defence team", which refers to counsel who are capable of understanding and presenting cases.[77] The defence team is actually the most crucial component of a fair trial. The significance of safeguarding the rights of the defence is mirrored in the founding instrument of the ICC, its Statute, as well as the related principles and provisions of the Court. Their intention is to effectively guarantee the implementation of proper criminal justice proceedings with due regard to the judicial powers of the independent judges of the Court. Two of the basic principles enshrined in the Rome Statute of the ICC for the protection of the accused by their lawyers are the presumption of innocence and the grounds for dismissing criminal responsibility. Article 67 of the Rome Statute guarantees the accused's right to a public, impartial, and fair hearing in addition to other minimum guarantees:

> 1. In the determination of any charge, the accused shall be entitled to a public hearing, having regard to the provisions of this Statute, to a fair hearing conducted impartially, and to the following minimum guarantees, in full equality: (a) To be informed promptly and in detail of the nature, cause and content of the charge, in a language which the accused fully understands and speaks; (b) To have adequate time and facilities for the preparation of the defence and to communicate freely with counsel of the accused's choosing in confidence; (c) To be tried without undue delay; (d)Subject to article 63, paragraph 2, to be present at the trial, to conduct the defence in person or through legal assistance of the accused's choosing, to be informed, if the accused does not have legal assistance, of this right and to have legal assistance assigned by the Court in any case where the interests of justice so require, and without payment if the accused lacks sufficient means to pay for it;(e)To

---

[77] William St-Michel, Chloé Grandon and Marlene Yahya Haage, 'Strengthening the Role of Defence at the International Criminal Court: Reflections on How Defence is and Can Be Supported for Greater Effectiveness and Efficiencies, 18 (3) *International Criminal Law Review* (2018), pp.517-539.

examine, or have examined, the witnesses against him or her and to obtain the attendance and examination of witnesses on his or her behalf under the same conditions as witnesses against him or her. The accused shall also be entitled to raise defences and to present other evidence admissible under this Statute; (f)To have, free of any cost, the assistance of a competent interpreter and such translations as are necessary to meet the requirements of fairness, if any of the proceedings of or documents presented to the Court are not in a language which the accused fully understands and speaks; (g)Not to be compelled to testify or to confess guilt and to remain silent, without such silence being a consideration in the determination of guilt or innocence; (h)To make an unsworn oral or written statement in his or her defence; and (i) Not to have imposed on him or her any reversal of the burden of proof or any onus of rebuttal.
2. In addition to any other disclosure provided for in this Statute, the Prosecutor shall, as soon as practicable, disclose to the defence evidence in the Prosecutor's possession or control which he or she believes shows or tends to show the innocence of the accused, or to mitigate the guilt of the accused, or which may affect the credibility of prosecution evidence. In case of doubt as to the application of this paragraph, the Court shall decide.[78]

The above are the rights of the accused as stated in the Rome Statute and the defence team is certainly responsible for the protection of these prescribed rights. These rights also have an international standard for the protection of all those who are accused of committing national or international crimes. Overall, the defence team is responsible for proving the innocence of the accused, if possible, or to present reasoning and argumentation which contribute to the mitigation of the guilt of the accused. However, all contributions made by the defence team must be made within the framework of the ethical construction of international standards and should not violate the judicial conscience of the Court or criminal justice. With this we also mean that the defence team is responsible for presenting all cases and arguments without any interference

[78] Consult also other provisions of Rome Statute.

and while maintaining their impartiality to the highest legal and moral standard.

4.2. Defence Attorneys' Crucial Duties

The defendant and their legal advisors or lawyers are together considered the defence team. The defence team's purpose is to protect the defendant during criminal proceedings and to attempt to have their punishment reduced or for them to be acquitted. That is why the ICC provides certain facilities for the defence team, including the chief defence attorney of the accused. Thus, the defence team may be referred to by several other terms such as defence lawyers, accumulation, joined, collection, or aggregation. One of the most indispensable duties of the defence team in the system of international criminal justice is to protect the consolidated human rights of the accused. These rights should be respected not only under *ad hoc* international criminal jurisdiction, but also by national or regional courts dealing with international crimes such as genocide, crimes against humanity, war crimes, and aggression.[79]

i. The defence team should explain the charges faced by the defendant in plain language,
ii. They should inform their client that they have the right to remain silent if no member of the defence team is present,
iii. The defence team should protect the rights of the defendant during the pre-indictment stages,
iv. The defendant has the legal right to be immediately informed of the charges against them, and the grounds for such charges,
v. The defence team should ensure that the right guaranteed in (iv) is fulfilled,

[79] Adopted from Malekian, 'Emasculating the Philosophy of International Criminal Justice in the Iraqi Special Tribunal,' note 48.

vi. The defence lawyers should ensure that the defendant receives appropriate treatment while in prison and awaiting court proceedings,

vii. The defence lawyer should ensure that the defendant is not discriminated against,

viii. The defence attorneys should ensure that the defendant is not insulted by guards or other prisoners,

ix. The defence attorneys should ensure that the accused is guaranteed appropriate sleep and rest before and during proceedings,

x. The defence team should ensure that the defendant has sufficient facilities in prison and receives enough food and other necessary daily needs,

xi. The defence team should ensure that if the defendant has children and/or a spouse, that they are able to meet them under the supervision of the ICC,

xii. The defence attorney should make sure that news reports, newspapers, and/or books are made available to the defendant,

xiii. The defence attorney should guarantee that the defendant is kept in sanitary conditions,

xiv. The defence team should make medical assistance available to the accused, if required,

xv. The defence team should ensure that the defendant is accompanied by a guard to the hospital,

xvi. All members of the defence team should collectively respect the political, judicial, economic, social, cultural, religious, and theoretical beliefs of the defendant,

xvii. The defence team, and particularly the main defence lawyer , should ensure that the defendant is not interrupted or ignored during the proceedings in the interest of time,

xviii. The defence attorney should do all within their power to ensure that the defendant is given enough time to prepare their arguments for proceedings,

xix. The defence attorney should guarantee that the accused's legal right to abstain from testifying during the proceedings is respected,

xx. The defence attorney should ensure that the defendant receives a fair trial,

xxi. The defendant has a right to a public hearing as dictated by international norms,

xxii. The defence attorney should guarantee that the defendant is presumed innocent until proven guilty,

xxiii. The defence attorney should inform the defendant that they have the right to be present for the duration of their trial,

xxiv. The defence attorney should not permit a political official to oversee the fulfilment of the rights of the defendant during the proceedings of the Court or Tribunal,

xxv. The defence attorney should inform the defendant that they have the right to ask for new attorneys if desired,

xxvi. The defence attorney should ensure that the right of the defendant to cross-examine witnesses is not ignored by a court,

xxvii. The defence attorney should ensure that the defendant is not convicted for an act or omission that was not a crime at the time it was committed according to the provisions of national criminal law, regional criminal law, and/or international criminal law,

xxviii. The defence attorney should reject any coerced confession made by the defendant,

xxix. The defence attorney should emphasise to the court that the threat or use of degrading and humiliating treatment against the defendant or their family for the purpose of extracting evidence is not admissible in fair and just proceedings of national, regional, or international criminal courts,

xxx. The defence attorney should protect the defendant's rights to appeal,

xxxi. The defence attorney should not let a national court applying the system of international criminal law apply capital punishment.[80]

4.3. Duties of the Defence Team

The following are some of the duties of the defence team or defence counsel:

1. The defence lawyers must maintain their objectivity concerning the given case at all times,
2. The defence team must work diligently on their cases in order to uncover all relevant information,
3. The defence team must be familiar with all rules and promote the victim's right to a reduction of punishment if possible. All arguments and presentations must be presented properly and objectively. Therefore, the defence must hear all information relevant to a given criminal case,
4. If there is any need to call more witnesses for the benefit of the accused, the defence team must inform the Court of this,
5. The duty of the defence team is not only to defend the accused, but also the independence of judicial conscience, ethical morality, and the presentation of facts that may be useful for the acquittal of the defendant,
6. The defence team is responsible for working to have the accusations against their client dismissed, without hiding facts or destroying evidence,
7. The defence team must conduct themselves morally and not get angry, frustrated, or use unprofessional language which could degrade the victims,

[80] See also *id.*, pp. 712-3

8. It is also essential that the defence team show their compassion toward all parties in the case and respect the rights of all victims equally,
9. The defence team must fully respect and accept the fundamental human rights of all involved in the case, regardless of the cultural, religious or ethnic backgrounds of the parties to the case,
10. A defence team should not ignore the rights of thousands of victims who have been brutally murdered during the commission of international crimes,
11. The defence team should acknowledge the devastation that has been caused by the accused and help the accused realise the impact of their criminality as much as possible,
12. The defence team must carry out their duties in consultation with the accused and with the hope of establishing the truth,
13. The defence team should be aware of the fact that any falsification or destruction of any document is unlawful and jeopardises the quest for the truth.

4.4. Code of Professional Conduct for Counsel

The ICC has to follow rules that are imperative for the presentation of its framework within the Court.[81] These rules have different characters and

[81] Yeun-Li Liang, The Establishment of an International Criminal Jurisdiction: The First Phase, 46 *American Journal of International Law* (1952); Quincy Wright, Proposal for an International Criminal Court, 46 *American Journal of International Law 60* (1952); Bienvenido C. Ambion, Organization of a Court of International Criminal Jurisdiction, 29 *Philippine Law Journal* 345 (1954); Fannie Klein & Daniel Wilkes, United Nations Draft Statute for an International Criminal Court: An American Evaluation, in *International Criminal Law* 526 (Gerhard O.W. Mueller & Edward M. Wise eds., 1965); Stone Julius and Robert Woetzel, *Toward 16 a Feasible International Criminal Court* (1970). Jean Dautricourt, The Concept of International Criminal Court Jurisdiction-Definition and Limitations of the Subject, in 1 *A Treatise on International Criminal Law* 636 (M.C. Bassiouni & V.P. Nanda eds., 1973); La Créationd'une Jurisdiction Pénale Internationale et la Coopération Internationale en Matière Pénale, 45 *Revue Internationale de Droit Penale* 435 (1974); Louis Kos-Rabcewicz-Zubrowski, The Creation of an International Criminal Court, in *International Terrorism and Political Crimes* 519 (M. Cherif Bassiouni ed., 1975); Benjamin Ferencz, *International Criminal Court* (2 vols. 1980); M. Cherif

different natures for the better implementation of the Court's duties within the system of international criminal justice. Similar conclusions may also be drawn about any other parts of the ICC, such as the counsel who work within its framework. However, it must be added that some aspects of the rules which should be exercised under the procedures of the ICC, are not only international in nature, but can also be found within the provisions of national criminal jurisdictions. An example of this is the Code of Professional Conduct for Counsel, which is practiced by various nations of the world (with minor reservations). This means that the provisions of the Code do not contradict national criminal justice jurisdictions or the functions and rules of the counsel in the administration of criminal justice.

The Code of Professional Conduct for Counsel aims to bring certain imperative rules to the recognition of those who are working in the ICC, although the independence of the jurisdiction of the Court should be respected. The duties of Counsel are to give appropriate advice to clients who seek assistance or are represented by the counsel. The Code makes it clear that with the term "associate", it refers to lawyers who practise in the same law firm as the counsel, and with the phrase "national authority", it refers to the Bar Association to which the counsel belongs.[82] The Code regulates what the system of professional conduct for counsel requires to be respected during proceedings under the system of international criminal law, and their roles in the maintenance of the independence of the Court and the counsel. However, the Code clearly underlines its primacy by stating that wherever "there is any inconsistency between this Code and any other code of ethics or professional responsibility which counsel are bound to honour, the terms of this Code shall prevail in respect of the practice and professional ethics of counsel when practising before the Court."[83]

Bassiouni & Daniel Derby, Final Report on the Establishment of an International Criminal Court for the Implementation of the Apartheid Convention and Other Relevant Instruments, 7 *Hofstra Law Review* 523 (1981).

[82] Article 2.

[83] Article 4: Primacy of the Code of Professional Conduct for counsel.

The lawyers, attorneys, or defence team working with the counsel must also take the same oath as judges of the Court. They solemnly declare that they will carry out their duties and obligations and exercise their "mission before the International Criminal Court with integrity and diligence, honourably, freely, independently, expeditiously and conscientiously." They should also carry out their functions appropriately and "scrupulously respect professional secrecy and the other duties imposed by the Code of Professional Conduct for Counsel before the International Criminal Court".[84] The members of the counsel exercise care to ensure the respect of professional secrecy and the confidentiality of information with due regard to the rules of the Statute. Counsel should also comply with the relevant provisions of the Code with due regard for the orders of the Court.

Any disclosure of information should be in accordance with the Statute; and subject to the Statute, counsel may only disclose information protected under the provisions of the Statute. The Counsel must not reveal the identity of protected victims and witnesses, as well as any other confidential information that could indirectly reveal their identity. In particular, the Code establishes the rule that discrimination between clients should not be exercised by the members of the counsel. This can be in relation to any other person, on the grounds of race, ethnic or national origin, nationality, citizenship, political opinions, religious convictions, gender, sexual orientation, disability status, marital status, or any other personal or economic factors. The counsel lawyer is also responsible for other behavioural matters such as respecting the circumstances of the client and not engaging in any improper conduct, such as demanding sexual favours.[85]

Certain significant provisions are also found within the Code which relate to certain situations where the Counsel should not represent a client in a given case. These include:

---

[84] Article 5.
[85] Articles 8 and 9.

1. Counsel shall not represent a client in a case:
(a) If the case is the same as or substantially related to another case in which counsel or his or her associates represents or formerly represented another client and the interests of the client are incompatible with the interests of the former client, unless the client and the former client consent after consultation; or
(b) In which counsel was involved or was privy to confidential information as a staff member of the Court relating to the case in which counsel seeks to appear. The lifting of this impediment may, however, at counsel's request, be ordered by the Court if deemed justified in the interests of justice. Counsel shall still be bound by the duties of confidentiality stemming from his or her former position as a staff member of the Court.
2. In the case of paragraph 1 (a) of this article, where consent has been obtained after consultation, counsel shall inform the Chamber of the Court seized with the situation or case of the conflict and the consent obtained. Such notice shall be provided in a manner consistent with counsel's duties of confidentiality pursuant to article 8 of this Code and rule 73, sub-rule 1 of the Rules of Procedure and Evidence.
3. Counsel shall not act in proceedings in which there is a substantial probability that counsel or an associate of counsel will be called to appear as a witness unless:
(a) The testimony relates to an uncontested issue; or
(b) The testimony relates to the nature and value of legal services rendered in the case.
4. This article is without prejudice to article 16 of this Code.[86]

Some other requests of the Code of Professional Conduct for Counsel which work to prevent violations of the Rome Statute and protect the merit of the integrity of international criminal justice from an international perspective are *inter alia*:

---

[86] Article 12.

a) Counsel has the right to refuse an agreement without stating their reasons why,[87]
b) Counsel has a duty to refuse an agreement where there is a conflict of interest as per Article 16 of the Code, if counsel is incapable of dealing with the matter diligently, or if they believe that they lack the required expertise,[88]
c) Counsel should maintain their objectivity while consulting with their client and act with fairness, integrity, and candour towards their client,[89]
d) All communication between counsel and their client should be carried out reasonably and counsel should inform their client about the decisions they make,[90]
e) When there is a conflict of interest between counsel and their clients, the interests of the latter should be prioritised as much as possible, and the client should be informed. In such cases, counsel should ensure that an equivalent replacement is found for their client,[91]
f) The duration of the counsel-client relationship is to be determined per agreement before proceedings begin. The duties of counsel towards the client continue until the agreement expires, except for those duties which concern the Code,[92]
g) Respect of certain rules concerning the fee charged by counsel is considered important. The rate of compensation should be established in written form. Remuneration in cash should be refused by the counsel,[93]
h) Counsel should not have contact with the Chambers and judges unless the judge or the Chamber dealing with a case permits it in exceptional circumstances,[94]

---

[87] Article 12.
[88] Article 13.
[89] Article 14.
[90] Article 15.
[91] Article 16.
[92] Article 17.
[93] Article 20-22.
[94] Article 23.

i) Any form of humiliation by the counsel is prohibited,[95]
j) Counsels should treat each other and their clients fairly,[96]
k) Any relationships between counsel and unrepresented individuals should only occur with the expressed consent of their clients,[97]
l) The integrity of all evidence, in written, oral, or any other form should be respected, [98]
m) The counsel should not be prejudiced and should take personal responsibility for their conduct.

4.5. Counsel Misconduct

The notion of misconduct in the system of international criminal law refers to acts which are not permitted due to the regulations, provisions, or principles of the law. Misconduct comes in different forms, varies in degree of gravity, and may even be justified in certain situations. Misconduct thus refers to an action which is not identified as being correct in the social or cultural relations of groups or individuals. However, despite prohibitions within the context of law and ethics, misconduct continues to be carried out and committed to varying degrees of severity, particularly by governments, superiors, and state organs.

In other words, misconduct refers to unjust, unfair, inappropriate, or unlawful conduct carried out in order to prevent certain situations. This means misconduct, whether it has positive or negative consequences, remains wrongful conduct. The intention of misconduct is certainly to change the course of events in order to benefit the culprit. Certain acts are also recognised as misconduct within the system of international criminal justice, including falsification, sexual misconduct, and other acts of misconduct carried out by the parties involved in proceedings. The Code of Professional Conduct for Counsel has foreseen the situation in which

---

[95] Article 29.
[96] Article 27.
[97] Article 26.
[98] Article 25.

counsel or one of the members of the defence team commit actions which may mislead the judges of Chambers, the prosecutor's office, witnesses, victims, or the accused. While misconduct may not be a serious criminal offence, it can still impact the direction of a case and be qualified as a crime.

The Code of Professional Conduct for Counsel requires that a commissioner responsible for investigating complaints of misconduct be established following reports of such.[99] A number of articles of the Code deal with acts of misconduct carried out by counsel. Accordingly, Article 31 deals with misconduct committed by counsel including violations or attempts to violate any provisions of the Code, the Statute, or any other legal provisions. Counsel may also encourage others to carry out prohibited acts or fail to comply with disciplinary decisions.[100] In such cases, the counsel orders or approves the relevant misconduct or is at least aware of it. Therefore, the Code requires that counsel assist staff in uncovering and reporting misconduct.

Any failure to report misconduct may be investigated by the Chamber dealing with the case, the prosecutor, or any person or group of persons whose rights or interests may have been affected by the alleged misconduct against the counsel.[101] It is the duty of the registrar to inform the commissioner of any complaints. All complaints should be kept confidential by the registrar. The statute of limitations for complaints against counsel for misconduct is five years.[102] Based on this, the Code also describes how a Disciplinary Board set up to investigate such misconduct should look and act.[103] The disciplinary procedure in the Code should be applied by the Board.[104] The Code includes comprehensive suggestions concerning how to deal with misconduct and its prevention. The duties of the Disciplinary Board and its decisions play important roles, and the Board may conclude the investigation and decide that there was no

---

[99] Article 33.
[100] Article 32.
[101] Article 34.
[102] Article 35.
[103] Article 36.
[104] Article 38.

misconduct based on the evidence provided. The Board may also conclude that the counsel should be subject to disciplinary proceedings. These decisions of the Board should be made public and relayed to the individual subject of the disciplinary procedures and to the registrar. It should also be published in the Official Journal of the Court and transmitted to the national authority.[105] The proof of misconduct on the part of the counsel may ultimately result in payment of fine, suspension of the right to practise before the Court for a period not exceeding two years, or may even lead to a permanent ban.[106]

The Code also describes in detail the composition and functions of the Disciplinary Appeals Board during their investigations of misconduct.[107] During the investigation, the Code of Professional Conduct for Counsel grants certain rights to the counsel regarding their defence. The Code therefore recognises the rights of counsel who are subject to the disciplinary procedure following alleged misconduct. The defence lawyer is hence entitled to receive assistance from another counsel if they wish. Additionally, counsel has the right to remain silent before the Disciplinary Board, which may draw any inferences it considers constructive and reasonable from such silence while taking into account all the available information. The defence counsel has the right to the full disclosure of any evidence or information in the possession of the Commissioner as well as their report. The defence counsel should be given adequate time to prepare their defence. They must also have the right to question, personally or through their own counsel, any person appearing before the Disciplinary Board in order to testify.[108] The Code also provides the right to appeal the decision of the Disciplinary Board by the sanctioned counsel and the commissioner as per certain regulations.

---

[105] Article 41.
[106] Article 42.
[107] Article 44.
[108] Article 40.

4.6. Moral Obligations of Lawyers Regarding the Truth

The rules of ethics in criminal justice play a very significant role in the proper and fair outcome of justice. Due to this, those who are working within the system of criminal justice should realise that their decisions, actions, approaches, and arguments play important roles in the lives of all parties, can change people's lives, and can even frame the innocent as guilty and the innocent as guilty. That is why the system of the administration of justice seeks the truth and should be based in it. The truth must not only come out at the end of proceedings, but must be present throughout in the actions of all parties to a case. However, this may be very difficult for the judges, prosecutors, and members of jury based on the fact that they do not have access to the truth if they are unable to view and analyse authentic evidence. They are therefore obliged to work wisely and with open eyes as much as possible in order to uncover the true nature of the criminal case.

This is why criminal cases are complicated, especially cases involving international crimes. However, the fact is that the most difficult task facing any court and its judges is to ensure that their findings do not infringe upon the rights of any party and that their statements are based on verified evidence. Therefore, moral obligations are not only a necessary corollary element in the administration of criminal jurisdiction for judges and prosecutors, but also for those who are working as defence lawyers, defence attorneys, or who are an integral part of the defence team. The ethical and moral responsibility of lawyers becomes more serious when they present certain documents, witnesses, or evidence which impact the final judgement and outcome of the case.

Since a lawyer or defence attorney meets their client and gathers all the information about a case before accepting it, they must be sure that their client is not lying. Therefore, a lawyer is responsible for ensuring that what they are presenting in civil or criminal courts does not harm the other side of the case. This is the same in the case of international criminal law and its implementation within national and international criminal courts. Based on reasonable facts, a lawyer must evaluate all matters and arguments made by their client and determine whether they are true and not in violation of ethical and moral codes. Moreover, an international human rights or criminal lawyer must be skilled and should have the capacity to recognise when their client is lying, which arguments do not make sense, and when the truth is missing from the narrative of a case. Additionally, moral, ethical, legal, and professional conscience requires judges to evaluate all matters with due regard to the fact that there may be some invisible part of the case that cannot be revealed as it would impact the client's position and even support the opposition

All this means that there are certain duties incumbent on lawyers before accepting any case. There are therefore a considerable number of questions relating to the moral responsibility of lawyers who represent their client in a civil or a criminal court with flawed or insufficient evidence. The responsibility here becomes more serious for the lawyer when the other parties to the case suffer as a result of a wrong decision on the part of the court. The lawyer obviously cannot claim that certain factors were outside of their control. This is because the moral responsibility of lawyers does not end with the end of the case. Certainly, any lawyer working in the system of national or international criminal courts should realise that their engagement and argumentation may have led to the wrong decision and that it could have been prevented. The key to understanding these elementary questions of moral responsibility therefore does not rely on how we explain the cases, but rather on how we ignore the sensitive parts of cases and fail to dig deeper into the arguments of our clients regarding certain very important questions of humanity.

4.7. Ethical Responsibility for Lawyers Regarding Wrongful Presentation

A criminal defence lawyer in a criminal court acts in accordance with basic criminal law. However, if a defence lawyer does not have the necessary background in criminal law to represent their client, they cannot be a good lawyer and could jeopardise the quality of criminal justice. As their client's representative, a lawyer functions as a person who knows the law and presumes they can win the case. This means that from the start of the case, it is expected that the lawyer has the full moral capacity to understand both sides, and to understand that their client speaks the truth. If a lawyer or a criminal defence lawyer does not realise that their client is lying and hiding the truth, how can they defend their client in front of judges, prosecutors, or members of jury?

Defence lawyers therefore function as advisors and provide informed legal guidance to their clients. This means that they must be able to recognise which statements made by their client are lies and which are the truth. As a negotiator in a civil case, or a defence lawyer in a criminal case, lawyers seek the best result for their client. However, this does not necessarily mean that lawyers should ignore their moral or ethical responsibilities towards other parties who may become victims of the wrongful presentation of the case by the lawyer in a civil or a criminal court. This is more obvious when lawyers defend clients in an international court such as in the ICC or even in the International Court of Justice (ICJ) in The Hague.

Although we fully understand that lawyers must first and foremost represent their clients, this does not mean that lawyers should ignore the facts or ignore the commission of international crimes by their clients only because they are receiving money. This occurred, for example, in the case of genocide against the Rohingya minority in Myanmar brought before the ICJ. The defence lawyer in this case actually encouraged the ongoing commission of genocide and crimes against humanity by supporting the brutal criminal authorities of the government of Myanmar.[109]

---

[109] For much analysing about genocide consult Farhad Malekian, 'Armenian Genocide and the Questions of Responsibility of the Turkish Government,' *House of Commons Conference on the Armenian Genocide, Armenian Solidarity, British-Armenian All-Party Parliamentary Group, No Security Publication* (2007), pp.31-9; J. Duffett, *Against the Crime of Silence* (New York, London, 1968). W. Michael Reisman, 'Legal Responses to Genocide and Other Massive Violations of Human Rights', 59 *Law and Contemporary Problems* (1996), p.75; Beth van Schaack, 'The Crime of Political Genocide: Repairing the Genocide Convention's Blind Spot', 106 *Yale Law Journal* (1997), p.2259; John D. van

As a result, the members of the government of Myanmar understood that they were permitted to continue their actions since an international criminal lawyer argued in an established international court that said acts did not constitute genocide. This means that the moral responsibility, ethical duties, judicial conscience, and legal obligations which constitute integral parts of the legal profession were totally ignored by the defence lawyer and the criminal Myanmar government. As an evaluator, a criminal defence lawyer or attorney acts by examining all conducts of their client, and if this significant principle of criminal justice or professional jurisdiction is not met by an international criminal lawyer who has a lot of experience with international criminal norms, what can we expect from other lawyers who acts as lawyers of fees and not as lawyers of the truth?

4.8. Lacking Moral Conscience

Any lawyer who modifies the principles of the systems of international criminal law and international human rights law, or the definition of genocide in exchange for money, is not a good lawyer and cannot be trusted. As Nelson Mandela asserted: "for anybody who changes their principles depending on whom he is dealing, that is not a man who can lead nation," or international criminal justice. Under the system of international criminal law, particularly when it comes to serious international crimes, it is assumed that a defence lawyer has the clear moral capacity to not deal justice with payments, not modify rules to serve personal interests, and to not deny elements of the crime of genocide in order to satisfy their client's political, economic, and evil interests.

---

der Vyver, 'Prosecution and Punishment of the Crime of Genocide', 25 *Fordham International Law Journal* (1999), p.286; Mary Robinson, 'Genocide, War Crimes, Crimes Against Humanity', 25 *Fordham International Law Journal* (1999), p.275; William A. Schabas, Genocide in International Law, the Crime of Crimes (2000); Matthew Lippman, 'Genocide', in *International Criminal Law*, Vol. I (M. Cherif Bassiouni, ed., 2008) pp.405-455. In particular, see the statements of Bertrand Russell and the Russell International War Tribunal held in Stockholm, Sweden, May 2-10, 1967 and Roskilde, Denmark from November 20 to December 1, 1967.

The conducts of a (defence) lawyer must align with the requirements of the judicial conscience of the law for which the law has been codified. All professional lawyers should make clear to their client that there is a big difference between the national concept of crimes and the established concept of international crimes. In other words, a number of crimes under national criminal law may be listed under their criminal jurisdiction and may be dealt with using different propositions, arguments, and provisions which imply the fact that the definitions of certain crimes vary slightly from state-to-state.

However, under the system of international criminal law, we have an established a framework for recognising genocide, which is quite different from the national concept of crimes based on the fact that the theory, principles, and definitions of international crimes are the same for all states of the world. This means that a defence lawyer or a defence attorney should not offer their own definition or explanation of the elements of crimes which have already been codified. An international lawyer should refer to the elements of crimes of genocide through the confirmation, and not the rejection, of the given facts. A systematic commission of certain criminal conducts against a particular group with the intention of ending their lives and social existence cannot be interpreted as anything other than genocide, and such acts should not be ignored to serve political or economic interests.

Such arguments may not only be rejected under the system of international criminal law, but they also deny the immoral achievement of defence lawyers, who ignore the rights of the victims to serve their own interest. This constitutes the rejection of the principle of legality within international criminal law and justice. As Phil Robertson, Deputy Director of Human Rights Watch's Asia Division stated *"William Schabas is basically selling out the Rohingya for some Myanmar gov't $$$. Really the worst sort of behaviour, how totally immoral and two-faced," And the defence attorney protected his position by stating: "I am an international lawyer. I do international law cases."*

According to which logic, if any, can we destroy a country, and then announce that we are pulling our troops out? Is this not a clear and

> *convincing proof of our animality? How can we employ secretive private companies such as Blackwater in the fight against injustice?* How can an international criminal lawyer defend criminals, a criminal government, or a brutal military regime (such as was the case with the genocide committed by Myanmar against the Muslim Rohingya population) and then go on to state: *"I am hired as a lawyer, they're my client" as a justification for that support?* Where are the values behind this reasoning?[110]

Schabas also stated that his position concerning Myanmar was not emotional, but rather professional, adding: regarding genocide "the debates can be not only quite robust, but people get angry very quickly…I am hired as a lawyer, they're my client." [111] This means that one could violate the systems of international criminal justice, international human rights law, and international humanitarian law whenever they deem fit in order to pursue financial interests. Stephen Rapp, a former United States war crimes ambassador, sharply criticised William Schabas for his wrong and immoral achievements and intentionally false interpretation of the term genocide in order to protect his client and ignore the rights of victims. *Rapp rightly concluded: "We have heard this morning from my friend Bill Schabas, I was just with him 10 days ago. I prosecuted genocide, we obtained convictions for this crime. He is wrong about the law: this was a genocide."* In addition, it is not without reason that Schabas was criticised for the violation of the principle of impartiality and the immorality of accepting such criminal conducts and painting them as non-criminal. Accordingly, the defence lawyer "had breached his duty of impartiality as head of the UN Human Rights Council inquiry" based on the fact that through accepting this case he made prejudicial statements "including his call to indict Israel's prime minister as his 'favourite' defendant ..."[112] This implies that lawyers can sell the system of international criminal justice and the body of international human rights, even regarding the brutal

---

[110] Malekian, *Trading Virginity of International Criminal Justice*, note 19, p.18.

[111] Anthony Deutsch, Myanmar's lawyer to critics on genocide case: Everyone has right to defence, https://www.reuters.com/article/us-myanmar-rohingya-profile-schabas-idUSKBN1YH02J.

[112] Stated by Hillel Neuer, the director of the United Nations Watch.

international crimes committed in Palestine by the Israeli government, as long as money continues to flow into the bank account of William Schabas. For some international criminal lawyers, money constitutes a combination of the fragrant liquid provisions of the rules of criminal law made from the blood of the victims of genocide which has been extracted from their dead bodies and the destruction of their houses.

4.9. AFFIRMATIVE DEFENCES BY THE DEFENCE TEAM

In the system of international criminal justice under the authority of the ICC, the prosecution ought to introduce evidence that denotes the commission of an international crime or crimes under the superior order of the defendant. This means that certain charges against the defendant under the control of the ICC are established by the Court. The defendant, with the assistance of their defence lawyer, challenges the evidence by questioning its reliability, interpretation, relevance, and its legal value. This is because all crimes which have been investigated under the authority of the ICC against certain African leaders have been political in nature. In such cases, one political party accuses another political party, and normally there are profound arguments about certain crimes which have been denied by the defence team. As a result, the burden of proof becomes more difficult to overcome when international crimes have been committed in response to the actions of another political party.

While the prosecutor's obligation is to prove that the defendant is guilty, the defence team's obligation is to prove the contrary. Thus, the burden of proof remains with both sides i.e., prosecutor and the defence team. The prosecutors and the defence team therefore work parallelly to each other, yet in opposition. The prosecutor produces evidence on every element of the alleged crime. It is here that the prosecutors must meet the "burden of production" and if they can't, the defendant will be entitled to an acquittal. For example, if the prosecutor states that the accused has committed genocide, they have to prove the existence of the elements of crimes of genocide such as intention to destroy and a systematic nature of the crimes. These are two of the requirements which prove that the defendant intended to wipe out a certain race, culture, religion, or ethnic group with their actions. Thus, the defence team may reject the evidence and argue that the evidence points to crimes against humanity but not genocide.

Certainly, the prosecutor of an international criminal court should gather all the evidence required for trying an international crime. Thus, convincing the judges of the Chambers of the Court is the job of two opposing sides— which means that the prosecutor must prove to the judges that the evidence is sufficient, while the defence must prove that it is not. The truth of the crime must be established beyond a reasonable doubt, and the relevant evidence must meet the necessary requirements of the crime. Consequently, the standard of proof in international criminal law and justice is "beyond a reasonable doubt". This principle is required to confirm a criminal conviction in connection with the presumption of innocence. This is what the ICC has been engaged with in a number of cases where evidence has proven that the defendant was guilty. Here, the defendant may concede that the prosecution has proven every element of the charged crime or genocide but still presents an argument why they should nevertheless not be convicted. Here, the defence team provides "affirmative defences," with the intention of proving that the crimes were committed in self-defence.

Here again, it is up to the defence team to provide evidence that the defendant did not intend to commit acts of genocide or crimes against humanity, but was forced to do so in order to save the lives of others. Thus, affirmative defences do not reject that the defendant carried out the alleged crimes, but question their motivation for doing so. It is here again the duty of the prosecution to prove beyond a reasonable doubt that the evidence produced by the defendant's team is insufficient and does not meet the standard of the prosecution's evidence. The defence team not has only the burden of producing evidence, but the burden of persuasion as well. The defence lawyer therefore must prove the validity of their claim by a standard less rigorous than "beyond a reasonable doubt," which implies the need for much stronger evidence that the defendant had no intention of committing the international crime of genocide.

Chapter 5

DEFENDING INTERNATIONAL CRIMES THROUGH THE ABSENCE OF APPARENT MOTIVE

5.1. LAWYERS PAINTING BIG POWERS AS VICTIMS

When the morality of international criminal lawyers is weighed on the scale of payment and fees or when the ethical questions of judicial conscience become a code of interests of defence lawyers, then the whole merit of criminal independence fails, justice becomes a game, and the knowledge of international criminal law becomes a privilege for all those who sell justice. As previously stated, we have seen similar problems with the show Tribunal for Saddam Hussein, where a number of well-known international criminal lawyers were working with the CIA and comparing their work to the work of Nobel Prize winners.[113] All this indicates the shortcomings of our knowledge of humanity and how that knowledge is

[113] Malekian, *The Mirage of International Criminal Law*, note 15; p.104; Mona Rishimawi, 'A Reality or a Mirage: Judicial Review of Detention,' in Charles Riziki Majinge (ed.), Rule of Law Through Human Rights and International criminal justice: Essays in Honour of Adama Dieng (Cambridge Scholars publishing, 2015), pp.507-522; Parish Matthew, International criminal law – Justice or Mirage? Transconflict (2013). Available online at http://www.transconflict.com/2013/05/international-criminal-law-justice-or-mirage-025/.

used, not to help humanity, but to serve our economic interests. The Saddam Husain Tribunal was not only wrong, but was largely supported by those who were working for the interests of big political and criminal governments of the world— namely the American and British governments.[114] The tribunal has been criticised for the following fundamental reasons which should have been understood by the lawyers working the case:

1. The Tribunal's statute was not drafted by a group of international lawyers chosen under the authority and supervision of the United Nations, but rather exclusively by lawyers chosen by the United States government,
2. Given that the newly formed Iraqi government had no independent political or legal character, especially governing certain serious questions of law, politics, and economics, the judicial effect of the Tribunal diminished automatically,
3. The Statute of the IST was not compatible with the United Nations Charter,
4. Unlike international tribunals such as the ICTY, the Tribunal could not function as an independent national or international criminal court having freedom of action regarding different judicial, historical, and political questions,
5. The Tribunal's ability to employ certain principles of justice was limited by procedure,
6. The proceedings of the Tribunal were subject to the will of the occupying power at all times,
7. Since Saddam Hussein was the most important subject of the tribunal, and since the Tribunal was in large part established to

[114] *Id*. The most significant fact is that after committing grave international crimes, the big international criminals write books about their history and go to church to ask for forgiveness. They have now bathed their crimes with holy water, even violating verses of repentance. For instance see Winston S. Churchill and Dr Martin Gilbert, *Churchill: The Power of Words: His remarkable life recounted through his writings and speeches* (2014); Bill Clinton, *My Life* (2005); Tony Blair, *A Journey* (2010); Barak Obama, *A Promised Land* (2020); George W. Bush, *A Decision Points* (2010). But, examine also Clarke Rountree, *George W. Bush: A Biography* (2010).

exercise its jurisdiction over him, the function and the significance of the Tribunal were compromised,

8. The judges of the Tribunal were not elected in accordance with international norms, as is done in the ICTY, but were rather chosen by the occupying power.
9. The judges of the Tribunal had far less experience regarding criminal cases involving serious human rights violations compared to the ICTY or ICTR judges,
10. Since the judges of the Tribunal were chosen by the Iraqi Governing Council, which lacked the power to pass legislation, the power of all judges remained a question of politics and policies of the occupying power and authority within the territorial jurisdiction of another state,
11. Given that the Tribunal judges were trained in London by the occupying power, they were likely to have found it difficult to remain impartial,
12. Since the former Iraqi government was known to have seized power with the political assistance of the United States, the Tribunal could not open any discussions that could divulge secret international political facts that could harm the position of the occupying power,
13. The cases that came before the Tribunal were selective and not exhaustive,
14. The limitations on the presentation of different cases as a result of political concerns that would affect the Hussein case and those of others accused of international crimes,
15. Due to bias, the Tribunal would be unable to consider those evidentiary rules that are supposed to control decisions of the court,
16. The judges, and the Tribunal as a whole, could not, in any way, guarantee a just outcome of the monopolized court,
17. The principles of international human rights could not appropriately be respected in a Tribunal that exclusively followed the rules of the victorious state,

18. The rights of the accused recognized by general principles of law were not free from political ties and therefore could not function under the proceedings of the forum,
19. The Tribunal prosecutors were not free from monopolisation by the victorious states, especially the United States.[115]

Moreover, there are a large number of international human rights conventions and provisions which demand the protection of human rights norms by the public and particularly by lawyers, regardless of the fact that lawyers sometimes assist criminals through their roles as criminal defence attorneys. Defence lawyers must not only protect their clients, but more significantly, the rights of the victims and the established facts. While it is the duty of the lawyer to protect the offender from accusations, it is also the professional duty of the lawyer to challenge the rectitude of established elements of crimes in order to not violate the moral ethics of the law under procedures of justice, particularly when it comes to the commission of international crimes by the big powers.

5.2. Shakespeare against Myanmar

It is relevant to state that although Shakespeare did not study law or the systems of international criminal law, justice, or human rights law, his discussions of the law show a profound knowledge of legal terminology and a sympathy with the universal principles underlying the rule of law, whether in Europe, the United States, or in the Islamic world. "The first thing we do, let's kill all the lawyers," that is, if they do not express love for the pure philosophy of reasonable justice. "When law can do no right, let it be lawful that law bar no wrong: Law cannot give my child his kingdom here, for he that holds his kingdom holds the law." It should be the main duty of law, lawyers, judges, prosecutors, and the systems of

[115] Malekian, 'Emasculating the Philosophy of International criminal justice in the Iraqi Special Tribunal,' note 48, pp.707-708.

national and international courts to respect the principles of ethical morality and purity for the just and fair application of justice in their judgments.

> *A lawyer is not a lawyer if she does not realise that her elegance of knowledge is not based on her income, position occupied, academic institutions, orations, or degrees. Knowledge of the law is not the knowledge of law if it cannot understand that the law does not need a lawyer with the knowledge of its laws but one with the knowledge of its substance for the morality of justice and for the love of justice. As Plato asserts, justice is "one's capacity to think rationally and to be able to follow the proper reasoning based on superior knowledge." These principles are in place in order to find a way to put an end to most reasons that are the basic source for the commission of grave violations of the system of international criminal human rights law.*[116]

Lawyers should make sure that their clients are conscious of the moral requirements of the case and that they should not ignore the requirements of truth and faithfulness. "Lawyers need to be able to engage their clients in a moral dialogue, which requires some familiarity with, and sensitivity to, moral reasoning." Lawyers clearly do not need to determine the moral requirements of the case for their clients. However, they should help their clients to find the correct answers to any moral questions through upholding a pure love for justice. The legal profession should avoid creating lawyers whose morality is based on payments, whose arguments are coloured by the power of criminals, and who not skilled at upholding the morality of criminal justice and its ethical standard of impartiality. This does not necessarily mean that lawyers should chose clients with moral skill, but the fact is that the big criminals, state crimes, the crimes of soldiers, the sexual exploitation of women and children during war, the torture of innocent civilians, and the destruction of their homes, villages and installations do not require the evaluation of moral skill. This should

---

[116] Malekian, *Judgments of Love in Criminal Justice*, note 52 p.101.

be clear to any lawyer who works for the integrity of justice, the humanity of rules, and as a minister of human rights law.

5.3. ICJ Judgment on Genocide

The ICJ came to a different conclusion than what was presented by the Myanmar government and its Canadian lawyer. The ICJ declared:

> 8. In the present case, having considered the terms of the provisional measures requested by The Gambia and the circumstances of the case, the Court finds that the measures to be indicated need not be identical to those requested.
>
> 79. Bearing in mind Myanmar's duty to comply with its obligations under the Genocide Convention, the Court considers that, with regard to the situation described above, Myanmar must, in accordance with its obligations under the Convention, in relation to the members of the Rohingya group in its territory, take all measures within its power to prevent the commission of all acts within the scope of Article II of the Convention, in particular: (a) killing members of the group; (b) causing serious bodily or mental harm to the members of the group; (c) deliberately inflicting on the group conditions of life calculated to bring about its physical destruction in whole or in part; and (d) imposing measures intended to prevent births within the group.
>
> 80. Myanmar must also, in relation to the members of the Rohingya group in its territory, ensure that its military, as well as any irregular armed units which may be directed or supported by it and any organizations and persons which may be subject to its control, direction or influence, do not commit acts of genocide, or of conspiracy to commit genocide, of direct and public incitement to commit genocide, of attempt to commit genocide, or of complicity in genocide.
>
> 81. The Court is also of the view that Myanmar must take effective measures to prevent the destruction and ensure the preservation of any

evidence related to allegations of acts within the scope of Article II of the Genocide Convention.[117]

It is interesting to see how an international criminal lawyer, whose duties are to respect the principles of international criminal law and justice and the principles of human rights, was able to reject them in one of the most brutal case of genocide in Europe since the crimes of the Nazis and Stalin.[118] Schabas rejected the establishment of the International Criminal Tribunal for the former Yugoslavia (ICTY) which was a United Nations court which investigated the Srebrenica genocide.[119] According to Schabas "Your old debate about Srebrenica was not whether it happened or not, it's not about that. It's about whether the legal qualification should be crimes against humanity rather than genocide." This interpretation of the lawyer, surely implies that Stalinism or Nazism must be present in order for crimes to be recognised as acts of genocide. This means that the statement of the ICTY was wrong when the ICTY President, Theodor Meron, an excellent and well-established international lawyer, correctly asserted:

> Among the grievous crimes this Tribunal has the duty to punish, the crime of genocide is singled out for special condemnation and opprobrium. The crime is horrific in its scope; its perpetrators identify entire human groups for extinction. Those who devise and implement genocide seek to deprive humanity of the manifold richness its

[117] Application of the Convention on the Prevention and Punishment of the Crime of Genocide (The Gambia v. Myanmar), available on website at https://www.icj-cij.org/en/case/178 and https://www.icj-cij.org/files/case-related/178/178-20200123-ORD-01-00-EN.pdf. See also Statement attributable to the Spokesman for the Secretary-General - on the International Court of Justice Order in the case "The Gambia vs. Myanmar Available online at "https://www.un.org/sg/en/content/sg/statement/2020-01-23/statement-attributable-the-spokesman-for-the-secretary-general-the-international-court-of-justice-order-the-case-the-gambia-vs-myanmar.

[118] Consult Antonio Cassese, *Cassese's International Criminal Law* (3rd Edition, Oxford Press, 2013).

[119] William L. Hurlock, 'The International Court of Justice: Effectively Providing a Long Overdue Remedy for Ending State-Sponsored Genocide (Bosnia-Herzegovina v. Yugoslavia)', 12 *American University Journal of International Law and Policy* (1997), p.299; Giulia Bigi, 'Joint Criminal Enterprise in the Jurisprudence of the International Criminal Tribunal for the former Yugoslavia and the Prosecution of Senior Political and Military Leaders: The Krajišnik Case' 14 *Max Planck United Nations Yearbook* (2010), pp.51-83.

> nationalities, races, ethnicities and religions provide. This is a crime against all of humankind, its harm being felt not only by the group targeted for destruction, but by all of humanity. The gravity of genocide is reflected in the stringent requirements which must be satisfied before this conviction is imposed. These requirements – the demanding proof of specific intent and the showing that the group was targeted for destruction in its entirety or in substantial part – guard against a danger that convictions for this crime will be imposed lightly. Where these requirements are satisfied, however, the law must not shy away from referring to the crime committed by its proper name. By seeking to eliminate a part of the Bosnian Muslims, the Bosnian Serb forces committed genocide. They targeted for extinction the forty thousand Bosnian Muslims living in Srebrenica, a group which was emblematic of the Bosnian Muslims in general. They stripped all the male Muslim prisoners, military and civilian, elderly and young, of their personal belongings and identification, and deliberately and methodically killed them solely on the basis of their identity. The Bosnian Serb forces were aware, when they embarked on this genocidal venture that the harm they caused would continue to plague the Bosnian Muslims. The Appeals Chamber states unequivocally that the law condemns, in appropriate terms, the deep and lasting injury inflicted, and calls the massacre at Srebrenica by its proper name: genocide. Those responsible will bear this stigma, and it will serve as a warning to those who may in future contemplate the commission of such a heinous act.[120]

It is not without reason that other lawyers call Schabas a "*genocide denier*", since he has denied the genocide which was committed in the middle of Europe in the presence of UN soldiers by the Serbs against the Muslims of Bosnia. The Bosnian Serb forces attempted to annihilate a group of the Bosnian Muslims by carrying out acts of genocide against its population. In 1995, over 8,000 Muslim were killed and thousands of Muslim women were brutally raped. The international criminal lawyer denied these crimes and opposed the ICTY's conclusions. This represents

[120] Statement by https://www.icty.org/en/press/address-icty-president-theodor-meron-potocari-memorial-cemetery Address by ICTY President Theodor Meron, at Potocari Memorial Cemetery

the killing of humanity, killing of justice, killing of the principles of international human rights conventions, and killing of the universality of the principles of *jus cogens* norms.[121] It seems that the Myanmar defence lawyer is, in one way or another, fighting against the Muslim population of the world, and surely for him the Chinese genocide against Muslims in Uighurs does not constitute genocide either.[122]

5.4. Unwise Arguments of Defence Lawyers

Delivering reliable judgments and confidence in justice does not necessitate witnesses, but rather wisdom. This wisdom should exist within every single judge and lawyer. If the defence lawyer has not understood the value of justice and the value of ethical norms in supporting the rights of victims in the system of international criminal justice, they are surely not aware of the value of ethical norms. Any legal representative who fights for the rights of their client without using their intuition for true and wise justice is not loyal to the soul of justice, but is rather an individual who is blind to fairness. If a system of justice is fair, it has to be fair not

---

121 On jus cogens consult O'Connell, ME 'Jus cogens: International Law's Higher Ethical Norms' in Childress, DE III (ed.), *The Role of Ethics in International Law* (2012); Alexander Orakhelashvili, *Peremptory Norms in International Law* (2006); A. Pellet, 'Comments in Response to Christine Chinking and in Defense of *Jus cogens* as the Best Bastion against the Excesses of Fragmentation' *Finnish Yearbook of International Law* (2008), p. 83; Paust, J 'The Reality of Jus cogens' 7 *Connecticut Journal of International Law* (1991), p. 81; Saul, M 'Identifying Jus cogens Norms: The Interaction of Scholars and International Judges' *Asian Journal of International Law* (2014); Shelton, D 'Normative Hierarchy of International Law' 80 *American Journal of International Law* (1986), p. 1; Suy, E 'Article 53: Treaties Conflicting with a Peremptory Norm of General International Law ('jus cogens')' in Corten, O and Klein, P (Eds.) *The Vienna Convention on the Law of Treaties: A Commentary*, Vol.II (2011); Tomuschat, C and Thouveinin, JM (eds.) *The Fundamental Rules of the International Legal Order: Jus cogens and Obligations Erga Omnes* (2006). For further examination of jus cogens norms see the bibliography of the book.

122 Farhad Malekian, 'Conundrums of *Jus cogens:* In Case Law' (Part II), No.13 *Вісник Південного регіонального центру Національної академії правових наук України, No.13 Journal of the South regional Center of National Academy of Legal Sciences of Ukraine (*2017), pp.12-21; Malekian, 'Conundrums of *Jus cogens*: in International Criminal Law' (Part I), *Вісник Південного регіонального центру Національної академії правових наук України No.12 Journal of the South regional Center of National Academy of Legal Sciences of Ukraine (*2017), pp.8-16.

just for its subjects, but also for the targets of its subjects. If a subject's voice has not been heeded in the system of international criminal justice and in the sphere of the International Court of Justice for the love of justice, for the truth to be realised and released, or for the protection of victims and witnesses, how can we proclaim that our criminal system of jurisdiction is reasonable?

> A lawyer should realise the fact that it is not the compulsory power of law which makes it law. On the contrary, it is reason, truth, purity, and harmony which make justice reliable, desirable, and digestible. If the nature and the character of a legal norm is true, if the legal norm is not a collection of savage norms, if the spirit of moral norms in the culture of the law is not monopolised by bad norms, if the law understands the difference between the vocabulary of justice and injustice, then such norms are love norms. If a norm realises the reasons for hearing and non-hearing or admission and non-admission of a case in a court, the dominance of the rich, weak, and the position of the accused persons, then such law ought to also understand that prosecuting the big criminals is not solely a duty but a mission of justice for love.[123]

How can a lawyer claim that they are working for the sake of justice and the truth if they are not? How can we assert that the law is organised by the system of positivist and naturalist morality? If the concept of love for justice is not contemplated in the system of international criminal justice, in the territory of International Court of Justice, and in the system of international human rights law and criminal law, then the relevant law is not an accurate law, but rather represents serious allegations of the principles of morality and legality.[124] This is particularly notable when an international criminal lawyer violates the conscience of humanity in the name of defending the rights of their client.

There is already excessive competition among lawyers in the world regarding earning positions at the ICC. A considerable number of these lawyers are seeking the large salary that comes with the position and

---

[123] Malekian, *Judgments of Love in Criminal Justice*, note 52, p.219.
[124] Malekian, *Allegations by Political Laundering*, note 48, p.115-120.

choose to ignore the questionable justice that emanates from the Court. The transparency of a sanction that deserves the appellation of justice should not take its inspiration from financial interests, from the Court, or from having a prestigious position in the Court, it should rather be based on the theory of love in order to establish the power of secure justice for all of humanity, for ethical norms, and for the pure conscience of humanity. This may come at the price of someone losing their job and income forever. Mannheim correctly explained the situation with the following statement:

> During the seventeenth and eighteenth centuries the earlier attempts to define the conception of bellum justum and jus ad bellum had to give way to discussions on the jus in bello – i.e., on the rules applicable to warfare without any regard to the justness of a particular war. In other words, ever hope had to be abandoned of solving the real problem of war. Working out in immense detail the technical rules of the jus in bello, international lawyers had found a field of activities where they could engaged themselves with less personal risk and more profit...Apparently international lawyers of certain previous generations found themselves too much handicapped by the fact of their being appointed by the princes whose actions they were expected to justify. If the teachers of criminal law had had to depend for their livelihood upon the generosity of the most successful criminals in their districts, the results of their labours might well have been equally unsatisfactory. Today we are inclined to be angry at the manifest failure of all those experiments, made before the present conflagration, to outlaw unjust wars.[125]

An international criminal lawyer or criminal defence lawyer may disagree that it is not prohibited to commit genocide based on the fact that the provisions of the 1948 Genocide Convention contradict the provisions of many international conventions which permit the manufacturing of most types of weapons. This argument may be true, since we cannot have an international convention that strongly prohibits the commission of acts of genocide and concurrently have international conventions which permit the production of weapons of mass destruction. This implies that we have

---

[125] H. Mannheim, War and crime, *AJIL* (1940), pp. 19–20.

educated our lawyers to present arguments that are true, even if they are not in practice, and that is the reality of the relevant laws.

That is why an international criminal lawyer may easily escape from their responsibility and argue that certain acts committed against the Rohingya did not constitute genocide, and were therefore lawful. This is how our policy of criminal justice really functions regarding the commission of serious international crimes. A wise man, a wise individual, a wise criminal defence lawyer, and a wise international criminal lawyer would not justify the crimes of the big criminals, for instance in Iraq, and then condemn the crimes that were committed by the dictator of the country. This would represent double morality which stems from working for the rich, powerful criminals, and for brutal policy as was carried out against Iraq by the United States and the United Kingdom. There are many lawyers with double morality, and their arguments surely violate the ethical morality of the jurisdiction of criminal law and therefore aggressively violate the ethical code of justice.

5.5. DEFENCE LAWYERS DISGUISING JUSTICE

Generally, every lawyer or legal academic carries the legacy of their cultural training. Thomas More describes lawyers in his book *Utopia* as "a sort of people, whose profession it is to disguise matters."[126] According to a Japanese proverb, “only lawyers and painters can turn white to black”. This may be broadly true within the criminal machinery of many nations. A number of our lawyers in international criminal law not only trade criminal justice, but they also help to develop and empower misguided international criminal policy. This is the way in which many international criminal defence lawyers assist the establishment of a corrupt court by falsifying arguments to serve the big political parties and their own personal interests. It is rightly asserted that:

---

[126] T. More, *Utopia* 128 (G. Burnet trans. 1821) (1516).

> But they do not as individuals seem so very different from the rest of the population as to justify the special level of animosity that the profession seems to arouse in the general public. One thinks, for example, of the present genre of what has come to be called "lawyer jokes." For instance: Question: What is the difference between a dead lawyer in the road and a dead skunk? Answer: There are skid marks by the skunk. Or: Question: Why did the research scientist substitute lawyers for rats in his laboratory experiments? Answer: Lawyers breed more rapidly, scientists became less attached to them, and there are some things that rats just won't do. Lawyer bashing is of course nothing new.[127]

The recent argument of an international criminal lawyer in the International Court of Justice in The Hague will certainly be complemented in the future by the arguments of other sold international defence attorneys. A good lawyer does not beg on their knees for money and prestige and claim to be the defender of the rights of victims. When a criminal lawyer or a criminal law professor speaks about criminal justice and the abolition of capital punishment, but then does not engage in the actual prevention of unfair criminal justice, they are by extension engaging in the trade of criminal justice. Furthermore, they are empowering another form of capital punishment which is more dangerous than the traditional one—ignoring the murder of thousands of innocent victims.

How can we call ourselves criminal lawyers, defence lawyers, international criminal lawyers, or the supporters of criminal justice and the equal protection of victims and the accused, but not see the violations of criminal law caused by our own interpretations of crimes committed in China, Myanmar, Palestine, Iraq, Afghanistan, and Libya? These defence lawyers do not find any reason to object to the relevant criminal systems because of their personal interests or out of fear of losing their jobs.[128] This is what many of those who assert to be criminal lawyers or defence lawyers do. This also is the reality in most countries, and not only in those of a dictatorial nature. In the Islamic Republic of Iran, a number of lawyers

---

[127] Robert C. Post, 'On the Popular Image of the Lawyer: Reflections in a Dark Glass', 75 California Law Review (1987), 379-389, at 379.

[128] Malekian, *Trading Virginity of International Criminal Justice*, note 19, pp.34-35.

defend victims in a non-political manner. However, when it comes to the crimes of government leaders, they are not only silent, but also hide the truth in order not to lose their position by disappointing government officials who exert great influence over the administration of the Bar.

Internationally, the fact is that a large number of lawyers get recommendations and violate the ethical conscience and morality of the law in order to gain certain positions, including entering into the office of the international prosecutor. These methods do not represent the justice of the law, but the justice of politics. A lawyer serving as a prosecutor, judge, or attorney needs to be a member of particular political party in order to fulfil their interests. Whether you are presumed to be a good lawyer or not usually comes down to technicalities rather than substance.

The trade of the rights of the victims, criminal justice, criminal judgments, criminal behaviour, criminal actions, criminal investigations, criminal judges, criminal prosecutors, and the judicial conscience of criminal procedures are integral parts of the behaviours of many international lawyers. A number of international criminal lawyers and international human rights lawyers are paid just to defend the big political parties and the big criminal governments in the world. Many of these international lawyers do not see the serious criminal violations of big governments which have occupied the territories of other nations and they support criminal regimes by one means or another, including through the establishment of human rights centres or institutions in their support. We are criminals with varying degrees of criminality, and we are the traders of the rights of victims with different volumes of cargo. This means that the trade of the rights of victims cannot end since the interests of our wallets do not cease. Furthermore, in the system of criminal justice, under which many defence lawyers function for the rights of victims or the accused, lawyers are controlled and directed by criminal governments and their capital. Are we not selling the rights of victims to serve our own personal interests?

How can we assert that our criminal justice and defence lawyers are honest when the political system of the same country is engaged in trading weapons? Was the trade of weapons between the United States and Saudi

Arabia morally, or even legally permissible when it was known that said weapons would be used against the Yemeni population? Did the Yemeni or Syrian population commit any crimes against the United States government through military attacks on American soil?[129]Obviously, a law which trades the lives of its subjects is not pure. Certainly, positive criminal law which argues about *de lege lata* and its power of enforceability is fundamentally flawed when it gives weight to the political and economic power of the perpetrators. Indubitably, criminal law may be a type of criminal organisation supported by judges, prosecutors, lawyers, defence lawyers, and the court when it comes to the democratic division of the values of positive criminal law, and its essence of one-sided justice.

5.6. Lawyers Complicating International Crimes

For the sake of saying something that at least one other international criminal lawyer might understand, certain international criminal provisions attempt to draw lines between what is understood as crimes against humanity and the notion of genocide. However, both types of crimes have the same legal definitions, and drawing this line makes certain conducts of states, groups, or individuals absolutely impermissible and inhumane. In such cases, lawyers are not permitted to protect the guilty parties and their criminal actions.

In other words, sometimes violations of the system of international criminal law are so grave and obvious, that they allow for a final distinction between crimes against humanity and genocide in order to respect international criminal law. This means that the system of international criminal law draws distinctions between such crimes and comes to the conclusion that they are similar. This is what international criminal lawyers must understand. Here we are speaking about lawyers who object to capital punishment and find the Iranian or North Korean governments guilty of

---

[129] Fein Bruce, 'Hillary Clinton's 5 lies about Syria, Terror Threat', *The Washington Times* (25 October, 2016).

crimes against humanity, but not the American, British, or Israeli governments—as long as they continue to pay enough.

Therefore, international criminal lawyers have to rely on their own conscience and decide whether or not to use their words to obfuscate the provisions governing genocide and crimes against humanity— which would constitute fraud on their part. Such international criminal lawyers not only harm the present system of international criminal law, but also create chaos for the future development of international criminal justice and the pure interpretation and recognition of international crimes. Although we understand that lawyers under national criminal systems have different interpretations of the law, we should realise the fact that national criminal law is not the law of reason, but the law of the relevant country. This should not be the same in the system of international criminal law.

The fact is that there are more specific international conventions and agreements about the nature of international crimes and the definition of genocide which should not be ignored by lawyers in exchange for payment, as that would be equivalent to fraud. This implies the fact that not much will be left of our system of international criminal justice and the integrity of the system will become contingent on economics and politics. The function of international criminal lawyers should not be to exonerate the guilty, but to uphold the principles of international criminal law in order to recognise international crimes. It is the important ethical and legal duty of lawyers to ensure that the principles concerning the recognition of international crimes are fully respected without interference from personal interests.

5.7. Lacking Purity of International Lawyers

Unfortunately, the purity of our criminal law, criminal judges, and criminal lawyers is largely based on power politics. That is why in many Latin American countries, the big criminals have escaped from being designated as such. The fact is that the truth is hidden in the offices of many lawyers dealing with international crimes while engaging with in relations with the intelligence agencies of their countries. Furthermore, we ignore the rights of victims ourselves, as do lawyers whose duty it is to work against the ethical duties of judicial conscience and defend our criminal conducts. Even our lawyers and judges have lost their purity when it comes to big financial questions.[130] Thus, there are a considerable number of lawyers who should really be advocates of peace and justice, of truth, and of love for the implementation of international human rights law, but are not.[131] Rather, international criminal law, international criminal justice, and human rights law function based on income, and consequently the trading of criminal law, the cargo of which are the weak individuals or victims, is guaranteed.[132]

With all this, I am not trying to say that our criminal system is wrong, nor am I trying to say that criminal law always lacks independence. My goal is rather to say that we are forced to understand that our criminal law is allowing for the execution of serious crimes through systematic violations of international criminal law, for example in occupied countries, while lawyers remain silent or even write in support of such crimes for financial gain.

Many national and international lawyers may attack my reasoning and not appreciate this interpretation, but the truth is the truth, and it cannot be altered. The fact is that even in democratic Scandinavian countries, certain lawyers only serve politicians and carry out deals behind closed doors. This is why human beings must be aware of the consequences of such behaviour. Once upon a time, we had Palme, a Swedish state minister with a strong voice who spoke out against certain criminality in the world and was subsequently shot to death for it. If our national lawyers do not understand that justice has become a forum for trading its rules, then they are driving the system of judicial conscience through other means.

The unfortunate fact is that our national criminal laws and lawyers are usually at the behest of our superiors. This is because our lawyers dance with the music of the mechanisms of Chapter VII of the United Nations

---

[130] Malekian, *Trading Virginity of International Criminal Justice*, note 19, p.107.
[131] *Id.*
[132] *Id.*, p.108.

Charter. I am not posing these statements for the measurement of criminal justice and the moral mentality of our lawyers— particularly our international criminal lawyers claiming to be the defenders of justice, nor do I question the conduct of human beings or seek to find a window into what truly goes on in international criminal justice and the crimes committed under its guise. What I am describing is the standard of our morality and of international movements within the system of international criminal justice. We must therefore ask why we are playing games with the definitions of criminal law and justice and the ethical norms of prosecution which should be respected by lawyers of high morality.[133]

If we are not playing games with the theory of criminal justice and our pretend international criminal lawyers, then why is it that when someone is killed in our own territory, we take legal measures against the offender and help the victims, but when millions are killed, raped, and tortured elsewhere, we turn a blind eye, with lawyers asserting: "I am just protecting my client"?[134] Are we really professors of law and justice? Are we really honest defence lawyers? Unfortunately today, many lawyers are members of the academic mafia which is much more dangerous than the traditional Italian mafia due to their international reach. If we cannot make sense of this classical suite, then we have a Van Gogh ear for music and a blind minds-eye concerning those who interpret clear acts of genocide in different countries not as genocide, but as political shortcomings.[135]

---

[133] See also the discussion in footnote 24.

[134] It is interesting to note here that in 2016, a 9-year-old boy with Autism was arrested at School (US), but not the killers of millions. However, in this regard, William Schabas, the writer of Abolition of Capital Punishment or the author of genocide is silent. Money money money must be funny.

[135] See Farhad Malekian, An open letter to the leading arms exporters and others: *Barbarity in Yemen* (1st October 2019). A letter send to the Secretary General of the United Nations – António Guterres; The President of the United States – Donald John Trump; The President of Russia – Vladimir Vladimirovich Putin; The President of France – Emmanuel Macron; The German Chancellor – Angela Dorothea Merkel; The British Prime Minister – Alexander Boris de Pfeffel Johnson; The Prime Minister of Spain – Pedro Sánchez Pérez-Castejón; The Prime Minister of Israel – Benjamin Netanyahu; The Prime Minister of Italy – Giuseppe Conte; The Prime Minister of the Kingdom of the Netherlands – Mark Rutte; The Crown Prince of Saudi Arabia Mohammad Bin Salman Al Saud; The Prime Minister of the United Arab Emirates Mohammed Al Maktoum.

5.8. SELF-INTERPRETATION OF THE LAW BY LAWYERS

Since lawyers are considered to be ambassadors of justice, their duties continue for as long they continue to work in the system of jurisdiction, and in particular in the systems of criminal justice and international criminal justice. As a public citizen, a lawyer has the duty to seek the improvement of the rules of law wherever necessary. This is because if a lawyer is truly working for the system of justice, its developments, and its equal demands, then they have to realise that they are one of the people who recognise the significant function and role of law in our social system. Moreover, a lawyer has access to the legal system, the administration of justice, and the quality of the provisions of the law rendered by the legal profession. This means that an international criminal lawyer is not only bound to respect the body of the existing legal system, but also to question its moral dimension in the criminal legal system of jurisdiction.

A lawyer with deep understanding should promote the knowledge of the law beyond its use for defendants and impartially protect them. In particular, in the system of international criminal justice, lawyers should be aware of the fact that it is not only their clients or victims who are seeking justice under the authority of the Court, but also the international public and the spirit of justice which has been harmed because its principles were ignored. Thus, a lawyer should employ sufficient knowledge not only for the benefit of their clients, but also for the benefit of the rule of law and its reform where it lacks certain provisions or appropriate framework. This means strengthening its basic foundation in order to decrease violations and prevent the future commission of international crimes. All this is also based on the flexibility of the lawyer and their confidence in the rule of international criminal law for the protection of man from brutal crimes.

A lawyer should be mindful of absences or shortcomings of such provisions that are necessary for victims of international crimes as well as for the protection of defendants in the international sphere. This is not only the duty of lawyers under the international criminal system, but it should also be considered important under national criminal jurisdiction, based on the fact that a lawyer should realise that not all victims of international crimes or national crimes are able to pay large fees, which can impact the fulfilment of their rights. This is however regardless of the fact that under the system of ICC, the victims and the accused are both protected, even if they are unable to pay.

A lawyer should understand all these symptoms concerning the economic position of potential clients under national and international systems. The responsibilities of a lawyer are more significant towards the innocent or the victims who are unable to advocate for their own rights in cases where the lawyer feels that an opposing party in the system of international criminal court is well-represented and better equipped to reject the rights of the victims. However, while we understand that the possibilities of lawyer may be limited, this does not mean that they should not protect their clients. The duties of lawyers are normally based on professional responsibilities and a lawyer should be also guided by the capacity of their personal conscience and the admiration of professional peers.[136]

Thus, we are referring at the same time to all the challenging and complicated ethical problems arising from conflicts between the responsibilities of a lawyer towards their clients, and the lawyer's personal interests. It is true that the rules of professional conduct under national and international criminal justice may differ to a slight degree, but the theory is the same in both legal systems and it concerns the protection of the rights of the accused or victims. Therefore, a number of complicated issues regarding professional discretion can arise when considering the appropriate measures to take in the case of the economic or political poverty of a client whose rights have been infringed upon by a strong party.

At the same time, we must assert that the notion of the legal profession and its legal ethics and rules, although outlined in certain legal documents,

---

[136] "What surely is most needed in order to make men clear sighted in confronting the official abuse of power, is that they should preserve the sense that the certification of something as legally valid is not conclusive of the question of obedience, and that, however great the aura of majesty or authority which the official system may have, its demands must in the end be submitted to a *moral scrutiny*." L.A. Hart, *The Concept of Law* (Oxford University Press, 1961), p. 206. Emphasis added.

are largely left up to interpretation. This is because it is very difficult to demand precise rules of ethics and their practical implementation when lawyers are working for their own self-interest. Thus, a lawyer is indeed their own judge, and most matters are based on the moral conscience of the lawyer. A lawyer functioning in an international criminal court may be satisfied with their performance and what they have done for their clients— however this is based on their own interpretation. That is why we have different understandings of legal ethics.

It is true that lawyers play a vital role in the preservation of international criminal justice and international human rights law. This means that an international lawyer must understand the needs of the international population in order to feel justice, to see justice, and to own justice based on the plain truth. The legal profession within the system of national and international criminal justice is thus a presentation of policy which aims at the protection of the international human rights discipline and its promotion for the needs of the diverse international society. Consequently, the duties of lawyers are generally to protect and support an independent legal profession which promotes peace.

That is why when we speak about protection of the law, rules of law, rules of justice and rules of impartiality of the system of justice, we are referring to the autonomy of a system which can serve all nations without any particular difference concerning culture, language, religion, ethnic origin, or other superficial values. It is actually a duty encompassed in all legal professions, particularly for lawyers and judges, to ensure that the rules of law are respected in the international criminal justice system, without allowing personal interests to interfere. This is a difficult job— but a necessary one.

Chapter 6

Conundrums Facing International Criminal Lawyers

6.1. Competence among International Criminal Lawyers

One of the problems that the system of international criminal law is facing is the competition between lawyers concerning positions on international courts.[137] The situation is certainly obvious, and has become unavoidable based on the current international political situation. Therefore, political authorities have a definite role in the selection of all matters relating to international criminal tribunals, particularly the ICC. This is not only regarding defence attorneys, but also with the selection of judges. The states parties to the Statute of the ICC therefore have strong influence over the nomination of judges to the Court, and although there are certain requirements judges must meet in order to be selected, it is still the votes of the political parties which make the final decision. That is why different regions have different voting rights, and the judges all come from nations which have ratified the Rome Statute. Thus, one may say that

137 Consult Jonathan Power, *Conundrums of Humanity: The Quest for Global Justice* (Brill, 2007). Reiss Hans Siegbert, *Kant: Political Writings* (University Press, 2003).

although judges are completely independent from the political parties of their governments, it is still the political parties which recommend judges to be nominated. This means that judges are appointed to the ICC by the Assembly of States Parties, the court's governing body. All judges must be nationals of states parties to the Rome Statute, and no two judges may be nationals of the same state. Although judges and lawyers of the Court must be qualified, their selection is a political decision in the end. This is even the case in *ad hoc* tribunals or other temporary courts. For instance, Milosevic's lawyers came at the recommendation of the Serbian government.[138]

Despite all these influences and recommendations, lawyers should respect certain rules of ethics in their relations with other lawyers. Whereas victim participation in proceedings before the International Criminal Court (ICC) is a central innovation in international justice, they also have a right to be represented by lawyers. This means that there may be lawyers fighting against one another during the proceedings of the Court. One of the main reasons for the participation of victims in the ICC proceedings is to ensure that *justice is not only done, but is also being seen* by those impacted by the crimes being prosecuted by the court. The intention of all these new rules of the ICC concerning the participation of victims in the procedures of the Court is to establish a more reliable system of international criminal justice for victims who have been the target of crimes against humanity, war crimes, aggression, or genocide.

6.2. Evaluating Affirmative Defences

There are no specific decisions of the ICC which demonstrate the elements of the defence. It may be said that the elements for affirmative defences according to the defence team may consist of several elements.

---

[138] See also N. Kandic, The ICTY Trials and Transitional Justice in Former Yugoslavia, 38 (3) *Cornell International Law Journal* (2005), pp. 789-792; J. Post and L. Panis, Tyranny on Trial: Personality and Courtroom Conduct of Defendants Slobodan Milosevic and Saddam Hussein, 38 (3) *Cornell International Law Journal* (2005).

In 2020, in a case before the ICC, the defence team for Mr. Al Hassan asserted the following affirmative defence of duress (Article 31(1)(d)), in addition to mistake of fact or law, and superior orders pursuant to Articles 32 and 33 respectively, which Counsel ascertained from the record of the proceedings.[139] According to the defence team, the affirmative defence of duress, while not a justification for committing a crime, serves as mitigating factor:

a) The defendant was obliged to obey the orders of the superior
b) The defendant did not know that the orders were unlawful
c) The orders were not manifestly unlawful
d) When a defendant committed a crime because they were facing the threat or use of physical force.
e) An imminent threat of death or serious harm through the actions or words of another person existed
f) Existence of duress
g) Duress was present as the result of a continuing threat of imminent death and imminent threat of serious bodily harm
h) A threat of death or serious bodily harm was directed at the perpetrator or another individual
i) The conduct carried out to avoid the threat was reasonable and necessary under the given circumstances
j) The alleged conduct by the defendant did not cause greater harm than conduct which was avoided
k) The defendant lacked the guarantees considered by law to be indispensable to a fair trial
l) The defendant was not aware that the sanctions ordered would not constitute lawful sanctions
m) They were not aware that certain measures constituted sentencing
n) They were not aware that the individuals, who were the subject of proceedings were "protected persons"
o) They were not aware of the connection to an armed conflict

[139] https://www.icc-cpi.int/CourtRecords/CR2020_04571.PDF.

p) They were not aware that certain conduct constituted a prescribed form of ownership
q) They were not aware that the application of certain rules was contrary to international law
r) They were not aware of the protected status of certain historical/cultural sites
s) They were not aware that the removal of elements of certain historical monuments constituted an attack

Generally, affirmative defences are defences presented by the defence team which explain why the court misunderstood or misinterpreted the conducts of their client. An affirmative defence may be partially or fully rejected by the prosecution, and judges may not accept the reasoning presented by the defence team on behalf of the defendant. In certain situations, affirmative defences may reduce the international criminal responsibility of the defendant and cause them to receive lighter punishment. Affirmative defences are also sometimes presented to prove that all matters presented by the accusers are baseless allegations and that the presented evidence has been falsely interpreted or does not represent the (whole) truth.

The presentation of an affirmative defence by the defence team within international criminal courts constitutes an integral part of the response to charges, through which a defendant with different arguments, reasonings, analysis, evidences, witnesses, and motivations rejects the deduction or conclusion of the prosecutor. Affirmative defences may not help the accused in being acquitted, but may in rare situations be useful for the reduction of their criminal responsibility regarding the relevant crimes. Overall, the defence team or the defendant should have known that committing war crimes, genocide, and crimes against humanity or acts of torture, rape, or sexual assault, or using children of young age as soldiers, violates national, regional, and international standards, regardless of whether or not certain criminal conducts were carried out under superior orders.

It has also been claimed that affirmative defences are based on facts other than those provided by the prosecution. However, if the presentation of facts and evidence and witness statements are strong and substantive, they may successfully release the defendant from international criminal responsibility. This is regardless of whether or not the allegations against the defendant were true and occurs in cases involving self-defence. However, while the notion of self-defence is only applicable for some cases under national criminal law, the possibility of proportionate self-defence under the system of international criminal law is very rare due to technological advancements in weapons.

6.3. Prevailing Principles among Defence Attorneys

Some of the prevailing principles which should be respected by attorneys or lawyers are as follows:

a) They should have respect for their profession,
b) They should demonstrate professional solidarity,
c) Every defence attorney should foster loyal relationships with other attorneys,
d) They should not cause disagreements because professional quarrels have a negative impact on everyone involved,
e) They should harmonise and respect each other's work,
f) They should not violate the code of conscience in their relations,
g) They should not compete for clients,
h) The defence attorney should not act immorally against the attorney of the accusers
i) The accuser's attorney should not act immorally against the defence attorney,
j) Attorneys may offer professional opinions and advice based on the given rules of the Court,

k) Any discrepancy between attorneys must not be hidden from the judges of the Court,
l) Any discussions between attorneys must be friendly and the attorney of the defendant should not threaten the attorney of the victims,
m) Lawyers should respect the judicial independence of the Court during all procedures,
n) The principle of truth and the impartiality of the lawyers should not be violated by any of the lawyers in the Court,
o) The ethical code of the relevant criminal jurisdiction should be respected by the lawyers of both sides,
p) International crimes committed by the accused should not be ignored by lawyers or the accused,
q) Attorneys must act responsibly following misunderstandings,
r) Defence attorneys in international criminal courts should respect each other's integrity,
s) Defence attorneys in international criminal courts should not make any agreements or deals among themselves in order to gain money,
t) The defence attorneys of the accused or accusers should not exchange or destroy evidence in order to win a case,
u) A defence attorney shall treat the opposing attorney with professional respect,
v) Any hostility, insult, slight, belittlement, or abuse is not permitted in the professional conduct of attorneys,
w) Attorneys should not speak poorly of the opposing party and attack their integrity in public,
x) Any communication during proceedings between attorneys should be peaceful,
y) Victims of international crimes have a right under Court rules to choose a lawyer, which means that the defence attorney should not interfere with their work in any way,
z) Victims must have the possibility to share their views and concerns during proceedings, and to be represented by a lawyer in

the courtroom. The defence attorney of the accused should not cause any practical difficulty for the lawyers of the victims,

aa) The lawyers of the victims should be permitted to express their views to the judge without interruption from the defence team,

bb) The attorneys of the opposing parties should not have any close relationships or be related,

cc) An attorney should not agree to represent a client who is already being represented by another attorney unless the client has already dismissed their first attorney.

6.4. Permissible Objections by Defence Attorneys

The defence rights of the accused in the system of international criminal law express that the accused have the right to object to evidence that has been presented in the Court or the Chamber of the Court. This is one of the established rights of the accused in the proceedings of international criminal courts, and these objections may be presented or submitted either orally or in writing. There are some common reasons for objecting to evidence presented by the prosecutor or witnesses. The defence team may object to the relevance of evidence which has been submitted by witnesses, prosecutors, or victims. Generally, the theory of objection relates to a lawyer or a party to a legal case objecting in order to prevent the opposing party from asking a witness a specific question.

Objections thus prevent witnesses from answering a question or prevent questionable evidence from being presented. Normally, it is the judge who rules on an objection and either overrules or sustains it. By “overruling the objection”, the trial judge permits the relevant question to be heard as evidence in the Court. If a judge of the Court confirms the objection, it means they "sustain" the objection and do not agree with the question or presented evidence. Objection normally helps the case in very crucial situations where the evidence may be misleading. We must emphasise that the ability to object is available to all parties in the Court. A defendant's attorney, a plaintiff's lawyer, and a victim's attorney all have the right to make an objection.

6.5. Reasons for Objections by Defence

Some of the reasons which give rise to objection by one of the parties can include:

a) The evidence is misleading,
b) False evidence has been presented,
c) A document is unfair, prejudiced, and unethically reflects the feelings of the judge of the Court concerning the accused,
d) It may be possible that by asking several questions, the opposing attorney psychologically influences the witnesses and leads them to have a false view of the case,
e) Pictures that could make the witnesses feel threatened have been presented,
f) Objection can also be made to confusing questions that are presented by any of the parties to the Court,
g) Objections cannot be made to cross-examination questions which seek to clarify the situation,
h) Cross-examining a witness must be done ethically and not lead to arguments, if this is not upheld then there can be an objection,
i) The intention of cross-examination should be to prove uncertainty about the truthfulness of the testimony of witness, otherwise it may be objectionable,
j) The cross-examination questions should differ from the direct examination of the witnesses, victims, or accused in order to discover if they have the correct picture of the case. Otherwise, these questions may be objected to by the lawyers,

k) Objection can also be made to complex questions which were posed to confuse everyone, including the judges,
l) Objections should be made to irrelevant questions,
m) An objection can also be made to questions which address a hypothetical situation,
n) Indirect evidence or hearsay is impermissible and objectionable,
o) Objections can be made when one of the defence attorneys or opposing attorneys bases their arguments on pure opinion,
p) If a lawyer jumps to a conclusion before explaining a situation, their statements can be objected to,
q) Objection is acceptable if the evidence was extracted illegally by threat, terror, or torture,
r) Evidence which was provided as the result of corruption or payment is objectionable,
s) If a person failed to explain the background circumstances of how they know the information they are testifying about, these statements are objectionable. When answering about specific facts, the witness has to be able to explain why they know these facts,
t) Repetition of the same question in order to get another answer creates ground for objection,
u) Objection can be made to unclear, vague, or ambiguous questions,
v) A defence attorney may object to a question based on the wording of the question,
w) An objection may not be permitted if the witness strays from the original question,
x) An objection is permissible where the rules of procedure of the Court are violated,
y) Unethical or immoral questions are objectionable,
z) Violating any norm of independence of the Court is objectionable,
aa) An objection may be overruled by a judge of an international criminal court,
bb) Objection may be accepted if the lawyer is badgering the witness.

6.6. Problematic Solution of Ethical Standards with Counsel

Any attempt to create and establish an international ethical profession for lawyers is indeed a very difficult task since most matters relating to ethical principles are strongly connected to the cultural values of different nations.[140] One understands that the substantial influence of the jurisprudence of international criminal tribunals and the Court concerning the development of international humanitarian criminal justice has many causes. The goal is to move in the right direction and create a legacy of norms applicable to, and respected by, all nations. However, the questions of ethical considerations are not as strong as they should be based on the ethical background of judges, prosecutors, and counsels of the tribunals and the Court. The reason for this may be that the international legal community has different perspectives of the mirror of justice and highlighting which nations have more criminal values than others is legally and ethically wrong and would lead to the discrimination between values. That is why the legacy of the ICC and other international criminal tribunals has been to create a fair balance between different values and to not give priority to any one nation.

The situation is particularly important regarding the position of lawyers and their attitudes of understanding, which is more difficult to create balance between, although the ICC has tried to do so. Another factor is that the international courts have chosen to follow the principles of civil law systems rather than common law systems regarding their final decisions. This means that there are no juries present during proceedings. This is regardless of the fact that the statutes of international criminal tribunals and the Court contain a mixed-method of jurisdiction which

[140] Joseph Raz, *Ethics in the Public Domain: Essays in the Morality of Law and Politics* (Oxford: Oxford University Press, 1994); Lon Luvios Fuller, *The Morality of Law* (Yale Law University, 2nd ed., 1969). Joseph Raz, *The Morality of Freedom* (Oxford University Press, 1986); Examine the natural and moral theory by John Finnis (ed.), *Natural Law* (1991); John Finnis, *Aquinas: Moral, Political and Legal Theory* (1998); Finnis John, *Fundamentals of Ethics* (1985).

employs principles from both legal systems.[141] In this sense, the tribunals and courts have created a common understanding of the criminal issues mixed with the background of judges and lawyers, as it is their views and interpretations of cases which impact the ultimate outcomes, although the decisions of the Court are independent of the culture or background of lawyers.

The fact is that the judges of the Court do not pursue evidence, but rather base their judgements on the evidence presented by the prosecutor or other parties to the Court. Therefore, the *game* of picking out certain pieces of evidence, arguments, or moral principles, comes down to personal understanding. In the courtroom, one does not reach consensus by accident, but rather through carrying out ethical and professional conducts. However, *generosity has seldom been seen among lawyers and the intention of the majority of lawyers is the absolute protection of their clients and the fee at any cost. There is no attention paid to the questions of mens rea or actus reus.*

> We should keep in mind that with the concept of criminal liability and the notion of *actus reus*, our intention is not only to find a person liable for punishment and bring them under our jurisdiction, but we are also seeking the proper subject of criminal responsibility for accurate prosecution, and the correct servicing of justice. The body of our criminal law and the social integrity of our cultures cannot permit the punishment of a person who is only a physical body, without a clear mind and undamaged soul. Were those the case, our criminal law would no longer be a healthy body of law, but rather a set of revenge-based regulations. Certainly, this is not our intention, and such intent would violate the basic provisions of human rights law. Comparison may be drawn to English law, which allows for a 10-year-old child to be found responsible for a crime, but not a legal adult, such as Tony Blair, for the commission of grave crimes in other countries, including Afghanistan and Iraq during

141 Consult Konstantinos D. Magliveras, The Special Court for Sierra Leone: A New Type of Regional Criminal Court for the International Community? 17 *International Enforcement Law Rep*. (Feb. 2001); David M. Crane, The Special Court for Sierra Leone, in International Criminal Law, Vol. III (M. Cherif Bassiouni, ed. 2008) pp. 195-218; C. Sriram, Wrong-sizing International Justice? The Hybrid Tribunal in Sierra Leone, 29 (3) *Fordham International Law Journal* (2006), pp.472-506.

> the Gulf War. Are we fair in our justice? Are our systems of criminal law, criminal justice, criminal jurisdiction, criminal proceedings, and criminal judgements legislated purely for national, regional, and international justice? An administration of criminal justice has to not only be fair within its own territorial jurisdiction, and beyond it, but it must also be kept pure for future generations.
> The question is, why do we speak about case law and its significance? If our administration of criminal justice is not pure in every sense today, how can case law be created and relied upon by future generations? The question is, who should be brought before a criminal court – a 10-year-old child? Tony Blair? Barack Obama? Leaders of Russia, North Korea, Iran, Israel, Saudi Arabia, or the United States? Have political *games*, political collectivism, and political dinners not traded the rights of our children by permitting the production of weapons? Who is really in need of treatment?[142]

One cannot deny the fact that international criminal courts and tribunals have developed and codified a number of standards of ethical codes in order to further specify the obligations inherent in the exercise of the judicial criminal jurisdiction and the duties of parties involved in a case. The ICC has established and institutionalised detailed rules and procedures governing the independence of the Court and the impartiality of its judges from all angles. These rules of ethical standards can be seen in the Rules of Procedure and Evidence, and its relation to the Code of Professional Conduct of Counsel, including the binding Code of Judicial Ethics. These codes, along with many other codes, have established comprehensive ethical standards for defence counsels, which are also similar to those codified by other international criminal courts such as the International Criminal Tribunal for the former Yugoslavia and the International Criminal Tribunal for Rwanda.

---

[142] Malekian, *Trading Virginity of International Criminal Justice*, note 19, pp.62-63.

The facts still remain the same even though we have codified a large number of provisions regarding the values of ethical norms. This is because ethical norms imply the value of their content and do not necessarily reflect our personal values. While both ethical values and personal values may have the same intention, the quality of personal context and its vision varies, particularly when it comes to the evaluation of the principles of criminal justice. The Court has recently shown that even judges who are supposed to respect the most recognised elements of international crimes, may, depending on the perpetrator, change their opinions on genocide.[143] This means that we have a similar problem as with counsel who are paid, the former may be invisible but the latter is certainly obvious. This implies the reality that the value of ethical codes, although high, still remains open to differing clarifications, deductions, interpretations, and orientations depending on the cultural values, social values, and legal knowledge of criminal jurisdiction and their connection with ethical norms.

6.7. Failings on the Part of Lawyers

It often seems that the solutions to ethical standards are very difficult to reach concerning counsel, judges, and prosecutors. For example, Article 4 of the Code of Judicial Ethics provides that judges shall "ensure the appearance of impartiality in the discharge of their judicial functions," while Article 5 of the same Code emphasises that judges should "conduct themselves with probity and integrity." The wording of these articles denotes that the significance and connotation of impartiality, probity, and integrity might diverge in different legal systems or across different national social, cultural, and ethnic traditions. There are obviously great differences between what is understood as the necessity of the notion of impartiality between nations and the minority cultures prevailing within

---

143 Malekian, *Conscience of Judges in International Criminal Law, The Heart of Judgements*, note 10.

the same nation. That is why the interpretation of ethical values in the office of the counsel may be more problematic than on the benches of judges, based on the very significant fact that they are paid and charge different rates for their services. Here, we are not dealing with lawyers who are doppelgängers or puppets, which means they may have different incomes coming from the same given case under their protection.

Considering the fact that our evaluations vary, the review of the way in which we deal with legal problems may therefore be very difficult. The many cases under investigation by international criminal courts and tribunals confirm that there may be serious failings on the part of the all parties, but most significantly on the part of lawyers. An international criminal lawyer or an international human rights lawyer may have doppelgänger attitudes towards similar cases. It has been seen that a counsel who is against the internal criminal policy of one state may have different ethical norms and attitudes concerning a similar case towards which they have different cultural ties and feelings. This leads to the lawyer expressing a contrasting view or not reacting, thereby supporting the criminal reason or policy of the preferred government. We are not here promoting bad faith toward any counsel, but rather highlighting the fact that cultural dependency is the most serious ethical issue in certain given international criminal cases.

> *If, by reason, we mean that international criminal justice is unable to bring all criminals under its jurisdiction because of their military and political powers, and is consequently unable to require accurate accountability by an inductive and efficient process of criminal justice, the Court will face many problems in the establishment of moral obligations. It will then follow that moral judgment is not a pressing act of the Statute of the Court, and therefore the true nature of its judgment remains short of morality. The fact is that morality of truth should be a faculty within the Court's jurisdiction, as it is within us for discovering of the truth, seeing the truth, and dealing with the truth. This is the substance of all morality. The Court should not separate its conclusions from the truth. If a single judgment of the Court is correct, this does not necessary mean that the moral policy of the Court is correct. This is what*

> *we may call the faculty of understanding of the truth in all relevant cases. It includes cases which are submitted to the Court and cases which are not submitted to the Court. The duties of this faculty are the notions from which we form solidarity, equality, equivalent accountability, receiving compensation, dealing with the substance of morality, and full understanding of the position of victims.*[144]

This legal problem facing the profession of lawyers stems from the fact that the scope of morality has different ethical definitions and does not coincide with the ethical norms of judicial conscience as it should. The reason for this stems from the profession's commitment to advocacy as the sole valid intention of the profession, and not purely the establishment of criminal justice, although the profession works for the institution of justice as well. The defence counsel, the defence lawyer, or the defence attorney may have the intention to pursue the truth, but upholding truth is not always the sole intention of lawyer. This should be compared with the consciences of prosecutors and judges who are working for the system of criminal justice as the permanent ambassadors of justice and truth. Within the ethical rules of criminal jurisdictions, a lawyer should play the moral content of justice in the procedures of criminal justice. However, this notion of morality, which simply represents the truth about the given case, does not exist or is ignored.

6.8. Truth Pleading for the Truth

Obviously, and without any hesitation, lawyers are employed to defend their clients by all means necessary, regardless of what the truth is and who is aware of it. Thus, although legal ethics are essential in the profession of lawyers and play an imperative role in the expression of fair and reliable judgments, the knowledge of the truth remains in the possession of the fee and its power of hiding the truth or eventually revealing it. That is why we seek good, professional lawyers who know

---

[144] Malekian, *Judgments of Love in Criminal Justice*, note 52, p.288.

the law, and who know how to play the game for their client. Of course, when the truth is hidden, lies become dominant and drive the entire system of the law and complicate the situation.[145] A clear example of this is the recent scandal in the United States regarding the occupation of Congress by citizens in response to the lies told by a team of lawyers who were hiding the truth. Thus, lawyers can be paid to be part of the destruction of democratic and legislative buildings, as seen in the US in 2021. This event demonstrated that lawyers follow lies.

The fact is that that no one supports a system of justice where the examination of the truth reaches a judgment which contradicted one's own specific personal sense of what is right. It has righty been asserted that "for centuries we have lived by a system of justice that finds innocent men 'Guilty' and guilty men 'No guilty' – with no uniform sense of outrage."[146] This has become a habit amongst most populations— to believe that someone is innocent until proven guilty. As a result, we really believe that an individual is innocent until proven guilty beyond a reasonable doubt. This is the way in which our criminal procedures of justice function and how an innocent person becomes a criminal while the strong are portrayed as weak in court proceedings. This implies the fact that our system of criminal justice does not search for the truth, but rather seeks for justice to be done and seen. Despite this notion of criminal justice that we live by, we still believe that law is the only way to find the truth, i.e., the law is the truth.

The situation is more critical when it comes to accusations made by one state against another state in the international sphere. Even though thousands of children have been killed as a result of our criminal policies and with the assistance of our lawyers, we still believe that the stronger political parties control the truth about criminal justice and make the weak appear criminal in their place. These acts are all promoted by our lawyers under the international legal system. Thus, any defence on the part of the weak is designate as terrorism, and our international criminal lawyers

---

[145] Consult Fein Bruce, 'Hillary Clinton's 5 lies about Syria, Terror Threat', The *Washington Times* (25 October, 2016).

[146] Mellinkoff, *The Conscience of a Lawyer*, note 1, p.4.

defend the statements of the strong, thereby completely disarming the weak. Therefore, lawyers jail the innocent and find them guilty of violations of international law and the strong get stronger through their impunity.

The duties of a lawyer include searching for the truth and finding the whole truth. If this truth is not proven in practice, and our conscious expressions about the truth are modified in order to win a case and get paid, then justice is no longer about finding the truth, but rather about hiding it. This has unfortunately become part of the profession and the practical aspects of the code of ethics, since the code of ethics is nothing more than conscience, and conscience is nothing more than a person, and a person is nothing more than their wishes and the limits of their personal desires. Justice and the code of the profession are rules, but these rules twist, screw, and bend cases of criminal law such that lawyers get paid well while the victims are robbed of reparations and justice. Despite the reality that justice cannot be achieved in most situations, we still proceed with the current system of justice with the hope that we will never be the victims of injustice ourselves.

Still, with all these shortcomings of our legal and criminal systems concerning appropriate criminal justice and finding the truth, international criminal lawyers do not care, and they all believe that they are performing their duties well. They do not see the bitterness of the system of international criminal law and the harm it causes the world of justice and humanity as a whole. The main trick that international lawyers have is that they have understood how the fundamental challenges threaten their personal incomes when they pursue the notorious "bad guys". The fact is that the majority of international criminal lawyers do not want to face the real definition and purpose of international criminal justice. This is because their only goal is to satisfy their clients, including when they are governments or political authorities.

6.9. Moral Conundrums Facing International Lawyers

Whilst all principles of the code of ethics imply the very significant value of judicial conscience and judicial independence, this independence naturally disappears and becomes impossible to maintain when politicians enter into the Court.[147] The Court is then unable to function without interference on their part and judicial independence is lost. Against great odds in the system of international criminal justice, international criminal lawyers have succeeded in convincing the population of the world that the system of international criminal law contains good provisions and promotes good policies concerning the attribution of international criminal responsibility to criminals. However, these criminals do not include the clients of the relevant lawyers, but rather those who are struggling and fighting against the injustices of the big criminals in the world.

Thus, for these international lawyers, the rules and principles of international law are only clear when they want them to be and when they can use them to attribute guilt to the great men of history. However, when it comes to the crimes of their favourite criminals or clients, this interpretation and deduction of the lawyers is certainly different. That is what international criminal lawyers work for, and that is what the scope of international criminal responsibility encompasses. A number of those who struggle for the rights of self-defence and independence become criminals, and a number of those who kill in the millions become innocent protectors of international human rights law. Three well-known examples of the former include the cases of Mahatma Gandhi, Patrice Lumumba, and Martin Luther King Jr. and their fights against criminal governments.

The fact is that international human rights lawyers have convinced the international community for over 70 years now that there are certain principles and rules of human rights law which are fundamental and should be respected by everyone. However, the same lawyers cannot convince

---

[147] Consult Jonathan Power, *Conundrums of Humanity: The Quest for Global Justice* (Brill, 2007). Reiss Hans Siegbert, *Kant: Political Writings* (University Press, 2003).

themselves of the existence of such law and protective principles. That is what we have created fees and justice for. Even our judges, because of their salary, have to be sure that they make decisions beyond a reasonable doubt, and are therefore right.

We should not forget the fact that international criminal lawyers are nothing more than individuals who are familiar with a particular aspect of the law. This means that they are not special or different from other individuals. It also means that knowing the law does not necessarily mean that you also have morality. Actually, their morality may even be restricted because of the narrow limitation of their scope. Comparatively, a mother or father, without any knowledge of the law or even the alphabet, may understand the definition of moral law better than a lawyer. Morality is not dependent upon our knowledge of the legal discipline, but on the way in which we treat people as human beings, and not as the objects of income. Morality implies an understanding of the problems of others without expecting any personal gain in return. You may knock on the door of a villager and receive assistance, but you may knock the door of a law firm and regret it for the rest of your life. A lawyer does not have time for the establishment of justice without receiving payment. Payment for them is justice; however justice may not be achieved even after payment. Justice needs special moral requirements that do not rest and cannot be established without properly understanding the common needs of all human beings.

> I really wonder what the nature of law is. Is law the manifestation of the concept of morality? Or, is morality the law? Can a violation of law be qualified as a violation of a legal system? Or, may non-violation of law be qualified as a violation of moral norms? Obviously, the law may not represent morality, but morality definitely symbolizes the real virtue of the law. By all these, I mean that the norms of law which present injustice, and even those norms which apparently present justice, may not be considered the obvious norms of legality if they do not fulfil the standard of international legalisation of law. This means, inter alia, good faith in the natural substance of the law; the intention of achieving good results regardless of the purpose of the law; demanding the full standard

> of human justice for the subjects of the law; and creating the atmosphere of objectivity for the law. The standard of international legalisation of law also means not containing any political deceptions; giving birth to the creation of justice with tolerance for other ideologies; quality of pure human rights law over quantity of the same law; and preventing criminal justice from any possible criminal behaviour against the machinery of judgment, i.e., the pillar of acquisition with love.[148]

An international human rights lawyer who works for justice based on the expectations of the big powers' needs and interests in any international organisation and who claims to support and protect human beings and their rights while directly and indirectly supporting the policy of criminal regimes, cannot be trusted at all. An international human rights lawyer who sincerely fights against the atrocities carried out against members of the Bahia faith in Iran, while simultaneously denying the rights of the Palestinians and the systematic genocide of their territories, children, people, and dignity, cannot be trusted based on principles of morality and of professional ethics. Simply, one should not work with the Israeli, Saudi Arabian, British, Canadian, or American governments without speaking out against their brutal acts in Iraq, Afghanistan, Palestine, and other parts of the world. The professional ethical principles of such lawyers reduce and conceal acts of genocide, crimes against humanity, and war crimes committed by governments in exchange for payment. These human rights lawyers have worsened the dilemma of human rights law by spreading the lie that a non-international human rights lawyer believes that the system of international criminal justice has no special moral requirements at all.

6.10. Turning the Case Upside Down

Unlike abstract principles, all forms of criminal jurisdiction have the intention of reaching the sphere of moral understanding, not only for the accused, but also for the public, in order to establish that certain conducts

---

[148] Malekian, *Classical Morality in International Peremptory Criminal Law*, note 8, pp.239-240.

are impermissible within the moral frame of law. This is particularly significant when we speak about the scope of morality in the system of international human rights law which is solely based on the moral requirements of law and the ethics of judicial conscience.[149] That is why an international criminal lawyer should know that the system of international criminal law is solely working for and supporting the principles of international human rights law, and those principles should not be violated. It is therefore misleading to pretend that we are supporting rights and ensuring that we are implementing the system of international human rights law and its requirements while we are not, and our claims to morality are much lower than the high morality of our villager in the earlier example.[150]

When the villager looks outside of themselves, they can easily recognise that the parties that claimed to implement the true principles of international human rights law were certainly wrong. It may be true and obvious that we are all aware of the fact that human rights principles are orchestrated optimistically with full harmony, but we do not wish to face the reality of those principles and their manipulation by governments and our international human rights lawyers.[151]

An international human rights lawyer who does not realise that the entire system of international human rights law has been monopolised by

---

149 Examine Farhad Malekian, *Documents on the Principles of International Human Rights* (Stockholm: Norstedts Juridik Student, 2007); Steven Greer, The Interpretation of the European Convention on Human Rights: Universal Principle or Margin of Appreciation, 3 UCL Human Rights Review (2010); Paolo G. Carozza, 'Uses and Misuses of Comparative Law in International Human Rights: Some Reflections on the Jurisprudence of the European Court of Human Rights,' 73 NOTRE DAME L. REV. (1998), pp. 1217-1237; Steven Greer, The Interpretation of the European Convention on Human Rights: Universal Principle or Margin of Appreciation, 3 UCL Human Rights Review (2010).

150 Examine sub-section above paragraph before quotation.

151 "I have touched upon these aspects of intellectual development for the sake of completeness. I cannot consider them in any detail, but we should note that they obviously have a central place in the acquisition of moral views. How well the art of perceiving the person is learned is bound to affect one's moral sensibility; and it is equally important to understand the intricacies of social cooperation. *But these abilities are not sufficient. Someone whose designs are purely manipulative, and who wishes to exploit others for his own advantage, must likewise, if he lacks overwhelming force, possess these skills*. The tricks of persuasion and gamesmanship call upon the same intellectual accomplishments." Rawls John, *A Theory of Justice* (1999) p.411.

many governments, is ignoring the truth.[152] The fact is that human rights principles are only enforceable when our governments wish them to be, or when international human rights lawyer consider it necessary. This is based on the very obvious fact that human rights principles only apply to those who the Security Council allow them to. This means that contributions to human rights principles and their enforcement are made selectively, and are not always wished for by the Security Council and the lawyers working with the Council. The enforcement of human rights principles was not, and is not, for example, necessary for the American, British, and Israeli governments in most political situations, nor for the Chinese or Russian governments.

The discussions surrounding the system of international human rights law among many international human rights lawyers and international criminal lawyers represent an old repeated story of the humiliation of man by man, the humiliation of man by lawyers, and the humiliation of the truth by the legal profession. This is a reality that we are constantly facing. Our profession is simply based on personal ethics and the existence of various codes of ethics which deal with the needs of human beings. Respecting their high value is indeed a matter of personal understanding, and is not representative of an appropriate enthusiasm for the rights of people of the world. This is regardless of how many times someone gives a solemn oath that they will protect the victims and not violate the moral and ethical requirements of the profession for any reason or at any price. These oaths have proven to be more than wrong and just a habit among lawyers. When the old hag Avarice went to the King's Court and became an advocate, she honestly declared:

But first I wear without a doubt,
My tongue I shall not put it out,
For right nor wrong, nor for nothing,
But where I see right great winning
Avarice goes further for gold and silver and says

---

152 Farhad Malekian, *Monopolization of International Criminal Law in the United Nations, A Jurisprudential Approach* (2nd ed., Almqvist & Wiksell International, 1995).

the fact that criminal justice requires the presentation of the truth from all parties. If this basic principle is not respected, then it will be very difficult to find the truth as long as people continue to only work to protect their own interests. All of us ought to take responsibility for the consequences of our conducts, and if this is not respected, then irresponsibility takes control and morality disappears.

If we do not find our international criminal lawyers ethically and legally responsible for their misconduct, then we will continue to face big problems with the philosophy of morality, and morality will continue to decrease in the most significant institutes of criminal justice i.e., the ICC and other international criminal courts. We should thus assert that there is always a tighter dimension of morality within which a lawyer functions. This is because lawyers generally do not accept responsibility in practice and try, as much as possible, to avoid taking any responsibility for their conduct at all. That is why we need to make clear to all criminal lawyers, in particular international criminal lawyers, that the criminal justice which constitutes a hope for the victims, should not be subject to corruption which identifies innocence based on power and money. The code of morality and ethics must be better formulated to fit lawyers or defence lawyers in international criminal courts with reference to their very sensitive role in the lives of the victims of international crimes.

7.2. Moral Dilemma of Lawyers

During both national and international criminal procedures, lawyers may promote the fairness of procedures or they may create panic and unfairness. As a result, how judgments turn out depends on how the parties involved in the procedures of criminal justice see and interpret the moral and ethical standards of criminal justice. The function of defence lawyers is therefore very significant in the evaluation of fairness and is equivalent to the function of a judge who decides whether or not someone is guilty. An opinion of a judge or lawyer who hides the truth may lose its value in similar cases. A clear example of this is the position of the Hungarian judge, Péter Kovács, and his dissenting view in 2021 written in support of crimes committed by the Israeli government in Palestine. The recent international crimes committed by the Israeli government in May 2021 demonstrate the fact that the relevant judge had his mind on one-eyed-justice and did not preserve fairness in the procedures of criminal justice.

That is why one must be very cautious and avoid promoting false evidence under the system of administration of criminal justice. Additionally, one should remember the fact that the purpose of international criminal jurisdiction is the overall satisfaction of the victims and not the condemned, although the rights of the latter should not be violated by any means. The moral duties integrated into the system of criminal justice inherently need the support of prosecutors, judges, and lawyers, regardless of what the opposing groups feels. Establishing fairness is not difficult, and is rather actually very simple as long as we do not neglect potential evidence and continue to present the entire truth. This is not only the duty of the prosecutors and judges of the Court, but also the imperative duty of defence lawyers or defence attorneys if ethical morality or the morality of ethics is in focus for the judicial impartiality of international criminal justice.

The acknowledgment that procedural fairness in the system of international criminal justice largely depends on the evidence presented by the defence team suggests the need to explore the appropriate definition of fair procedures and their principles in the context of criminal jurisdiction. It is a great task, as well as an intensive moral duty, for defence lawyers not to jeopardise fair procedures or create international dissatisfaction within the system of international criminal law. In the case of morality, we are, without a doubt, all strongly affected by our own judgments. These judgments should not impact the morality of various criminal laws with reference to the fact that the definitions of international crimes and the development of the system of international criminal justice were all founded upon respect for the universal criteria of morality.

The international criminal justice system, and particularly the ICC, require increased morality in their principles. This means that we should teach all lawyers the principles of true morality based on the truth as the essential condition for establishing true justice, which would not be possible if it were not based on true wisdom. Trust in the truth comes not only with oaths or knowledge of international criminal law, but also through framing international criminal law in terms of achieving morality in the rules of the law and framing the real nature of the codes of morality in the Court. This must all still be based on the nature of our personal honesty and impartiality. However, we believe that all this must occur if the victims' rights have value in the system of international human rights law. To this end, we need a better understanding of the notion of morality, within both national and international criminal codes.

7.3. LAWYERS CONCEALING THE TRUTH

These claims of morality by our international criminal lawyers and international human rights lawyers have become so clear that all of us believe we have the master key of morality in our minds and can easily follow the judges, if they follow our legal discipline and our interpretation of morality, legality, and justice. For instance, the international criminal lawyers who helped with the establishment of the fake Saddam Hussein tribunal believed, and continue to believe, that the tribunal was acting appropriately and in accordance with the principles of international criminal law. That is why the judges of the tribunal were appreciated by Michael Scharf who served as a mediator between judges, lawyers, the CIA, and the American government throughout proceedings. However, this lawyer has not accepted the truth that the Swedish international lawyer, Hans Blix, uncovered concerning the conduct of the big powers in Iraq. The fact is that the basic complaint of this American international criminal lawyer in the Iraqi case represents an indifference to truth in which the maliciousness of the brutal acts of American and British governments has been hidden.[156] The fact is that not only did this American international

[156] Farhad Malekian, *Gravity of Wisdom in International Criminal Law* (New York: Nova Science Publishers, 2021); Leila Nadya Sadat, 'International Legal Issues Surrounding the Mistreatment of Iraqi Detainees by American Forces', vol. 8, *Issue 10 Insights* (May 21,

criminal lawyer succeed in hiding the truth from the judges of the tribunal who were sincerely engaged for charges against Hussein, but he also succeeded in hiding the truth from the general public and pretended that the independent judicial conscience of criminal justice was fully respected and therefore, authentic.

Regrettably, in the judgments of lawyers, money represents the first principle of the code of ethics. In other words, the fee for hiding the truth and pulling the wool over the eyes of the public is a primary principle of the code of ethics. This is a fact and reality. A well-known international criminal lawyer who passed away, although not before earning a lot of money, never spoke out against the criminal conducts of Obama administration in Palestine, nor against the Saudi Arabian King concerning his crimes against the Yemeni population in order to preserve his wealth. Although this international criminal lawyer was against occupation and other international crimes, he preferred to earn money by knowingly or unknowingly protecting criminals. This double morality of international human rights lawyers i.e. doppelgänger behaviour, is not new. The fact is that morality principles are as cold as charity.

We should not also put aside the fact that Barak Obama should have respected international criminal regulations and international human rights law in Afghanistan, Iraq, and Palestine. We should remember that he and his wife were both practicing lawyers who worked with the Bar.[157] As a civil rights attorney, he should have been aware of the fact that torturing nationals of various nations in Guantanamo Bay was not only illegal, but

---

2004); Clark Ramsey, *War Crimes – A Report on United States War Crimes against Iraq* (Maisonneuve Press, 1992).

[157] See *Investigation into the Situation in the Islamic Republic of Afghanistan,* Pre-Trial Chamber of the ICC, No.ICC-02/17, 12 April 2019, p.30, Para. 96, Available online at https://www.icc-cpi.int/CourtRecords/CR2019_02068.PDF; Examine *also* C. Perelman, *The Idea of Justice and the Problem of Argument* (Humanities Press, 1963); David Sugarman (ed.), *Legality, Ideology and the State*(Academic Press, 1983); Peter Goodrich, *Languages of Law* From Logics of Memory to Nomadic Masks (Cambridge University Press,1990); D. Kennedy, *'Law and Ideology'* 3 *Tikkun* (1988); R. Unger, 'The Critical Legal Studies Movement,' 96 Harvard Law Review 561 (1983); J. Derrida, 'Force of Law: Mystical Foundation of Authority,' 11 *Cardozo Law Review* 919 (1990); S. Fuller, 'Playing Without a Full Deck: Scientific Realism and the Cognitive Limits of Legal Theory,' 97 *Yale Law Journal* 549 (1988); Alasdair MacIntyre, *After Virtue: A Study in Moral Theory,* (University of Notre Dame Press, 1982).

in violation of the entire system of international criminal law and justice. He was also clearly aware of serious crimes committed in Abu Ghraib by American soldiers against Iraqi prisoners. However, Obama was a very good lawyer when it came to lying, hiding, and destroying evidence. As a result of his orders, hundreds of thousands of documents and pictures showing acts of torture in Abu Gharib were destroyed. His contribution to humanity is negative, with due regard to the fact that he was a practicing lawyer and knew how the professional conscience of a lawyer should function to prevent any violations of ethical norms. However, his international commitments violated many ethical norms. We are referring to a person who believes that he was educated at Harvard Law School. The true lawyers include Nelson Mandela, Mahatma Gandhi, Martin Luther King Jr., and Mohammad Mossadegh. All four were lawyers, but with very excellent personalities, characters, dignities, and sincere commitments to moral and ethical jurisdiction.

7.4. Attorneys as the Puppets of Ventriloquist Politicians

Ventriloquy, as I have stated in two of my other volumes about the judicial conscience, is an art form in which one projects their voice to make it seem as though it is originating from somewhere else, usually from someone else's mouth—and in our case, within a courtroom.[158] Traditionally, there have been a number of ventriloquists in the cultures of most nations of the world who perform with puppets. However, in certain cases, the ventriloquist's position has been dictated by a politician to a lawyer. A lawyer who is the puppet of a ventriloquist is quite different from an independent lawyer or attorney. Puppet lawyers serve as the tools of politicians or tyrannical authorities who pretend to be moral, trustworthy lawyers.

---

[158] Malekian, *Conscience of Prosecutors in International Criminal Law: The Heart of the Matter*, note 14, pp.137-148; Farhad Malekian, *Conscience of Judges in International Criminal Law*, pp.185-188.

Puppet lawyers are the real doppelgängers, as they are both puppets and ventriloquists. This means they perform two functions at the same time. However, the lawyer is the voice of politicians, and the lawyer fulfils the needs of politics i.e., the interests of the government. The lawyer or puppet is a tool of the politicians. Their task is to accuse certain people and hide certain questions and thus to conceal the truth from the public. The lawyer does their job and gets paid simply for defending their client and fulfilling their responsibility to protect. Thus, an innocent man represented by such lawyers may be found guilty, and the guilty may be exonerated. The lawyer may still demonstrate this voice of the politicians as their own and be complicit in hiding the truth.[159]

The fact is that a large number of lawyers around the world act as ventriloquist lawyers or even worse. They are puppets, ventriloquists, lawyers, the voice of the law, and the final word of justice. One can search the territories of dictatorial governments to find them as they can easily be seen in the jurisdiction of all states in the world. However, in certain countries, there is systematic cooperation between prosecutors, judges, and lawyers, which means that ventriloquist lawyers take orders from their masters (politicians) to ensure that certain individuals end up in prison.

As human beings, lawyers have enough difficulty reconciling their personal necessities with the different requests of a system of criminal justice which pretends to be impartial. Lawyers contribute to the attribution of the notion of criminal responsibility to innocent individuals, whose crime is simply the desire for the establishment for their rights, freedoms, *somebodiness*, and the respect of their essence by political authorities. Lawyers help to put the innocent in jail for wishing to have their human rights respected. There are a number of such lawyers who function as the puppets of politicians and carry out their final wishes. These lawyers do not see anything wrong with their profession and even believe that they

[159] Richard Falk, 'The Accountability of Leaders: A Challenge to Civil Government and Society' in Jeremy Brecher, Jill Cutler, Smith Brendan, *In the Name of Democracy: American War Crimes in Iraq and Beyond (American Empire Project)*, (New York: Metropolitan Books, Henry Holt and Company, 2005); John Farmer, *The Ground Truth: The Story Behind America's Defense on 9/11* (New York: Riverhead Books, 2009); Ramsey Clark, *War Crimes – A Report on United States War Crimes against Iraq* (Maisonneuve Press, 1992).

have respected professional ethics and morality to a very high degree with their actions.

The function of attorneys as the puppets of ventriloquist politicians is the same as that of ventriloquist lawyers. This is because ventriloquist lawyers have different faces and different characters and their functions change based on the circumstances and the payments they are promised. They can thus even be the politician themselves. Since the words of the law are difficult to understand, and the terms of the law can have different interpretations and definitions, and since they are the only ones who understand the content of the law and its complicated terms, they can manipulate it with different expressions and give different definitions to the terms. This is particularly obvious in the examination of international crimes and the scope of their definitions. In particular, I am referring here to crimes against humanity, war crimes, genocide, and aggression, and even to the definition of rape. For a large number of international criminal lawyers, it took over 80 years to define the term "aggression", and the term was finally defined—albeit with the caveat that it is subject to debate when it comes into use.

A recent example of this is with the term "genocide" which has a clear definition; however it has become the most complicated international crime when it comes to its definition, due to lawyers prioritising their paychecks over justice. Lawyers are not only puppets, but are also ventriloquists. That is why different definitions and notions of genocide have been created and are still not complete based on the fact that *the deep pockets of ventriloquist lawyers are bottomless, and thus the definition of genocide can vary depending on the day*. As was clearly expressed by the Canadian lawyer William Schabas regarding the case of brutal genocide in Myanmar, "I am paid and I have to defend my client".

In other words, the terminology of the international crime of genocide, or the crime of crimes against the civilisation of human beings, did not apply in this case for Schabas, and the brutal crimes of the government of Myanmar clearly do not constitute genocide. This is what we call the power of the fee. This means that we modify our understanding of all the definitions within the legal discipline based on the customer's ability to pay. Thus, if the payment comes from a government, and the ventriloquist lawyer is actually serving as the voice of the Myanmar government, then the fee is much higher and the defence attorney must reject the structure of the system of international criminal law and the definition of genocide as a whole. The result is that we will have different definitions for the brutal crime of genocide from time-to-time and from fee-to-fee and so forth.

7.5. Ventriloquist Lawyers Ignoring the Truth

Ventriloquist lawyers may also work with ventriloquist judges in certain situations, such as in the case of the brutal crimes in Palestine and the dissenting view of Hungarian judge Péter Kovács in the Chamber of the ICC, in which he claimed that the Palestinian territory does not constitute an independent state, and therefore Palestine has no international legal personality. Although the question of the international legal personality of a state is up to some level of interpretation, the fact is that a classic state does not need confirmation of their international legal personality according to the customary system of international law. Under this system, the confirmation of the personality of state is simply a political decision and does not reduce the traditional personality of a state under the system of international law. The judge through his dissent, as I have stated elsewhere, was used as a ventriloquist judge for the voice of the big political parties.

More surprising are the statements of Latin American international criminal lawyer Kai Ambos regarding the statement of Judge Péter Kovács. Ambos, after some examination of the work of the dissent, situated himself in the middle, able to play both sides. He took the dissent into consideration, but still believes that Palestine does not meet the standards for state personality in international law. He therefore places more weight on political views than legal ones. Thus, here, Ambos understands the reality but nevertheless invalidates the customary principles of international law and the fact that the occupation of a state has nothing to do with its international legal personality and occupation does not modify the international traditional personality of a state which has been the target of political attacks and international intrigues.

This is particularly evident in the case of Palestine, which has been hunted by different governments, including the American and British ones. In comparison, the South African black population did not lose their independence, even though they were subject to apartheid for several decades and their sovereignty was infringed upon by the brutal acts of the white citizens and their barbarous conducts against the Africans. In other words, occupation does not take away the value of the international legal personality of a state, and evidently the vast majority of states of the world support the international legal personality of Palestine. However, the problem is the support of the brutal Israeli government by the Security Council and the United States, which was affirmed by the killings and destruction carried out in Gaza in May 2021. The question is, how can a state like Israel, which is just seventy years-old, receive international legal personality in accordance with the words of Judge Péter Kovács and Kai Ambos, but a state which has existed for thousands of years is said to have no international legal personality?[160]

The views of ventriloquist judges or lawyers are invalid because of their bias resulting from economic and political factors. However, this does not mean that national or international criminal courts are empowered to make such decisions invalid. Although we understand that the systems of international criminal law and justice are both integral parts of the moral requirements in the profession of law, their professional rules or ethical rules of criminal justice have nothing to empower when it comes to the questions of power politics and the enforcement of their rules over the accused or offenders. Thus, the language of law has foreseen the way in which we find the guilty innocent and the innocent guilty. In addition, a ventriloquist lawyer is also aware of the fact that some of the judges of *ad hoc* or permanent tribunals also act as ventriloquist judges and have

---

160 Farhad Malekian, *Paralysing International Criminal Justice* (New York: Nova Science Publishers, 2021), pp. 39, 70, 76, 79, 85-86, 88, 95, 102-103, ff; Malekian, *Gravity of Wisdom in International Criminal Law*, note 156.

doppelgänger characters. In other words, lawyers and judges may appear to be in opposition, but are actually working together. They may conspire with each other in various ways. Their task may be to cover up each other's mistakes or secrets in order to protect their interests. Therefore, this is done in order to promote their own personal financial or political interests and as a result, the rights of the international population are ignored.

It is not without reason that Emperor Justinian issued this warning: "let all attorneys and judges refrain from taking money, and let them not regard the controversies of others as a source of plunder." This statement is still valid today and will continue to be valid considering that international criminal lawyers and international human rights lawyers exploit millions of victims to support their own wishes and demands, their own children, their own families, and their own interests. They ignore the fact that the blood of children has paid for their luxurious lives.

7.6. Doppelgänger Character of Ventriloquist Lawyers

In national or international criminal jurisdictions, it is lawyers who play with words and have definitions for every word, which may change based on the case and even be used as an excuse if a lawyer loses a case. This is the doppelgänger character of a ventriloquist lawyer. For instance, under the procedures of a criminal court, when a decision is announced, the decision may be stated that the losing argument was without merit. This is clear for ordinary people, and refers to the finding at the conclusion of an inquiry, that the alleged abuse did not occur, which in turn implies that the alleged perpetrator is not criminally responsible for the abuse or the neglect as charged. This clear language of the rules of criminal law may still be interpreted differently by the lawyer and allow them to argue that they did not make a mistake, but rather that their client did not provide enough evidence.

The lawyer or the puppet in this situation addresses the mistake to the ventriloquist, who is again a scapegoat, in order to release themselves from any kind of responsibility or liability towards the accused. This is the case concerning a large number of international lawyers who argue that they believed that the information they presented about certain crimes was correct and authentic since it was given to them by our own governments. In other words, one passes responsibility on to someone else, who passes it on again to someone else and so on, and thus in the end the situation becomes too confusing and the essence of the case is lost.

In such cases, lawyers become puppets and make sure to always find someone else guilty in exchange for payment. This is exactly the situation seen with another Canadian lawyer who was invited along with 14 others to express their views about the tribunal for Saddam Hussein at the Cornell Law School in 2004. However, since the situation was politically clear and all dances of destruction with Iraq by the British and the American armed forces were carried out in order to gain access to oil, the Canadian lawyer did not speak about the tribunal but rather about the difficulty he himself faced thanks to the Iranian regime when he was younger. Here, I am referring to Payam Akhavan. He had several intentions. First, he did not want not to say a word against the establishment of the tribunal in Iraq. Such a statement could jeopardise the interests of his powerful criminal clients and cause him to lose the one million dollars that he had received in the name of protecting human rights in Iran. Secondly, he sought to indirectly support the criminal attacks of British and American forces during the Gulf War. Thirdly, he wanted to secure his position with the big powers by only talking about the domestic criminal regime of Iran, despite this not being the subject of the international conference. Fourthly, he secured future financial support from the big powers and their allies such as Saudi Arabia, Israel, and Canada through his statements.

Although the system of international criminal law condemned the crimes against humanity committed against members of the Bahia faith by the Iranian regime, a considerable number of criminal lawyers still sought to escape from speaking the truth and getting on the bad side of the big powers—by pleading ignorance. This is an excuse which is not permissible considering that the system of international human rights law, with the assistance of doppelgänger lawyers or ventriloquist lawyers, is violating the system of judicial conscience and no one has been punished for the deaths of over 550,000 children.[161]

Therefore, an international criminal lawyer who does not understand that the crimes committed in the Iraqi territories by the superpower states were crimes which violated the foundation of civilisation of mankind, does not have knowledge of law for justice but the knowledge of law for the payments. Similarly, an international criminal lawyer who does not realise that the crimes committed in Palestine were crimes of the state and evoke the international criminal responsibility of the relevant state, is surely supporting the power of guns and the royalty of money. Again, an international criminal lawyer who speaks about the criminal acts of the Chinese government, the Iranian government, the Russian government, the Myanmar government, the Cuban government, the Chilean government, the Lebanese government, or the Syrian government, but does not see the barbarous crimes of the American government, the British government, and the Israeli government, is surely ignoring the essence of the conscience of criminal justice and the truth.[162]

The fact is that an international criminal lawyer is responsible for recognising all government crimes and to fight against all injustices without discrimination. The American, British, and Israeli governments brand any movement of any lawyer or any government against their criminal policy as terrorist movements, and unfair understandings of their criminal policies. For these fundamental reasons, a number of international criminal lawyers turn a blind eye to, and are silent about, the criminal activities of the big political powers of the Security Council and devote their time to the cases from which they can make the most money. The same can be said about Chinese or North Korean lawyers who work with full political conscience rather than with judicial conscience and morality.

---

[161] Jordan J Paust, *Beyond the law: the Bush Administration's Unlawful responses in the "War" on Terror* (Cambridge, 2007).

[162] Malekian, *Orchestrating Diversity in International Criminal Justice*, note 14 pp.50, 61, 83, 113, 134, 203 and 221.

This is unfortunately the reality of our international human rights system, which has become a tool with which many international criminal lawyers can make money.

7.7. International Lawyers Ignoring Common Understanding

An international criminal lawyer or an international human rights lawyer approaches the depth of moral degradation as a natural consequence of their indifference to truth. They know where the truth is, but they ignore it in favour of supporting the side of evil and painting it as good. Thus, they continue to defend the evil conducts of big powerful states in order to earn more money. In fact, a person who has lost their conscience and sold justice, does not have judicial conscience and strongly believes that it is the public who do not have the ability to recognise the truth.

Thus, we have very few good international criminal lawyers or international human rights lawyers who struggle for real justice and for the real truth. It is avarice which causes lawyers to represent evil big political parties even after witnessing the brutality of their crimes. For instance, as we have stated elsewhere, in the case of Saddam Hussein, the situation of the relevant lawyer was able to secure his position by working for the evil governments, evil military actions, evil military attacks, and the evil destruction of a country. As a legitimate platform for defending the evil conducts of the British government, or Tony Blair who became known internationally for the killing over half a million children with the assistance of George W. Bush, the lawyer pointed to Hussein and his murder of 4,000 Kurds, and thus found a legitimate argument to cover the truth about the big criminals.[163]

In other words, a lawyer can hit several targets with one shot, and any time they face any problems, they have the support of the big criminals.

---

[163] *Id.*, note 162.

Therefore, they cannot face any legal or political consequences. Additionally, ethical qualms or those relating judicial conscience do not exist for such a lawyer, and therefore they do not mind that the judicial independence had been violated from the very beginning of the fake Saddam Hussein Tribunal through the intervention of big political parties of the United Nations. The situation was very clear: the use of force during the Gulf War by the big powers against Iraq was condemned internationally and resulted in the devastation of one of the oldest civilisations of the world.[164] Despite this, avarice encouraged lawyers to side with evil. Inevitably, those who pay are affluent; they are the big powers who believe that they are the representatives of the universe and must therefore settle the rules of heaven in all countries through killing innocent people and establishing international criminal courts. It is therefore rightly asserted that the classical embodiment of the lawyer arose and spread throughout the "*Western world.*"[165] This implies "a consummate malevolence, callousness to truth the basic vice, hardened with the sine of avarice, and a consequence denial of God's favoured – the downtrodden poor."[166] It is also noted that even the big criminals know and agree with the fact that "in a classless damnation: the lawyer is the immoralist, denying truth for a fee. With that agreed, subsidiary evils fall quickly into place."[167]

The motivations of international criminal lawyers and international human rights lawyers are also clear, they have to work for human rights and should hide the truth from the international public for several reasons; among which are to keep the international public in the dark, allow the criminals to continue carrying out their crimes, and ignore crimes in order to preserve their power. This means that international lawyers are not thieves, but something almost beyond belief. That is why good lawyers are painters who can turn black to white and white to black. *That is also why the honest international criminal lawyers or the international human*

---

[164] Farhad Malekian, *Condemning the Use of Force in the Gulf Crisis* (Almqvist & Wiksell International, 1st ed., 1992, republished 1994).
[165] Mellinkoff, *The Conscience of a Lawyer*, note 1, p.13.
[166] *Id.*
[167] *Id.*

rights lawyers of dignity who sleep in their sleeping bags in graveyards and forests are jailed in the prisons of the big powers. However, poverty here implies highest degree of their somebodiness, *and not the support of injustice.*

7.8. Lawyers as the Puppets of Super Powers

In certain very hopeless situations when brutal international crimes have been committed by super powerful states, international human rights lawyers may act on their own accord and establish non-governmental tribunals which may have no power of implementation, but nevertheless wish to draw attention to international crimes. One example of such a tribunal is the Bertrand Russell Tribunal and its sincere lawyers seeking to record the barbarity of the crimes committed by the US Armed Forces in Vietnam.[168] The sessions of the Tribunal took place in London, Copenhagen, and Stockholm. It was planned to have one session in Paris; however this was hindered by the political authorities at the time because of their alliance with the CIA and the American government. The Tribunal's purpose was to call for the truth based on judicial conscience and the dignity and impartiality of certain international lawyers.

However, the merit of the Russell Tribunal has been misused by the current generation of lawyers whose main objective is to preserve their financial, military, and political interests. The Russell Tribunal was not supported by any superpowers in the Security Council nor by their allies. Nor did the President of any superpower deliver a welcome address for the Tribunal, and all ignored some of the most serious crimes committed in the civilisation of mankind against the weak by the strong nations of the world, namely the United States. One of the clear examples of the *misuse* of the

---

[168] Examine Bertrand Russell and the Russell International War Tribunal held in Stockholm, Sweden, May 2-10, 1967 and Roskilde, Denmark from November 20 to December 1, 1967. The Tribunal was essentially created as a result of different meetings in London in 1966. J. Duffett, Against the Crime of Silence (New York, London, 1968). See also See *The Belmarsh Tribunal: The War On Terror is Put on Trial,* https://www.youtube.com/watch?v=E_xxGWAxlGc.

legacy of the Bertrand Russell Tribunal is the recent puppet Uighur Tribunal which was established by President Biden in order to exploit the brutal situation of Uighur victims who have long suffered under the authoritarian regime of the Chinese government.

This puppet tribunal has been investigating the humiliated victims of the Uighur genocide committed by the Chinese government and has several goals. The first major intention of these international human rights lawyers is politics, and the second is to make the victims believe that their voices have been heard. Since the ICC could not investigate the crimes in China because China is not a member of the Court, the door opened immediately after the rejection of the Case by the ICC for the big powers to use Geoffrey Nice, a British lawyer, to protect their political and economic interests in the name of human rights. Of course, he was prepared for this for many invisible reasons, and his engagement not only will not help the victims, but the case is also being ignored by a group of Western lawyers who do not realise that the blood of victims is being exploited for political aims. This is an example of acts of genocide against poor victims being exploited to serve political interests.

The Western cats cannot reach the Chinese cat's power; they use the mutilated bodies of mice to put pressure on the Chinese cat. This is exactly the story of Tom and Jerry, albeit with more than one Tom. We should also emphasise that the USA and the UK have some nerve talking about China, considering that they have committed genocide against populations in North America, Afghanistan, Australia, New Zealand, and Africa. Similarly, thousands of aboriginal children were forced into Catholic boarding schools by the government of Ottawa and then raped, abused, tortured, and murdered. No voice was heard by any lawyer. The UK has never held a tribunal for their crimes of colonisation and mass torture, mass murder, and mass slavery in their African colonies. "The self-righteous scream judgments against others to hide the noise of skeletons dancing in their own closets."[169] We have forgotten the fact that all human beings have the right to live with dignity concerning their *somebodiness.*

---

[169] John Mark Green.

Everybody should live in peace, harmony, regardless of which religion, belief, or race we belong to.

Here, again, the system of international criminal justice faces another doppelgänger lawyer like William Schabas. However, in this case, the doppelgänger lawyer is investigating the brutal crimes against the Uighur race. In the first case, the lawyer did not protect international political views, but rather the opinion of Myanmar government. In the second case, the British lawyers are generally protecting the political views of most states in the world, but in reality, they are actually protecting the economic, political, and military interests of certain powerful states.[170] What is really the marginal of definition of conscience for Nice?[171] Therefore, this lawyer is a doppelgänger lawyer and a puppet who is hiding the truth about the barbarity of the Chinese government's criminal conducts and is also promoting the interests of other states. This case is, without any hesitation, a political case, and the lawyers are being used as puppet-judges.

There is no doubt that the authoritarian Chinese government is committing crimes against the Uighur population, however the fake examination of the case is destroying the legal validity of the system of international criminal justice and abusing the rights of the innocent Uighur victims. Here our intention is not to speak out against Michael Scharf concealing the crimes of the United States and the United Kingdom against the innocent Iraqi population, nor William Schabas advocating injustice as justice in the Myanmar genocide case, nor other lawyers creating a puppet Iran Tribunal against Iranian *criminal* regime, nor Geoffrey Nice and his colleagues protecting Uighur's victims while voicing the political slogan

---

[170] Consult the statements of the judges in the *Belmarsh Tribunal: The War On Terror is Put on Trial,* https://www.youtube.com/watch?v=E_xxGWAxlGc.

[171] Kant says "One oughtn't to venture anything that risks being wrong — that is a moral principle that needs no proof. Hence, the consciousness that an action that I intend to perform is right is an unconditional duty. Whether an action is over-all right or wrong is judged by the understanding, not by conscience. And it's not absolutely necessary to know, concerning all possible actions, whether they are right or wrong. But concerning the action that I am planning to perform I must not only judge and form an opinion that it is not wrong but be certain of this; and this requirement is a postulate of conscience, to which is opposed probabilism, i.e. the principle that the mere opinion that an action may well be right is a good enough reason for performing it. So conscience could also be defined as follows: Conscience is the moral faculty of judgment." Quoted in Malekian *Judgments of Love in Criminal Justice*, note 52, p.35.

of big powerful states, as they are just a few representative examples of international human rights and international criminal law lawyers. Thus, our arrow is pointed to all those who are using the plight of victims for personal gain. However, the judges of the non-governmental Belmarsh Tribunal in London correctly clarified: "What and whom are we putting on trial? The bloody crimes that have been committed by Western governments: the United States, the United Kingdom, Australia, Sweden, Ecuador and …"[172] It is in response to this tribunal that "the British lawyer Sir Geoffrey Nice, the American Lawyer Michael Scharf, and the Swedish lawyers should reflect upon their professional licenses, including their morality of conscience, not only concerning Julian Assange but also concerning all crimes committed by big powers and their governments."[173]

Our intention is to ask all the aforementioned lawyers and all other national or international criminal lawyers of such nature the following:

a) Why do these doppelgängers not speak about the brutal atrocities committed by the American and British governments in Iraq?
b) Why do the same lawyers remain silent about the same criminal governments' crimes in Afghanistan?
c) Why are these very elegant and intelligent people, who seem to not be politicians, not the lawyers of the truth concerning Yemen and Syria?
d) How can Nice not see that the crime of genocide did not originate with Hitler, but rather with the British government in Africa and Persia, where between 12 and 16 million Persians were killed as a result of the British government's actions at the beginning of the 21st century?
e) Does Nice, this knowledgeable British lawyer, have any knowledge about the four million Indians who were killed through acts of genocide by the government of Winston Churchill after the

---

[172] 22 October, 2021. See *The Belmarsh Tribunal: The War On Terror is Put on Trial,* https://www.youtube.com/watch?v=E_xxGWAxlGc.

[173] Malekian, *Conscience of Judges in International Criminal Law, the Heart of Judgements*, note 10, p.p.153-154.

Second World War? Why does he not retroactively fight for the rights of these victims?

f) Why did this British lawyer not defend Julian Assange with his skills as an international human rights lawyer?[174]

g) Why have these promoters of human rights not made any claims against the brutal crimes of the Israeli government against the Palestinians over the last seventy years?

h) Why does Nice or anyone else not bring the Israeli government case to the General Assembly *based on full conscience of human united essence*, since the Security Council does not work because of the veto power and the General Assembly functions much better as seen with the case of Apartheid in South Africa?

The function of an international criminal lawyer or an international human rights lawyer is not to convict people, but to sincerely work for the entire international community in order to promote what we have decided is an abstract principle: that all people are equal.[175] It is a lawyer's significant duty to see that this principle is adhered to despite pure international willingness for the truth, and without any regard for the interests of national or international political authorities, and without any hidden political interests or any hate for the accused, in particular when we are talking about big criminal states or governments of the Security Council, even if the plaintiff tells their counsel that the state is guilty.

---

[174] Should Nice be paid for his service to humanity? Examine Malekian, *Allegations by Political Laundering*, note 48; Nice is known as "Sir Geoffrey Nice is one of the country's most distinguished human rights lawyers." See *also* 'The University of Buckingham', available online at https://www.buckingham.ac.uk/research/hri/fellows/nice. Assange Case Interview with Lawyer Mads Andenæs', http://www.pravdareport .com/world/europe/15-03-2016/133811-assange_lawyer-0/ [visited 12 September 2017].

[175] For example "One of the serious practical problems of the Swedish academic system, in cases of violations of human rights, is that most professors are silent unless they can see that a group of writers has collectively condemned a particular violation; then, they feel that they can speak. For instance, in the case of serious violations of human rights in Palestine by Israeli armed attacks, they practised silent diplomacy until they noticed that, e.g., Professor Iran Brownlie was active; then, they started to write their names on the relevant website lists." Malekian, *Allegations by Political Laundering*, note 48, p.29.

7.9. Honest, Unsold International Lawyers

An international attorney with full true conscience should protect the whole truth concerning the principles of implementation of justice. This is an essential duty of any elegant and unsold international lawyer. However, if an international lawyer can promote the truth and the virtue of the essence of joint humanity as a whole, they are definitely more appreciated within the pure inspiration of conscience. The expertise of a lawyer does not only rely on a deep knowledge of the provisions of law, but also on a higher morality concerning the presentation of the whole truth from both sides, particularly when a lawyer wants to act as a non-governmental code of legislation and ethics based on the fact that if the conducts are truly independent of politics and the Security Council members influence, they must meet certain moral requirements.

The fact is that many resolutions of the Security Council have caused thousands and thousands of people to be killed and, similarly, millions and millions of people have become refugees. The reality, however, is that we ignore these events and do not pay particular attention to them, because we are used to believing that the Security Council is doing good and the right things." International political laundering needs an invisible judicial horse with a tailor-made riding boots. We never dare to answer the simple questions below, since they would damage the *lawyer's* income, the *lawyer's* international or academic position, and the *lawyer's* future. Many of those who work in international juridical entities, such as the Conundrum of Allegation by Political Laundering permanent International Criminal Court, would like to reach the apex without giving sufficient ethical and moral thought to their writings and without properly understanding the fact that moral elegance is not a seat. They rarely answer the following questions and when they answer, they answer with four shoes, four heads, and four pencils: Have the permanent members been active in the territories of Iraq or the contrary? Has the Iraqi military power destroyed the homes and installations of the United States/the United Kingdom or the contrary? Did an estimated 550,000 children die in the United States/the United Kingdom or in Iraq because of the Security Council sanctions during the first Gulf War? Does the Iraqi

> government have the intention to occupy the territories of the permanent members or the contrary? Do the Iraqi and Libyan governments intend to take the oil resources of the United States/the United Kingdom or the contrary? Has ISIS really been created by the Iraqi government or the contrary? Did the Abu Ghraib events perpetrate by the Iraqi Army against the United States civilians or the contrary? Did Afghan armies rape the New York's civilian population or the contrary? Have the provisions of international criminal law been seriously violated by the government of the permanent members or by the government of Iraq? Were the questionable events of September 11 2001 against the Muslim world or the contrary? Was the intention to occupy Iraq, Libya, Afghanistan, and Iran or was it to occupy Israel, the United Kingdom, and the United States? Ultimately, the question is: did Wikileaks release news about the criminal acts of Iraq in the United States or the contrary? Anyone who calls himself an international *lawyer* should know the difference between political justice, juridical justice, and the pure nature of justice.[176]

If the client's humanitarian conscience is restricted solely to themselves and the lawyer is bound to follow such conscience, even at the price of exploiting the bloodshed of the victims, then we do not have lawyers and clients, but rather pirates of law and morality.[177] *The main duty of an international criminal lawyer is not to establish or disprove guilt, but to ensure that the normal procedures of justice remain independent. How can a lawyer be a defender of guilty states? How can a lawyer argue for the condemnation of a guilty state like China and for the acquittal of other guilty states such as Canada, the United States, and the United Kingdom for their crimes against indigenous populations across the globe, including in Palestine?*

International criminal justice, and particularly the body of international human rights law or even the natural rights of human beings, do not need doppelgänger lawyers, but rather lawyers who suffer for the truth, who speak the truth, who fight peacefully for the truth, who would go to jail for the truth, who would sacrifice their life for the truth, and

[176] Malekian, *Allegations by Political Laundering*, note 48, pp.26-27.
[177] Malekian, *The Mirage of International Criminal Law*, note 55, p.44.

would be willing to be killed for the truth. *Here my love arrow is obviously pointed to Martin Luther King Jr. Speaking about the brutal crimes of the Chinese government is obviously appreciated by any wise individual, even if they are not a lawyer. The truth is that while the Chinese government is demolishing the essence of humanity, the victims' rights should not be exploited by other politicians in order to solve their differences with the Chinese government. Consequently, the main advice I have for any pretend human rights law supporter is: if your theory is pure, if your arguments are based on the rules of ethics and judicial conscience, and if judicial conscience has any real value for your organisation at all, you must question the whole structure of the United Nations and the monopolised rules of Chapter VII of the UN Charter.*[178]

The system of international criminal justice is not *hocus pocus,* even if it appears to be since a considerable number of international criminal and international human rights lawyers' positions are based on following the politics of the colonial or authoritarian powers. This is also certainly true for all those lawyers who blindly represent the dictatorial governments of North Korea, China, Russia, Turkey, Saudi Arabia, and Egypt, to name but a few. The system of international human rights and its relevant conscience can never see the freedom of their principles as long as the lawyers who are invited to speak the truth speak about the way in which

---

178 Consult *also The Belmarsh Tribunal: The War On Terror is Put on Trial,* https://www.youtube.com/watch?v=E_xxGWAxlGc. For the whole Julian Assange case consult Malekian, *Allegations by Political Laundering,* note 48. "More or less similar questions may also be drafted about Cambodia, Egypt, Palestine, Syria, Yemen, Vietnam, and many other countries. Certainly, a large number of people have been killed and became homeless, because it is obviously impossible to provide a precise statistic of the killings based on the Security Council resolutions. A rapid glance at the books by Richard Falk, particularly the four volumes in The Vietnam War and International Law, implies the miserable facts of bad maxims in the practice of the permanent members of the United Nations. His books say precisely what Kant says, and he tries to prevent the universalisation of these horrible maxims. According to Kant, only one type of motive is consistent with the notion of morality. This is what he calls the motive of duty. One may describe this duty as performing or acting for the right thing for the right reason. Certainly, the right thing here does not mean violation or commission of crimes or adopting certain resolutions for the sake of secret superpower interests. Kant believes that there are different types of motives when a decision is taken. This is the same in the case of the Security Council resolutions, the content of which implies the nature of the motive. Kant sums up different types of motives in the category of inclination, which exists in the content of various resolutions of the Security Council or even the General Assembly." *Id.*, pp.44-45.

they can protect the interests of the big power, and how victims are used as the instruments of politics.

7.10. THE DEPENDENT CONSCIENCE OF LAWYERS

The dependent conscience of lawyers causes lawyers to appear as beautiful white lilies representing lofty ideals and powerful intellect, but without passion or practicality. A considerable number of professors of human rights, justices, and lawyers are representatives of justice for the fundamental human rights law. However, they have been involved in the actions of criminal organisations such as SAVAK, the CIA, Herasat, or the Ministry of Intelligence and Security (MOIS) in dictatorial regimes. They have acted as diplomats, but in reality, when the regime was overthrown (the Shah of Iran who is named the puppet of big powers)[179], they came to Europe or other states to lecture on international or human rights law.

Their only goal is to keep their deep pockets full. When one asks them about the substance of their justice, they ignore the question. They actually have at least two types of morality. This is what one of the lawyers in international criminal law and the judge of International Criminal Tribunal for the former Yugoslavia, Albin Eser, called "double morality." He explained how one of his best tutors taught the class about natural law and justice with love, but later on it was revealed to the students that he had been a member of the Nazi party.

As we will see, there exists tension within the dependent conscience of lawyers between the motive and logic of reason which is answerable, and the motive or logic which is unanswerable. Therefore, there exist different methods of interpretation within the fundamental reasoning of the conscience of lawyers. There also exist different values among all presented values that are associated with particular habits of evaluation held by lawyers. It may be said that in the system of justice, and particularly in the system of criminal justice, the betrayal of lawyers and

[179] https://www.youtube.com/watch?v=elWD1rwWG6w.

their various natures and characters and treatment of their clients is not solely a matter of corruption or hostility, but is related to the financial compensation they will receive. The Amsterdam's Trial Manual, one of the recognised criminal trial manuals clearly points out that:

> Counsel may and must give the client the benefit of counsel's professional advice on this crucial decision; and often counsel can protect the client from disaster only by using a considerable amount of persuasion to convince the client that a plea which the client instinctively disfavours is, in fact, in his or her best interest. This persuasion is most often needed to convince the client that s/he should plead guilty in a case in which a not guilty plea would be destructive. The limits of allowable persuasion are fixed by the lawyer's conscience.[180]

The spontaneous, coherent system of values in the system of criminal justice originating from different interpretations results in the division of interests, affects the judgments of cases, and destroys impartiality. We must also emphasise the fact that the corner in which a lawyer represents their client, is in reality the corner which has been created by the members of society to support unrestricted interests through violating other people's rights, and even killing them. This competition is even greater in the system of international relations, and is wild without any wisdom. That is why lawyers from across the globe are fighting invisible fights within the system of international criminal justice.

7.11. A Few Examples of the Morality of Lawyers

The picture of the morality of lawyers is indeed very complicated, considering that even their morality goes beyond God's will. They believe themselves to be the original key to all notions of immorality, while their

---

180 Anthony G. Amsterdam, *Trial Manual 5 for the Defense of Criminal Cases* § 201, at 339 (5th ed. 1988), § 201, at 339.

morality has no limit when it comes to payments and hiding the truth from the public. "Instead of stopping to explain that they are helping to administer a continue system of justice rather than searching for truth, lawyers do the very thing needed to bring down the moral judgment upon their heads. They fall over themselves rushing to line up on the side of the angels, insisting that their morality is the same as the common morality."[181]

Therefore, it is noted that "there is no difference between personal and professional ethics."[182] Beyond this, it is also essential to know that lawyers have a morality which is a notch higher than that of the general public, and claim that theirs is a profession "dedicated to a spirit of public service."[183] "That underneath, most lawyers are boy scouts,"[184] that law is a "public profession."[185] A few examples of the notion of morality of lawyers include the following:

In 1985 in Sweden, I brought a case to a lawyer, and he charged me 350 euros at that time. After an hour he advised me: "*you should never bring a case against any of those who work with the law in any capacity, since your case will never succeed due to the personal relationships of lawyers. Thus, your complaint is a waste of time--this is simply how the profession of lawyers works.*"[186]

In 2003, the topics of discussion at the meeting of almost 900, lawyers at the International Criminal Association in Beijing were *ne bis in idem* and sexual violations against children. The meeting took place in a well-known hotel which had shops and casinos under it where children were trafficked. I used to go jogging at 11 pm after all the ceremonies had ended

---

181 Mellinkoff, The Conscience of a Lawyer, note 1, p. lost.

182 *Id.*, p.9.

183 M. Pirsig, Cases and Materials on Professional Responsibility 38 (1965; 2d ed., p.46, 1970).

184 G. Haar, Reflections on Four Studies of the Legal Profession, Law and Society (1965), p.48.

185 R Smith, Survey of the Legal Profession Its Scope, Methods and Objectives,

186 Advokaten Henning Elof Sjöström (1985). Sweden is a small familial nation; you can find cousins wherever you turn. It is important to note that Sweden is also considered to be a democratic country, despite the fact the majority of academic positions in the legal field are granted to individuals based on personal recommendations or through back-door dealings. For instance, applicants for professor positions in law should legally not intervene in the election of the experts who judge their academic merits, but they do in reality. These experts then submit a list of names of those with whom they have good relations to the person in charge such that they can choose three or five of the people from the list to give the job to. This is called the necessity of the proceedings for democracy in the faculties of law!

for the day. The Chinese had exercise equipment placed alongside streets and you could easily access the equipment. One night when I had come back and was about to go into my room, I witnessed two international lawyers (one from the US) who attended meetings in the morning, taking trafficked children back to their rooms.

I had just come into my room when someone knocked at the door. When I opened it, I was surprised to see the Chief of the Bar Association of Lawyers in Iran. He had wine in one hand and a packet of pistachios in the other.[187] He told me: "when I came to China, I did not like Chinese girls since they have small hips, but now after a week, I love to see them and have realised that they are marvellous. It is very cheap under this hotel and there are many very young girls who charge only ten dollars for a whole night. We can take two or three together" and while pointing to his hands "I have these, we can have a fun night." I looked at him and said: "Dear colleague; I am a married man, have four children, and am very loyal to my family. Sorry, but I have to sleep. I would never do such a thing, under any condition."

This was the head lawyer of the main Bar Association of Lawyers in Iran. The Bar has the authority to decide who is ethically and morally eligible to enter into the profession of first-class advocacy. In 2018, I was at the Max Planck Institute of International Criminal Law in Freiburg, Germany. There were many lawyers from Tehran there as well. I told the story of Beijing to every Persian lady I met, and they unanimously agreed that it was true. All had bad memories concerning the Chief of the Bar and called him a "dirty-man" or a "dirty character".

In 2015, when I had gone home to attend my mother's funeral, I decided to visit her grave very late at night. I took a taxi and sat in the front passenger seat because there were two female passengers in the back. They talk and discussed working as assistants of the lawyers of the city's largest court. They had come from a wedding party which had just finished. The discussion was as follows: "Did you hear what the judge gave as a dowry for his daughter?" "Yes, I have known for long time. I was working in his

[187] This is an old tradition in Persia when you want to have some fun.

morality in practice. According to different national, regional, and international codes of ethics, lawyers, attorneys, defence lawyers, defence attorneys, and defence counsels must not violate these codes and must carry out their duties with full legal, professional, and personal conscience. This means that their impartiality, dignity, and ability to respect the rights of victims is highly significant, and the rights of the victims should not be intentionally violated in the pursuit of other interests or to support the rights of the accused. The reasoning of lawyers may be fully supported by various arguments, but cannot be supported by the united essence of man and humanity which seeks the truth. In other words, the entire system of international criminal justice was established to protect millions of victims across the globe, not to fill the deep pockets of lawyers.

8.2. Lawyers Promoting Procedural Fairness

Both the system of criminal justice and the system of international criminal justice are characterised by their fair natures. Fairness encourages public confidence in the system of criminal justice and creates trust in the administration of criminal justice. The intention of the whole system of the ICC is to establish fairness within international standards for those who have been the subject of attacks and violations by criminal systems or governments. This means that the idea behind creating the ICC was not to promote criminal law, but rather to restrict its development as a result of the systematic violation of its principles. Thus, the notion of fairness is also combined with the procedures of criminal justice and the scope of its application to all those who have committed international crimes. The purpose is to avoid impunity and thereby establish greater levels of confidence in the effectiveness of international criminal justice and its framework for justice for all, as well as in the imposition of justice at the international level.[191] Thus, the intention of the ICJ is to provide an

[191] For example, it is noted that the International Court of Justice "has been particularly assiduous in protecting states and state agents from accountability for major crimes, a predilection witnessed not only by *Arrest Warrant* and *Germany v. Italy* but also by the *Genocide Case*

appropriate voice and a sense that an international legal body is responding to international crimes including as genocide, crimes against humanity, and war crimes. Increasing international public confidence is thus the primary function of international criminal norms. However, this confidence cannot be maintained if fairness and equality are not present throughout all proceedings. [192]

The theory of fairness is itself subject to many factors that are necessary corollaries for the identification and evaluation of its nature and substance. Fairness in the procedures of justice does not come from fair regulations or a number of rules dealing with code of ethics and morality. Although these are important factors for initiating an understanding of the theory of fairness, they are not by themselves satisfactory for the establishment of fair procedures. The theory of fairness has a collective definition and is a collective presentation of the integrity of the court.

The whole theory of fairness is based on the manner in which the prosecutors, judges, and lawyers act and perform their legal, ethical, moral, and conscience-related duties in relation to the parties involved in a case. Justice in the system of ICC is thus based on the capacity of the understanding of individuals who represent the voices of the victims and the criminals, and on the re-establishment of fair treatment for all without any discrimination between victims and criminals. This means that the fairness of the ICC can only be measured through its commitments to creating substantive fairness for all victims and the equal treatment of all

---

(*Application of the Convention on the Prevention and Punishment of the Crime of Genocide (Bosnia and Herzegovina v. Serbia and Montenegro)*), 26 February 2007." David Luban, 'After the Honeymoon: Reflections on the Current State of International Criminal Justice', 11 (3) *Journal of International Criminal Justice* (2013), pp.505–515, p.514, available online at https://academic.oup.com/jicj/article/11/3/505/814469.

[192] The dissenting opinion of Judge Cançado Trinidadein in *Al Adsani* case is surely powerful. "What jeopardizes or destabilizes the international legal order, are the international crimes, and not the individual suits for reparation in the search for justice. What troubles the international legal order, are the cover-up of such international crimes accompanied by the impunity of the perpetrators, and not the victims' search for justice." ICJ, *Germany v. Italy*, § 305, *id*., p.514. See *also* Luban, 'After the Honeymoon: Reflections on the Current State of International Criminal Justice', note 191, referring to the European Court of Human Rights *Al Adsani v. United Kingdom*, Appl. No. 35763/97, 21 November 2001; UK House of Lords, *Jones v. Saudi Arabia*, 14 June 2006; *Case Concerning the Arrest Warrant of 11 April 2000 (DRC v. Belgium)*, 14 February 2002, separate opinion of Judge ad hoc Bula-Bula; ICJ, *Jurisdictional Immunities of the State (Germany v. Italy)*, 3 February 2012.

criminals. As a result, selectivity between criminals is not permitted under the Rome Statute. Nor is it permitted to prioritise victims based on the political or financial interests of superior powers. All these matters are the duties of prosecutors, judges, and lawyers functioning for the implementation of criminal justice in the world. With superior, I do not mean that they are superior regarding their humanity and in their knowledge of civilisation, but rather they are superior when it comes to killing, destruction, and creating inequality and impunity. [193]

It is therefore a major duty of defence attorneys to establish trust in their statements and to not act immorally or damage the integrity and independence of the court by accepting bribes or succumbing to pressure from any party. Nonetheless, in order to understand what constitutes procedural fairness, one must consider the general mechanisms of procedural fairness. According to one author, fairness requires that procedures include six essential components:

(i) consistency across circumstances, persons and over time;
(ii) impartiality and/or maintaining a suppression of bias in a key decision-maker;
(iii) accuracy, i.e., being based on a full range of reliable information;
(iv) 'correctability', i.e., subjection to a correction mechanism or an appeal of the final decision;
(v) representation of the interests of groups affected by the procedure; and

---

[193] "It turns out that there is no immaculate jurisdiction either. Attempts to exercise universal jurisdiction often seemed like heavy-handed efforts by former colonial masters like Belgium and Spain to define their former colonies' history for them - as Congolese Judge Bula-Bula furiously argued in his separate opinion in the Arrest Warrant case. On the other side, there was no chance that powerful states and corporations would regard exercises of universal jurisdiction against them as 'immaculate'. Here, one need consider only the thuggish US reaction to Belgium, or the leaked Wikileaks cables reporting US pressure on Spain in the case of the 'Bush Six'. For that matter, serious efforts to crush the US ATS began only when human rights litigators began suing multinational corporations rather than ousted warlords and fugitive hoodlums with no assets to attach. In the end, then, universal jurisdiction has succeeded in antagonizing both weak and strong powers - a recipe for political failure." Luban, 'After the Honeymoon: Reflections on the Current State of International Criminal Justice', note 191, p.513.

(vi) ethicality, i.e., conformity with commonly held moral values.[194]

These six principles are believed to create procedural fairness through obeying the standards of procedures and the safeguards of ethical demands. Nonetheless, it is also widely understood that procedural fairness tends to be subjective concerning certain matters and people who act in their own self-interest. This means that the interpretation and scope of these six principles are based on the perception of those affected by, or involved in, a given case, which can include victims, witnesses, judges, prosecutors, and the defence team. Objective principles preserve their connotation only insofar as they have a certain connection with individuals and what the relevant parities in a given case believe indicates a fair procedure.[195]

8.3. Freedom of Choice of an Attorney

Choosing an attorney in civil or criminal cases should not be forced upon the defendant or accused by any means. The accused should be free to decide which defence lawyer is going to represent them during criminal proceedings. The position concerning the choice of a defence lawyer constitutes a principal right of the accused and cannot be ignored under any circumstances. This also implies the impartiality of the criminal jurisdiction, which requires the full respect of the right of the accused to select their own defence lawyer. This principle is therefore undisputed in all criminal jurisdictions adhering to, and striving for, the improvement of the rules of procedures and the codes of ethics in national and international criminal courts. The respect of this principle is also required by the Statute of the ICC and its impartiality regarding the choice of defence lawyer.

---

[194] G. Leventhal, 'What Should be Done about Equity Theory?' in K.J. Gergen et al. (eds), Social Exchange Advances in Theory and Research (Springer, 1980), at 40–45. Extracted by Birju Kotecha, 'The International Criminal Court's Selectivity and Procedural Justice', 18*JICJ*(2020), 107–139, at 116; Robert Cryer, *Prosecuting International Crimes, Selectivity and the International Criminal Law Regime* (Cambridge University Press, Cambridge, 2005).

[195] Birju Kotecha, *id.*

Appointment of counsel and freedom of choice as principles demand that the Court assist the defendant in finding the appropriate lawyer for them. The right to freely choose counsel for suspects and accused persons is a principle that is safeguarded and deeply entrenched in the legal regime of international criminal courts such as the ICTY and the ICC. If a suspect or accused person requires legal representation and is willing to choose their own lawyer, the international criminal courts or tribunals should not deny them this right.[196] This right is also protected by national criminal courts which deal with the prosecution of international crimes.

Concerning the system of the International Criminal Court, the Registry of the Court simplifies this process and offers a considerable number of qualified counsellors to defendants to choose from. These lawyers from around the globe have been accepted to be on the list of the Registry. The Court has no responsibility for the performance of the counsel, and they are therefore not connected to the members of the ICJ, rather they are independent and exercise their duties in accordance with the Code of Professional Conduct for counsel practicing before the proceedings of the Court. This means that the chosen counsel is responsible for creating their team and choosing their associate counsel, case-managers, legal assistants, resource-people, and professional investigators.[197]

Therefore, these lawyers should have certain qualifications in order to ensure that they can support and protect the defendant. They should successfully and professionally protect the defendant's rights at the highest international standards. The Registrar may also appoint a duty counsel, or a temporary counsel, if urgent legal support is needed prior to the suspect selecting their permanent counsel. This role of duty consul may also be

---

[196] Examine also See Ronald Slye, *The Nuremberg Principles in Non-western Societies: A Reflection on their Universality, Legitimacy and Application* (International Nuremberg Principles Academy, 2017); George Augustus Finch, 'The Nuremberg Trial and International Law,' 41 *American Journal of International Law* (1947); Farhad Malekian, 'Comparative Substantive International Criminal Justice', in Ronald Slye (ed.),*The Nuremberg Principles in Non-western Societies: A Reflection on their Universality, Legitimacy and Application (*2017), pp.10-44.

[197] Examine also Beverley, G. Smith (author), Elizabeth M.A. Turgeon (editor), *Professional Conduct for Lawyers and Judges* (1998).

suggested by the Chambers of the ICC. That means that a Chamber may appoint counsel where the protections of the interests of justice require their engagement. Therefore, by appointing counsel the Chamber acknowledges that there are procedural matters which require the intervention of the counsel for the protection of the accused.

8.4. Courtesy of the Defence Attorney in Court

Although lawyers work independently and do not take any orders from other legal disciplines, this does not mean that they can act as they wish in the system of international criminal courts. They have certain obligations in their relations with international courts and their judges and prosecutors. Lawyers are to respect the power of the ICC and not carry out acts which are incompatible with the legal profession. Defence lawyers should always protect the authority of the Court and should express full respect for the legal independence and power of the Court at all times. The defence team and its main attorney should always justify and maintain a full understanding of the rules of the Court and its procedures. Furthermore, they should not violate any rules of the Court and should work to always protect the fundamental rights of all judges, officers, and the office of the Prosecutor.

The defence team should maintain its neutrality while communicating with the judge, and should not exploit relationships with the judges in order to influence their decisions concerning the outcome of criminal proceedings. The defence team must also inform the accused about the rules of the Court and remind them to act in accordance with the legal regulations of the Court and Court orders. Thus, the defence attorney should not attempt to violate the rule of law and nor should their clients. The dignity of the Court and judges should especially be respected. Furthermore, the defence attorney should maintain courteous moral, legal, and ethical behaviour before the Court at all times. This also includes during their oral arguments and speeches, which means that the lawyer should speak the truth and treat all those involved in the proceedings with respect. The defence attorney should not blame the judges of the Court for any financial or political issues. Any insulting statements or derogatory comments made about the decisions or comments by the judges are wrong and violate the discipline of the criminal justice. Therefore, the attorney must be careful to not jeopardise the case or the position of their client by employing questionable tactics. This means that all principles of international human rights law in the Court must be enforced.

In addition, attorneys should respect judges and not interrupt their speeches or statements. Furthermore, they must respect the impartiality of the Court and recognise that the Court is not trying to reach a certain verdict regarding the commission of international crimes such as crimes against humanity, war crimes, aggression, and genocide.[198] The defence lawyer should not occupy the entire time of the Court in order to control the case and sway the judges in a certain direction or disrespect the rights of the opposing parties, victims, witnesses, or other individuals involved. Furthermore, if a case is complicated or unique in nature, the defence attorney should not change how they handle the case or how they conduct themselves in order to influence the final judgement.

Therefore, the defence attorney and their team should exert maximum effort to ensure that their submissions and statements are concise and realistic. They should require the understanding of judges with due regard to the impartial character of judges and the final judgments. This means that attorneys should speak in an eloquent, expressive, and fluent matter which adheres to the norms of the law. The defence team should also provide definitions or translations of any foreign words and idioms they may use.

In all cases, the defence attorney is responsible for ensuring that the rights of the accused are respected along with the independence of the Court and judges. This means that the defence team should be sure that the client conscientiously evokes the rights they are entitled to throughout the proceedings of the Court or Chambers. The way in which the Court

---

[198] Consult also Mark J. Findlay, *International and Comparative Criminal Justice: A Critical Introduction* (Routledge, London, 2013). Also Mark Osiel, *The End of Reciprocity* (Cambridge University Press, 2009), p.125-ff.

respects the rights of the accused should also be the way in which the accused and their defence team respect the Court. This respect also includes treating witnesses and victims in a very polite manner and refraining from acting aggressively toward other parties involved in proceedings, including judges. It is imperative that the defence team avoids influencing witnesses for the purpose of releasing the accused from accusations or reducing the length of punishment or to use the theory of one-eyed justice.[199]

8.5. The Case of the ICTY Regarding the Free Choice of Counsel

Some of the most well-known cases concerning choosing an attorney in international criminal courts or tribunals occurred during the proceedings of the International Criminal Tribunal for the former Yugoslavia. The Chambers of the Tribunal also upheld the principle of freedom of choice of the counsel by the accused or defendant. The statements of the Appeals Chamber[200] are as follows:

> 7. The Registrar has the primary responsibility of determining matters relating to the assignment of counsel under the legal aid system. The Trial Chamber, however, considered that it had a statutory obligation to ensure a fair and expeditious conduct of the proceedings, and that from this obligation it derived the power to decide on the Prosecution's motion

---

[199] For example, because of victims of the World War Second, "the world could not observe the murder of innocent Jews with a one-eyed justice and rely solely on positive international criminal law. *A one-eyed justice* needed to be combined with other rules of social conduct, with the intention of fulfilling the basic requirements of a legal philosophy. *This meant that the ethical and moral understanding of the case had to have priority over the positive circumstances of the legal philosophy, such as its body of legislation*. We could not ignore the claims of the love of humanity, love of justice, and the duty of protecting the innocent. Although different juridical questions have arisen in my previous interpretations of the judgments of the Nuremberg Tribunal, the fact is that the future generation of human beings would have interpreted the non-establishment of the Tribunal as as a great insult to the foundations of both legal positivism and moral naturalism and as a grave dereliction of love for man." Malekian, *Judgments of Love in Criminal Justice*, note 52, p.281.

[200] https://cld.irmct.org/notions/show/833/right-to-counsel-of-ones-choosing#.

alleging a conflict of interest.[201] The approach of the Trial Chamber is consistent with the Appeals Chamber's decision in the case *Prosecutor v. Blagojević* of 7 November 2003.[202] In that decision, the Appeals Chamber confirmed that the Trial Chamber has an inherent power to ensure that the trial of an accused is fair. However, the Appeals Chamber warned that in exercising this power the Trial Chamber cannot appropriate for itself a power that is conferred elsewhere.[203] The Directive on Assignment of Defence Counsel[204] does not provide any specific procedure for the removal of Defence Counsel in the case of a conflict of interest at the request of the Prosecution, and as such, the Trial Chamber could rely on its inherent power to review the assignment of Mr. Simić.

8. The right to choose counsel is a fundamental right of the accused and is recognized by Article 21(4) (b) and (d) of the Statute of the International Tribunal ("Statute"). However, this right is not without limits. The Appeals Chamber has on several occasions stated that "the right to free legal assistance by counsel does not confer the right to counsel of one's own choosing."[205] One of the limits to the accused's choice is a conflict of interest affecting his counsel. Under Article 14 of the Code of Conduct,[206] a counsel may not represent a client when this representation affects or can affect the representation of another client.

[….]

This requirement is reflected by Article 16 (E) of the Directive on Assignment of Defence Counsel: E. No counsel shall be assigned to more than one suspect or accused at a time, unless an assignment to more than one suspect or accused would neither cause prejudice to the defence of either accused, nor a potential conflict of interest.[207] Mr. Simić had acknowledged a potential conflict of interest and, following the procedure laid out under Article 14 of the Code of Conduct, obtained the

---

[201] First Decision [Decision on Prosecution motion to resolve conflict of interest regarding attorney Jovan Simić, 18 September 2003], p. 2.

[202] *Prosecutor v. Blagojević,* Case no. IT-02-60-AR73.4, Public and redacted reasons for Decision on Appeal by Vidoje Blagojević to replace his Defence team, 7 November 2003.

[203] *Idem*, para.7.

[204] Directive on Assignment of Defence Counsel, IT/73, Rev 9, as amended on 12 July 2002.

[205] *Prosecutor v. Akayesu*, Case No. ICTR-96-4A, Appeals Chamber Judgement, 1 June 2001, para.61.

[206] Code of professional conduct for counsel appearing before the International Tribunal, IT/125 rev. 1, as amended on 12 July 2002.

[207] This provision was amended with entry into force on 11 July 2006 of the directive on the assignment of Defence Counsel, IT/73 Rev 11. AS AMENDED.]

written consent of both Mr. Mejakić and Mr. Prcać to represent each of them.[…]

12. The Appeals Chamber finds that a conflict of interests does exist at the present stage of the proceedings. It is not contested that Mr. Mejakić was the direct superior of Mr. Prcać in the Omarska camp. Mr. Mejakić is charged with crimes committed in the Omarska camp under Article 7 (1) of the Statute for participating in a joint criminal enterprise. In addition, he is charged under Article 7 (3) of the Statute, on the basis that he was the commander of the camp and had effective control over the guard shift commanders, camp guards, and other persons working within or visiting the Omarska camp. Further, the Prosecution claims that Mr. Prcać has given evidence incriminating Mr. Mejakić in an interview with the Prosecution in the *Kvočka et al.* case. It was for this reason that the Trial Chamber considered Mr. Prcać's evidence significant and allowed the Prosecution to include Mr. Prcać in its witness list.[208][…]

14. The Appeals Chamber further finds that, if the conflict of interest regarding the representation of Mr. Prcać and Mr. Mejakić is not resolved at the present stage of proceedings, the administration of justice may be irreversibly prejudiced. The Appeals Chamber considers that the conflict of interest is an important one. The Trial Chamber noted in its First Decision that Mr. Mejakić did not deny that he was in a position of authority at the Omarska camp, and that he acknowledged that Mr. Prcać spent some time there under his command.[209] Mr. Mejakić is charged with command responsibility under Article 7(3) of the Statute. Mr. Prcać may give evidence on the command structure of the Omarska camp as well as on the particular offences committed in this camp. The evidence given by Mr. Prcać may therefore have a significant impact on the trial of Mr. Mejakić.

15. The decision by Mr. Prcać whether to cooperate with the Prosecution has to be taken presently, and it may impact on the potential benefits for Mr. Prcać and on the conduct of the *Mejakić* trial. Moreover, the conflict of interest may influence the Defence strategy of Mr. Mejakić, for example, by preventing his counsel from calling certain witnesses in order not to prejudice the interests of Mr. Prcać. There is finally the risk

---

[208] Decision on Prosecution motion for leave to amend its Rule 65*ter* witness and exhibit lists, 18 February 2004.

[209] First Decision, p. 3.

that Mr. Simić might withdraw in the course of the trial because of the conflict of interest, thus delaying the proceedings. For these reasons also the Appeals Chamber finds that the representation of both Mr. Mejakić and Mr. Prcać by Mr. Simić is likely to irreversibly prejudice the administration of justice.

8.6. Prerequisites for the Ambassadors of Truth

The fact is that our system of international criminal justice needs to promote cooperation and protection in order to create loyal individuals who are the ambassadors of truth and not the representatives of the strong against the weak i.e., lawyers. Such ambassadors should be the representatives of the love for justice, the love for the truth, and the love for the victims. There is no doubt that all victims have to be protected, including those who are the victims of the crimes of the Security Council members, and not only those whose cases are already under investigation by the ICC. If the crimes of the members of the Security Council are investigated, then the evil in the world will be put on trial. However, finding an ideal ambassador of love is rare.[210]

A lawyer who is faithful to their clients is unfaithful to the victims, not only because they are orchestrating the strong powers' demands and conditions of justice, but because they are playing both sides. Here, we do not mean that these lawyers receive money from both sides, but that they receive money from the big powers in exchange for completely ignoring

---

210 "We cannot accept at any rate that violators of legalized/illegalised conduct go without prosecution and punishment. This is what I call the criminal law of morality, the criminal law of our international human conscience, the invisible criminal law expressed by the human mentality of love that the offenders of grave atrocities have to be prosecuted and punished in accordance with the principles of natural law, human rights law, justice without law, and ethics. One may ask what the nature of justice without law is. This is a justice which not only relies on the statutory law that is suggested by Hart but also relies on much more. It is a law that relies on the substance of all laws, on the statutes of all legislation, on the natural existence of man, on the core principles of the substance of human rights law, and on the strength of justice to achieve its essence. This is what should be called the encouragement and the strength of all laws of human beings demanding the implementation of criminal justice in accordance with love for human beings." Malekian, *Judgments of Love in Criminal Justice*, note 52, p.103.

the victims and their rights. If the system of international criminal justice is really going to be effective, and the body of international human rights law and its provisions are going to be applied correctly, then we are forced by the united essence of human beings to bring all criminals under prosecution and hold them accountable for their crimes. The ICC can no longer only try African leaders; it is time to realise that all those Western leaders who have committed serious international crimes are responsible for their crimes and must be held accountable before the population of the world.

If international lawyers cannot understand this simple logic of criminal justice, and if our doppelgänger lawyers are incapable of realising the truth, then we will always witness the victimisation of the innocent without any legal or moral doubt. The conscience of lawyers and legal ethics must be unqualified theories since they are not successful in reality. My hope is that conscientious international lawyers understand the fact that our current system of lawyers and their way of working with human rights principles and criminal jurisdictions cannot be correct and will never help the victims. This is not just a problem within international criminal justice but is also an epidemic within national criminal jurisdictions.

A truthful lawyer can surely understand that rich oppressors are protected and have been for hundreds of years. Even in the middle of Europe, the rich are always protected, and almost all lawyers prefer to have them as their clients. Almost no lawyer would reject an offer by a rich individual to take on a case, and they drop everything to help them. Any lawyer who claims the contrary is surely lying. However, if the client is not rich or if they are a foreigner, the lawyer will refuse the case before even hearing about it because such cases never make it past the secretary.[211]

This all means that lawyers look for rich clients and big pay outs. This is also the case in the international criminal system. *If a victim has been oppressed and cannot pay well, lawyers will refuse their case, saying they do not have enough time or knowledge to help them. This has indeed occurred time and time again. A similar criticism may apply to all our*

---

[211] Examine also L Scott Cummings, 'Introduction: What Good are Lawyers?' in Scott L. Cummings (ed.), Paradox of Professionalism Lawyers and the Possibility of Justice (2011).

preceding discussions, even in the case of permanent values of peremptory norms of international criminal law.[212] *The fact is that the truth lies in the appearance of big or tiny payments. A lawyer may therefore be as flexible as the fee is. When the fee increases, a lawyer ignores their conscience and could even find their own mother or father guilty for enough money. This is how the system of international law works in reality, and demonstrates how international lawyers are completely defenceless and leave the minimal stage of conscience. That is why it is commonly said that everyone has a price. This is particularly true concerning the majority of lawyers, both in the past and in the future.*

8.7. Fundamental Obligations of Counsel in the ICC

The role of advocate and even counsellor within criminal jurisdictions, and particularly within international criminal jurisdiction, may require attorneys to withhold the truth. It is through the search for the truth that justice may be felt by the victims. The system of the ICC is meant to facilitate uncovering the truth, not hiding it. In criminal proceedings, the Chambers cannot proceed without the truth. The burden of proof is on the prosecution to prove beyond a reasonable doubt that the defendant is guilty of the crimes they are accused of.

Consequently, the obligations of defence lawyers may well be to advise their clients or the accused to withhold the truth, not only for the sake of the international public, but also for themselves. That is why the system of international criminal law speaks about criminal responsibility

---

212 "That is to say, the phrase peremptory norm is poor. It should be omitted and be rephrased with the term "ought to moral eligibility" or "peremptory-moral" norms with the future generation of man including lawyers who work for justice, who struggle for humanity and who fight not to lose self-restraint for financing their own house with the problems of genocide and rape of victims. If moral principle is not shown in the phrase of the law, if the law is not fixed with a moral understanding of the norm, if the moral accusation is not given for certain violations of the indispensable basic construction of the value of man, then we are swimming in a sea without water." Malekian, *Classical Morality in International Peremptory Criminal Law*, note 8, p.159.

and criminal accountability. Presenting the reality of truth is emphasised in the codes of professional ethics of all states. Unfortunately however, these questions of truth remain serious, unresolved questions. In particular, we should remember that defence counsels and prosecutors have significantly different roles and functions in the proceedings of international criminal courts and tribunals because of their ethical duties.[213]

The defence counsel has obligations deriving from the importance of ethical duties, partially based on the order of the ICC, and partially because they are functioning independently of the policy of the Court. In other words, the duties of lawyers are based on several factors and they therefore have much greater ethical responsibility than the Court itself. The Court functions upon international legal personality and does not take orders or obey the rules of other member states. Its duties are already prescribed. However, the duties of lawyers arise from many rules and the principles of ethics as codified in national or international legislations. The prosecutor of the Court does not represent the accused and is not affected by these contemplations in the same way. Likewise, it is ethical for defence counsel to cross-examine a witness to make them appear trustworthy. The defence should not hide the truth if they know that the witness is testifying truthfully and accurately. It is a general principle that an international criminal lawyer should never mislead the Court in any way in order to protect their interests or to protect the accused over the victims.[214]

---

[213] The notion of ethical duties constitutes very important principle. Consult W. F. R. Hardie, Aristotle's Ethical Theory (Oxford, The Clarendon Press, 1968), ch. X. Particularly examine Immanuel Kant, *Critique of Pure Reason* (1781); Immanuel Kant, *Answering the Question: What is Enlightenment?* (1784); Immanuel Kant, *Groundwork of the Metaphysic of Morals* (1785); Immanuel Kant, *The Critique of Practical Reason* (1788); Immanuel Kant, *Critique of Judgment* (1790); Immanuel Kant, *The Metaphysics of Morals* (1797); Immanuel Kant, *Practical Philosophy* (editor: Mary J. Gregor, 1999).

[214] "Obviously, a police officer cannot demand respect for a law that he does not respect himself. Similarly, a lawyer or scholar of international criminal law cannot demand full respect of peremptory law if he himself, for individual reasons and benefits, works with the violators, writes for the violators and protects the violators by one means or another. This means when a writer writes a book on genocide, moans, and weeps for the victims for his own interests, this is not support for the prevention of genocide but uses the victims for his own economic interests." Malekian, *Classical Morality in International Peremptory Criminal Law*, note 8, p.226.

There is actually a big difference between lawyers who represent the accused under national criminal law, and lawyers representing individuals under international criminal justice. If a lawyer misleads a national criminal court, the hiding of the truth may affect a few victims. However, if they mislead an international criminal court, their statements can harm hundreds or thousands of victims. Nonetheless, we are aware of the fact that there is no difference between national victims and international victims, and no number of victims permits a defence lawyer to misrepresent a case. Victims should always face the truth. However, in cases involving the crime of genocide, we are speaking about a very serious crime which implies an attempt to annihilate an entire group. I base the same conclusion on the necessities of speaking the truth on the part of the defence lawyer if it concerns crimes against humanity, war crimes, aggression, torture, and rape. The lawyer should not lie about evidence on the basis of the confidentiality of certain matters. The fact is that in the systems of international criminal justice and national criminal justice, all evidence must be released and its authentic integrity should be maintained.

8.8. Security of Life for Lawyers

All those who are engaged in the procedures of a criminal case should be protected from all forms of danger which could impact their social or personal lives. Security of life is not only necessary for national attorneys or lawyers, but also for judges, prosecutors, and members of the courts, as well as for those who are working to protect the accused or defendants in an international criminal court. Therefore, the members of defence teams should be guaranteed security and should not be put in danger through the threat of force or other matters. This is also one of the essential principles of prosecution in *ad hoc* and permanent international criminal courts. The principle applies regardless of to which side of the case the lawyer gives judicial assistance, and what arguments the lawyer, defence attorney, or members of the defence team make. Some of the measures which should be taken to protect lawyers include:

- Protection of the lives of the members of the defence team
- Protection of the life of the main attorney
- Defence of the lives of the lawyers in the office or in the ICC
- Defence of the lives of lawyers in *ad hoc* tribunals
- Security of the lives of all members of the defence team
- Protection of all family members of the defence team
- Protect of the integrity of the defence team
- Protection of the defence team against insult
- Security of lawyers in social life
- Prevention of attacks on the life of the defence attorney
- Prevention of any attack against members of the defence team
- Prevention of any discrimination against the defence attorney
- Prevention of any discrimination of any kind against the members of the defence team
- Security of all members of the defence team against any aggressive threats made per phone, email, or mail

Despite the existence of human rights norms and the freedom of lawyers to defend their client, the protection of this freedom has been violated in certain cases. In certain countries and regions the protection of the lives of lawyers, judges, or prosecutors becomes particularly difficult when the constitution of the relevant country is under the control of an authoritarian regime. For example, many lawyers under the system of Islamic Republic of Iran have been jailed because of their views. The same has also occurred in Russia, China, North Korea, Egypt, Turkey, Saudi Arabia, and Nicaragua. Additionally, lawyers may be murdered by certain national or international groups. For instance, Dragoslav Ognjanović, who was part of the legal team for Slobodan Milosevic at the ICTY in The Hague, was murdered in Belgrade, Serbia in 2018. The attacker even injured his son. According to the head of the Bar Association of Serbia, there have been three murders and 50 attacks against attorneys in the country over the past 10 years, including 95 unsolved attacks. In addition, between 2012 and May 2018, there were a total of 115 murders in Serbia and Montenegro which were tied to organized crime. Milosevic was prosecuted for war crimes committed during the Balkan Wars of the 1990s and was also called a warlord, however he died from an alleged heart attack before the conclusion of his trial.[215]

[215] N. Kandic, The ICTY Trials and Transitional Justice in Former Yugoslavia, 38 (3) *Cornell International Law Journal* (2005), pp. 789-792; J. Post and L. Panis, Tyranny on Trial: Personality and Courtroom Conduct of Defendants Slobodan Milosevic and Saddam Hussein, 38 (3) *Cornell International Law Journal* (2005), pp. 823-836; William A. Schabas, The UN International Criminal Tribunals: the Former Yugoslavia, Rwanda and Sierra Leone (Cambridge: Cambridge University Press, 2006).

Chapter 9

CONCLUSION

Lawyers derive their title from the law and are meant to be the representatives, interpreters, and voices of the law. The lack of objectivity in the conscience of lawyers in a judicial context is a huge distraction from the results of ethical norms. In the pejorative anatomy of lawyers we do not find the system of international criminal law or international human rights law, but rather the system of large payments. Lawyers measure the gravity of crimes by the fees they charge. This means they fail to respect the fact that ethical codes of conducts have to be respected. However, lawyers are obliged to follow moral and ethical rules in order to truly practice law. Despite this, this has not been widely seen in practice and the fact is that all lawyers defend their positions and reject any criticism against their characters or offices. Moreover, no lawyer would ever admit that they have violated the ethical codes of conscience and morality. Evidently, lawyers who follow the system of international criminal law in order to pursue truth and justice actually empower righteousness for the victims.

Nonetheless, the problem is that many international criminal lawyers decide whether someone is guilty or not before the trial begins, and if they cannot establish this, they use the phrase “not proven”. This denotes the fact that the client has already demonstrated to the lawyer what their wishes are and how they want the lawyer to handle their case. With expressions such as "not proven", "did not occur", or "the law does not cover such acts", the lawyer plays a game in order to win the case and thus get paid well. They try to convince the court that their client is innocent and has not committed the crime of genocide by utilising their mastery of semantics. This is the unfortunate feature and weakness of certain international criminal procedures.

Moreover, lawyers are not the subjects of criminal law--however the subjects give them recognition and money. This means that lawyers are almost never loyal in their interpretations of the system of international criminal law. They are one of the essential reasons why the provisions of international law have been developed and reinterpreted and also why the system has never been properly implemented. It has become routine behaviour for most lawyers to craft arguments in order to fulfil the interests of their clients— without due regard for the fact that the rights of the victims may be ignored, particularly when it comes to massive violations of the system of international criminal justice and the commission of international crimes such as genocide, crimes against humanity, war crimes, and aggression.

With the phrase "interpretation", we do not mean to imply that the lawyer is unaware of the discussions surrounding law, but to highlight the fact that they are able to argue and prove that they actually did not know about the crime and can thus shift the blame to others. An international criminal lawyer actually sees all evidence of criminality and has to take an extra step to access evidence which has been hidden by governments due to certain economic or political reasons. However, lawyers usually ignore this evidence or deny knowledge of it. Thus, there are always open windows for lawyers to escape through, and if there is no scapegoat, the doppelgänger lawyer creates it in their image, not only for themselves but also in order to convince the international public. International human rights lawyers can always find a scapegoat to blame in order to help criminals wash their hands of the blood of millions of innocent victims. This fact has not yet been acknowledged by the lawyers of criminal justice, but has been proven through the conviction of weak criminals while big criminals have hidden the truth and received impunity.

Hiding the truth and empowering lies in the system of international criminal justice has become an important duty of lawyers, which is carried out regardless of to what degree doing so could harm the rights of the international community and the undeniable rights of the victims. The virtue of all matters of criminal justice in the eyes of certain international criminal lawyers is to prove that they are the only ones who truly understand the law and know the truth, and therefore their views and knowledge should be trusted in order to bring the real criminals to justice. Again, it is lawyers who intentionally confuse the facts through their arguments in order to fulfil the wishes of serious criminals and the big powers.

The falsification of the truth has actually become common practice among international human rights lawyers, although some may be unaware of who the real criminals are. However, others may know and simply play along in order to assist the Western nations. These lawyers then receive aid, assistance, and funds from different bodies such as human rights bodies, governmental bodies, or private organisations, or certain funds to fight counter-terrorism movements, which are all just covers for the pursuit of their own interests. Hardly any lawyers have spoken out about the serious crimes committed by the members of the Security Council and their dangerous terrorist acts.

> Once upon a time, Alexander the Great captured one of the most infamous pirates and asked him, why are you plundering the high seas? The pirate turned the question back at him and asked Alexander the Great, why are you plundering the land? He said I am the king. The pirate answered, if you are the king of the land, in that case, I am the king of the high seas. What is the difference? The business is the same for both of us. Obviously, Alexander presented the law and morality as independent personal norms of his own, and the pirate used the same code

of conduct. Both loved the law but with the power of a one-eyed justice.[216]

The terrorist governments become the good governments, the criminal governments become the innocent governments, and the huge criminal brutal activities of armies are classified as acts of self-defence, while all actual acts of defence are classified as acts of terrorism. Most lawyers believe in these acts of "self-defence" and defend them sincerely, while others do so for the financial gain. Furthermore, still others speak the truth and are removed from the public sphere. As a result, the innocent become terrorists, fighting for self-determination becomes terrorism, any resistance against occupation is labelled as terrorism, and any protest is labelled as anti-imperialist, anti-Zionist, anti-Communist, anti-Western, or anti-Islamist.[217] Therefore, lawyers find scapegoats to blame for the crimes of the big criminals and defend this position in their writings and statements. Such governments and lawyers are also praised as heroes.

The fact is that lawyers help to hide the real truth in the systems of international human rights law, international criminal law, and international criminal justice. The result is that we not only ignore the judicial conscience, but also all the ethical norms and principles of jurisdiction. Lawyers trust the notion of morality, and then in certain situations, lay blame on others in order to serve their own interests. That is why lawyers are always criticised, and will forever be as a result of their experiences and attempts to conceal the truth by presenting the truth as false and vice versa. Although we do not reject the fact that there has been increasing development concerning ethical norms and principles, these norms and principles have no value in their practical implementation, and are therefore only empty words.

The conscience of an international criminal lawyer which is connected with fees cannot embody the true essence of humanity and help establish the rights of the victims in the international sphere. Such lawyers will also

---

[216] Malekian, *Judgments of Love in Criminal Justice*, note 52, p.249.

[217] However, consult *also* Maurists Berger, A brief history of Islam in Europe: Thirteen Centuries of Creed, Conflict and Coexistence (2014).

always face serious questions concerning morality, ethical codes, and legality. Although we do not reject the fact that there are a considerable number of good international human rights lawyers, including international criminal lawyers, the definition of good here is still subject to debate when it comes to the big criminals and their right to criticise the system of international criminal justice or the ICC as they wish. This has been seen time and again, and almost none of the lawyers who support the artificial legitimacy of the special tribunals of the big powers, which punish other leaders so that the big powers can get away with their crimes, have criticised the behaviour of the big criminals.

We must bear in mind that the system of international criminal law is not the presentation of justice alone, but rather the presentation of the injustices which have been committed by those who believe that their actions do not constitute violence. The situation is the same under national criminal jurisdictions as well. Both criminal legal systems, national and international, have the intention of finding the truth, and this truth cannot be uncovered as long as there is not a system of criminal justice in place which works to implement the provisions of criminal law and international criminal law as practical theories of justice, rather than as tools to punish other nations in order to grant impunity to the big criminals. In other words, criminal codes, criminal legislations, and criminal resolutions within both systems are invalid if they are not effectively empowered under the body of their criminal justice. That is why the system of international criminal law has never been strong, and why the ICC continues to act, for whatever reason, with one-eyed-justice and one-eyed-policies.

The problem of international criminal justice certainly does not rest on the shoulders of lawyers; rather they are to blame for the corruption present within the system. The policy of the system of international criminal law is not only weak, but this weak policy is also controlled by the strong superior political parties. Thus, it is of no essential importance to identify who works for the truth and who does not. This is because if the foundation of criminal jurisdiction is flawed, then the whole structure of the house of justice is affected and as a result, truth disappears from the structure of the legal system. Although this is evident to international lawyers, they do not mind hiding the truth and promoting injustice because helping criminal states gain impunity brings them money and success. All lawyers of international criminal law know this, and that is why they also hide the truth, including concerning the crimes of genocide committed in Myanmar and the brutal crimes committed in Palestine. Similarly, the crimes committed against the Uighurs by the Chinese government have not been protested against by Chinese lawyers who are faithful to the government. If they were to protest, they would be killed or imprisoned.

The fact remains that the powerful states know that the acts of genocide in Palestine will not be acknowledged by the perpetrators and the oppressed will remain under their power. Thus, the genocide against the Palestinians has not been addressed by human rights organisations because the oppressors target organisations who dare to speak the truth. However, if there is any reaction by national or international organisation against the genocide in Palestine, it is mostly superficial and no one has yet demanded an end to the criminal occupation. This is what we call the quality of international criminal justice and the quality of international lawyers. Furthermore, counterterrorism institutes which were established to fight terrorists after the events of 11 September are funded by the big powers such that they are able to wage wars against non-Western nations to serve their interests.[218]

---

[218] Consult Thierry Meyssan, 11 September 2001: L'effroyable imposture (2002); Arthur Naiman, *9/11: The Simple Facts - Why the Official Story can't Possibly be True* (US: Soft Skull Press, 2011); John Farmer, *The Ground Truth: The Story Behind America's Defence on 9/11* (New York: Riverhead Books, 2009); Don Paul and Jim Hoffman, *Waking Up from Our Nightmare, the 9/11/01 Crimes in New York City* (New York: I/R Press, 2004); Paul Zarembka, *The Hidden History of 9-11-2001* (New York: Seven Stories Press, 2008). Watch also his very powerful lecture concerning 11 September on https://www.youtube.com/watch?v=PinWplT-4vY (Accessed: 15th October 2017); See *also* https://sputniknews.com/us/201607021042349218-obama-riyadh-washington-terror-911/. See *also* an excellent French book *L'effroyable imposture* which was translated into 28 languages and had a print run of 300,000 copies. Thierry Meyssan, 11 September 2001: L'effroyable imposture (2002); Arthur Naiman, *9/11: The Simple Facts – Why the Official Story can't Possibly be True* (US: Soft Skull Press, 2011). Robert F. Kennedy, Why the Arabs don't want us in Syria: They don't hate 'our freedoms.' They hate that we've betrayed our ideals in their own countries — for oil in http://www.politico.eu/book/why-the-arabs-dont-want-us-in-syria-mideast-conflict-oil-intervention/(Accessed 4 May 2017); Washington's Secret Agendas – Truth is being Disguised to Suit, available online at http://www.oneworldofnations.com/2014/09/washingtons-secret-agendas-truth-is.html (Accessed 11 May 2017); 'Former Liberian dictator Charles Taylor had US spy

We should therefore not be surprised when lawyers take orders from the big criminals and support their criminal actions. This does not mean that they should necessarily support the criminal conducts of big criminal states or those who empower the system of international criminal law when they want and extinguish its power when they wish. Powerful states continue to establish national and *ad hoc* tribunals through various resolutions of the Security Council in order to address the crimes of all states except their own. This simply means that *the systems of international human rights law and international criminal justice are under their control, and lawyers are also potentially under their control as well*. As a result, it is very difficult to find a trustworthy lawyer who is not after a big payment from Western powers. This means that whatever we do, and whatever argument we present, the theory is the same since the international legal and political community is based on inequality, and the unequal division of power in the Security Council affects all aspects of the legal discipline and the consciences of lawyers as well.

We are therefore forced to realise that habits, double moralities, and the doppelgänger mentality of international lawyers, as well as the commission of international crimes will not cease as long as we are applying the systems of human rights law and international criminal justice under the power of the Security Council. The theory is very simple: a lawyer's conscience is learned from the dictated power of the Council and their conducts cannot be independent from the exercise of power by the big governments. This is what is also called the monopolised conscience of lawyers. In other words, ethical codes for lawyers are sold and directed

---

agency ties' available online at http://www.bostonglobe.com/metro/2012/01/17/mass-escapee-turned-liberian-dictator-had-spy-agency-ties/DGBhSfjxPVrtoo4WT95bBI/story.html. Niels H. Harrit, et al., 'Active Thermitic Material Discovered in Dust from the 9/11 World Trade Center Catastrophe' available online at http://911review.com/evidence/wtc_explosives.html; www.bentham-open.org/pages/content.php?TOCPJ/2009/00000002/00000001/7TOCPJ.SGM (last accessed 24 October, 2018); See also U.S. Professor Zarembka's very powerful lecture concerning September 11, available online at https://www.youtube.com/watch?v=PinWplT-4vY; David Ray Griffin – 9/11 Myths and Reality Lecture on https://www.youtube.com/watch?v =hQBsWT1xF0w. Watch also his very powerful lecture concerning 11 September on https://www.youtube.com/watch?v=PinWplT-4vY. See *also* https://www.youtube.com/watch?v=1W6QLfXE3wA; https://www.youtube.com/watch?v=ySAUjvWgnws.

by the political power of governments. Every wise lawyer should be aware of the fact that resolutions of the UNSC which permit the unlimited use of force by the most powerful nations of the world against weaker nations are unjust. The false accusation of nations for any reason is not only wrong, but also represents criminal conspiracy to commit international crimes.

The conscience of lawyers therefore plays a significant role in the presentation of the truth. Simply put, a good lawyer should address the roots of the problems of international criminal justice and dare to speak out about problems, including why we cannot prevent the commission of international crimes by various states. If the house of justice were firmly built on rights, principles, and/or the equal applications of norms, the commission of many international crimes and violations would decrease. A human rights activist or a human rights lawyer is supposed to work for the establishment of the principle of equality in the United Nations and should not water the fruits of injustice. If justice enters the provisions of the United Nations, injustice within the provisions will decrease and we would have to identify any additional rotting fruit.

In agriculture, even if you treat a sick plant, the illness will linger for as long as the root remains infected. This implies the fact that establishing hundreds of institutions and regulating thousands of rules and principles of human rights law and international criminal justice cannot be effective since the root, the UN Charter, remains infected and must be cured first. A human rights lawyer should clearly understand that the problems plaguing human rights and causing violations are coming from the inequality embodied in Chapter VII of the UN Charter. The problem is that our international criminal lawyers and international human rights lawyers take pride in the institutions with which they are affiliated, and these institutions and work come first, which hinders any progress in international law when it comes to the truth.

When the members of the UNSC cannot reach an agreement, one vote can freeze the establishment of a particular court and paralyse any legal intentions. However, the unwise decisions of the body are also seen in the form of the political pressure exerted by the members of the Council. Although all five permanent members may commit crimes, one member may consider the international crimes of other governments more brutal than its own brutal crimes and those of its allies. A big member of the Security Council never acknowledges that international crimes have been committed under their authority. They instead blame other big criminals. In such cases, international human rights or criminal lawyers target superficial issues instead of addressing the problems plaguing the root i.e., the inequality within the UN Charter. As a result, lawyers accept the inequality within the Charter and promote unequal politics. They ignore major issues in favour of receiving payment. This denotes the fact that we continually violate the independence of judicial conscience and its very high integrity. Inequality thus refers to the non-existence of judicial conscience.[219]

---

219 "Conscience is therefore our intuition or judgment regarding certain matters with moral reasoning, moral argumentation, and sometimes a superior moral justification for selfishness. This is a synonym for evil. Consequently, it is not a matter of choice but a matter of what is just and what is unjust for humanity." Malekian, *Judgments of Love in Criminal Justice*, note 52, p.35.

APPENDIX: CODE OF PROFESSIONAL CONDUCT FOR COUNSEL

Resolution ICC-ASP/4/Res.1

Adopted at the 3rd plenary meeting on 2 December 2005, by consensus

ICC-ASP/4/Res.1

Code of Professional Conduct for counsel

The Assembly of State Parties,

Having regard to rule 8 of the Rules of Procedure and Evidence;

Having regard to rule 20, sub-rule 3;

Having regard to the consultations conducted by the Registrar with independent representative bodies of counsel or legal associations;

Recognizing the general principles governing the practice and ethics of the legal profession;

Recalling resolution ICC-ASP/3/Res.3, of 10 September 2004, whereby the Assembly of States Parties requested the Bureau of Assembly of States Parties to prepare an amended draft Code for adoption by the Assembly at its fourth session;

Having regard to the Report of the Bureau on the draft Code of Professional Conduct for counsel, submitted pursuant to the above resolution;

Decides to adopt the Code of Professional Conduct for counsel, the text of which is annexed hereto.

Chapter 1. General Provisions

Article 1. Scope

This Code shall apply to defence counsel, counsel acting for States, amici curiae and counsel or legal representatives for victims and witnesses practising at the International Criminal Court, hereinafter referred to as "counsel".

Article 2. Use of Terms

1. Unless otherwise defined in this Code, all terms are used as defined in the Statute, the Rules of Procedure and Evidence and the Regulations of the Court.

2. In this Code:

– "Court" refers to the International Criminal Court;

– "associate" refers to lawyers who practise in the same law firm as counsel;

– "national authority" refers to the bar association of which counsel is a member or any other organ competent to regulate and control the activity of lawyers, judges, prosecutors or professors of law, or other qualified counsel according to rule 22, paragraph 1, of the Rules of Procedure and Evidence;

– "client" refers to all those assisted or represented by counsel;

– "defence team" refers to counsel and all persons working under his or her oversight; and

– "agreement" refers to the oral or written legal relationship which binds counsel to his or her client before the Court.

Article 3. Amendment Procedure

1. States Parties, judges, the Registrar, counsel and independent organizations representing lawyers' associations and counsel may submit proposals for amendments to this Code. Any proposal for amendments to this Code shall be submitted to the Registrar, together with explanatory material, in one or both working languages of the Court.

2. The Registrar shall transmit the proposals to the Presidency, together with a reasoned report prepared after consultation with the Prosecutor and, as appropriate, with any independent organization representing lawyers' associations and counsel.

3. Any proposal to amend this Code, submitted by one or more States Parties, shall be transmitted by the Presidency to the Assembly of States Parties together with any comments the Presidency may have, taking into account the report of the Registrar.

4. Any proposal to amend this Code, other than one submitted by one or more States Parties, shall be transmitted by the Presidency to the Assembly of States Parties together with any comments the Presidency may have, taking into account the report of the Registrar. In such circumstances, the Presidency shall provide the Assembly of States Parties with the Presidency's reasoned recommendations as to whether or not any such proposal should be adopted. If the Presidency recommends adoption, it shall submit a draft amendment in relation to that proposal to the Assembly of States Parties for the purpose of adoption.

5. Amendments to this Code shall be adopted by the Assembly of States Parties in accordance with article 112, paragraph 7, of the Statute.

Article 4. Primacy of the Code of Professional Conduct for Counsel

Where there is any inconsistency between this Code and any other code of ethics or professional responsibility which counsel are bound to honour, the terms of this Code shall prevail in respect of the practice and professional ethics of counsel when practising before the Court.

Article 5. Solemn Undertaking by Counsel

Before taking office, counsel shall give the following solemn undertaking before the Court: “I solemnly declare that I will perform my duties and exercise my mission before the International Criminal Court with integrity and diligence, honourably, freely, independently, expeditiously and conscientiously, and that I will scrupulously respect professional secrecy and the other duties imposed by the Code of Professional Conduct for Counsel before the International Criminal Court”.

Article 6. Independence of Counsel

1. Counsel shall act honourably, independently and freely.

2. Counsel shall not: (a) Permit his or her independence, integrity or freedom to be compromised by external pressure; or (b) Do anything which may lead to any reasonable inference that his or her independence has been compromised.

Article 7. Professional Conduct of Counsel

1. Counsel shall be respectful and courteous in his or her relations with the Chamber, the Prosecutor and the members of the Office of the Prosecutor, the Registrar and the members of the Registry, the client, opposing counsel, accused persons, victims, witnesses and any other person involved in the proceedings.

2. Counsel shall maintain a high level of competence in the law applicable before the Court. He or she shall participate in training initiatives required to maintain such competence.

3. Counsel shall comply at all times with the Statute, the Rules of Procedure and Evidence, the Regulations of the Court and such rulings as to conduct and procedure as may be made by the Court, including the enforcement of this Code.

4. Counsel shall supervise the work of his or her assistants and other staff, including investigators, clerks and researchers, to ensure that they comply with this Code.

Article 8. Respect for Professional Secrecy and Confidentiality

1. Counsel shall respect and actively exercise all care to ensure respect for professional secrecy and the confidentiality of information in accordance with the Statute, the Rules of Procedure and Evidence and the Regulations of the Court.

2. The relevant provisions referred to in paragraph 1 of this article include, inter alia, article 64, paragraph 6 (c), article 64, paragraph 7, article 67, paragraph 1 (b), article 68, and article 72 of the Statute, rules 72, 73, and 81 of the Rules of Procedure and Evidence and regulation 97 of the Regulations of the Court. Counsel shall also comply with the relevant provisions of this Code and any order of the Court.

3. Counsel may only reveal the information protected under paragraphs 1 and 2 of this article to co-counsel, assistants and other staff working on the particular case to which the information relates and solely to enable the exercise of his or her functions in relation to that case.

4. Subject to paragraph 3 of this article, counsel may only disclose the information protected under paragraphs 1 and 2 of this article, where such disclosure is provided for by a particular provision of the Statute, the Rules of Procedure and Evidence, the Regulations of the Court or this Code or where such disclosure is ordered by the Court. In particular, Counsel shall not reveal the identity of protected victims and witnesses, or any

confidential information that may reveal their identity and whereabouts, unless he or she has been authorized to do so by an order of the Court.

Article 9. Counsel-Client Relationship

1. Counsel shall not engage in any discriminatory conduct in relation to any other person, in particular his or her client, on grounds of race, colour, ethnic or national origin, nationality, citizenship, political opinions, religious convictions, gender, sexual orientation, disability, marital status or any other personal or economic status.

2. In his or her relations with the client, counsel shall take into account the client's personal circumstances and specific needs, in particular where counsel is representing victims of torture or of physical, psychological or sexual violence, or children, the elderly or the disabled.

3. Where a client's ability to make decisions concerning representation is impaired because of mental disability or for any other reason, counsel shall inform the Registrar and the relevant Chamber. Counsel shall also take the steps necessary to ensure proper legal representation of the client according to the Statute and the Rules of Procedure and Evidence.

4. Counsel shall not engage in any improper conduct, such as demanding sexual relations, coercion, intimidation, or exercise any other undue influence in his or her relations with a client.

Article 10. Advertising

Counsel may advertise provided the information is:

(a) Accurate; and

(b) Respectful of counsel's obligations regarding confidentiality and privilege.

Chapter 2. Representation by Counsel

Article 11. Establishment of the Representation Agreement

The agreement is established when counsel accepts a request from a client seeking representation or from the Chamber.

Article 12. Impediments to Representation

1. Counsel shall not represent a client in a case:

(a) If the case is the same as or substantially related to another case in which counsel or his or her associates represents or formerly represented another client and the interests of the client are incompatible with the interests of the former client, unless the client and the former client consent after consultation; or

(b) In which counsel was involved or was privy to confidential information as a staff member of the Court relating to the case in which counsel seeks to appear. The lifting of this impediment may, however, at counsel's request, be ordered by the Court if deemed justified in the interests of justice. Counsel shall still be bound by the duties of confidentiality stemming from his or her former position as a staff member of the Court.

2. In the case of paragraph 1 (a) of this article, where consent has been obtained after consultation, counsel shall inform the Chamber of the Court seized with the situation or case of the conflict and the consent obtained. Such notice shall be provided in a manner consistent with counsel's duties of confidentiality pursuant to article 8 of this Code and rule 73, sub-rule 1 of the Rules of Procedure and Evidence.

3. Counsel shall not act in proceedings in which there is a substantial probability that counsel or an associate of counsel will be called to appear as a witness unless:

(a) The testimony relates to an uncontested issue; or

(b) The testimony relates to the nature and value of legal services rendered in the case.

4. This article is without prejudice to article 16 of this Code.

Article 13. Refusal by Counsel of a Representation Agreement

1. Counsel has the right to refuse an agreement without stating reasons. 2. Counsel has a duty to refuse an agreement where: (a) There is a conflict of interest under article 16 of this Code; (b) Counsel is incapable of dealing with the matter diligently; or (c) Counsel does not consider that he or she has the requisite expertise.

Article 14. Performance in Good Faith of a Representation Agreement

1. The relationship of client and counsel is one of candid exchange and trust, binding counsel to act in good faith when dealing with the client. In discharging that duty, counsel shall act at all times with fairness, integrity and candour towards the client.

2. When representing a client, counsel shall:

(a) Abide by the client's decisions concerning the objectives of his or her representation as long as they are not inconsistent with counsel's duties under the Statute, the Rules of Procedure and Evidence, and this Code; and

(b) Consult the client on the means by which the objectives of his or her representation are to be pursued.

Article 15. Communication between Counsel and the Client

1. Counsel shall provide the client with all explanations reasonably needed to make informed decisions regarding his or her representation.

2. When counsel is discharged from or terminates the agreement, he or she shall convey as promptly as possible to the former client or replacement counsel any communication that counsel received relating to the representation, without prejudice to the duties which subsist after the end of the representation.

3. When communicating with the client, counsel shall ensure the confidentiality of such communication.

Article 16. Conflict of Interest

1. Counsel shall exercise all care to ensure that no conflict of interest arises. Counsel shall put the client's interests before counsel's own interests or those of any other person, organization or State, having due regard to the provisions of the Statute, the Rules of Procedure and Evidence, and this Code.

2. Where counsel has been retained or appointed as a common legal representative for victims or particular groups of victims, he or she shall advise his or her clients at the outset of the nature of the representation and the potential conflicting interests within the group. Counsel shall exercise all care to ensure a fair representation of the different yet consistent positions of his or her clients.

3. Where a conflict of interest arises, counsel shall at once inform all potentially affected clients of the existence of the conflict and either:

(a) Withdraw from the representation of one or more clients with the prior consent of the Chamber; or

(b) Seek the full and informed consent in writing of all potentially affected clients to continue representation.

Article 17. Duration of the Representation Agreement

1. Counsel shall advise and represent a client until:

(a) The case before the Court has been finally determined, including all appeals;

(b) Counsel has withdrawn from the agreement in accordance with article 16 or 18 of this Code; or

(c) A counsel assigned by the Court has been withdrawn.

2. The duties of counsel towards the client continue until the representation has ended, except for those duties which subsist under this Code.

Article 18. Termination of the Representation

1. With the prior consent of the Chamber, counsel may withdraw from the agreement in accordance with the Regulations of the Court if:

(a) The client insists on pursuing an objective that counsel considers repugnant; or

(b) The client fails to fulfil an obligation to counsel regarding counsel's services and has been given reasonable warning that counsel will withdraw unless the obligation is fulfilled.

2. Where counsel withdraws from the agreement, he or she remains subject to article 8 of this Code, as well as any provisions of the Statute and the Rules of Procedure and Evidence relating to confidentiality.

3. Where counsel is discharged by the client, counsel may be discharged in accordance with the Regulations of the Court.

4. Where counsel's physical or mental condition materially impairs his or her ability to represent the client, counsel may be withdrawn by the Chamber at his or her request or at the request of the client or the Registrar.

5. In addition to complying with the duties imposed by article 15, paragraph 2, of this Code, counsel shall convey to replacement counsel the entire case file, including any material or document relating to it.

Article 19. Conservation of Files

Following the termination of the representation, counsel shall keep files containing documents and records of work carried out in fulfilment of the agreement for five years. Counsel shall allow the former client to inspect the file unless he or she has substantial grounds for refusing to do so. After this time counsel shall seek instructions from the former client, his or her heirs or the Registrar on the disposal of the files, with due regard to confidentiality.

Article 20. Counsel's fees

Prior to establishing an agreement, counsel shall inform the client in writing of the rate of fees to be charged and the criteria for setting them, the basis for calculating the costs, the billing arrangements and the client's right to receive a bill of costs.

Article 21. Prohibitions

1. Notwithstanding article 22, counsel shall not accept remuneration, in cash or in kind, from a source other than the client unless the client consents thereto in writing after consultation and counsel's independence and relationship with the client are not thereby affected.

2. Counsel shall never make his or her fees contingent on the outcome of a case in which he or she is involved.

3. Counsel shall not mix funds of a client with his or her own funds, or with funds of counsel's employer or associates. Counsel shall not retain money received on behalf of a client.

4. Counsel shall not borrow monies or assets from the client.

Article 22. Remuneration of Counsel in the Framework of Legal Assistance

1. The fees of counsel where his or her client benefits from legal assistance shall be paid exclusively by the Registry of the Court. Counsel shall not accept remuneration in cash or in kind from any other source.

2. Counsel shall neither transfer nor lend all or part of the fees received for representation of a client or any other assets or monies to a client, his or her relatives, acquaintances, or any other third person or organization in relation to which the client has a personal interest.

3. Counsel shall sign an undertaking to respect the obligations under this article when accepting the appointment to provide legal assistance. The signed undertaking shall be sent to the Registry.

4. Where counsel is requested, induced or encouraged to violate the obligations under this article, counsel shall advise the client of the prohibition of such conduct.

5. Breach of any obligations under this article by Counsel shall amount to misconduct and shall be subject to a disciplinary procedure pursuant to this Code. This may lead to a permanent ban on practising before the Court and being struck off the list of counsel, with transmission to the respective national authority.

Chapter 3. Relations with the Court and Others

Article 23. Communications with the Chambers and Judges

Unless the judge or the Chamber dealing with a case permits counsel to do so in exceptional circumstances, counsel shall not:

(a) Make contact with a judge or Chamber relative to the merits of a particular case other than within the proper context of the proceedings; or

(b) Transmit evidence, notes or documents to a judge or Chamber except through the Registry.

Article 24. Duties towards the Court

1. Counsel shall take all necessary steps to ensure that his or her actions or those of counsel's assistants or staff are not prejudicial to the ongoing proceedings and do not bring the Court into disrepute.

2. Counsel is personally responsible for the conduct and presentation of the client's case and shall exercise personal judgement on the substance and purpose of statements made and questions asked.

3. Counsel shall not deceive or knowingly mislead the Court. He or she shall take all steps necessary to correct an erroneous statement made by him or her or by assistants or staff as soon as possible after becoming aware that the statement was erroneous.

4. Counsel shall not submit any request or document with the sole aim of harming one or more of the participants in the proceedings.

5. Counsel shall represent the client expeditiously with the purpose of avoiding unnecessary expense or delay in the conduct of the proceedings.

Article 25. Evidence

1. Counsel shall at all times maintain the integrity of evidence, whether in written, oral or any other form, which is submitted to the Court. He or she shall not introduce evidence which he or she knows to be incorrect.

2. If counsel, while collecting evidence, reasonably believes that the evidence found may be destroyed or tampered with, counsel shall request the Chamber to issue an order to collect the evidence pursuant to rule 116 of the Rules of Procedure and Evidence.

Article 26. Relations with Unrepresented Persons

1. When required in the course of representation, counsel may communicate with and meet an unrepresented person in the client's interest.

2. When counsel communicates with unrepresented persons he or she shall:

(a) Inform them of their right to assistance from counsel and, if applicable, to their right to legal assistance; and

(b) Without infringing upon the confidentiality of counsel-client privilege, inform them of the interest that counsel represents and the purpose of the communication.

3. If counsel becomes aware of a potential conflict of interest in the course of a communication or meeting with an unrepresented person, he or she shall, notwithstanding paragraph 1 of this article, refrain immediately from engaging in any further contact or communication with the person.

Article 27. Relations with Other Counsel

1. In dealing with other counsel and their clients, counsel shall act fairly, in good faith and courteously.

2. All correspondence between counsel representing clients with a common interest in a litigated or non-litigated matter and who agree on exchanging information concerning the matter, shall be presumed confidential and privileged by counsel.

3. When counsel does not expect particular correspondence between counsel to be confidential, he or she shall state clearly at the outset that such correspondence is not confidential.

Article 28. Relations with Persons Already Represented by Counsel

Counsel shall not address directly the client of another counsel except through or with the permission of that counsel.

Article 29. Relations with Witnesses and Victims

1. Counsel shall refrain from intimidating, harassing or humiliating witnesses or victims or from subjecting them to disproportionate or unnecessary pressure within or outside the courtroom.

2. Counsel shall have particular consideration for victims of torture or of physical, psychological or sexual violence, or children, the elderly or the disabled.

CHAPTER 4. DISCIPLINARY REGIME

Article 30. Conflict with Other Disciplinary Regimes

Subject to article 38 of this Code, the present chapter is without prejudice to the disciplinary powers of any other disciplinary authority that may apply to counsel subject to this Code.

Article 31. Misconduct

Counsel commits misconduct when he or she:

(a) Violates or attempts to violate any provisions of this Code, the Statute, the Rules of Procedure and Evidence and the Regulations of the Court or of the Registry in force imposing a substantial ethical or professional duty on him or her;

(b) Knowingly assists or induces another person to commit any misconduct, referred to in paragraph (a) of this article, or does so through the acts of another person; or

(c) Fails to comply with a disciplinary decision rendered pursuant to this chapter.

Article 32. Liability for Conduct of Assistants or Other Staff

1. Counsel shall be liable for misconduct under article 31 of this Code by his or her assistants or staff when he or she:

(a) Orders or approves the conduct involved; or

(b) Knows or has information suggesting that violations may be committed and takes no reasonable remedial action.

2. Counsel shall instruct his or her assistants or staff in the standards set by this Code.

Article 33. The Commissioner

1. A Commissioner responsible for investigating complaints of misconduct in accordance with this chapter shall be appointed for four years by the Presidency. The Commissioner shall be chosen from amongst persons with established competence in professional ethics and legal matters.

2. The Commissioner shall not be eligible for re-appointment. A Commissioner who is involved in an investigation when his or her mandate expires shall continue to conduct such an investigation until it is concluded.

Article 34. Filing a Complaint of Misconduct

1. Complaints against counsel regarding misconduct as referred to in articles 31 and 32 of this Code may be submitted to the Registry by:

(a) The Chamber dealing with the case;

(b) The Prosecutor; or

(c) Any person or group of persons whose rights or interests may have been affected by the alleged misconduct.

2. The complaint shall be made in writing or, if the complainant is unable to do so, orally before a staff member of the Registry. It shall

identify the complainant and the counsel against whom the complaint is made and shall describe in sufficient detail the alleged misconduct.

3. The Registrar shall transmit the complaint to the Commissioner.

4. The Registrar may, on his or her own initiative, make complaints to the Commissioner regarding the misconduct referred to in articles 31 and 32 of this Code.

5. All complaints shall be kept confidential by the Registry.

Article 35. Limitation Period

The right to file a complaint against counsel for misconduct shall lapse five years after the termination of the representation agreement.

Article 36. Composition and Management of the Disciplinary Board

1. The Disciplinary Board shall comprise three members, two of whom shall be permanent and one *ad hoc*.

2. The members of the Disciplinary Board shall perform their functions under this Code in an independent and impartial manner.

3. The Registry shall make appropriate arrangements for the elections, provided for in paragraph 4 of this article, in consultation with counsel and, as appropriate, national authorities.

4. The two permanent members, as well as one alternate member who may serve as a replacement in accordance with paragraph 10 of this article, shall be elected for four years by all counsel entitled to practise before the Court. They shall be chosen from amongst persons with established competence in professional ethics and legal matters.

5. The *ad hoc* member shall be a person appointed by the national authority competent to regulate and control the activities of counsel subject to the disciplinary procedure.

6. The permanent members shall not be eligible for re-election.

7. Notwithstanding paragraph 4 of this article, at the first election one of the permanent members shall be selected by lot to serve for a term of six years.

8. After each election and in advance of the first meeting of the newly-elected Disciplinary Board, the permanent and alternate members shall elect one of the permanent members as a chairperson.

9. All members of the Disciplinary Board shall have the same rights and votes. The Disciplinary Board shall decide by majority vote. An alternate member serving on a case pursuant to paragraph 10 of this article shall have the same rights and votes as permanent and *ad hoc* members serving on the same case.

10. If one of the permanent members is unavailable to deal with the case or serve on the Disciplinary Board, the chairperson or, where the chairperson is the permanent member concerned, the other permanent member, shall request the alternate member to serve as a replacement on the Disciplinary Board.

11. Permanent members or the alternate member whose mandates have expired shall continue to deal with the cases they already have under consideration until such cases are finally determined including all appeals.

12. The Registrar shall appoint a staff member of the Registry who will render secretariat services to the Disciplinary Board. Once appointed, the relevant staff member of the Registry shall act at arm's length from the Registry and, subject to article 44, paragraph 12 of this Code, solely as the secretariat of the Disciplinary Board.

Article 37. Preliminary Procedures

1. If the complaint filed meets the requirements in article 34 of this Code, the Commissioner shall forward it to counsel subject to the disciplinary procedure, who shall submit a response within sixty days from the date the complaint is forwarded.

2. The response shall indicate whether the alleged misconduct has been or is the subject of a disciplinary procedure before the national authority. If so, it shall include:

(a) The identity of the national authority deciding on the alleged misconduct; and

(b) A certified communication by the national authority stating the alleged facts that are the basis of the disciplinary procedure before it.

Article 38. Complementarity of Disciplinary Measures

1. The disciplinary procedure in this Code shall be applied by the Disciplinary Board.

2. The *ad hoc* member of the Disciplinary Board shall serve as the contact point with the relevant national authority for all communication and consultation regarding the procedure.

3. Counsel subject to the disciplinary procedure shall request the national authority dealing with the matter to inform the Disciplinary Board of the progress of any national disciplinary procedure concerning the alleged misconduct and of its final decision, and shall take all measures necessary to facilitate such communication.

4. When the alleged misconduct is the basis of a disciplinary procedure which has already been initiated before the relevant national authority, the procedure before the Disciplinary Board shall be suspended until a final decision is reached regarding the former procedure, unless:

(a) the national authority does not respond to communications and consultations in accordance with paragraph 2 of this article within a reasonable time;

(b) the Disciplinary Board considers that the information received is not satisfactory; or

(c) the Disciplinary Board considers that, in the light of the information received, the national authority is unable or unwilling to conclude the disciplinary procedure.

5. As soon as it receives the decision of the national authority, the Disciplinary Board shall:

(a) declare the procedure closed, unless the decision adopted does not adequately address a complaint of misconduct under this Code; or

(b) declare that the decision of the national authority does not cover or only partially covers the misconduct brought before the Disciplinary Board and that therefore the procedure is to be continued.

6. In the case of paragraphs 3 and paragraph 4 (b) of this article, the Disciplinary Board may ask counsel subject to the disciplinary procedure to provide detailed information about the procedure, including any minute or evidence which might have been submitted.

7. A decision by the Disciplinary Board based on this article may be appealed before the Disciplinary Appeals Board.

Article 39. Disciplinary Procedure

1. The Commissioner conducting the investigation may dismiss a complaint without any further investigation if he or she considers on the basis of the information at his or her disposal that the allegation of misconduct is unfounded in fact or in law. He or she shall notify the complainant accordingly.

2. Should the Commissioner consider otherwise, he or she shall promptly investigate the counsel's alleged misconduct and decide either to submit a report to the Disciplinary Board or to bring the procedure to an end.

3. The Commissioner shall take into consideration all evidence, whether oral, written or any other form, which is relevant and has probative value. He or she shall keep all information concerning the disciplinary procedure confidential.

4. The Commissioner may try to find an amicable settlement if he or she deems it appropriate. The Commissioner shall report the outcome of any such efforts to reach an amicable settlement to the Disciplinary Board, which may take it into consideration. Any amicable settlement shall be

without prejudice to the competence or powers of the Disciplinary Board under this Code.

5. The report of the Commissioner shall be submitted to the Disciplinary Board.

6. The Disciplinary Board hearing shall be public. However, the Disciplinary Board may decide to hold a hearing or parts of it in closed session, in particular to safeguard the confidentiality of information in the report of the Commissioner or to protect victims and witnesses.

7. The Commissioner and the counsel subject to the disciplinary procedure shall be called and heard. The Disciplinary Board may also call and hear any other person deemed useful for the establishment of the truth.8. In exceptional cases, where the alleged misconduct is of such a nature as to seriously prejudice the interests of justice, the Commissioner may lodge an urgent motion with the Chamber before which the counsel who is the subject of the complaint is appearing, so that it may, as appropriate, declare a temporary suspension of such counsel.

Article 40. Rights of Counsel Subject to the Disciplinary Procedure

1. Counsel subject to the disciplinary procedure shall be entitled to assistance from other counsel. 2. Counsel shall have the right to remain silent before the Disciplinary Board, which may draw any inferences it deems appropriate and reasonable from such silence in the light of all the information submitted to it.

3. Counsel shall have the right to full disclosure of the information and evidence gathered by the Commissioner as well as the Commissioner's report.

4. Counsel shall be given the time required to prepare his or her defence.

5. Counsel shall have the right to question, personally or through his or her counsel, any person called by the Disciplinary Board to testify before it.

Article 41. Decisions by the Disciplinary Board

1. The Disciplinary Board may conclude the procedure finding no misconduct on the basis of the evidence submitted to it or finding that counsel subject to disciplinary procedure committed the alleged misconduct.

2. The decision shall be made public. It shall be reasoned and issued in writing.

3. The decision shall be notified to counsel subject to the disciplinary procedure and to the Registrar.

4. When the decision is final, it shall be published in the Official Journal of the Court and transmitted to the national authority.

Article 42. Sanctions

1. When misconduct has been established, the Disciplinary Board may impose one or more of the following sanctions:

(a) Admonishment;

(b) Public reprimand with an entry in counsel's personal file;

(c) Payment of a fine of up to €30,000;

(d) Suspension of the right to practise before the Court for a period not exceeding two years; and (e) Permanent ban on practising before the Court and striking off the list of counsel.

2. The admonishment may include recommendations by the Disciplinary Board.

3. The costs of the disciplinary procedure shall be within the discretion of the Disciplinary Board.

Article 43. Appeals

1. Sanctioned counsel and the Commissioner shall have the right to appeal the decision of the Disciplinary Board on factual or legal grounds.

2. The appeal shall be notified to the secretariat of the Disciplinary Board within thirty days from the day on which the decision has been delivered.

3. The secretariat of the Disciplinary Board shall transmit the notification of the appeal to the secretariat of the Disciplinary Appeals Board.

4. The Disciplinary Appeals Board shall decide on the appeal according to the procedure followed before the Disciplinary Board.

Article 44. Composition and Management of the Disciplinary Appeals Board

1. The Disciplinary Appeals Board shall decide on appeals against decisions of the Disciplinary Board.

2. The members of the Disciplinary Appeals Board shall perform their functions under this Code in an independent and impartial manner.

3. The Registry shall make appropriate arrangements for the elections provided for in paragraph 5 of this article, in consultation with counsel and, as appropriate, national authorities.

4. The Disciplinary Appeals Board shall comprise five members:

(a) The three judges of the Court who take precedence under regulation 10 of the Regulations of the Court, not including:

(i) the judges dealing with the case from which the complaint subject to the disciplinary procedure arose; or

(ii) any members or former members of the Presidency who appointed the Commissioner.

(b) Two persons elected in accordance with paragraph 5 of this article.

5. The two members of the Disciplinary Appeals Board referred to in paragraph 4 (b) of this article, as well as an alternate member who may serve as a replacement in accordance with paragraph 6 of this article, shall be elected for four years by all counsel entitled to practise before the Court. They shall be chosen from amongst persons with established competence in professional ethics and legal matters.

6. If one of the elected members is unavailable to deal with the case or serve on the Disciplinary Appeal Board, the chairperson shall request the alternate member to serve as a replacement on the Disciplinary Appeals Board.

7. The functions of members of the Disciplinary Appeals Board are incompatible with those of members of the Disciplinary Board.

8. The elected members shall not be eligible for re-election.

9. The judge who takes precedence among the three judges referred to in paragraph 4 (a) of this article shall be the chairperson of the Disciplinary Appeals Board.

10. All members of the Disciplinary Appeals Board shall have the same rights and votes. The Disciplinary Appeals Board shall decide by majority vote. An alternate member serving on a case pursuant to paragraph 6 of this article shall have the same rights and votes as other members serving on the same case.

11. Members whose mandates have expired shall continue to deal with the cases they already have under consideration until such cases are finally determined.

12. The staff member of the Registry appointed by the Registrar pursuant to article 36, paragraph 12, of this Code to provide secretariat services to the Disciplinary Board shall also act as the secretariat of the Disciplinary Appeals Board. Once appointed, the relevant staff member of the Registry shall act at arm's length from the Registry.

CHAPTER 5. FINAL PROVISIONS

Article 45. Entry into Force

This Code and any amendments to it shall enter into force 30 days after their adoption by the Assembly of States Parties in accordance with article 112, paragraph 2, of the Rome Statute.

Article 46. Publication

The Code adopted by the Assembly of States Parties shall be published in the Official Journal of the Court.

REFERENCES*

Allison Henry, *Kant's Theory of Freedom* (Cambridge University Press, 1990).

Andreopoulos George J. (ed.), *Genocide: Conceptual and Historical Dimensions* (Philadelphia, 1994).

Annacker C 'The Legal Régime of erga omnes Obligations in International Law' 46 *Austrian Journal of Public International Law* (1994), pp.131–66.

Aquila Richard E., *Matter in Mind: A Study of Kant's Transcendental Deduction*. (Indiana University Press, 1989).

Araujo, 'Anti-Personnel Mines and Peremptory International Law: Argument and Catalyst' 30 *Vanderbilt J Transnat'l L* (1997).

Arif Sardar MA, Waqar Khan, 'Judicial precedent and its authority under international law', 3 (6) *International Journal of Law* (2017), pp.75-81.

Arthur Naiman, '*9/11: The Simple Facts – Why the Official Story can't Possibly be True',* (US: Soft Skull Press, 2011).

Arts Karin and Vesselin Popovski (eds.), *International Criminal Accountability and the Rights of Children* (Heidelberg: Springer, 2006), pp. 37–52 and 53–65.

* Mention here neither includes nor excludes in the text.

Ashman Allan and David L. Lee, 'Non-Lawyer Judges: The Long Road North' 53 (3) Chicago Kant Law Review (1977), pp.565-595.

Ashworth A., Four Threats to Presumption of Innocence' *South African Journal* (2006), pp.63–97.

Asimow Michael, 'When the Lawyer Knows the Client is Guilty: David Mellinkoff's 'The Conscience of a Lawyer'', Legal Ethics, Literature, and Popular Culture, *SSRN Electronic Journal* DOI:10.2139/ssrn.948291.

Baderin Mashood A., *International Human Rights and Islamic Law* (New York, NY: Oxford University Press, 2005).

Baderin Mashood, A., 'A Comparative Analysis of the Right to a Fair Trial and due Process under International Human Rights Law and Saudi Arabian Domestic Law', 10 (3) *The International Journal of Human Rights* (2006).

Baderin Mashood A., 'Effective Legal Representation in '*Shariah*' Courts as a Means of Addressing Human Rights Concerns in the Islamic Criminal Justice System of Muslim States.' 11 *Yearbook of Islamic and Middle Eastern Law* (2006), pp. 135-167.

Baderin Mashood A., *International Law and Islamic Law* (Ashgate, 2008).

Ballin Ernst Hirsch, 'The Value of International Criminal Justice: How Much International Criminal Justice Can the World Afford?' *International Criminal Law Review* (online publication, 2019), pp.201-213, available online at https://brill.com/view/journals/icla/19/2/article-p201_201.xml?language=en.

Bantekas Ilias and Susan Nash, *International Criminal Law* (2007).

Bartlett Eva, *How We Were Mislead about Syria*, available at https://timhayward.wordpress.com/2017/02/06/how-we-were-misled-about-syria-channel-4-news/.

Bartlett Eva, 'What's Happening in Syria? The Media 'Kills the Truth', 'Terrorism' is Described as 'Moderate Opposition.' (Global Research, February 05, 2017).

Bassiouni M. Cherif, Islam: Concept, Law and Word *Habeas Corpus*, 2 *Rutgers Camden Law Journal* (1970).

Bassiouni M. Cherif (ed.), *International Terrorism and Political Crimes* (1975).

Bassiouni M. Cherif, *Studies in Early Hadith Literature* (Indianapolis, 1978).

Bassiouni M. Cherif, 'Protection of Diplomats under Islamic Law', 74 *American Journal of International Law* (1980), pp.609-655.

Bassiouni M. Cherif, (ed.), *The Islamic Criminal Justice System* (London, Rome, New York, Oceana Publications, 1982).

Bassiouni M. Cherif, 'A Comprehensive Strategic Approach on International Cooperation for the Prevention, Control and Suppression of International and Transnational Criminality, Including the Establishment of an International Criminal Court', 15 *Nova Law Review* 353 (1991).

Bassiouni M. Cherif, 'Draft Statute of International Criminal Tribunal', 9 *Nouvellese Etudes Penales* (1993).

Bassiouni, C 'International Crimes: *Jus cogens* and *Obligatio Erga Omnes*' 59 *Law and Contemporary Problems* (1996) 63.

Bassiouni M. Cherif (ed.), *International Criminal Law* (US: Ocean Publication, 3 vols., 1999).

Bassiouni M. Cherif, *Crimes Against Humanity in International law* (1999).

Bassiouni M. Cherif, *Introduction to International Criminal Law* (2005).

Bassiouni M. Cherif and Benjamin B. Ferencz, *The Crime Against Peace and Aggression: From Its Origins to the ICC, in International Criminal Law*, vol. I, (M. Cherif Bassiouni, ed. 2008).

Bassiouni M. Cherif, 'International Recognition of Victims' Rights,' in Bassiouni (ed.), III *International Criminal Law* (2008).

Bassiouni M. Cherif, 'The Discipline of International Criminal Law', in M. Cherif Bassiouni (ed.), *International Criminal Law*, Vol. 1 (2008), pp.5-40.

Bassiouni M. Cherif, 'The Subjects of International Criminal Law: Ratione Personae' in M. Bassiouni Cherif (ed.), *International Criminal Law*, Vol. 1 (2008) pp.41-70.

Bassiouni M. Cherif, 'The Subjects of International Criminal Law: Ratione Personae,' in *International Criminal Law*, Vol. I (M. Cherif Bassiouni, ed. 2008) pp.41-70.

Bassiouni M. Cherif, *Criminal Justice in the Time of War and Peace* (Cambridge University Press, Cambridge, 2014).

Bassiouni M. Cherif, *The Shariah and Islamic Criminal Justice in the Time of War and Peace* (Cambridge University Press, Cambridge, 2014).

Bassiouni M. Cherif & Christopher Blakesley, 'The Need for an International Criminal Court in the New International World Order', 25 *Vand. J. Transnat'l* 151 (1992).

Bassiouni M. Cherif & Daniel Derby, 'Final Report on the Establishment of an International Criminal Court for the Implementation of the Apartheid Convention and Other Relevant Instruments', 7 *Hofstra Law Review* 525 (1981).

Bassiouni M. Cherif and Ved P. Nanda (eds.), *A Treatise on International Criminal Law: Crimes and Punishment* (2 vols. 1973).

Baum L. M., 'Pursuing Justice in a Climate of Moral Outrage: An Evaluation of the Rights of the Accused in the Rome Statute of the International Criminal Court,' 19 *Wisconsin International Law Journal* (2001), 197.

Baumgartner Elisabeth, 'Aspects of Victim Participation in the Proceedings of the International Criminal Court', 90 (870) *International Review of the Red Cross* (2008), pp.409-440. Available online at https://www.corteidh.or.cr/tablas/R21692.pdf.

Beattie J. M., *Policing and Punishment in London, 1660-1750: Urban Crime and the Limits of Terror* (Oxford: Oxford University Press, 2001).

Beccaria Cesare, *On Crimes and Punishments* (1764).

Beccaria Il caso. *A 250 anni dalla pubblicazione del "Dei delitti e delle pene"* [*250 years after the publication of "Crimes and Punishment"*] (Società editrice il Mulino, 2016).

Beck Lewis White, *Kant Studies Today* (Open Court, 1969).

Bekker P. M., 'The undefended accused/defendant: a brief overview of the development of the American , American Indian and South African Positions' *XXIV CILSA* (1991), pp. 151-188.

Bell Richard, *Introduction to the Quran* (Edinburgh University Press, 1955).

Bellamy A., *Responsibility to Protect: the Global Effort to End Mass Atrocities* (Polity Press, Cambridge, 2009).

Bellamy R (ed.), C Beccaria, *On Crimes and Punishments*, (1995).

Benazir Bhutto, Reconciliation, Islam, Democracy, and the West (Simon & Schuster, 2008).

Benneh, EY 'Sovereignty Immunity and International Crimes' 22 *Ghana Law Journal* (2002–2004), 112.

Bennett Jonathan, *Kant's Analytic* (Cambridge University Press, 1966).

Bennett Jonathan, *Kant's Dialectic* (Cambridge University Press, 1974).

Bennoune Karima, 'As-Salamu 'Alykum? Humanitarian Law in Islamic Jurisprudence', 15 *Michigan Journal of International Law* (1994), pp. 605-643.

Benny Philip Berger, *Criminal Code of the Jews: According to the Talmud* (New Jersey: The Law Book Exchange, LTD., 2005).

Bentley D., *English Criminal Justice in the Nineteenth Century* (London: Bloomsbury Academic, 1998).

Benvenisti Eyal & George W. Downs, 'Prospects for the Increased Independence of International Tribunals', 12 (5) *German Law Journal* (2011), pp.1057-1081.

Benvenisti Eyal and George W. Downs, Prospects for the Increased Independence of International Tribunals (2019).

Berger Maurists, A brief history of Islam in Europe: Thirteen Centuries of Creed, Conflict and Coexistence (2014).

Berman Schiff (ed.), *The Oxford Handbook of Legal Pluralism* (Oxford University Press, 2019).

Berman Schiff, *Global Legal Pluralism: A Jurisprudence of Law Beyond Borders* (2012).

Bernstein Richard J, *Radical Evil: A Philosophical Interrogation* (New York: Blackwell Publisher, 2002).

Bianchi A., 'Human Rights and the Magic of *Jus cogens*', 19 *European Journal of International Law* (2008), pp. 491-508.

Bigi Giulia, 'Joint Criminal Enterprise in the Jurisprudence of the International Criminal Tribunal for the Former Yugoslavia and the Prosecution of Senior Political and Military Leaders: The Krajišnik Case' 14 *Max Planck United Nations Yearbook* (2010), pp.51-83.

Bird Graham, *Kant's Theory of Knowledge* (Humanities Press, 1962).

Bix Brian, 'Natural Law: The Modern Tradition' in Jules Coleman and Schott Shapiro (eds.), *The Oxford Handbook of Jurisprudence and Philosophy of Law* (2002).

Blackstone W., COMMENTARIES (reprint 1978), pp. 66-7.

Bloxham Donald, *Genocide on Trial: War Crimes Trials and the Formation of Holocaust History and Memory* (2001).

Boas Gideon, *International Criminal Law Developments in the Case Caw of the ICTY* (2004).

Boas Gideon, *International Criminal Justice: Legitimacy and Coherence* (2012).

Boerefijn Ineke, 'Towards a Strong System of Supervision: The Human Rights Committee 's Role in Reforming the Reporting Procedure under Article 40 of the Covenant on Civil and Political Rights', *Human Rights Quarterly* 17.4 (1995), pp.766-793.

Boot Machteld, *Genocide, Crimes against Humanity, War Crimes: Nullum Crimen Sine Lege and the Subjective Matter of Jurisdiction of the International Criminal Court* (2002).

Bosworth-Smith R, *Mohammad and Mohammadanism* (London, 1889).

Boyle James D. A., ed., *Critical Legal Studies* (1992).

Boyle James, 'Is Subjectivity Possible? The Postmodern Subject in Legal Theory', 62 *University of Colorado Law Review* 489 (1991).

Browning Christopher, *The path to genocide: Essays on Launching the Final Solution* (2002).

Browning Don (eds.), *Universalism vs. Relativism: Making Moral Judgements in a Changing, Pluralistic, and Threatening World* (Rowman and Littlefield Publishers, United Kingdom, 2006).

Brownlie, Ian, *International Law and the* Use of Force *by States* (Oxford: Oxford University Press, 1996).

Brownlie Ian, *Principles of Public International Law* (Oxford: Clarendon Press, 5th ed., 1998).

Brunnée J, 'The Prohibition on Torture: Driving *Jus cogens* Home?' 104 *Proceedings of the Annual Meeting of the American Society of International Law* (2010).

Brunstetter Daniel R. and Arturo Jimenez-Bacardi, 'Clashing over Drones: The Legal and Normative Gap between the United States and the Human Rights Community,' 19 (2) *International Journal of Human Rights* (2015), pp. 176–198.

Buchanan Allen, 'Toward a Drone Accountability Regime,' 29 (1) *Ethics and International Affairs (2015)*, pp. 15–70.

Burke-White William W., 'Implementing a Policy of Positive Complementarity in the Rome System of Justice,' 19 *Criminal Law Forum* (2008), 59-89.

Burgess Pete, Susan Corby, and Paul L. Latreille, 'Lay Judges and Labour Courts: A Question of Legitimacy', 35 *Comparative Labour Law and Policy Journal* (2014), pp.191-215.

Burns Peter, 'An International Criminal Tribunal: The Difficult Union of Principle and Politics', 5 *Criminal Law Forum* (1994).

Byers M, 'Conceptualising the Relationship Between *Jus cogens* and *Erga Omnes Rules*' 66 *Nordic Journal of International Law* (1997).

Byrd B. Sharon and Joachim Hruschka, *Kant and Law* (Ashgate, 2005).

Caenegem R. C. van, *European Law in the Past and the Future: Unity and Diversity over Two Millennia* (Cambridge: Cambridge University Press, 2001).

Cançado Trindade, A '*Jus cogens* in Contemporary International Law', UN Audiovisual Library, (http://www.un.org/law/avl).

Cannizzaro E., 'A Higher Law for Treaties?', in E. Cannizzaro (ed.), *The Law of Treaties Beyond the Vienna Convention* (2011).

Carvin Stephanie, 'Getting Drones Wrong', 19 (2) *International Journal of Human Rights* (2015), pp. 127–141.

Cassese Antonio, 'For an Enhanced Role of *Jus cogens*' in Cassese, A (ed.), *Realizing Utopia* (2012).

Cassese Antonio (ed.), *The New Humanitarian Law of Armed Conflict* (Naples: Editoriale Scientifica, 1979).

Cassese Antonio, 'First Annual Report of the ICTY', *Yearbook* of *International Law Commission* (1994).

Cassese Antonio, *International Criminal Law* (Oxford: Oxford University Press, 2nd, ed., 2008).

Cassese Antonio, 'For an Enhanced Role of *Jus cogens*' in Cassese, A (ed.), *Realizing Utopia* (2012).

Chinkin Christine, '*Jus cogens*, Article 103 of the UN Charter and other Hierarchical Techniques of Conflict Solution' *Finnish Yearbook of International Law* (2006).

Chinkin Christine, '*Jus cogens*, Article 103 of the UN Charter and Other Hierarchical Techniques of Conflict Solution,' 17 *Finnish Yearbook of International Law* (2008), pp. 63-90.

Chinkin Christine, Mary Kaldor, *International Law and New Wars* (New York: Cambridge University Press, 2017).

Chossudovsky Michel, *War and Globalisation: The Truth Behind September 11* (Global Outlook, *2002).*

Christian Wolff., *Jus Gentium Methodo Scientifica Pertractatum* translated by Joseph H. Drake (Oxford: Clarendon Press at London (1934).

Cicero, *De Finibus Bonorum et Malorum*, Book V, XXIII.

Cima Elena, 'Ethical Conduct in International Criminal Courts: Whose Ethics?', *American Journal of International Law*(2019), pp.296-301. Available online at https://www.researchgate.net/publication/335848353_Ethical_Conduct_in_International_Criminal_Courts_Whose_Ethics.

Clooney Amal, Philippa Webb, Right to a Fair Trial in International Law (Oxford Publication, 2020).

Cohen Morris, 'Moral Aspects of the Criminal Law,' 49 *Yale Law Journal* (1949), pp. 987-1026.

Colbran Stephen, 'Diligent as a Criterion for Judicial Performance Evaluation', 11 (1) *Griffith Law Review* (2002), pp.198-222Coleman Francis, X. J., *The Harmony of Reason: A Study in Kant's Aesthetics*. (University of Pittsburgh Press, 1974).

Combs Nancy, *Fact-Finding Without Facts* (Cambridge: Cambridge University Press, 2010).

Combs Nancy, 'Grave Crimes and Weak Evidence: A Fact-Finding Evolution in International Criminal Law' 38 *Harvard International Law Review* (2016), pp.47-125.

Corten Olivier, 'La rébellion et le droit international: Le principe de neutralité en tension' ['Rebellion and International Law: The Principle of Neutrality in Tension'], 374 *Recueil des Cours: Académie de Droit International de la Haye* (2014), pp. 53–312.

Coulson, N. J, *Conflict and Tensions in Islamic Jurisprudence* (University of Chicago Press, 1969).

Cox, J. Gray, *The Will at the Crossroads: A Reconstruction of Kant's Moral Philosophy* (University Press of America, 1984).

Crane David M., 'The Special Court for Sierra Leone, in International Criminal Law', Vol. III (M. Cherif Bassiouni, ed. 2008) pp. 195-218.

Cranston R. (ed) *Legal Ethics and Professional Responsibility* (Oxford: Clarendon Press, 1995).

Craven Sarah M. R., *In Good Conscience: Expressions of Judicial Conscience in Federal Appellate Opinions,* (Akron Law Publication, 2012), pp.1-67.

Crawford J and S Olleson 'The Continuing Debate on a UN Convention on State Responsibility' *54 ICLQ* (2005) 959–71.

Crawford J., *The ILC's Articles on State Responsibility: Introduction, Text and Commentaries* (CUP Cambridge 2002).

Cryer Robert, *Prosecuting International Crimes, Selectivity and the International Criminal Law Regime* (Cambridge University Press, Cambridge, 2005).

Cryer Robert, 'The Doctrinal Foundations of International Criminalization,' in *International Criminal Law*, Vol. 1 (M. Cherif Bassiouni, ed., 2008), pp. 107-128.

D'Amato A., 'The Moral Dilemma of Positivism', 20 *Valparaiso University Law Review* (1985-86), 43-53.

D'Amato A., 'It's a Bird, It's a Plane, It's *Jus cogens'* 6 *Connecticut Journal of International Law* (1990).

Danilenko G, 'International *Jus cogens*: Issues of Law-Making' 2 *European Journal of International Law* (1991).

Danilenko G. M., 'International *Jus cogens*: Issues of Law Making', *European Journal of International Law* (1991).

David Eric, 'The Belgin Experince', in M. Cherif Bassiouni, *International Criminal Law*, Vol. III (Netherlands: Brill, 2008), pp.359-384.

David Lyons, 'Moral Aspects of Legal Theory' in Kenneth Himma and Brian Bix (eds) *Law and Morality* (2005).

David MacGregor, "September 11 as 'Machiavellian State Terrorism'", in Paul Zarembka, *The Hidden History of 9-11-2001* (New York: Seven Stories Press, 2008).

Davis Michael C., Dietrich Wolfgang, Bettina Schoolman and Sepp. Dieter, *International Intervention in the Post-Cold War World: Moral Responsibility and Power Politics* (M. E. Sharpe, Inc., 2003).

de Hoog AJJ, 'The Relationship between *Jus cogens*, Obligations *Erga Omnes* and International Crimes: Peremptory Norms in Perspective' 42 *Österreichische Zeitschrift für öffentliches Recht und Völkerrecht* (1991).

de Hoogh A, *Obligations erga omnes and International Crimes: A Theoretical Inquiry into the Implementation and Enforcement of the International Responsibility of States* (Kluwer The Hague , 1996).

de Wet, Erika '*Jus cogens* and Obligations Erga Omnes' in de Wet, E and Vidmar (eds.), J *Hierarchy in International Law: The Place of Human Rights* (2012).

de Wet Erika, 'The Prohibition of Torture as an International Norm of *Jus cogens* and its Implementation for National and Customary Law,' 15 (1) *European Journal of International Law* (2014), Vol. 15, No.1, 97-121.

Delmas-Marty Mireille, The Contribution of Comparative Law to a Pluralist Conception of International Criminal Law, 1 *Journal of International Criminal Justice* (2003), pp. 13-25.

DeSon Jason S., 'Automating the Right Stuff? The Hidden Ramifications of Ensuring Autonomous Aerial Weapon Systems Comply with International Humanitarian Law,' 72 *Air Force Law Review* (2015), pp. 85–122.

Despland Michael, *Kant on History and Religion* (McGill-Queen's University Press, 1973).

Detmold M. J., *The Unity of Law and Morality: A Refutation of Legal Positivism* (Canada: Law Book Co. of Australasia, 1984).

Dhanapala Jayantha, *Under-Secretary-General for Disarmament Affairs United Nations, International Law, Security, and Weapons of Mass Destruction* (New York, 9 May 2002).

Dhokalia, 'Problems Relating to *Jus cogens'*, in S. Agrawala (ed.), *Essays on the Law of Treaties* (1972).

Dickson Julie, *Evaluation and Legal Theory* (2001).

Don Paul and Jim Hoffman, Waking Up from Our Nightmare, the 9/11/01 Crimes in New York City (New York: I/R Press, 2004).

Drost Pieter Nicolaas, *The Crime of State: Genocide* (Original from Indiana University, 1959).

Drost Pieter Nicolaas, *The Crime of State: Humanicide* (Original from Indiana University, 1959).

Dryer Douglas P., *Kant's Solution for Verification in Metaphysics* (Allen and Unwin, 1966).

Dugard John, 'Lifting the Guise of Occupation and Recourse to Action before the ICJ and ICC', Palestine Yearbook of International Law, Vol. 17, 2013–14, pp. 9–27.

Duncan A. R. C., *Practical Reason and Morality* (Nelson, 1957).

Dupuy P. M, 'Reviewing the Difficulties of Codification: On Ago's Classification of Obligations of Means and Obligations of Result in Relation to State Responsibility' 10 *EJIL* (1999), pp. 371–85.

Dupuy, P 'Some Reflections on Contemporary International Law and the Appeal to Universal Values: a Response to Marti Koskenniemi' 16 *European Journal of International Law* (2005), 131.

Duțu Mircea, Vespasian V. Pella (1897-1952): *Founder of International Criminal law, Promoter of the Unification of the Criminal Law, Architect of the International Criminal Justice* (Universul Juridic, Bucharest, 2012).

Eberle Edward J., 'The German Idea of Freedom', 10 *Orgon Review of Int'L Law* (2008), pp. 1-76.

Economides K. (ed) *Ethical Challenges to Legal Education and Conduct* (Oxford: Hart Publishing, 1998).

Edgeworth F. Y., *Mathematical Psychics: An Essay on the Application of Mathematics to the Moral Sciences*, (London: C. Kegan Paul & Co. 1881).

Emil L., 'Fackenheim, Kant and Radical Evil', in Immanuel Kant: *Critical Assessments.* 3 ed., Chadwick Ruth. (Routledge, 1992), 259-273.

Engelhardt Jordan, *The Pre-eminent State: National Dominance in the Effort to Try Saddam Hussein, Cornell Journal of International Law*, (2009).

Eric David, *Principes de Droit des Conflits Armés* [*Principles of the Law of Armed Conflict*] (2nd, ed. 1999).

Ewald F., 'Unger's Philosophy: A Critical Legal Study' 5 *Yale Law Journal* (1988), 665.

Ewing A. C., *A Short Commentary on Kant's 'Critique of Pure Reason'* (Methuen, 1978).

Falk Richard, *The Vietnam War and International Law* (Princeton University Press, 1968).

Falk Richard, 'The Accountability of Leaders: A Challenge to Civil Government and Society' in Jeremy Brecher, Jill Cutler, Smith Brendan, *In the Name of Democracy: American War Crimes in Iraq and Beyond (American Empire Project)*, (New York: Metropolitan Books, Henry Holt and Company, 2005).

Falk Richard, *Slouching Toward a Palestinian Holocaust*, www.transnational.org/Area.../Falk Palestine Genocide.html, 20 October 2010.

Farmer John, *The Ground Truth: The Story behind America's Defense on 9/11* (New York: Riverhead Books, 2009).

Fein Bruce, 'Hillary Clinton's 5 lies about Syria, Terror Threat,' The *Washington Times* (25 October, 2016).

Ferencz Benjamin, *International Criminal Court* (2 vols. 1980).

Ferencz Benjamin, *An International Criminal Code and Court: Why They Stand and Where They're Going,* 30 *Columbia Journal of Transnational Law* (1992), 375.

Ferencz Benjamin B., 'Ending Impunity for the Crime of Aggression,' 41 *Case W. Res. J* (2009), pp.281-290.

Finch George Augustus, 'The Nuremberg Trial and International Law,' 41 *American Journal of International Law* (1947), 20.

Finch George A., 'Draft Statute for an International Court', editorial comment 46 *American Journal of International Law* (1952), pp. 89-98.

Finch George, 'Draft Statute for an International Criminal Court,' 46 *American Journal of International Law* (1990), 67.

Findlay Escrito por Mark J., *International and Comparative Criminal Justice: A Critical Introduction* (Routledge, London, 2013).

Finnis John (ed.), *Natural Law* (1991).

Finnis John, *Fundamentals of Ethics* (1985).

Finnis John, *Aquinas: Moral, Political and Legal Theory* (1998).

Fischer-Lescano A. and G. Teubner, 'Regime Collision: The Vain Search for Legal Unity in the Fragmentation of Global Law,' 25 *Michigan Journal of International Law* (2004), pp. 999-104.

Fitzmaurice Gerald, 'The General Principles of International Law Considered from the Standpoint of the Rules of Law,' 92 *Recuel des Cours* (1957).

Focarelli C, 'Promotional *Jus cogens*: A Critical Appraisal of *Jus cogens*' Legal Effects' 77 *Nordic Journal of International Law* (2008), 429.

Fouladvand, S. *Complementarity and cultural sensitivity: Decision-making by the International Criminal Court (ICC) Prosecutor in Relation to the Situations in the Darfur Region of the Sudan and the Democratic Republic of Congo (DRC)* (2012).

Fuller Lon Luvios., The Morality of Law (Yale Law University, 2nd ed., 1969).

Gardiner Gerald, *Capital Punishment as a Deterrent: And the Alternative* (London: Victor Gollancz, 1956).

Garland David; Randall McGowen; Michael Meranze, *America's Death Penalty: Between Past and Present* (2011).

Gavison Ruth (ed.), *Legal Philosophy: The Influence of H.L.A. Hart* (1987).

George Robert P. (ed.), *The Autonomy Of Law: Essays On Legal Positivism* (1995).

George Robert P., *Natural Law Theory: Contemporary Essays* (1994).

Gideon Boas and William A. Schabas (eds.), *International Criminal Law Developments in the Case Law of the ICTY* (2005).

Glennon, MJ "De l'Absurdité du Droit Impératif (*Jus cogens*)' 110 *Revue Générale de Droit International Public* (2006), 529.

Gómez Robledo, A "Le *Jus cogens* International: Sa Genése, sa Nature, ses Fonctions' 172, *Recueil des Cours de l'Académie de Droit International de la Haye* ["*Jus cogens* International: Its Genesis, its Nature, its Functions' 172, *Compendium of Courses of the Hague Academy of International Law*] (1982), 9.

Gottfried Martin, *Kant's Metaphysics and Theory of Science* (Manchester University Press, 1974).

Gram Moltke S. (ed.), *Kant: Disputed Questions* (Quadrangle, 1967).

Gray C., *International Law and the Use of Force* (2000).

Grayeff Felix, *Kant's Theoretical Philosophy* (Barnes & Noble, 1970).

Greenawalt Alexander K. A., The Pluralism of International Criminal Law, 86 *Indiana Law Journal* (2011), 1063-1130.

Gross Michael L., 'Nonlethal Weapons, Non-Combatant Immunity, and the Principle of Participatory Liability', 47 *Case Western Reserve Journal of International Law* (2015), pp. 201–216.

Grover Sonja, *Prosecuting International Crimes and Human Rights Abuses Committed Against Children – Leading International Court Cases* (2010), pp. 169–279.

Guyer Paul, *The Cambridge Companion to Kant* (1992).

Guyer Paul, *Kant and the Experience of Freedom* (Cambridge University Press, 1993).

Haas Jacob De, *History of Palestine - The Last Two Thousand Years* (USA: Macmillan, 1934).

Hacker P. M. S. and J. Raz, (eds.), Law, *Morality and Society: Essays in Honour of H. L. A. Hart* (1977).

Hakim Khalifa Abdul, *Fundamental Human Rights* (1952).

Hall W. A., *Treatise of International Law* (8th ed., 1924).

Hannikainen, L., *Peremptory Norms (jus cogens) in International Law: Historical Development, Criteria, Present Status* (1988).

Harees Lukman, *The Mirage of Dignity on the highways of Human 'Progress': - the Bystanders Perspective* (2012).

Harhoff Frederik, 'It's All in the Process: Reflections on the Relation between International Criminal Trials and International Humanitarian Law', 78 Nordic Journal of International Law (2010).

Harle Vilho, *Ideas of Social Order in the Ancient World* (1998).

Harrit, Niels H. Jeffrey Farrer, Steven E. Jones, Kevin R. Ryan, Frank M. Legge, Daniel Farnsworth, Gregg Roberts, James R. Gourley, Bradley R. Larsen, 'Active Thermitic Material Discovered in Dust from the 9/11 World Trade Center Catastrophe' in http://911review.com/evidence/wtcexplosives.html and www.benthamopen.org/pages/content.php?TOCPJ/2009/00000002/00000001/7TOCPJ.SGM.

Hart H. L. A., *The Concept of Law* (1961).

Hart H. L. A., *Essays in Jurisprudence and Philosophy* (1985).

Hart H. L. A., *The Concept of Law,* 2nd ed., (P.A. Bulloch and J. Raz, eds., 1994).

Hartnack Justus, *Kant's Theory of Knowledge* (Harcourt, Brace and World, 1967).

Head Michael, *The Legal Power to Launch War: Who Decides?* (2009).

Head Michael; Kristian Boehringer, *Domestic Deployment of the Armed Forces: Military Powers, Law and Human Rights* (Routledge, 2019).

Head Michael, Domestic Military Powers, Law and Human Rights: Calling out the Armed Forces (2021).

Heidegger Martin, *Kant and the Problem of Metaphysics* (Indiana University Press, 1962).

Heikkilä Mikaela, International Criminal Tribunals and Victims of Crime: A Study of the Status of Victims before International Criminal Tribunals and of Factors affecting this Status (Institute for Human Rights, Abo Akademi University, Turku, 2004).

Heller Kevin Jon, *The Nuremberg Military Tribunals and the origins of international criminal law* (2010).

Heller Kevin Jon, 'What Is an International Crime? (A Revisionist History)', 58 *Harvard International Law Journal* (2017), pp. 353-420.

Hendeled C. W., (ed.), *The Philosophy of Kant and Our Modern World* (Liberal Arts, 1957).

Hersh Seymour M., *The Killing of Osama Bin Laden (2016).*

Higgins, 'Derogations under Human Rights Treaties' *BYIL* (1976–1977), 282.

Hoffe Otfried, *Immanuel Kant* (State University of New York Press, 1994).

Hoover Joseph, Moral Practices: Assigning Responsibility in the International Criminal Court, 76 *Law and Contemporary Problems* (2014), pp.263-86.

Hugo Adam Bedau, Paul G. Cassell, *Debating the Death Penalty: Should America Have Capital Punishment? The Experts on Both Sides Make Their Best Case* (2004).

Huntington Cairns, *Plato's Theory of Law*, 56 Harvard Law Review (1942), pp. 559-587.

Husabø Erling Johannes and Ingvild Bruce, *Fighting Terrorism through Multilevel Criminal Legislation: Security Council Resolution 1373, the EU Framework Decision on Combating Terrorism and their Implementation in Nordic, Dutch and German Criminal Law* (Martinus Nijhoff Publishers, 2009).

Hutchings Patricia A. E., *Kant on Absolute Value* (Wayne State University Press, 1972).

Jacovides A., *Treaties Conflicting with Peremptory Norms of International Law and the Zurich-London 'Agreements'* (1966).

James Paul, Jonathan Friedman, *Globalization and Violence, Vol. 3: Globalizing War and Intervention* (London: Sage Publications, 2006).

Janis, MW 'The Nature of *Jus cogens*' 3 *Connecticut Journal of International Law* (1988) 59.

Jeffreys-Jones Rhodri, In *Spies We Trust: The Story of Western Intelligence* (Oxford: Oxford University Press, 2013).

Jevons W. S., *The Theory of Political Economy* (London: Macmillan and Co., 1871).

Jones Hardy E., *Kant's Principle of Personality* (University of Wisconsin Press, 1971).

Jørgensen, *The Responsibility of States for International Crimes* (OUP Oxford 2000).

Jori Mario (ed.), *Legal Positivism* (1992).

Kant Immanuel, *The Only Possible Argument in Support of a Demonstration of the Existence of God* (1763).

Kant Immanuel, *Critique of Pure Reason* (1781).

Kant Immanuel, *Prolegomena to Any Future Metaphysics* (1783).

Kant Immanuel, *Answering the Question: What is Enlightenment?* (1784).

Kant Immanuel, *Perpetual Peace, and Other Essays on Politics, History, and Morals* (1784).

Kant Immanuel, *Groundwork of the Metaphysic of Morals* (1785).

Kant Immanuel, *Metaphysical Foundations of Natural Science* (1786).

Kant Immanuel, *The Critique of Practical Reason* (1788).

Kant Immanuel, *Critique of Judgment* (1790).

Kant Immanuel, *The Science of Right* (1790).

Kant Immanuel, *Religion within the Bounds of Bare Reason* (1793).

Kant Immanuel, *Perpetual Peace: A Philosophical Sketch* (1795).

Kant Immanuel, *The Metaphysics of Morals* (1797).

Kant Immanuel, *Opus Postumum* (1995).

Kant Immanuel, 'Religion within the Limits of Reason Alone,' in *Religion and Rational Theology*, ed. and transl. Allen Wood and George di Giovanni (Cambridge University Press, 1996), 93.

Kant Immanuel, *Practical Philosophy* (editor: Mary J. Gregor, 1999).

Kawasaki KYOJI, 'A brief Note on the Legal Effects of *Jus cogens* in International Law', 34 *Hitotsubashi Journal of Law and Politics* (2006), pp. 27-43.

Kelsen Hans, 'Will the Judgement of the Nürenberg Trial Constitute a Precedent in International Law,' 1 *International Law Quarterly* (1947), 153.

Kelsen Hans, *What is Justice? Justice, Law and Politics in the Mirror of Science* (1957).

Kelsen Hans, *Pure Theory of Law* (transl. Maz Knight, 1967).

Kemal Salim., *Kant's Aesthetic Theory: An Introduction* (St. Martin's Press, 1992).

Kennedy D, 'Law and Ideology' 5 *Tikkun* (1988).

Kent Greenawalt, *Statutory and Common Law Interpretation* (Oxford: Oxford University Press, 2013).

Khadduri Majid, (ed.), *War and Peace in the Law of Islam* (Baltimore: The Johan Hopkins Press, 1955).

Khadduri Majid, 'The Islamic Theory of International Relations and its Contemporary Relevance in Proctor' in J. Harris Protector, *Islam and International Relations* (New York, 1965), pp. 24-39.

Khadduri Majid, (ed.), (transl.) *The Islamic Law of Nations: Shaybani's Siyar* (Transl. with an introduction, notes, and appendices, Baltimore, 1966).

Khadduri Majid, *Major Middle Eastern Problems in International Law* (1972).

Kitcher Patricia, *Kant's Transcendental Psychology* (Oxford University Press, 1990).

Klamberg Mark, 'The Alternative Hypothesis Approach, Robustness and International Criminal Justice: A Plea for a "Combined Approach" to Evaluation of Evidence', 13(3) *Journal of International Criminal Justice* (2015), pp. 535-553.

Klein A., Theory for the Application of the Customary International Law of Human Rights by Domestic Courts 13 *Yale Journal of International Law* (1988).

Klein David F., 'A Theory for the Application of the Customary International Law of Human Rights by Domestic Courts,' 13 (2) *Yale Journal of International Law* (1988), pp. 332-365.

Klincewicz Michal, 'Autonomous Weapons Systems, the Frame Problem and Computer Security,' 14 (2) *Journal of Military Ethics* (2015), pp. 162–176.

Kolb, R *Théorie du Jus cogens International: Essai de Relecture du Concept* [*Jus cogens International Theory: Concept Proofreading Essay*] (2001).

Kolb, Robert "*Jus cogens*, Intangibilité, Intransgressibilité, Dérogation 'Positive' et 'Négative'" 109 *Revue Générale de Droit International Public* ["*Jus cogens*, Intangibility, Intransgressibility, Derogation 'Positive' and 'Negative'"] 109 *Revue Générale de Droit International Public*] (2005).

Kolb, R 'Observations sur l'évolution du concept de jus cogens' ['Observations on the evolution of the concept of jus cogens'] in *Revue générale de droit international public* (2009), pp. 837-850.

Komicker Uhlmann, EM 'The State Community Interests, *Jus cogens* and the Protection of the Global Environment: Developing Criteria for Peremptory Norms' *Georgetown International Environmental Law Review* (1998), 101.

Kornicker, 'State Community Interests, *Jus cogens* and Protection of the Global Environment' 11 *Georgetown Int'l Environmental L Rev* (1998).

Koskenniemi M., 'Solidarity Measures: State Responsibility as a New International Order?' 72 *BYIL* (2001), pp. 337–56.

Koskenniemi Martti, *The Gentle Civilizer of Nations: the Rise and Fall of International Law*, 1870-1960 (Cambridge University Press 2002).

Koskenniem Martti, *The Politics of International Law* (Hart, 2011).

Koskenniemi Martti, Mónica García-Salmones Rovira, and Paolo Amorosa, *International Law and Religion: Historical and Contemporary Perspectives* (2017).

Kress Claus, 'Aggression and the Use of Force in International Law', *Proceedings of the 108th Annual Meeting of the American Society of International Law* (2014), pp. 325–346.

Kuper Leo, *International Action against Genocide* (Minority Rights Group Report No. 53, London, 1982).

Kuper Leo, *The Prevention of Genocide* (New Haven and London, 1985).

Lefenya Kesolofetse, 'Use of Explosive Weapons in Densely Populated Areas: Implications for International Humanitarian Law,' *African Yearbook on International Humanitarian Law* (2014), pp. 68–86.

Legal *Consequences of the Construction of a Wall in the Occupied Palestinian Territory* (I.C.J. Reports, 2004).

Leiboff Marett and Mark Thomas, *Legal Theories in Principle* (2004).

Limbach Jutta, Pedro Cruz Villalón, Roger Errera, Lord Lester, Tamara Morschtschakowa, Lord Justice Sedley, Andrzej Zol., 'Judicial Independence: Law and Practice of Appointments to the European Court of Human Rights' (2003). Available online at https://www.corteidh.or.cr/tablas/32795.pdf.

Linderfalk Ulf, 'The Creation of *Jus cogens* – Making Sense of Article 53 of the Vienna Convention,' Max-Planck-Institut für ausländisches öffentliches Recht und Völkerrecht (2011), pp.259-278.

Luban David, 'After the Honeymoon: Reflections on the Current State of International Criminal Justice', 11 (3) *Journal of International Criminal Justice* (2013), pp.505–515, available online at https://academic.oup.com/jicj/article/11/3/505/814469.

Luper-Foy, Steven 'Introduction: Global Distributive Justice' in Steven Luper-Foy (ed.), *Problems of International Justice* (London: Westview Press, 1988), pp. 1-24.

Luther King Martin, *The Quest for Peace and Justice, a Nobel Lecture delivered by Martin Luther King in December* 11, 1964.

MacGregor, 'State Immunity and *Jus cogens*' 55 *International & Comparative Law Quarterly* (2006), 437.

MacIntyre Alasdair, *A Short History of Ethics : a History of Moral Philosophy from the Homeric Age to the Twentieth Century* (1965).

MacIntyre Alasdair, *After Virtue: A Study in Moral Theory* (University of Notre Dame Press, 1982).

Macleod Peter R., 'Latin in Legal Writing: An Inquiry into the Use of Latin in the Modern Legal World', 39 (1) *Boston College Law Review* (1997), pp.235-251, available online at https://lawdigitalcommons.bc.edu/cgi/viewcontent.cgi?referer=&httpsredir=1&article=2089&context=bclr.

Madsen Wayne, Jean-Charles and Guillaume Dasquie, *Forbidden Truth: U.S.-Taliban Secret Oil Diplomacy, Saudi Arabia and the Failed Search for bin Laden* (2002).

Magliveras Konstantinos D., 'The Special Court for Sierra Leone: A New Type of Regional Criminal Court for the International Community?' 17 *International Enforcement Law Rep*orter (Feb. 2001).

Majd Mohammad Gholi, *The Great Famine & Genocide in Iran: 1917-1919* (2nd ed., University Press of America, 2013).

Majd Mohammad Gholi, *Victorian Holocaust Iran in the Great Famine of 1869-1873* (Hamilton Books, 2018).

Majinge Charles Riziki, 'Peaceful Settlement of Disputes among States and the Rules of Regional Judicial Institutions in Africa ' in Charles Riziki Majinge (ed.), *Rule of Law Through Human Rights and International Criminal Justice : Essays in Honour of Adama Dieng* (Cambridge: Cambridge Scholars publishing (Cambridge Scholars Publishing, 2015), pp. 523-52.

Malekian Farhad, *International Criminal Responsibility of States: A Study on the Evolution of International Responsibility of States with particular Emphasis on the Concept of Crime and Criminal Responsibility* (Stockholm, 1985).

Malekian Farhad, *System of International Law: Formation, Treaties, Responsibility* (Uppsala, 1987).

Malekian Farhad, *International Criminal Law: The Legal and Critical Analysis of International Crimes* (Almqvist & Wiksell International,2 vols. 1991).

Malekian Farhad, *Condemning the Use of Force in the Gulf Crisis* (Almqvist & Wiksell International, 1st ed., 1992).

Malekian Farhad, *The Monopolization of International Criminal Law in the United Nations, A Jurisprudential Approach* (Almqvist Wiksell International, 1st ed., 1993).

Malekian Farhad, *Condemning the Use of Force in the Gulf Crisis* (Almqvist & Wiksell International, 2nd ed. 1994).

Malekian Farhad, *The Concept of Islamic International Criminal Law, A Comparative Study* (Netherlands: Brill, 1994).

Malekian Farhad, *The Monopolization of International Criminal Law in the United Nations, A Jurisprudential Approach* (Almqvist Wiksell International, 2nd ed., 1995).

Malekian Farhad, '*International Criminal Responsibility', in International Criminal Law* (M. Cherif Bassiouni, 2ed, ed., 1999).

Malekian Farhad, 'International Criminal Responsibility: International Criminal Responsibility of Individuals' in M. Cherif Bassiouni, *International Criminal Law,* Vol. *Crimes* (2ed, ed., New York: Transnational Publishers, 1999).

Malekian Farhad, 'Emasculating the Philosophy of International Criminal Justice in the Iraqi Special Tribunal,' *Cornell International Law Journal*, 58/5 (2005), pp.675-725.

Malekian Farhad, *Prohibition Governing Child Soldiers Constituting an Integral Part of Jus cogens and Obligatio Erga Omnes*, XVII *World Congress of the International Association of Youth and Family Judges and Magistrates*, Belfast, Northern Ireland, 27 August – 2 September (2006).

Malekian Farhad, 'Armenian Genocide and the Questions of Responsibility of the Turkish Government,' *House of Commons Conference on the Armenian Genocide, Armenian Solidarity, British-Armenian All-Party Parliamentary Group, No Security Publication* (2007), pp.31-9.

Malekian Farhad, *Documents on the Principles of International Human Rights* (Stockholm: Norstedts Juridik AB, 2007).

Malekian Farhad, 'Mutilating the Philosophy of Justice in the Time of Armed Conflicts,' *Contemporary Journal of International Criminal Law* (Publication of the Institute of International Criminal Law, Uppsala, 2007).

Malekian Farhad, 'The Functions of International Criminal Law and the Problem of Positivism and Neutralism Philosophy', *Contemporary Journal of International Criminal Law* Publication of the Institute of International Criminal Law, Uppsala, 2007, 2007).

Malekian Farhad, 'The Homogeneity of International Criminal Court with Islamic Jurisprudence,' 9 (4) *International Criminal Law Review* (2009), pp.595-621.

Malekian Farhad, 'The Miserable Wedding of Naturalism into Positivism,' 2 *ID EST Journal* (2009).

Malekian Farhad, *Principles of Islamic International Criminal Law: A Comparative Search* (Netherlands: Brill & Nijhoff, 2011).

Malekian Farhad, 'The Laws Governing Crimes against Women Constituting *Obligatio Erga Omnes*' in David Wingeate Pike, Crimes Against Women (New York: Nova Science Publishers, 2011).

Malekian Farhad, 'Judging International Criminal Justice in the Occupied Territories,' 12 *International Criminal Law Review* (2012), pp.627-869.

Malekian Farhad, 'The Child as an Autonomous Subject of Justice' in Farhad Malekian, Kerstin Nordlöf, *Sovereignty of Children in Law* (Newcastle: Cambridge Scholars Publishing, 2012), pp. 2-55.

Malekian Farhad., *'Islamic Law Justice Systems' in* Jay S. Albanese, *The Encyclopaedia of Criminology and Criminal Justice* (United States: Wiley-Blackwell (5 volumes, 2013), vol. III, pp.1220-1225.

Malekian Farhad, *Jurisprudence of International Criminal Justice* (Introduction by Professor Benjamin Ferencz, the former Prosecutor of the Nuremberg Tribunal (Newcastle: Cambridge Scholars Publishing, Cambridge Scholars Publishing, 2014).

Malekian Farhad, 'Consolidating the International Criminal Law of Children', 26, (3) *Criminal Law Forum* (2015), pp. 569-593.

Malekian Farhad, 'The Canon of Love against the Use of Force in Islamic and Public International Law: Part II: The Anatomy of Love Against Violations,' 15 *International Criminal Law Review*, 2015), pp. 861-895.

Malekian Farhad, 'The Canon of Love against the Use of Force in Islamic and Public International Law: Part I: The Chamber of Love within Legal Discipline,' 15 *International Criminal Law Review*, 2015), pp. 591-628.

Malekian Farhad, 'Comparative Substantive International Criminal Justice,' in Ronald Slye (ed.), *The Nuremberg Principles in Non-western Societies: A Reflection on their Universality, Legitimacy and Application* (2017), pp. 10-44.

Malekian Farhad, 'Conundrums of *Jus cogens:* In Case Law' (Part II), No. 13 *Вісник Південного регіонального центру Національної академії правових наук України,* [No. 13 *Journal of the South regional Center of National Academy of Legal Sciences of Ukraine*] (2017), pp. 12-21.

Malekian Farhad, 'Conundrums of *Jus cogens*: in International Criminal Law' (Part I), *Вісник Південного регіонального центру Національної академії правових наук України* [*No.12 Journal of the South regional Center of National Academy of Legal Sciences of Ukraine*] (2017), pp. 8-16.

Malekian Farhad, *Corpus Juris of Islamic International Criminal Justice* (Newcastle: Cambridge Scholars Publishing, 2017).

Malekian Farhad, *Judgments of Love in Criminal Justice* (Switzerland: Springer: 2017).

Malekian Farhad, 'The Heaven of Justice with Love,' *The Journal of the Henry Martyn Institute* (2017), pp. 5-29.

Malekian Farhad, *Classical Morality in International Peremptory Criminal Law* (Newcastle: Cambridge Scholars Publishing, 2018).

Malekian Farhad, *Judgments of Love in Criminal Justice* (Switzerland: Springer: 2018).

Malekian Farhad, *The Mirage of International Criminal Law: Kant Metaphysics of Mens Rea* (Newcastle: Cambridge Scholars Publishing, 2018).

Malekian Farhad, *Allegations by Political Laundering* (Newcastle: Scholars Publishing, 2019).

Malekian Farhad, *Trading Virginity of International Criminal Justice* (New York: Nova Science Publishers, 2020).

Malekian Farhad, *Classical Morality in International Peremptory Criminal Law* (Newcastle: Cambridge Scholars Publishing, 2021).

Malekian Farhad, *Conscience of Judges in International Criminal Law, the Heart of Judgements* (New York: Nova Science Publishers, 2021).

Malekian Farhad, *Conscience of Lawyers in International Criminal Law, the Burden of Doppelgängers* (New York: Nova Science Publishers, 2021).

Malekian Farhad, *Conscience of Prosecutors in International Criminal Law, the Heart of the Matter* (New York: Nova Science Publishers, 2021).

Malekian Farhad, *Gravity of Wisdom in International Criminal Law* (New York: Nova Science Publishers, 2021).

Malekian Farhad, *International Criminal Law of Children* (New York: Nova Science Publishers, 2021).

Malekian Farhad, *International Criminal Law, the Law of Somebodiness, the Law of Nobodiness* (New York: Nova Science Publishers, 2021).

Malekian Farhad, *Orchestrating Diversity in International Criminal Justice* (New York: Nova Science Publishers, 2021).

Malekian Farhad, *Paralysing International Criminal Justice* (New York: Nova Science Publishers, 2021).

Malekian Farhad and Kerstin Nordlöf, *Confessing the International Rights of Children: The Basic documents with Analysis (*Cambridge: Cambridge Scholars Publishing, 2012).

Malekian Farhad, Kerstin Nordlöf, *The Sovereignty of Children in Law* (Cambridge: Cambridge Scholars Publishing, 2012).

Malekian Farhad and Kerstin Nordlöf, 'International Legal Status of Children' in Jay S. Albanese (ed.), *The Encyclopaedia of Criminology*

& Criminal Justice (United States: Wiley-Blackwell (5 volumes, 2013), vol. III, pp. 1173-1178.

Malekian Farhad, Kerstin Nordlöf, *Prohibition of Sexual Exploitation of Children Constituting Obligation Erga Omnes* (Newcastle: Cambridge Scholars Publishing, 2013).

Manacorda Stefano, '*Cesare Beccaria e la pena dell'ergastolo.' Jus* [*Cesare Beccaria and the sentence of life imprisonment*] (2015), pp. 165–182.

Marc Weller, *Iraq and the Use of Force in International Law* (Oxford: Oxford University Press, 2010).

Markovic Milan, 'International Criminal Trials and the Disqualification of Judges on International Criminal Trials and the Disqualification of Judges on the Basis of Nationality the Basis of Nationality', 13 (1) *Washington University Global Studies Law Review* (2014), pp.1-48. Available online at https://openscholarship.wustl.edu/cgi/viewcontent.cgi?article=1472&context=law_globalstudies

Max Maxwell, *A Socratic Perspective on the Nature of Human Evil*, available online at http://www.socraticmethod.net/socratic_essay_nature_of_ human_evil.htm.

May Lary, *'Habeas Corpus as* Jus cogens *in International Law' 4 (3)* Criminal Law and Philosophy *(2010), 249–265.*

McAuley Finbarr and J Pail McCutcheon, *Criminal Liability* (Round Hall Sweet and Maxwell, 2000).

McInerny Ralph, 'Thomistic Natural Law and Aristotelian Philosophy' in John Goyette, Mark Latkovic and Richard Myers (eds.) *St Thomas Aquinas and the Natural Law Tradition: Contemporary Perspectives* (2004).

Mellinkoff David, *The Conscience of a Lawyer* (West Publishing Co., 1973).

Mendus Susan, 'The Importance of Love in Rawls's Theory of Justice' 29 (1) *British Journal of Political Science* (1999), pp. 57-75.

Meron Theodor, 'Judicial Independence and Impartiality in International Criminal Tribunals'. 99 (2) *American Journal of International Law* (2005), pp.359-369.

Meron Theodor, *The Humanization of International Law* (Netherlands: The Hague Academy, 2006).

Meron, T 'On Hierarchy of International Human Rights' 80 *American Journal of International Law* (1986).

Meyssan Thierry, *11 September 2001: L'effroyable Imposture* (2002).

Mill J. S., *Collected Works of John Stuart Mill*, Gen. Ed. J. M. Robson, Toronto: University of Toronto Press, 1963-91).

Milmed Bella K., *Kant and Current Philosophical Issues* (New York University Press, 1961).

Mokhtar Ali, '*Nullum Crimen, Nulla Poena, Sine Lege*: Aspects and Prospects', 26 *Statute Law Review,* pp. 41-55.

Moyn Samuel, *Not Enough: Human Rights in an Unequal World* (2018).

Muchnik Pablo, *Kant's Theory of Evil: An Essay on the Dangers of Self-love and the Aperiodicity of History* (Lexington Books, 2010).

Mueller Gerhard O. W., 'International Criminal Law: Civitas Maxima,' 15 *Case Western Reserve Journal of International Law* (1985).

Murphy Peter, 'No Free Lunch, No Free Proof: The Indiscriminate Admission of Evidence is a Serious Flaw in International Criminal Trials', 8(2) *Journal of International Criminal Justice* (2010), pp. 539-573.

Murphy S., 'Nation-Building: A Look at Somalia,' 3 *Tul J Int'l & Comp L* (1995).

Nafeez Mosaddeq Ahmed, *'Terrorism and Statecraft: Al-Qaeda and Western Covert Operations after the Cold War,'* in Paul Zarembka (ed.), pp. 143-182.

Neal J., *Principles of Legislation: From the Ms. of Jeremy Bentham*; *By M. Dumont … With Notes and a Biographical Notice of Jeremy Bentham and of M. Dumont*, Boston, MA: Wells and Lilly, 1830).

Newton Michael A., 'Back to the Future: Reflections on the Advent of Autonomous Weapons Systems', 47 (1) *Case Western Reserve Journal of International Law* (2015), pp. 5–23.

Nicolas A. J., 'Croquet the International Criminal Court and the Treatment of Defence Rights: A Mirror of the European Court of Human Rights' Jurisprudence?', *Human Rights Law Review* (2011), pp.91-131.

Nicolson Donald, 'Making Lawyers Moral? Ethical Codes and Moral Character', 25 (4) Legal Studies (2005), pp.601-626. DOI: https://doi.org/10.1111/j.1748-121X.2005.tb00686.x

Nieto-Navia, R *International Peremptory Norms (Jus cogens) and International Humanitarian Law* (2011).

Nikam N. A. *Sense, Understanding and Reason* (Asia Publishing House, 1966).

Noone Gregory P. and Diana C. Noone, 'The Debate over Autonomous Weapons Systems', 47 (1) *Case Western Reserve Journal of International Law* (2015), pp. 25–35.

O'Connell, '*Jus cogens*: International Law's Higher Ethical Norms' in Childress, DE III (ed.), *The Role of Ethics in International Law* (2012).

O'Connor Susan, 'Up in Arms: A Humanitarian Analysis of the Arms Trade Treaty and Its New Zealand Application,' *11 New Zealand Yearbook of International Law* (2013), pp. 73–105.

Ogletree Charles J., Austin Sarat, *The Road to Abolition? The Future of Capital Punishment in the United States* (2009).

Ogunfolu Adedokun and Oludayo Fagbemi, 'I Have a Drone: The Implications of American Drone Policy for Africa and International Humanitarian Law,' 23 (1) *Revue Africaine de Droit International et Comparé* (2015), pp. 106–128.

Oliver Covey, 'The Attorney-General of the Government of Israel v. Eichmann,' 56 (3) *The American Journal of International Law* (1962), pp. 805-845.

Oliver Covey, 'Attorney-General of the Government of Israel v. Adolf Eichmann,' 36 *Israeli Law Review* (1968).

Olson Peter M., 'The Lawfulness of Russian Use of Force in Crimea', 53 (1) *Revue de Droit Militaire et de Droit de la Guerre* (2014), pp. 17–40.

O'Neill Onora, *Constructions of Reason: Explorations of Kant's Practical Philosophy* (Cambridge University Press, 1989).

Orakhelashvili Alexander, 'The Impact of Peremptory Norms on the Interpretation and Application of United Nations Security Council

Resolutions,' 16 (1) *The European Journal of International Law* (2005), pp. 59-88.

Orakhelashvili Alexander, *Peremptory Norms in International Law* (2006).

Oriolo Anna, 'Codes of Conduct for International Prosecutors', *Max Planck Encyclopaedias of International Law*, https://opil.ouplaw.com/view/10.1093/law-mpeipro/e2656.013.2656/law-mpeipro-e2656.

Osiel Mark, *The End of Reciprocity: Terror, Torture, and the Law of War* (Cambridge University Press, 2009).

Pardo Pilar Villanueva Sainz, 'Is International Criminal Law a living discipline?', 3:4 *The International Journal of Human Rights* (1999), pp. 92-100.

Parish Matthew, *International criminal law – Justice or Mirage?* Transconflict (2013). http://www.transconflict.com/2013/05/international-criminal-law-justice-or-mirage-025/.

Parker S. and C. Sampford (eds) *Legal Ethics and Legal Practice* (Oxford: Clarendon Press, 1995).

Paton Herbert James, *Kant's Metaphysic of Experience* (Humanities Press, 1961).

Patrides C. A. and Joseph Anthony Wittreich, *The Apocalypse in English Renaissance Thought and Literature: Patterns, Antecedents, and Repercussions* (Manchester University Press, 1984).

Patterson Dennis (ed.), *Postmodernism and Law* (1994).

Paul Roberts, 'The Priority of Procedure and the Neglect of Evidence and Proof: Facing Facts in International Criminal Law', 13(3) *Journal of International Criminal Justice* (2015), pp. 479-506.

Paulus A., '*Jus cogens* in a Time of Hegemony and Fragmentation', 74 *Nordic Journal of International Law* (2005), pp. 297-334.

Paust, J 'The Reality of *Jus cogens,*' 7 *Connecticut Journal of International Law* (1991), 83.

Pella V. Vespasian, *La criminalité collective des états et le droit pénal de l'avenir* [*The collective criminality of states and the criminal law of the future*], Bucarest: Imprimerie de l'état, (1925).

Pella Vespasian V., *Revue Internationale de Droit Penal* (1928).

Pella Vespasian V., *La Guerre-Crime et les Criminels de Guerre* [*War-Crime and War Criminals*] (Paris, 1946).

Pella Vespasian V., Plan for World Criminal Code, 17 *Revue Internationale de Droit Penal* (1946).

Pella Vespasian V., "Fonctions Pacificatrices du Droit Pénal Supranational et Fin du Système Traditionnel des Traités de Paix" ["Peacemaking Functions of Supranational Criminal Law and End of the Traditional System of Peace Treaties"], 1 *Le Droit Internationale Public* (1947).

Pella Vespesian V., 'Towards an International Criminal Court', 44 *American Journal of International Law* (1950), 57.

Pella Vespasian V., Plan d'un Code Répressif Mondial [Plan of a Global Repressive Code], 6 *Rewe International de Droit Pénal* 1948 (1955).

Pellet A, 'Vive le crime! Remarques sur les degrés de l'illicité en droit international' in United Nations /International Law Commission (ed.), *International Law on the Eve of the Twenty-first Century: Views from the International Law Commission* (United Nations New York 1997), pp. 287–315.

Pellet A, 'Comments in Response to Christine Chinkin and in Defense of *Jus cogens* as the Best Bastion against the Excesses of Fragmentation' 83 *Finnish Yearbook of International Law* (2006).

Penrose Mary Margaret, 'Lest We Fail: The Importance of Enforcement in International Criminal Law: An Essay on the Nature and Immutability of Truth', 15 (2) *American University International Law Review* (1999), pp. 321-394.

Pepper S. L. 'The Lawyer's Amoral Ethical Role: A defence, a Problem, and Some Possibilities, *American Bar Foundation Research Journal*, (1986).

Peterson Jeremy, 'Unpacking Show Trials: Situating the Trial of Saddam Hussein,' 48 *Harvard International Law Journal* (2007).

Plaw Avery and João Franco Reis, 'Learning to Live with Drones: Answering Jeremy Waldron and the Neutralist Critique', 14 (2) *Journal of Military Ethics*, 2015, pp. 128–145.

Posner Eric A., A. O Sykes, *Economic Foundations of International Law* (Cambridge: Harvard University Press, 2013).

Potter R. B., War and Moral Discourse (Richmond, Va., John Knox Press, 1969).

Power Jonathan, *Conundrums of Humanity: The Quest for Global Justice* (2007).

Protector J. Harris, *Islam and International Relati*ons (New York, 1965).

Quadri Kafayat Motilewa, Hunud Abia Kadaouf, Mohammad Naqib Ishan Jan, Mohd. Iqbal AbdulWahab and Haniff Ahama, 'Adquisitorial: The Mixing of Two Legal Systems' 3 (1) *International Journal of Humanities and Management Sciences* (2015), pp.31-36.

Ragazzi M The Concept of International Obligations erga omnes (Clarendon Press Oxford 1997).

Rahmdel Mansour, 'Money Laundering in Iranian Law: Present and Future,' *Journal of Money Laundering Control* (2002).

Rahmdel Mansour, 'The Ne Bis In Idem Rule in Iranian Criminal Law,' *Journal of Financial Crime* (2004).

Rahmdel Mansour, The Role of the Courts in the Reform of Iranian Criminal Law Policy,' *Criminal Law Forum* (2006).

Ramadan Tariq, *Radical Reform: Islamic Ethics and Liberation* (Oxford: Oxford University Press, 2009).

Ramadan Tariq, *The Quest for Meaning, Developing a Philosophy of Pluralism* (London: Penguin, 2010).

Ramsey Clark, *War Crimes – A Report on United States War Crimes against Iraq* (Maisonneuve Press, 1992).

Ramsey Paul, War and the Christian Conscience (Durham, N.C., The Duke University Press, 1961).

Randall Kenneth C., 'Universal Jurisdiction under International Law' 66 *Texas Law Review* (1988).

Rawls John, *A Theory of Justice* (2ed.,1999).

Raz Joseph, *The Morality of Freedom* (1986).

Raz Joseph, *Ethics in the Public Domain: Essays in the Morality of Law and Politics* (Oxford: Oxford University Press, 1994).

Raz Joseph, 'Why the State?' in N. Roughan and A. Halpin (eds) *In Pursuit of a Pluralist Jurisprudence* (CUP 2017).

Rehman Javaid, *International Human Rights Law* (London and New York: Longman Pub Group, 2nd ed., 2010).

Reisman W. Michael, 'Legal Responses to Genocide and Other Massive Violations of Human Rights', 59 *Law and Contemporary Problems* (1996).

Reiss Hans Siegbert, *Kant: Political Writings* (2003).

Report of the Independent Inquiry into the actions of the United Nations during the 1994 genocide in Rwanda, *UN Doc S/1999/1257* (1999) [Rwanda Report].

Rinceanu, Johanna, 'Concept and Systematization of the Criminal Offense in Romania' in U. Sieber, S. Forster, & K. Jarvers (Eds.), *National Criminal Law in a Comparative Legal Context*, Vol. 3(1): Max-Planck-Institute Max-Planck-Institute für Ausländisches und Internationals Strafrecht (2011), pp. 73–85.

Rinceanu Johanna, 'The principle of legality (*Nullum crimen sine lege*) in Romania' in U. Sieber, S. Forster, & K. Jarvers (Eds.), *National Criminal Law in a Comparative Legal Context, vol. 2* (1): Max-Planck-Institute für Ausländisches und Internationals Strafrecht, (2011), pp. 89-10.

Rinceanu Johanna, 'Criminal Liability of Legal Persons in Romania' in *Riccardo Borsari, Responsabilita` da reato deli enti* (Padova: Padova University Press, 2016), pp. 407–418.

Rishimawi Mona., 'A Reality or a Mirage: Judicial Review of Detention,' in Charles Riziki Majinge (ed.), *Rule of Law Through Human Rights and International Criminal Justice: Essays in Honour of Adama Dieng* (Newcastle: Cambridge Scholars publishing, 2015), pp. 507-522.

Robertson Geoffrey, *Crimes Against Humanity – The Struggle for Global Justice* (Penguin Books, 3rd ed., 2006).

Roméo Dallaire's, *Shake Hands with the Devil: The Failure of Humanity in Rwanda* (Carroll & Graf, New York, 2003).

Rosen Allen D., *Kant's Theory of Justice* (Ithaca, London: Cornel University Press, 1996).

Rosenstock R., 'An International Criminal Responsibility of States?', in United Nations/International Law Commission (ed.), *International*

Law on the Eve of the Twenty-First Century: Views from the International Law Commission (United Nations New York, 1997), pp. 265–85.

Ruth Mackenzie & Philippe Sands, 'International Courts and Tribunals and the Independence of the International Judge', 44 *Harvard International Law Journal* (2003), pp.271-285.

Ruys Tom, 'Of Arms, Funding and Non-Lethal Assistance: Issues Surrounding Third-State Intervention in the Syrian Civil War,' 13 (1) *Chinese Journal of International Law* (2014), pp. 13–53.

Ryngaert Cedric, *Jurisdiction in International Law* (Oxford: Oxford University Press, 2009), PP. 42-84.

Ryngaert Cedtric, 'Territorial Jurisdiction Over Cross-frontier Offences: Revisiting a Classic Problem of International Criminal Law' 9 *International Criminal Law Review* 9 (2009), pp. 187–209.

Sacirbey Muhamed, *International Criminal Tribunal Born as Bastard?' The World Post*, available (https://www.huffingtonpost.com/ambassador-muhamed-sacirbey/international-criminal-tribunals_b_3344169.html.

Sadat Nadya Leila, Custom, 'Codification and Some Thoughts about the Relationship between the Two: Article 10 of the ICC Statute,' 49 *DePaul Law Review* (2000).

Sadat Nadya Leila and S. Richard, 'The New International Criminal Court: An Uneasy Revolution,' 88 *Georgetown Law Journal* 581 (2000).

Sadat Leila Nadya, 'Competing and Overlapping Jurisdictions', Bassiouni, ed., *International Criminal* Law (2008).

Sahovic Milan and William W. Bishop., 'The Authority of the State: Its Range with Respect to Persons and Places' in Max Sorensen, *Manual of Public International Law* (London : Macmillan, 1968), pp. 311-380.

Salter William Mackintire, *Anarchy or Government? An Inquiry in Fundamental Politics* (1895).

Salter William Mackintire, *Ethical Religion* (1889).

Salter William Mackintire, *The Conflict of the Catholic Church with the French Republic* (1907).

Saner Hans, *Kant's Political Thought* (University of Chicago Press, 1973).

Sassoli, 'State Responsibility for Violations of Humanitarian Law', 84 *IRCR* (2002).

Saul, M 'Identifying *Jus cogens* Norms: The Interaction of Scholars and International Judges,' *Asian Journal of International Law* (2014) (forthcoming).

Schabas William A., Justice, 'Democracy and Impunity in Post Genocide Rwanda: Searching for Solutions to Impossible Problems,' 7 *Criminal Law Forum* (1996).

Schabas William A., *The Abolition of the Death Penalty in International Law* (2002 and 2005).

Schabas William A., *The UN International Criminal Tribunals: The Former Yugoslavia, Rwanda and Sierra Leone* (Cambridge: Cambridge University Press, 2006).

Schabas William A., *Genocide in International Law: The Crimes of Crimes* (Cambridge University Press, 2000 and 2009).

Schabas William A., *An Introduction to the International Criminal Court* (Cambridge University Press, 2011).

Schachter Oscar, *International Law in Theory and Practice* (1991).

Schwarzenberger Georg, 'The Problem of an International Criminal Law,' 5 *Current Legal Problems* (1950).

Schwarzenberger G., *International Jus cogens*?, 43 Tax. L. Rev (1965).

Scott L Cummings, 'Introduction: What Good are Lawyers?' in Scott L. Cummings (ed.), *Paradox of Professionalism Lawyers and the Possibility of Justice* (2011).

Sevrine Knuche, 'State Immunity and the Promise of *Jus cogens*', *Northwestern Journal of International Human Rights (*2011), Vol. 9, No. 2, pp. 149-183.

Shaffer Thomas L., 'The Legal Ethics of Radical Individualism' 65 *Texas Law Review* (1997).

Shelton, D. 'Normative Hierarchy of International Law' 80 *American Journal of International Law* (1986).

Shytov Alexander Nikolaevich, Conscience and Love in Making Judicial Decisions (2001), p.xiv.

Sieber U., S. Forster, & K. Jarvers (Eds.), *National Criminal Law in a Comparative Legal Context*, Vol. 3(1): Max-Planck-Institute Max-Planck-Institute für Ausländisches und Internationals Strafrecht (2011).

Simma Bruno & Philip Alston, 'The Sources of Human Rights Law: Custom, *Jus cogens*, and General Principles' 90 *Australia Yearbook of International Law* (1992).

Simon William H., *The Practice of Justice: A Theory of Lawyers' Ethics* (1998).

Sinclair I., *The Vienna Convention on the Law of Treaties* (1986).

Sliedregt Elies van, Pluralism in International Criminal Law, 25 *Leiden Journal of International Law* (2012).

Sliedregt Elies van & Sergey Vasiliev eds., *Pluralism International Criminal Law* 3 (Oxford, 2014);

Smith Norman Kemp, '*Commentary to Kant's 'Critique of Pure Reason''* (Humanities Press, 1962).

Smith Alic Halford, *Kantian Studies* (Greenwood Press, 1974).

Smith T. S., *Lecture Delivered over the Remains of Jeremy Bentham, Esq., in the Webb-Street School of Anatomy & Medicine, on the 9th June, 1832* (London: Effingham Wilson, 1832).

Smith Beverley, G. (author), Elizabeth M.A. Turgeon (editor), *Professional Conduct for Lawyers and Judges* (1998).

Sowilet A., *The Problem of the Creation of a Permanent International Criminal Court* (1951).

Spiermann, 'Humanitarian Intervention as a Necessity and the Threat or Use of *Jus cogens*' 71 *Nordic Journal of International Law* (2002), 523.

Spooner Lysander , *Natural Law; or the Science of Justice: A Treatise on Natural Law, Natural Justice, Natural Rights, Natural Liberty, and Natural Society; showing that all Legislation whatsoever is an Absurdity, a Usurpation, and a Crime. Part First*. [1882], available at http://oll.libertyfund.org/titles/spooner-natural-law-or-the-science-of-justice-1882.

Sriram C., 'Wrong-sizing International Justice? The Hybrid Tribunal in Sierra Leone', 29 (3) *Fordham International Law Journal* (2006), pp.472-506.

Stahn Carsten (ed.), *The Law and Practice of the International Criminal Court* (Oxford University Press, 2015).

Stern Robert, *Understanding Moral Obligation: Kant, Hegel, Kierkegaard* (Cambridge, Cambridge University Press, 2012).

Stigall Dan E., 'The French military Intervention in Mali, Counter-Terrorism, and the Law of Armed Conflict,' 223 (1) *Military Law Review* (2015), pp. 1–40.

Strawson P. F., *The Bounds of Sense: An Essay on Kant's 'Critique of Pure Reason'* (Methuen, 1966).

Sugarman David, ed., *Legality, Ideology and the State* (1985).

Suy, E 'Article 53: Treaties Conflicting with a Peremptory Norm of General International Law ('*jus cogens*')' in Corten, O and Klein, P (Eds.) *The Vienna Convention on the Law of Treaties: A Commentary Volume II* (2011).

Talmon S., 'The Duty Not to 'Recognize as Lawful' a Situation Created by the Illegal Use of Force or Other Serious Breaches of a *Jus cogens* Obligation: An Obligation without Real Substance?', in C Tomuschat and J. M. Thouvenin (eds.), *The Fundamental Rules of the International Legal Order* (2005).

Thirlway H. W. A., *International Customary Law and Codification* (1972), pp. 70-94.

Thornberry Patrick, *International Law and the Rights of Minorities* (Oxford, 1991), pp. 57–109.

Thouvenin M. (eds.), *The Fundamental Rules of the International Legal Order* (2005).

Tomoko Yamashita 'Do *Jus cogens* Norms Invalidate State Immunity? International Restorative Justice and Japanese War Compensation Cases' Chinese (Taiwan) 31 *Yearbook of International Law and Affairs* (2013), pp. 160-194.

Tomuschat, C and Thouveinin, JM (eds.) *The Fundamental Rules of the International Legal Order: Jus cogens and Obligations* Erga Omnes (2006).

Tunkin G., "Soviet Theory of Sources of International Law", in *Volkerrecht und Rechtsphilosophet: Internationale Festchrift for Stefan Verosta* (1980).

Turner Jenia Iontcheva, Nationalizing International Criminal Law, 41 *Stanford Journal of International Law* (2005), pp. 1-52.

Tyler Tom R., 'Understanding the Force of Law', 51 *Tulsa Law Review* (2016), pp.507-519.

Van Schaack Beth, Ronald C. Slye, *International Criminal Law: The Essentials* (2008).

Van Schaack Beth, Ronald C. Slye, *International criminal law: intersections and contradictions* (2020).

Vanhullebusch Matthias, 'The Arab League and Military Operations: Prospects and Challenges in Syria', 22 (2) *International Peacekeeping* (2015), pp.151–168.

Verdross, A 'Forbidden Treaties in International Law: Comments on Professor Garner's Report on 'The Law of Treaties" 31 *American Journal of International Law* (1937), 571.

Verdross, A '*Jus Dispositivum* and *Jus cogens* in International Law' 60 *American Journal of International Law* (1966).

Vest Hans, 'A Structure-Based Concept of Genocidal *Intent'*, *Journal of International Criminal Justice* (2007), pp.781-797.

Vidmar, J 'Rethinking *Jus cogens* after Germany v. Italy: Back to Article 53?' 60 *Netherlands International Law Review* (2013).

Virally Michel, 'The Sources of International Law,' in M. Sorenson, *Manual of Public International Law* (2nd ed., 1968).

Virally, M 'Réflexions sur le *Jus cogens*' ['Reflections on *Jus cogens*'] 12 *Annuaire Français de Droit International* (1966), 5.

Vischer K. Robert, *Martin Luther King Jr. and the Morality of Legal Practice: Lessons in Love and Justice* (2014).

Vleeschauwer H. J., *The Development of Kantian Thought* (Nelson, 1962).

Vyver John D. van der, 'Prosecution and Punishment of the Crime of Genocide', 25 *Fordham International Law Journal* (1999), p.286.

Vyver Johan D. Van der, 'The International Criminal Court and the Concept of *Mens rea* in International Criminal Law,' 12 *U. Miami Int'l& Comp. L. Rev.* 57 (2005), pp.57-149, at 92. Available online at: http://repository.law.miami.edu/umiclr/vol12/iss1/3.

Waldock H., 'General Course on Public International Law,' 106 *Recueil Des Course* (1962), pp. 39-103.

Ward Keith, *The Development of Kant's View of Ethics* (Humanities Press, 1972).

Watson John, *The Philosophy of Kant Explained* (Garland, 1976).

Weatherhall Thomas, *Jus cogens International Law and Social Contract* (2015).

Weil, P 'Towards Relative Normativity in International Law' 77 *American Journal of International Law* (1983).

Weinrib Ernest J., 'Law as a Kantian Idea of Reason', 87 *Columbia Law Review* (1987), pp. 472-508.

Weinstein Jack B., Ian Dewsbury, 'Comment on the meaning of 'proof beyond a reasonable doubt' ', 5 (2) *Law, Probability and Risk* (2006), pp.167–173.

Weisburd M, 'The Emptiness of the Concept of *Jus cogens*, As Illustrated by the War in Bosnia-Herzegovina', 17 *Michigan Journal of International Law* (1995-1996), pp. 1-51.

Weiss T., *Military-Civilian Interactions: Humanitarian Crises and the Responsibility to Protect* (2nd ed., Rowman & Littlefield Publishers Inc, Lanham (MD), 2005).

Weller Marc, *Iraq and the Use of Force in International Law* (Oxford: Oxford University Press, 2010).

Wet De, 'The Prohibition of Torture as an International Norm of *jus cogens* and Its Implications for National and Customary Law,' 15 *European Journal of International Law* (2004).

Whiteman, MM '*Jus cogens* in International Law: With a Projected List' 7 *Georgia Journal of International and Comparative Law* (1977), p. 609.

Wigmore John Henry, *The Principles of Judicial Proof as given by Logic, Psychology, and General Experience, and Illustrated in Judicial Trials* (Chicago: Little Brown & Co., 1913).

Williamson Myra, *Terrorism, War and International Law, The Legality of the Use of Force Against Afghanistan in 2001* (London: Ashgate Publishing, 2009).

Wistrich Andrew J, Jeffrey J. Rachlinski & Chris Guthrie, 'Heart Versus Head: Do Judges Follow the Law or Follow Their Feelings?', 93 *Texas Law Review* (2015).

Wladyslaw Czaplinski, 'Concepts of Jus cogens and Obligations Erga Omnes in International Law in the Light of Recent Developments', 23 *Polish Yearbook of International Law* (1997–1998).

Wolff Christian, *Ius naturae et ius gentium [The law of nature and the law of nations]* (Halle, 1740–46). Available at http://oll.libertyfund.org/titles/vattel-the-law-of-nations-lf-ed.

Wolff R. P. (ed.), *Kant* (Doubleday, 1967).

Wood Allen W., *Kant's Moral Religion* (1970).

Wood Allen, *Kant's Ethical Thought* (Cambridge University Press, 1999).

Wood David, *Judicial Ethics: A Discussion Paper, Australian Institute of Judicial Administration* (1996).

Wright Quincy, 'Proposal for an International Criminal Court' 46 (1), *American Journal of International Law* (1952), pp. 60-72.

Wright Quincy, 'The Scope of International Criminal Law: A Conceptual Framework,' 15 *Virginia Journal of International Law* (1975).

Wägenbaur B., *Court of the European Union* (Hart, 2013).

Yvonne McDermott, 'Strengthening the Evaluation of Evidence in International Criminal Trials' 17(4) *International Criminal Law Review* (2017), pp. 682-702.

Zaman R., 'Playing the Ace? Jus cogens Crimes and Functional Immunity in National Courts,' 17 *Australian International Law Journal* (2010), 53.

Zammito Johan, *The Genesis of Kant's Critique of Judgment* (University of Chicago Press, 1992).

Zarembka Paul, *The Hidden History of 9-11-2001* (New York: Seven Stories Press, 2008).

INDEX

A

B

C

D

E

F

G

H

I

J

N

O

P

R

S

T

U

V

W

Y

Water Resource Planning, Development and Management

nova
science publishers
www.novapublishers.com

Water Resource Planning, Development and Management

Technical Systems of Protection of Hydro Resources, Management and Monitoring of Processes
David Gurgenidze, PhD
2024. ISBN: 979-8-89113-471-3 (Hardcover)
2024.ISBN: 979-8-89113-519-2 (eBook)

Water Supply and Drainage for Buildings
Syed Azizul Haq
2023. ISBN: 979-8-88697-607-6 (Hardcover)
2023. ISBN: 979-8-88697-761-5 (eBook)

Water Purification: Processes, Applications and Health Effects
Paul LeBlanc (Editor)
2022. ISBN: 978-1-68507-622-1 (Hardcover)
2022. ISBN: 978-1-68507-633-7 (eBook)

Solar Water Heating: Fundamentals and Applications
Khalil Kassmi (Editor)
2021. ISBN: 978-1-53619-320-6 (Hardcover)
2021. ISBN: 978-1-53619-356-5 (eBook)

More information about this series can be found at https://novapublishers.com/product-category/series/water-resource-planning-development-and-management/

David Gurgenidze

Technical Systems to Protect Water Resources

Process Management and Monitoring

nova
science publishers
www.novapublishers.com

DOI: https://doi.org/10.52305/MUAJ0541

Library of Congress Cataloging-in-Publication Data

ISBN: 979-8-89113-471-3

Published by Nova Science Publishers, Inc. † New York

Contents

List of Figures

List of Tables

Abstract

The monograph highlights the issues of monitoring and management of the conditions necessary for the proper operation of modern systems of engineering protection of water resources.

Ways to improve the economic efficiency of the environmental programs and integrated approaches to the creation of all-encompassing policies for the use of natural resources are discussed.

A new model describing technogenic disasters has been created to determine the trajectory of the flow of oil and oil products spilled in the rivers and their penetration into the soil. New highly effective methods to protect the hydraulic resources and environment against ecological damage and their economic evaluation are proposed.

Innovative hydrotechnical anti-mudflow structures designed to protect the ski jump structures are presented. Innovations are achieved by reducing the force of dynamic impact on them, simplifying existing structures and reducing the costs. Emphasis is placed on the new methodology of technical and economic calculation of innovative hydraulic structures and their economic effect.

The monograph addresses the pollution of water resources with the biogenic elements that affect the condition of water bodies, as well as nitrogen and phosphorus compounds. Information about the quality of wastewater arriving at treatment plants, as well as the concentration of biogenic elements in the treated wastewater is given.

The methods to remove biogenic elements are divided into two main groups: physical-chemical and biological. A detailed description of the processes occurring in wastewaters is given for the biological methods. The monograph describes the reliable and sustainable methods actively used today.

Keywords: water resources, environmental damage, wastewater, eutrophication of water resources, environmental protection structure, economic efficiency, functional-value analysis, sustainable management of water resources

Acknowledgment

List of Reviewers

Lech Dzienis, Doctor of Technical Sciences, Professor of Bialystok Technical University

Shalva Gagoshidze, Doctor of Technical Sciences, Professor Emeritus

Introduction

The protection of areas and population from natural and technogenic disasters is one of the many challenges of the twenty-first century needing particular attention. Responsible for the rise in the number, size, and frequency of natural disasters and catastrophic events on Earth is the current global natural and technogenic processes.

Economic, social and several other negative effects of the society's intellectual development and the rapid development and introduction of new technologies without first considering their impact on the environment often need the efforts by the state to eliminate.

Efficient population and environment protection measures are implemented by employing engineering systems and mechanisms, which are worthwhile among the engineering safety measures.

The disruption process of the natural balance in the Earth's hydrosphere is alarming; the natural and artificial water reservoirs, as well as ground and surface waters have all been contaminated; water levels have been drastically reduced; and numerous water sources have disappeared. Maintaining the balance of the environment is a goal that many international institutions have set, along with implementing the necessary corrective and mitigating actions to address the effects of anthropogenic, technological, and natural factors.

The sustainable management and development of water resources and sanitary systems is a global issue now rather than a country-specific one, but each country still has a crucial role to play.

The UN General Assembly Resolution 64/292 adopted in 2010 recognizing "the right to safe and clean drinking water and sanitation as a human right that is essential for the full enjoyment of life and all human rights" is historical indeed.

The data of various international organizations are alarming:

- About 90% of all natural disasters are water-related (UNESCO, 2017);

- Worldwide, over 80% of all wastewaters returns to the environment without being treated (WWAP, 2017);
- Some 2.2 billion people around the world do not have safely managed drinking water (WHO/UNICEF, 2019);
- More than half of the world population amounting to about 4.52 billion people do not have access to safe sanitary-hygienic services (WHO/UNICEF, 2019);
- Every year, 297 000 children under 5 years die due to diarrhea linked to inadequate wash, poor sanitation and contaminated water (WHO/UNICEF, 2019);
- Over two billion people live in countries experiencing high water stress (UN, 2019);
- Already four out of ten people experience water deficit (WHO);
- Almost two billion people depend on health care facilities without basic water services (WHO/UNICEF, 2020);
- About two-thirds of the world's transboundary rivers do not have a cooperative management framework (SIWI);
- Agriculture accounts for 70 percent of global freshwater (FAO).

Sources of pollution arising during accidents of oil and oil-product pipelines, resulting in the transported product getting into the aquatic environment, are identified as an independent group and studied. It is practically impossible to avoid such events, despite the contemporary requirements for reliability of oil and oil product pipelines. Moreover, it is very difficult to predict expected accidents.

Development of the power industry is related to the extensive use of high-pressure and large-diameter oil pipelines. The constant increase in production scales and processing of hydrocarbon raw materials lead to an increased specific capacity and need the use of technological and trunk pipelines of fire-explosive products. This, in turn, leads to an increase in the scale, number and severity of fires, strong emergency explosions and emergency complications in case of accidents. Damage from accidents and incidents on oil pipelines can be estimated from different points of view: ecological, economic, and even social, and each of these views in itself is complex. Accidents and leaks from oil pipelines may bring both economic and environmental damage to the country. If economic damage can be eliminated within a short period of time, restoration of the initial environment in the areas of accidents and pipeline failures sometimes takes many years. Oil spills from main oil pipelines have a significant impact on the environment. When a spill is near water resources, it can end in an ecological catastrophe. It is usually much more difficult to eliminate the consequences of an accident than to prevent it. Local prevention of oil and oil products spills involves a complex set of objectives, methods and technical means. Regardless of the type of an emergency oil and oil products spill, the first measures to eliminate it must be against spill propagations to form new hotbeds of pollution.

The dynamics of the earth's population migration, mostly to big cities, resulting in the abandonment of villages and settlements are an irreversible process today. Urbanization is one of the most important processes of global change, and related issues of land use are becoming increasingly important. Active exploitation of natural resources, growth of socio-demographic figures, and deterioration of public health due to emerging diseases contribute to the change of the environment and, consequently, to the pollution of water resources.

Pollution of the environment with wastewaters has reached catastrophic scales. Most water treatment facilities fall short of current standards, and organic pollutants, particularly biogenic elements (nitrogen, phosphorus), frequently enter natural water bodies and contribute to eutrophication. Experts place a high priority on the creation of novel techniques and the enhancement of currently used ones for the removal of biogenic elements from wastewater.

Man's negative influence on the environment does not manifest itself immediately, but its "silent and concealed" has the potential to unleash natural disasters and human catastrophes. Rehabilitating damaged agricultural lands, deteriorated vegetation cover, and damaged natural and man-made water basins and reservoirs is a lengthy and expensive process. Scientists, practitioners, and international environmental organizations all agree that prevention is the best course of action. The engineering structures to protect water systems are one of the components of engineering protection of the regions.

Innovative hydrotechnical structures that protect the environment are suggested for protecting the hydrosystems. Their scientific-technical novelty is proved by relevant patent licenses.

As noted in the monograph, the purpose of the novel open-end anti-mudflow springboard-type innovative structures is to reduce the impact of flows, especially those with catastrophic parameters, as well as to simplify the design and reduce the cost of the structures.

The advantages of the new structures over the existing ones are as follows: a) reliability and durability; b) efficient stabilization of mountain rivers; and

c) great economic effect. These structures are made of reinforced concrete and second-hand materials (written-off metal rails, depreciated metal cables, etc.) making 50÷80% of the total construction materials.

To determine the efficiency of innovative hydrotechnical structures, the methodology to assess the technical-economic effectiveness of the structures is given and the economic effect of each structure is assessed. The ways to improve the economic effect of implementation of environmental programs and integrated approached to develop complex plans while exploiting natural resources are also described.

Chapter 1

Some Issues of Wastewater and Water Reservoir Eutrophication

Protection of the environment from pollution and depletion is one of the most pressing global issues. Man's economic activities over the last few decades have had a significant impact on the planet's hydrosphere. Anthropogenic pollution of continental waters has reached global scales, disrupting the natural regimes of the world's largest lakes and rivers. The situation was exacerbated by the fact that humans were forced to build hydrotechnical systems (water reservoirs, irrigation channels, and water supply systems to transport water over long distances) in order to increase fertile lands, what, among other things, has resulted in the pollution of fresh waters with wastewaters. Virtually, there are almost no natural fresh water sources not polluted by humans. Water resources in many countries are unfit for agricultural, cultural, or household use due to sanitary and hygienic concerns.

The majority of existing water treatment plants fail to meet modern requirements, and organic pollutants, particularly biogenic elements (nitrogen and phosphorus), frequently enter natural water bodies. In recent years, scientists of many countries have paid close attention to the problem of purifying wastewaters from organic pollutants and biogenic elements. Nowadays, much emphasis is placed on the development of new methodologies and the enhancement of the existing ones to purify wastewaters from biogenic elements. The issue of Treatment from biogenic elements is the first step toward wastewater improvement.

One of the most pressing issues in the modern world is the protection of the environment, particularly water resources, from pollution and depletion.

Humans have had a significant impact on the planet's hydrosphere balance in recent decades. Anthropogenic pollution of continental waters has reached a global scale, disrupting the world's natural water regime. It was exacerbated by urbanization and wastewater pollution of fresh waters. This condition compelled humans to construct hydrotechnical structures (water reservoirs, irrigation channels, and water transfer systems) in order to increase the area of fertile lands at the expense of irrigating arid areas.

1.1. Biogenic Elements in Wastewaters and Eutrophication of Water Reservoirs

Biogenic is a component of organisms that is constantly performing certain biological functions. The following are some of the most important biogenic elements: oxygen, carbon dioxide, phosphor, sulfur, calcium, sodium, and chlorine. All of these elements play an important role in biochemical processes that occur all around us, including water reservoirs [1-5].

In the practice of Treatment of wastewaters, two basic biogenic elements are highlighted: nitrogen (*N*) and phosphorus (*P*). Biogenic substances (nitrogen and phosphorus) are major components of wastewaters that are constantly present in the composition of communal or household drinking water, close to the former with its composition. Nitrogen can be found in wastewater in several forms, including ammonium (NH_4^-), nitrates (NO_2^-), nitrites (NO_3^-), and organic nitrogen (in the composition of organic compounds). In drinking water, phosphorus can be found in organic compounds (organic phosphor), polyphosphates (P_2O_5) and orthophosphates (PO_4) [6-8].

The present world creates extremely unstable situations, such as the generation of excess wastes and the production of biodegradable materials, the assimilation and dissimilation of which by natural processes is rather complicated. Unstable conditions have become increasingly evident in densely populated and industrially developed areas of the continents, where water bodies are exposed to various types of severe pollution, including eutrophication [9, 10].

As is well known, biogenic elements found in water reservoirs promote the growth of algae, resulting in eutrophication. Eutrophication can be caused by both natural aging of water reservoirs and anthropogenic impact. To better grasp the issue of eutrophication, two types of algae life must be distinguished: benthic and phytoplanktonic. Benthic plants grow by attaching to or rooting in the bed of a water reservoir and can survive in water with scarce biogenic elements because they take the elements required for life, such as nitrogen and phosphor, from the sediments on the bed, but for photosynthesis, sufficient sun rays must penetrate through the water layer. The depth at which photosynthesis occurs is known as the "eutrophication zone," and it can reach

30 meters in clear water but may be reduced to 2.5 cm if the water is turbid [1, 8, 10].

Many algae species are classified as phytoplanktons: individual cells, their groups or threads, floating near or directly on the water surface. Turbid water has little effect on their development, and an abundance of plankton is the primary cause of water turbidity. Because phytoplankton has no contact with bed, it must obtain the biogenic elements required for viability from the water.

As a result, the nutrient concentration in water influences the ratio of plankton to benthic plants. Benthic plants not only provide food and shelter to aquatic life, but they also store high concentrations of water dissolved oxygen at depth, because the oxygen produced during photosynthesis is dissolved directly in the water [2, 3, 11].

In terms of erosion and leaching, a water reservoir gradually fills with sediments and becomes rich in biogenic elements, promoting the growth of planktons. As a result, water becomes turbid, resulting in the extinction of benthic plants, the impossibility of photosynthesis, and a decrease in the concentration of water dissolved oxygen. Consequently, conditions for eutrophication of water reservoirs develop [1, 12].

Eutropohication refers to an increase in the primary production level of water reservoirs, primarily as a result of increased nitrogen and phosphor concentrations. Increase of primary production to certain levels contributes to the creation of abundant food base for fish and other hydrobionts resulting in an increase in their population. Water quality deteriorates due to "discoloration," reduced transparency, and low oxygen content. As a result, the water reservoir suffers from severe eutrophication, which causes the extinction of fish and other hydrobionts due to a lack of oxygen [6, 7].

Anthropogenic eutrophication is caused by pollution of wastewater and floodwaters with biogenic elements; it differs from natural processes by high pace. When biogenic elements enter the water, plankton starts to grow quickly leading to water "blooming". Water "blooming" refers to the extensive growth of algae, as a result of which microscopic organisms become visible and give different colors to water; for example, blue-green algae (typical of moderate or warm climates) produce toxic substances. In this case, the water's quality deteriorates, the odor and taste become unpleasant, and the water becomes unfit for drinking. In the event of mass death of microsilt or macrovegetation, water quality deteriorates even further, oxygen content in water decreases, and an unpleasant odor appears. This phenomenon (change in water quality caused by disruption in the natural progression of biological processes) is known as "secondary (biological) pollution" [13, 14].

As a result of eutrophication and pollution of water reservoirs, their biological parameters change significantly; diversity of species increase; the number and biomass of non-photosynthesis microorganisms (bacteria, fungi) increase, and the number of species of algae and higher-class water plants decrease as their number and biomass increase. Metals, oil products and other compounds hazardous for human health accumulate in the cells of hydrobionts. The fauna of water reservoirs changes both qualitatively and quantitatively; many species of living organisms die; and the number and biomass of fish species, including valuable fish species, decrease. As a result of rapid propagation of parasitic organisms and pathogenic microflora, the sanitary and epidemiologic situation deteriorates. In such an environment, various diseases of hydrobionts, birds, and water animals proliferate. During the "blooming" period, the concentration of algae reaches 1-5 million cells per milliliter of water or 1000-5000 billion cells per cubic meter of water, giving the water a greenish color [14, 15].

The main causes of water "blooming" are a dramatic decrease in the speed of a water current, mixing, and the formation of stagnant zones. The intensity of algae development is greatly influenced by water temperature. Excessive nutrient saturation of water reservoirs (nitrogen, phosphorus, and organic compounds) is the third cause of algae growth intensification. Blue-green algae are extremely viable; they are the first to respond to any ecological disaster; they change their growth pattern and adapt to any conditions. Water "blooms" as a result of the combination of all of the aforementioned causes. This process repeats year after year, with varying intensity and scale, depending on the conditions established in the water reservoir. Climatic factors (lighting, pressure, temperature), hydrodynamic properties of water bodies, and the level of nutrient provision to algae all play a regulatory role [2, 9, 11, 16].

The deterioration of water's basic chemical parameters as it "blooms" is related to intravital growth of algae and decay of organic matter generated. Around 200 chemical compounds, including toxins, carcinogens, and allergens, were discovered and studied in "blooming" water. Acetone, butyric acid, and butyric spirit accumulate in algae accumulation areas as a result of processes that occur there. Water contains phenols (their concentration may exceed the acceptable sanitary norm by ten times), indole-containing components, mercaptans, and amines, and the pH level may drop to 4-5 or lower. As a result of the algae film that forms on the water surface, extensive water warming occurs (exceeding normal levels by 6-8°C), increasing evaporation and facilitating the transfer of volatile metabolites in air, thus polluting the atmosphere [14, 15].

A high concentration of organic compounds creates an unfavorable sanitary and epidemiological situation by providing a fertile environment for the development and preservation of pathogenic microflora, such as vibrio cholera. A hazardous situation develops when toxic algae forms proliferate in large numbers. Thus, the presence of algae in large numbers in a water reservoir has a wide range of negative consequences, including the transformation of water from a valuable and beneficial natural product into a liquid mass dangerous to all living organisms. Particularly serious consequences occur when biological pollution is combined with chemical and thermal pollution [1, 14, 17].

The chemical composition of water determines the qualitative and quantitative content of biocenosis and nutritional peculiarities (trophicity) in water reservoirs; for example, water from oligotrophic water reservoirs is low in mineral nitrogen and, especially, phosphor, which may appear only as a trace. Because of the low density of biocenosis, there is a lot of oxygen in the water and very little CO_2. As a result, iron compounds may not dissolve. The water is clear and has a light blue or green color. This type of water reservoir includes deep lakes with sandy shores. Atmospheric oxygen dissolves too slowly in water. Thus, benthic plants not only provide food and shelter to water reservoir habitants, but also maintain the required concentration of water dissolved oxygen in the depth and emit oxygen directly into water, as a result of which in such nutrient-poor water reservoirs, a rich, diverse biocenosis of fish and mollusks, as well as benthic plants, which the former feed on, may exist [3, 7, 18].

Nitrogen and phosphorus are abundant in eutrophic water reservoirs. During the stagnation phase, an abundance of organisms causes a scarcity of oxygen in deep water layers. The water is opaque and changes color from greenish to dark brown. In the event of erosion and leaching, the water reservoir gradually fills with sediments and becomes rich in biogens, the accumulation of which contributes to the development of phytoplankton, resulting in water turbidity and the shadowing of benthic plants. The oxygen produced by plankton during photosynthesis oversaturates the upper layers of water and evaporates. In bright sunlight, it is easy to see oxygen bubbles emerging from thread-shaped algae accumulation areas [2, 7, 9, 11, 18].

Phytoplankton has a very short life cycle. Its rapid reproduction is balanced by a high death rate, resulting in the accumulation of detritus. Dead phytoplankton is transferred to a deep zone, where decomposers use it as food; the decomposers also consume oxygen lowering its concentration in the water. When the dissolved oxygen in water is completely depleted, decomposing bacteria maintain viability through anaerobic fermentation for as long as there is detritus available as food. Thus, the amount of water dissolved oxygen on the water surface may be very high due to plankton photosynthesis, whereas its reserves in the deep layers of water may be very low due to intense oxygen use by decomposers. The digested biogenic elements are carried to the bottom by phytoplankton "rain," where they are released again simultaneously with the detritus decay process. Ascending convectional currents return biogenic elements to the water surface, and the processes described above are repeated many times [1, 3, 4, 10, 19].

According to the time geological scale, water reservoirs are continuously enriched with biogenic elements and filled with sediments from land. Silt and detritus accumulate in a water reservoir over many centuries, gradually filling its deep bed.

Natural aging of water reservoirs is also eutrophication and integral part of a natural process known as succession. A water reservoir can naturally change and transform from oligotrophic to eutrophic over millennia, or in other words, age. Anthropogenic activities, on the other hand, may produce similar results even after several decades. As a result, they refer to anthropogenic eutrophication as opposed to natural eutrophication. Eutrophication is a good example of how not all modern negative issues are related to industrial-toxic waste, as the case discussed here is a frequent cause of the occurrence of harmless substances, such as soil particles and nutrients, in natural ecosystems, i.e., any change in any ecological factor may disrupt the balance in the ecosystem.

1.2. Sources of Occurrence of Biogenic Elements in Water Bodies

The sources of nitrogen and phosphor occurrence in water bodies must be identified in order to take anti-eutrophication measures or control the general state of water reservoirs. The following are the general causes of occurrence of biogenic elements in water reservoirs:

- Land cultivation by humans using extensive agrichemical methods (use of mineral fertilizers);
- Formation of large water reservoirs with insufficient confluents;
- New streams of wastewaters, rich in nitrogen and phosphor;
- Development of industrial sectors (production of mineral fertilizers, household chemicals), resulting in an increase in industrial wastewaters rich in biogenic elements; wastewaters originating from the operation of food processing plants.
- Rainstorm water currents with low biogenic element concentrations (considering that during the rain, storm waters enter the water reservoirs for a short time and there are no strict regulations for their Treatment from biogenic elements) [1, 10, 17, 19].

Occurrence of pollutants in water reservoirs can be reduced by artificial limitation of biogenic elements in wastewaters or extensive Treatment of these waters from these substances.

As mentioned above, the basic biogenic elements having an impact on water reservoirs are nitrogen and phosphorus compounds. Consequently, the main sphere of interest is the identification of causes of occurrence of these same elements in water reservoirs.

The main source of phosphor ions occurring in water reservoirs is household wastewaters. Phosphates are an integral part of the common pollutants of household wastewaters (30-50% of phosphor is contained in household wastewaters). Another significant pollutant source is the widespread use (50-70%) of synthetic detergents containing polyphosphates.

Organic compounds of ortho- and polyphosphates are the most common form of phosphor in wastewaters, with hydrolysis occurring even before orthophosphate, where phosphor content is 70-90%. The remainder of phosphor is found in organic substances.

Most phosphor compounds in wastewaters are soluble in water, with only a minor portion given in the form of simple sediment. The biological Treatment uses biological processes to clear wastewaters of phosphor; nevertheless, its amount is much higher than permissible in the case of Treatment of wastewaters using biochemical processes. Consequently, only approximately 20-30% of phosphor is removed during the primary and secondary wastewater treatment, and phosphor concentration in treated wastewater significantly exceeds the legally permissible levels. Only few municipal wastewater treatment plants have technologies for complete phosphate removal; thus, the development of new technologies is required for the Treatment of agricultural and household waters from biogenic elements [20-22].

The primary sources of ammonia ions in water reservoirs are animal farms, household, agricultural-and-household food and wastewaters from chemical industry. An increase of ammonia nitrogen concentration is evidence of the water having been polluted recently. A limited indicator of harmfulness of such pollution is its toxicity.

Internal processes in water reservoirs, such as the action of nitrifying bacteria; atmospheric precipitation absorbing nitrogen oxides formed as a result of electric discharge in the atmosphere; and industrial, agricultural, and household wastewaters, particularly after biological treatment, all contribute to the natural presence of nitrate ions in water. A rise in nitrogen nitrates is a common indicator of previous pollution. The concentration of nitrate ions in surface waters varies significantly between seasons: it is lowest during the vegetation period, rises in autumn, and peaks in winter.

Nitrites are an intermediate state in the chain of oxidation bacterial processes to ammonia nitrates (nitrification in anaerobic conditions) and, vice versa, reduction of nitrates to nitrogen and ammonium (denitrification in terms of oxygen deficiency). An increase in nitrogen concentration is a sign of recent pollution. Seasonal variations in nitrate content are seen by their absence in winter and emergence in spring. By the end of summer, nitrate concentrations are at their peak, and decrease in fall. Looking at the occurrence of biogenic substances in water reservoirs in general, as well as the state of water reservoirs and the quality of wastewater treatment, we can conclude that, despite efforts, the main source of occurrence of biogenic substances in water reservoirs is insufficient Treatment of wastewater.

The concentration of pollutants in the wastewaters to be treated determines the quality of wastewater treatment. Biogenic elements are known to be used in the biological treatment of wastewaters to ensure the viability of microorganisms in active silt. Standard biological treatment processes, on the other hand, can effectively purify wastewaters from a small proportion of biogenic elements [1, 17, 21, 19].

It should be noted that the qualitative content of household wastewaters varies across countries, owing primarily to the degree of equipping of wastewater treatment plants, the state of water drainage systems, water drainage standards, the country's pollution rate per capita, climatic conditions, and so on. Table 1 displays data on wastewater pollution per capita in various countries around the world [7, 23-25].

Table 1. Wastewater pollution per capita in different world countries

Countries	Biochemical oxygen consumption BOC (kg/man.year)	Weighted substance (kg/man.year)	Total nitrogen (kg/man.year)	Total phosphor (kg/man.year)
Denmark	20-25	30-35	5-7	1.5-2
Germany	18-22	30-35	4-6	1.2-1,6
Italy	18-22	20-30	3-5	0.6-1
Sweden	25-30	30-35	4-6	0.8-1,2
USA	30-35	30-35	5-7	1.5-2
Russia	14.6	23.7	2.9	1.2

1.3. Quality Regulation/Normalization of Wastewaters Flowing into Water Reservoirs

The negative impacts of wastewaters on European and American water reservoirs, followed by eutrophication, were first seen in the 1950s. This necessitated the development of special conditions of wastewaters discharged into water reservoirs and regulation of biogenic substances in them. The first printed normative documents were based on the theory of limiting factors adopted from biology suggesting that lowering the concentration of one major biogenic substance to a certain level is sufficient to prevent eutrophication. As a result, it served as the foundation for the development of standards for the permissible contents of biogenic matter in treated wastewaters. Only phosphor was generally regarded as a limiting substance (in the United States, Switzerland, Finland, and so on), with only a few countries, such as Denmark, accepting nitrogen as another limiting factor. The first standards required that the phosphate content of treated water discharged into water reservoirs be no more than 2 mg/L. The established criteria were strictly followed [15, 26, 27].

In Georgia, as in other USSR republics, anthropogenic eutrophication of water bodies became apparent in the early 1970s as a result of the later introduction of synthetic detergents into everyday life. Three symposiums on anthropogenic eutrophication of natural water bodies were held in the USSR in the mid-1970s and early 1980s [28]. Following a thorough discussion of the current situation, the Commission of the USSR Academy of Sciences, in collaboration with the Council of Mutual Economic Assistance (CMEA), developed recommendations to implement measures to reduce eutrophication. Significant scientific research and engineering activities were carried out in CMEA countries to prevent the occurrence of biogenic substances in wastewaters and reduce their concentrations in water reservoirs. New technologies and wastewater treatment methods based on technical and biological means were introduced to protect natural water bodies from anthropogenic eutrophication, specifically to ensure the Treatment of wastewaters from nitrogen and phosphor. Simultaneously, new technologies were developed, and existing technologies were improved for the Treatment of wastewater from biogenic matter. At the same time, a new regulatory base was established, but as a result of society's transition to a new economic model, these innovations were not implemented [9, 10].

As the situation in water reservoirs worsened, the requirements for wastewater quality became more stringent globally, and these requirements became increasingly related not only to phosphor, but also to nitrogen. In foreign countries, nitrogen compounds are primarily controlled against total nitrogen concentration and ammonium salt concentration in less purified wastewaters; for example, in Switzerland, ammonium concentration in wastewaters before discharge into water reservoirs must be no more than 0.65 mg/L, and its concentration in a water reservoir, in the most unfavorable situation, must not exceed 0.5 mg/L. According to standard documents, the maximum permissible concentration of nitrogen in treated wastewater in the United States is 10 mg/L [29]. Denmark has established stringent requirements for nitrogen content of 8 mg/L in treated water, and 1.5 mg/L for total phosphor. It is illegal in the Netherlands to exceed 10 mg/L total nitrogen concentration and 1.0 mg/L total phosphor concentration [29]. In France, phosphor content requirements range from 5 to 50 mg/L depending on the type of water reservoir. In Germany, the legally mandated phosphor content is 1 mg/L for facilities with a capacity of more than 100,000 men·equivalent, and 2 mg/L for facilities with a capacity of 2000 to 100,000 men·equivalent [9, 19].

Working on not only national, but also international agreements – joint development of measures for reducing the discharge of biogenic substances in water reservoirs and norms for the discharge of pollutants, primarily biogenic substances, in water reservoirs – has been a feature of recent decades. The Helsinki Commission for the Protection of the Baltic Marine Environment developed individual recommendations for countries that discharge wastewaters in sea catchment basins reducing total phosphor content below 1.5 mg/L; later, a recommendation was developed implying that total nitrogen compounds be reduced to 10-15 mg/L. Furthermore, the same countries adopted a declaration aiming for a minimum 50% reduction in nitrogen and phosphorus in treated wastewaters [9, 19]. The North Sea Conference adopted recommendations for the basin's countries regarding total nitrogen reduction to 10 mg/L and total phosphor reduction to 1 mg/L [30] (Removal of Nitrogen and Phosphor Compounds from Wastewaters without Use of Reagents. Patent 134048 PNR 1986). According to this document, new regulations were enacted in the United Kingdom. An EU Directive, dated May 01,1991, is a later international document that relates to the establishment of requirements for treated wastewaters. The accepted form of the international agreement allows for the consideration of both national environmental laws and standard documents from EU member countries. The adopted directives are binding on EU member countries, but the methods and techniques for implementing them are not specified in the documents.

Directive 91/271 regulates urban wastewater treatment and sets the requirements for treated waters including the amount of water discharged in reservoirs, the degree of eutrophication, and the permanent population of a concrete settlement. For settlements with 10.000-100.000 conventional residents, N_{total} must be less than 15 mg/L or alternatively, treated by 70-80%) or P_{total} must be less than 2 mg/L (or alternatively, treated by 80%) for settlements with 10.000-100.000 conventional residents. For settlements with a population of more than 1.000.000, N_{total} must be less than 10 mg/L (or alternatively, treated by 70-80%), or P_{total} must be less than 1 mg/L (or alternatively, treated by 80%). In the case of wastewater discharge in an ordinary water reservoir, in both cases water treatment based with a biological method or its equivalent is admissible. For the settlement with 2000-10000 ordinary residents, the major requirement is that the biochemical oxygen demand for the given content of organic matters BOD5 = 25 mg/L, or alternatively treated by 70-90%, while chemical oxygen demand COD = 125 mg/L or alternatively treated by 75%.

As regards the publication of EU Directive, all countries revise their own national standards and begin looking for a solution to the problem at hand. It should be noted that the existing document does not include requirements for the simultaneous treatment of wastewaters from nitrogen and phosphorus, although is it critical for the environmental protection. As a result, studies were initiated in Western countries to find methods of simultaneous treatment of wastewaters containing nitrogen and phosphorus.

Table 2. Classification of household wastewaters

Parameter	Unit (mg/L)	Agricultural and household wastewaters		
		Concentrated	Medium	Light
BOD_{Total}	mg O_2/l	530	230	150
BOD_5	mg O_2/l	350	150	100
COD	mg O_2/l	740	320	210
Total organic carbon	mg C/ l	250	110	70
Total nitrogen	mg N/l	80	30	20
Ammonium nitrogen NH_4	mg NH_4/l	50	18	12
Nitrite NO_2^-	mg NO_2/l	0.1	0.1	0.1
Nitrate NO_3^-	mg NO_3/l	0.5	0.5	0.5
Organic nitrogen	mg/L	30	12	8
Total phosphor	mg P/l	23 (14)*	10 (6)	6 (4)*
Orthophosphates	mg P/l	14 (10)	6 (4)	4 (3)
Polyphosphates	mg P/l	5 (0)	2 (0)	11 (0)
Organic phosphates	mg P/l	4 (4)	2 (2)	1 (1)

The figures in brackets are for three regions, which use phosphate-free detergents [31].

1.4. Physical-Chemical Methods to Treat Wastewaters from Biogenic Elements

Treatment from Nitrogen Compounds

The treatment of wastewaters from nitrogen compounds using physical-chemical methods began in the 1960-1970s. It was not necessary at the time to clean wastewaters from nitrogen compounds to modern parameters; however, in some cases, physical-chemical methods were the most acceptable way to treat industrial wastewaters.

Many countries now use physical-chemical methods of wastewater treatment from nitrogen compounds, primarily at the final stage of treatment. This is because the quality requirements for treated water discharged into reservoirs are lax. Thus, in some cases, removing nitrogen compounds from wastewater is sufficient without further treatment of organic pollutants.

Let us look at the methods that are commonly used today to treat wastewater from nitrogen compounds with a 95-99% efficacy.

1.5. Chlorination with Active Chlorine

The active chlorination method relies on a chemical reaction that occurs in water when chlorine is added. Hypo- and hydro-chlorine acids are formed in this case. Chloramines are formed when ammonium reacts with hypo-chlorine acid. Chloramines are converted into nitrogen suboxide, a soluble gas, by the addition of active chlorine, which then evaporates into the atmosphere.

Chlorination to bending point is a major physical-chemical method of nitrogen wastewater treatment. The weight proportion of chlorine and ammonia to nitrogen required for wastewater chlorination to bending point ranges from 8:1 to 10:1; a lower weight proportion is permissible for wastewaters that have already received major preliminary treatment. The analysis revealed that chlorination to bending point within the pH range of 6.5-7.5 can treat wastewaters from ammonia by 95%, and in the case of original ammonia nitrogen concentrations of 8-15 mg/L, the content of tri-chlorine compounds of residual nitrogen does not exceed 0.5 mg/L. The disadvantage of excessive chlorination is that almost all of the chlorine introduced reduces to chloride ions, increasing the concentrations of salts dissolved in the treated waters. This problem, however, can be solved by passing chlorine-treated wastewaters through activated charcoal columns.

1.6. Reverse Osmosis

The use of semi-impenetrable membranes, specifically acetate-cellulose membranes, allows for a treatment effect of up to 98.5% from nitrogen compounds. However, the process, which is based on the free passage of dissolving molecules when filtering the membrane and capturing the molecules or ions of the substances dissolved in it, necessitates preliminary basic treatment and water softening. It was also discovered that in an acidic environment, acetate-cellulose membranes actively capture ammonium ions. Electrolyte reduction of water solution (at pH = 2-13) was considered permissible for disintegration of quaternary ammonium ions [22, 23, 29, 32].

1.7. Method of Ammonium Salts Oxidation Using Ozone

Ozonation is only appropriate for converting ammonium nitrogen to nitrate [33]. In nitrate, ammonia completely oxidizes. As a result, the use of oxygen for nitrogen oxidation in residues is no longer necessary. The primary reaction in wastewater depends on the ammonia concentration and the pH indicator. From 7-9, the speed of reaction increased as partial pressure increased. Furthermore, effective treatment from nitrogen can be achieved only by maintaining an alkaline environment.

1.8. Method of Ammonia Evaporation

When pH = 11, ammonia solution can be evaporated from the solution by air. Wastewaters are pumped to the upper section of the cooling tower and distributed in columns based on loadings after being treated with lime (for phosphor sedimentation) (Figure 1). To remove ammonia from water drops, pressurized air is passed through the loads. Because of its simplicity, this process is the most cost-effective denitrification method when wastewaters are pre-treated with lime to remove phosphorus. Thus, with air evaporation, it is possible to clean ammonia from nitrogen with 95% efficacy by using 3000 liters of air to treat 1 liter of wastewater. Working with cooling towers, on the other hand, revealed the following issues: Calcium carbonate deposits form in tower loaders and must be removed through acid washing or mechanical cleaning. In the winter, ice forms in the tower. Ammonia's solubility increases at low temperatures, reducing removal efficiency and possibly necessitating tower heating in the winter. Nitrate nitrogen formed during the biological treatment process cannot be evaporated by air.

The cooler constructed for extensive liquid spraying in wastewater treatment plant near Taho lake was filled with a wooden structure (wooden cover with planks arranged at 3.7 cm intervals vertically and 5 cm intervals horizontally). Water was supplied from the top, and air was supplied by fans from side shutters. Due to high water alkalinity caused by a high dose of lime, calcium carbonate was intensely formed on the internal surface of the tower, especially on the wooden structure during the cooler operation. For this reason, they had to deny this method. Presently, water spraying is done using fountain what has decreased the process efficiency (to 90%) in spite of increased air current to 6 000 m^3 per 1 m^3 of treated wastewater.

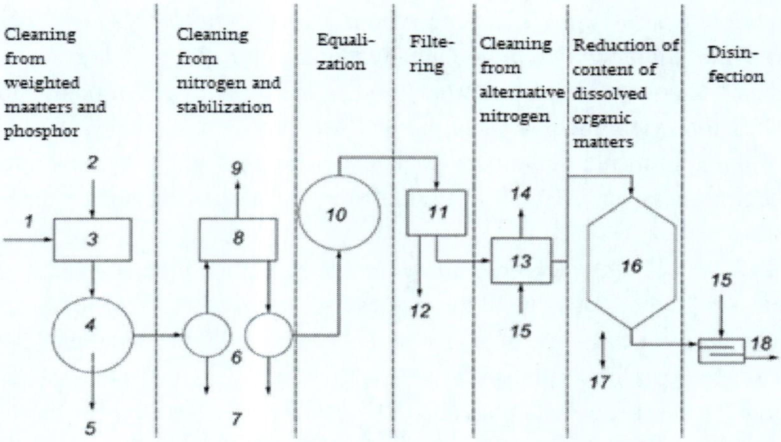

Figure 1. Flow diagram of cleaning wastewaters from ammonia using evaporation method.
1 – wastewater; 2 – lime; 3 – reservoir for mixing and flocculation; 4 – primary settlement tank; 5 – sediment from primary settlement tank; 6 – recarbonizers; 7 – sediment; 8 – air evaporation tower; 9 – ammonia; 10 – equalizer; 11 – filters; 12 – washing water; 13 – oxidation reservoir; 14 – gaseous nitrogen; 15 – chlorine 16 – coal absorbers; 17 – coal restoration; 18 – outlet.

1.9. Ion-Based Method

Unlike ammonia evaporation, the efficiency of the ion exchange process is not affected by the temperature of the wastewaters to be treated. Furthermore, when using the ion exchange method, the efficiency of cleaning from ammonia is much higher, and this process will be appropriate when a very low permanent nitrogen concentration is required after treatment.

The concentration of ammonium and nitrate ions in wastewater is very low, making ion exchange extraction difficult. Materials with high selection ability to inorganic nitrogen are required for the denitrification process to be efficient when the ion exchange method is used. Clintoptilolite is a natural, inorganic zeolite material with extremely high ammonium ion selectivity. Prior to cathion exchange, clarification and filtration using a coagulation method are performed. To convert ammonia to ammonium ion, the pH value must be brought to 6.5, as free ammonia is not absorbed and does not participate in the ion exchange reaction with clintoptilolite. One of the basic conditions for using the ion exchange method on the fixed sorbent layer during wastewater treatment is the presence of weighted substances at 10 mg/L and sulphide ions at 8-10 mg/L concentration. Treatment materials are generated using lime solution, which is then evaporated by air, and ammonium is dispersed in atmospheric air. Sorbent regeneration with 10% sulphuric acid is also possible, yielding a valuable product – ammonia sulphate [22, 23].

The experiments demonstrated that the use of zeolites where ammonia concentration is max. 100-150 mg/L is appropriate for further treatment of wastewaters [32, 34].

In Japan, a combined three-phase treatment method based on zeolites was developed. In the first stage of the process, zeolites are added to the waters to remove heavy metal ions; lime (150 mg/L CaO) and excess activated silt are also added to remove phosphor compounds and weighted solid materials. Sedimentation (second stage): clarified wastewater is directed for biological treatment, and the sediment formed is dehydrated, burned, and removed. Clinoptilolite is added to biologically treated wastewaters again in the third stage of the process in a dose that allows for a significant reduction in ammonium nitrogen concentration. To improve water quality the water should be routed to the absorption stage of treatment and disinfection after the third stage of the process. A thermal method is used to regenerate ceotile [35].

Studies dedicated to water problems were carried out at Oil and Gas Scientific Research Project Institute of Azerbaijan, where the natural zeolite-clinoptilolite with high absorption ability, as a filtering material to treat natural and wastewaters containing ammonium nitrogen was studied. High effect (94-97%) of clearing from ammonium nitrogen in water solutions was achieved by loading crushed clinoptilolite ($d_{equiv.} = 0.5$ mm).

The Scientific-Research and Engineering-Technological Institute of Municipal Economy of Ukraine carried out studies to identify the properties of different types of clinoptilolite in the complex of hydrolyze-absorption treatment during the municipal wastewater treatment, which consisted of the following steps: treatment with lime, pH: up to 11.5, and sedimentation; neutralization with carbon dioxide; filtration with a quartz filter; ionic exchange with a zeolite filter; absorption with a charcoal filter; and disinfection with chlorine. The process of wastewater biological treatment from biogenic elements was studied with a semi-industrial device. These are: a device for clearing from chlorine with a contact coagulation method, a device for clearing from ammonium nitrogen, reagent equipment, and regeneration liquid reservoirs. Structurally, all filters are metal columns: height: 3.5 m, cross-section: 0.3 x 0.3 m. The capacity of each filter was 0.5 m^3/hr, and the filtration rate is 6 m/hr. The studies demonstrated that in case of optimal filtration rate of 6 m/hr, the necessary liquid-zeolite contact time is 50 minutes.

This corresponds to the height of loading of 5 m high zeolite filter. In this regard, a two-phase consecutive regime of operation of ionic exchange filters was designed. At the first stage, liquid filtration was done from bottom to top, and from top to bottom at the second stage; after the saturation of exchange capacity, the filter loading was removed for regeneration. The clearing efficacy from ammonium nitrogen using zeolite filter was 95% [5].

Lime suspension yielding hydroxyl ions, shifting the balance between ammonia and ammonium ions towards the formation of alkaline ammonia solution like the solution used for ammonia removal, is used to regenerate the used clinoptilolite. The used solution is sent to the distillation column to distile ammonia. As a result, the regenerated solution can be used repeatedly. As the regenerated solution recirculates in the process, there is no need to remove liquid wastes [36].

Synthetic zeolites: NaA, NaX, NaY, NaM, NaP (philipsite-type zeolite), can be used for clearing the wastewaters from nitrogen compounds. For the final treatment of wastewaters, up to 0.25-0.5 fraction was used. These particles have quite a high mechanical strength, and they are resistant to water dissolved salts and pH changes within the range of 4-9.

Coke slag [37-39] and various types of hydro-thermally crystalized charcoal ash [28] can also be used as a sorbent to clear the wastewaters from ammonia nitrogen.

1.10. Electrochemical Method

The method is based on electrolysis of sea water, with the released magnesium hydroxide reacting with phosphor ions and ammonia contained in wastewaters and forming complex insoluble salts. At the same time, due to the release of Cl_2 on anode, the treatment of wastewaters and partial oxidation of organic pollutants take place. In the given case, lamellar graphite (anode) and stainless steel (cathode) are used. It was established that the most efficient and stable treatment, in particular, removal of up to 80-85% ammonium nitrogen and up to 90% orthophosphate is achieved in untreated wastewaters by adding 20% sea water. In case of 7V voltage, energy consumption is 200 Amp/h per 1 m^3 water to be treated. The sediment obtained in this process contains 1.1-2 g total phosphor per 100 g of dry substance evidencing its efficiency as a fertilizer.

First, the chlorination of wastewaters, and the use of electric coagulation-flotation method as final treatment is hampered due to frequent replacement of used electrodes and lack of sheet aluminum when operating the device, when the process parameters are: power consumption: 0.3 kWh/m^3, distance between electrodes: 20 mm, time of water treatment flowing into the device: 30 minutes, aluminum consumption: 8 g/m^3. In addition, reduction of pollution with weighted matters was fixed decreasing from 49 mg/L to 9 mg/L, chemical oxygen consumption (COD) decreasing from 50 mg/L to 12.8 mg/L, ammonium concentration decreasing from 2.6 mg/L to 0.1 mg/L, phosphate concentration decreasing from 2.8 mg/L to concentration without trace [40-42].

1.11. Treatment to Remove Phosphor Compounds

There are currently numerous methods for removing phosphates from wastewaters. Phosphate can be removed chemically (chemical, physical-chemical methods), biologically (biological method), by changing the biological process of phosphor incorporation into cellular substance, or by biochemical method [6, 7, 22, 29, 40, 43].

There are several methods for removing phosphor from wastewater, including chemical and physical-chemical methods. Utility companies avoid using chemical methods due to the high cost of reagents and secondary pollution caused by coagulant use. Physical-chemical methods are distinguished by high costs and process complexity. The use of sorptive materials necessitates fundamental preliminary preparation of wastewaters, as the presence of solid, weighted, and other pollutants in them reduces the absorption capacity of sorptive materials, complicating the treatment process. Regardless, physical-chemical methods of phosphor removal from wastewater are most commonly used at the final stage of wastewater treatment.

The chemical method of removing phosphor from wastewater is currently in use, and research into it is ongoing. This method is widely used in small to medium wastewater treatment plants.

With the chemical method, reactive ions interact with soluble phosphoric acid salts, resulting in water-dispersible colloidal phosphate sediment. Simultaneously, a chemical reagent reacts with alkali in water, forming sediment as large flakes. It causes the coagulation of fine water-dispersible colloidal phosphate sediment and weighted matters, as well as the absorption of organic compounds containing a certain amount of phosphor; the sediment is then removed from the system. As reagents, bivalent and trivalent metal salts are used. Coagulants such as aluminum and iron salts, as well as lime, are commonly used in wastewater treatment.

Sodium aluminate NaAlO2 is another source of aluminum ions. In general, this substance is a poor coagulant in soft water but much better in hard water [23, 40].

The sediment formed during the coagulation of high-color less turbid waters with aluminum sulphate in a water pipeline can be used as a coagulant used as a reagent for the purpose of clearing wastewaters of phosphor compounds [23, 25].

Mine waters containing bivalent iron salts may also be used as a de-phosphorizing agent. This method ensures consistent phosphor removal quality, and its implementation is feasible at wastewater treatment plants without halting them due to its simplicity of operation [34].

When lime is used as a coagulant, it interacts with bicarbonate ions in wastewater, forming calcium carbonate, and it also reacts with phosphates. Clearing from polyphosphates occurs via absorption on hydroxyapatite particles formed earlier when orthophosphate is surrounded by calcium ions and forms hydroxyapatite. The solubility of hydroxyapatites decreases rapidly as pH increases, but the efficiency of phosphor removal increases. When the pH exceeds 9.5, almost all orthoposphate settles. Phosphorus is absorbed on calcium carbonate at pH = 9.5 [40, 43]. According to British scientists, increasing the pH from 5 to 7 reduces the solubility of phosphates in wastewater by 1000 times [40, 43]. Furthermore, when lime is used, the biological process is inhibited, and as a result, a constant supply of lime at the stage preceding biological treatment is not acceptable, and the fact that such technology must be terminated by recarbonization complicates biological wastewater treatment.

A variety of *physical-chemical methods* have been developed to remove phosphor from wastewaters. These methods are:

- *Absorption method:* sorbent surface is used to absorb phosphor. Sorbents can be made of granulated aluminum oxide, activated aluminum oxide and aluminum sulphate, hydrated titanium dioxide, or activated metals from the periodic table of elements with oxides from the third and fourth groups of elements by applying them on a fiber material [6, 19, 35]. Dolomite was discovered to have a high absorption capacity for phosphor compound admixtures (removing over 95% of phosphor) [7, 22]; among other things, the use of light convex clay to remove phosphor from wastewaters is studied [16, 44]. The efficiency of phosphor removal in this process can be very high, even reaching 100% in some cases.

- *Removal of phosphates in magnetic field:* a reagent is used to bind phosphates in insoluble compounds, and then magnetic material is introduced to exert influence via the magnetic field. Phosphate-containing sediment is thus released [39]. German researchers propose using lime, iron, or aluminum salts as sediment-forming agents and fine-ground Fe_2O_3 powder as a magnetic material [37]. There is information that iron and copper flakes can be used instead of the reagent; in this case, sediment is separated using a magnetic field [5]. The method allows for up to 100% phosphate removal from wastewater while reducing the number of basic stages of the treatment process.
- *Electric coagulation–flotation treatment method.* Aluminum, as well as iron (steel) electrodes can be used [15]. This method allows for the total removal of phosphor from wastewaters.
- *Crystallization:* this method is based on the formation of phosphate crystals in crystallization centers, which, then, are removed from the system. Crystallization is performed on filters or the outer layer. For this method, calcium phosphate, containing minerals, bone coal, and blast furnace slag can be used as stock material, where phosphor binds with calcium ions and is released in the form of hardly soluble hydroxilapatite as sediment [27]. German scientists propose using calcium carbonate (calcite) for creation of crystallization centers [40]. The “Phosnix” method is interesting because it involves the simultaneous removal of nitrogen and phosphorus as a result of the chemical interaction of magnesium ions. In particular, in an ammonia environment, magnesium ions chemically act on phosphates, resulting in the formation of a double salt of insoluble crystal phosphate-magnesium-ammonium.

The sediment formed as a result of crystallization has low humidity. The effectiveness of phosphate removal is 80-90%. It should be noted that due to the high costs and complexity of operation, not all of the above-mentioned physical and chemical methods can be used.

1.12. Biological and Chemical Methods

In practice, various schemes that combine biological and chemical sedimentation processes are currently in use. This combination of processes allows for higher wastewater treatment quality than could be achieved by using each process individually. Biological and chemical treatment schemes differ depending on the area of introduction and reagent composition. The reagents used in biological and chemical treatment processes are being improved at the same time as the processes themselves. The most promising direction is the development of new reagents from industrial waste. As a result, we investigate the potential for using water supply plant sediments, grey charcoal ash extracts, and iron production byproducts as reagents. The process of reagent dosing is given special attention [13, 18, 25, 26].

The areas of reagent introduction may differ when conducting biological and chemical treatment processes. As a result, the following biological and chemical phosphate removal schemes are currently in use:

- Preliminary phosphor removal: a mechanical treatment stage. This scheme is used for the treatment of highly concentrated wastewaters, but it has several drawbacks: with this scheme, the reagent dose increases, which increases the amount of formed sediment, increasing the cost of the method.
- Treatment of biologically treated wastewaters using a reagent. The scheme uses additional settlement tanks what also increases its cost. For complete clearing of wastewaters from phosphor by using this method, as British scientists advise, the treatment of biologically treated wastewaters is necessary using lime (200 mg/L), flocculant (2-3 mg/L) and magnetite (Fe_2O_3 1 mg/L) [45].
- Introduction of reagent directly in the aeration reservoir (simultaneous sedimentation) is the most efficient method of reagent use during the biologic al treatment. This scheme improves the sedimentation characteristics of activated silt, according to experience. However, when a reagent enters a system where a biochemical process is in progress, precautions must be taken to ensure that the rate of formation of solid matter under the influenced of the chemical reagent does not exceed the rate of formation of activated silt.

German scientists propose reagent dosing in the returned activated silt in the primary and secondary settlement tanks, to ensure a long anaerobic phase for efficient phosphate removal [30, 40].

The method of producing iron ions around phosphor in the form of iron (III) phosphate proposed by Japanese scientists involves the circulation of biologically treated water around the electrode under voltage; additionally, the anode must be made of low-carbon steel, while the cathode must be made of stainless steel. The activated silt must be mixed with iron (III) phosphate and removed from the system [34].

British scientists studied the influence of periodical impact of additives such as acetate, protein and glucose on the wastewater treatment to remove phosphor in a biological reactor [35].

In addition to silt aeration, alum and trivalent iron can be used for chemical coagulation. Coagulant must be added to aeration liquid or the liquid that exits the aeration reservoir before it reaches the secondary settlement tank, according to this technology. Despite the presence of protozoans in such chemical-biological silt, the efficiency of reducing biochemical oxygen consumption is unaffected. Before being discharged to water reservoirs, treated wastewaters are filtered to remove flakes where required by quality standards.

The first studies of this process were conducted by Goodman, Bart, Ettinger, Eberhardt and Nesbit. They added reagents to the aeration reservoir and found that sodium aluminate, at 1.8 mg per 1 mg of phosphor, produced the best results. The residual phosphor content in the treated waters was approximately 0.5-1 mg/L in this case. Increased reagent dose increased the turbidity of treated wastewaters [34, 35, 46].

Similar results were obtained by Gregory Opoulos by using aluminum sulphate and sodium-aluminum as reagents. The reagents were introduced with the ratio of Ai:P 1.9 and 1.3, ensuring 85–90% phosphor removal from wastewaters.

Davis and Lavy recommend performing the clearing process in the aeration reservoir with "young" activated silt, as this results in better phosphate removal and sedimentation of weighted solid particles in the secondary settlement tank. Better sedimentation in a secondary settling tank with "old" silt can be achieved by adding polyelectrolytes or by installing a device with a weighted layer, or sand filters for extra water clarification.

A similar method, the use of iron sulphate as coagulant, was also developed. Titanium white produces iron sulphate as a byproduct. Iron sulphate solution (20-30% concentration) is introduced in the wastewater current between the primary settlement tank and the aeration reservoirs in a maximum amount of 150 g per 1 m^3 of wastewater. As a result of aeration and the activated silt impact, bivalent iron oxidizes to trivalent and chemically reacts with phosphor compounds, the products of which are removed from the system along with the activated silt.

The treatment of pollution by biological-chemical methods was investigated at Talin Polytechnic Institute using low-capacity equipment, i.e., for the working conditions of aeration reservoirs, settlement tanks, and in the mode of complete oxidation of pollution. As a reagent, commercial iron sulphate (iron alum) was used. It was determined that introducing the reagent once a day required 12.3-12.6 mg of reagent to remove 1 mg orthophosphate, whereas introducing the reagent twice a day required only 3.65 mg of reagent in 24 hours. With an initial phosphate concentration of 9.4 mg/L, the phosphate removal effect was 75%, and the phosphate removal effect without reagents in the reservoir of prolonged aeration was no more than 10% [25, 35].

Biological and chemical treatments were studied at the Utility Water Supply and Water Treatment Scientific-Research Institute of the K. Panfilov Academy of Utility Services in two variations: introducing the reagent before the aeration reservoir and before the secondary settlement tank. Iron sulphate (iron alum) was used as a coagulant in the former case, while iron (III) sulphate salt was used in the latter. Aeration reservoir with a capacity of 50 m^3/day worked with 1.2-1.7 hrs aeration period, with an activated silt dose of 4.5-7.5 g/L and silt loading change: biochemical oxygen consumption increased from 450 mg to 1000 mg per 1 g ashless silt substance. By keeping active silt for 0.5-1 hours, the sedimentation time was 1.5-2 hours. It has been established that the effectiveness of phosphor compound removal to a certain limit is dependent on the dose of coagulants. Furthermore, the maximum allowable dose of the reagent is determined by its introduction and BOC loading on silt. The maximum allowable dose of coagulant to introduce into the aeration reservoir with similar loads was 30 mg/L, and 10 mg/L for the secondary settlement tank. An increase in coagulation dose caused disruption during wastewater biochemical treatment in the former case and silt mixture separation in the latter. Loading the activated silt improves phosphor removal efficiency. So, increasing the BOC loading from 450 to 750 mg per 1 g ashless silt substance increased total phosphor removal efficiency from 85.7% to 90.4% at a coagulant dose of 30 mg/L.

When introducing coagulant before the secondary settlement tank, the installation of flocculators, whether built-in or autonomous, must be considered. Otherwise, the effectiveness of reagent treatment may be compromised due to an increase in the release of small flake-shaped sediments. The addition of 1-2 mg/L polyelectrolytes prevents such release. According to the level of removal of weighted solid matters from the secondary settlement tank, the addition of sand and gravel filters at the final stage of biological-chemical treatment by ascending waster current may increase the phosphor removal efficiency to 40%. The filter performance parameters are the same as for filtration of biologically treated wastewaters without coagulant treatment.

It should be noted that large volumes of poorly condensed silt are formed during wastewater treatment with aluminum and iron salts. It is recommended that 1 mg polyacrylamide be added per 1 liter of wastewater to increase condensation.

1.13. Theoretical Justification of Thorough Biological Treatment Processes to Remove Biological Elements from Wastewaters

Removal of Nitrogen Compounds

The chemical element nitrogen (N) is one of the essential elements supporting life on our planet. It is found in gases, liquids, solids, and organic and inorganic chemical compounds. Nitrogen removal from wastewaters must be considered only in the context of its overall impact on the ecological system. Thus, before thoroughly discussing the biological process of removal of nitrogen compounds from wastewaters, let us consider the nitrogen cycle on Earth [10, 12].

Nitrogen cycle is one of the most complex processes on Earth because it includes both gaseous and mineral phases, but it is also the most ideal gas.

The cycle of the atmospheric gas is unusual and slow. Nitrogen appears in a small percentage of living organisms.

Consider nitrogen cycle. The majority of nitrogen is found in air (N_2 molecules account for 78% of the volume of air). Plants cannot absorb nitrogen from the air, but only from ammonium ions (NH_4^-) or nitrates (NO_3). However, some bacteria and cyanobacteria can convert gaseous nitrogen fixation to ammonium.

The nitrogen cycle incorporates: biomass nitrogen, biological nitrogen fixation by bacteria and living organisms, juvenile (volcanogenic) nitrogen, atmospheric nitrogen (recorded during thunder) and technogenic nitrogen.

Nitrogen accounts for approximately 80% of the water in the atmosphere. A portion of it exists in soil and water as organic compounds (ammonium, nitrite, and nitrate ions), while another portion forms vegetable and animal proteins, amino acids, and DNA. There is a large nitrogen cycle between the Earth and the atmosphere, containing a small cycle as a part. It implies that organic nitrogen compounds undergo ammonization and nitrification processes after organism death, excretion, or food waste formation (with the participation of bacteria), and resultant ammonia, nitrates, and nitrites are formed [1, 9].

Some processes, such as accumulation in deep oceanic sediments, terminate the nitrogen cycle. When there is a lack of oxygen, a large volume of water (in humid loam), and saponification of organism remnants (the process of decomposition of fats under the influence of alkalis), the decay process may not start at all. In dry soils, the cycle also comes to an end (mummification of the remnants of organisms). In recent years, it has been established that environmental pollution with heavy metals has a negative impact on the mineralization process of nitrogen compounds. The disruption of nitrogen cycle is partially compensated by the release of volcanic gases [26].

Microorganisms, such as nitrogen fixators, nitrifiers and denitrifiers contribute significantly to the nitrogen cycle. All other organisms have an impact on nitrogen cycle only after it has been assimilated into the cells. Nitrogen is also found in purple and green photosynthetic bacteria, as well as other soil bacteria [14].

The bacterial cycle accounts for nearly 80% of global nitrogen cycle, with metazoan organisms accounting for the remaining 20%. However, ammonization decomposing bacteria and fungi primarily perform this cycle [25].

Nitrosomonas bacteria oxidize ammonia to nitrites, and Nitrobacter bacteria oxidize nitrates, so the nitrogen cycle continues. Simultaneously with the described processes, nitrogen is constantly returned to the atmosphere by denitrifying bacteria, which can decompose nitrates to nitrogen (N_2). These bacteria are typically found in fertile soils rich in nitrogen and carbon. Each year, these bacteria release 50 to 60 kg of nitrogen from a 1 ha soil surface into the atmosphere.

As most plants and animals cannot use atmospheric nitrogen (N_2), the latter is converted into nitrites by nitrogen fixing bacteria, root system of legumes and cyanobacteria (NO_2^-), and then into nitrates (NO_3^-). Nitrogen cycle implies that soil microorganisms consume animal and dead organism remains, releasing ammonium, which is converted to soluble nitrate salts by nitrifying bacteria used by plants to form proteins. As herbivorous animals eat grass, the vegetable proteins in their bodies are converted into animal proteins [7, 22].

Human activities have a significant impact on nitrogen cycle. On the one hand, the mass production and use of nitrogen fertilizers causes an excessive accumulation of nitrates. Nitrogen applied to soil as a fertilizer is lost during harvesting, alkalization and denitrification; on the other hand, a slower rate of transformation of ammonia into nitrate causes ammonium fertilizers to accumulate in the soil. Because of soil pollution caused by industrial waste, processes involving microorganisms are hampered [5, 15].

The nitrogen cycle is increasingly influenced by air pollution caused by the operation of industrial plants. Nitrogen oxides (NO and NO_2) are found only in intermediate phases and in low concentrations in most habitats. The combustion of various types of soil-derived fuel significantly increases the content of unstable oxides in the air, particularly in cities. They are hazardous for biotic components of ecosystems at such high concentrations; for example, under the influence of ultraviolet radiation from the sun, NO_2 reacts with incomplete combustion products of hydrocarbons contained in vehicle emissions in large amounts, resulting in photochemical emissions that irritate eyes. The development of new types of internal combustion engines, the transition to fuel cleaning, and the use of nuclear power stations instead of thermal power plants provide opportunities to eliminate these serious drawbacks in nitrogen cycle [1, 7, 10].

The global nitrogen cycle structure is extremely complex, consisting of several interconnected cycles, one of which is caused by photochemical reactions in the troposphere. In addition to N_2 , other gaseous nitrogen compounds, such as NH_2 , N_2O , are systematically emitted in the atmosphere, resulting in the formation of nitrous and nitrogen acids first followed by their nitrite and nitrate salts. They do not accumulate as a result of photochemical reactions. Ammonia [10], a reduced nitrogen compound, is found in the atmosphere alongside nitrogen oxides. Figure 2 depicts a diagram of biological nitrogen cycle.

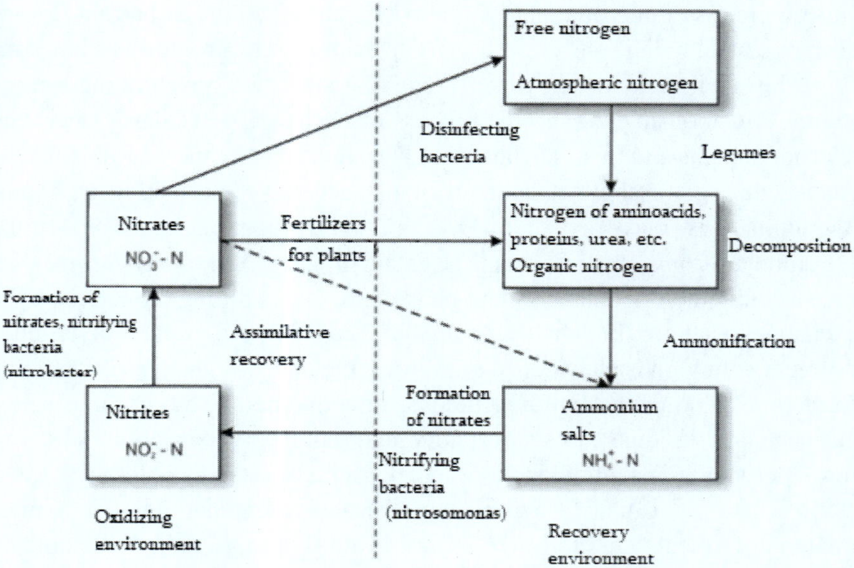

Figure 2. Scheme of nitrogen cycle in nature.

Biological transformation occurring in metabolic processes takes place in the presence of inorganic nitrogen, and includes, as previously states, nitrogen fixation, ammonization, nitrification, and denitrification processes that occur during the wastewater treatment in activated silt mixtures.

Activated silt of wastewater treatment plants is a living consortium with a complex structure. It primarily consists of microorganisms involved in trophic and metabolic processes serving the purpose of wastewater treatment.

A change in mixed controlled culture of microorganisms, which may develop during long-term, uninterrupted processes, is a promising way of making more extensive use of microorganism biological activity. The study of the kinetics of mixed microbial population growth and death is an urgent task, the solution to which would allow for a reduction in the amount of activated silt and its use more thoroughly and efficiently in the wastewater treatment technical chain [7, 22].

Activated silt bacteria are classified into several physiological groups. Each group brings together organisms that have similar food chains. Active silt contains ammonium-forming, cellulose-disintegrating, nitrifying, fat-disintegrating, and disinfecting bacteria, actinomycetes, fungi, and a large number of decomposers, primarily infusoria and sarcodina [16, 32, 44].

The biological process of wastewater treatment is accomplished by various groups of microorganisms. Microorganisms require a constant flow of energy to form living cells, as well as for life activity and growth. The nutrients from the environment, i.e., directly from wastewaters, provide the energy source. Metabolism refers to the process of exchanging substances between microorganisms and their surroundings. The nutrients in microorganism cells change during metabolism as a result of successive fermenting reactions. Metabolism is classified into three major groups: 1. *catabolism*, the breakdown of nutrients into small fragments (decay). The nutrients are then transformed into organic acids and phosphoric ethers during the intermediate exchange reactions known as 2. *amphibism*. The two processes produce different compounds (substrates) with low molecular weights, resulting in the formation of so-called building blocks, or monomers. They (amino acids, purine and pyrimidine bases, phosphorylated sugars, organic acids, and so on) form polymeric macromolecules (nucleic acids, proteins, polysaccharides, etc.). These two phases of biosynthesis of monomers and polymers (macromolecules) are followed by the third group called anabolism. Microorganisms generate energy as ATP bioenergy (adenosine triphosphate-$C_{10}H_{16}N_5O_{13}P_3$) during metabolism [9, 11, 20, 21].

Ferments are responsible for chemical transformations in the cell. A specific ferment is in charge of converting one substrate into another. Ferments are proteins with catalytic functions. Binding and further transfer of individual substrate fragments, such as hydrogen and amino-groups, together with ferment proteins, involve compounds with low molecular weight, so-called co-ferments and prosthetic groups (e.g., nicotinamide adeninedinucleotide phosphate NAD(P), cytochromes, etc.) [2, 3, 10, 21].

Thus, microorganisms require energy, a carbon (*C*) source, and inorganic elements such as nitrogen (*N*), phosphor (*P*), sulfur (*S*), potassium (*K*), calcium (*Ca*), and magnesium (*Mg*) for survival and development. Furthermore, they require trace amounts of elements such as *Zn, Mn, Mo, Se, Co, Ni, V, W*, and other organic nutrients, which are classified into three groups: amino acids, purines and pyrimidines, and vitamins. Organisms that use organic carbon (*C*) are known as heterotrophic; organisms that take carbon (*C*) from carbon dioxide (CO_2) are known as autotrophic; organisms that get energy from cell synthesis are known as phototrophic; and organisms that get energy from chemical reactions are known as chemotrophic (see Table 3).

Table 3. Microorganisms and classification of their energy sources

Classification	Energy source	Carbon source (C)
Autotrophic		
Photoautotrophic	Light	CO_2
Chemoautotrophic	Inorganic redox reactions	CO_2
Heterotrophic		
Chemoheterotrophic	Organic redox reactions	Organic carbon
Photoheterotrophic	Light	Inorganic carbon

Following the phosphorization associated with electron transfer, much more adenosine triphosphate (ATP) is produced as aerobic organisms respire than during fermentation at the substrate level. As a result, it is not surprising that, during the biochemical evolution, the type of metabolism that transfers hydrogen (H) from organic substrate with the help of so-called bound oxygen emerged and survived. In this case, nitrates (NO_3^-), sulphates (SO_3^-), and carbonates (CO_3^{2-}) can be the carriers of oxygen. They are reduced at the expense of substrate hydrogen. Electron transferring ability in these compounds allows bacteria to oxidize substrates without the participation of molecular oxygen.

Thus, if aerobic respiration (in which bacteria use oxygen as an external receiver of electrons) is considered a condition for substrate oxidation, then other conditions in which the substrate oxidizes using so-called bound oxygen must be understood as anaerobic respiration (bacteria use external receiver of electrons other than oxygen electrons). As a result, we can talk about nitrate, sulfate, or carbonate respiration. For the purpose of biological wastewater treatment, the term "anaerobic conditions" is used specifically, which implies that microorganisms respire not at the expense of dissolved oxygen (O_2), but nitrites (NO_2^-) and nitrates (NO_3^-). The term "anaerobic conditions" refers to respiration that does not use oxygen (O_2), nitrates (NO_3^-), or nitrites (NO_2^-) found in the air. Thus, the processes of "nitrate respiration" and "nitrite respiration" can occur under anaerobic conditions but not under aerobic conditions.

1.14. Organic Compound Removal from Wastewaters (Reduction of Biochemical Oxygen Consumption (BOC) under Aerobic Conditions) during the Traditional Biological Treatment

The reduction of biochemical oxygen consumption (BOC) with heterotrophic microorganisms can be represented by the two oxidation reactions given below:

$$C_{18}H_{19}O_9N + 17.5O_2 + H^+ = 18CO_2 + 8H_2O + NH_4^+ \quad (1)$$

(without nitrification)

$$C_{18}H_{19}O_9N + 19.5O_2 + H^+ = 18CO_2 + 9H_2O + H_4^+ + NO_3^- \quad (2)$$

(with nitrification)

The amount of oxygen needed for reaction (1), (2) will be 1.42 and 1.59 kg O_2 per 1 kg of organic substance, respectively.

Factors influencing the reduction of biochemical oxygen consumption (BOC):

The most important factors influencing the reduction of biochemical oxygen consumption are:

- Temperature, T, °C;
- Oxygen;
- Toxic substances;
- Nitrogen (*N*) and phosphor (*P*).

1. The temperature effect can be described by the following exponential equation:

$$\mu_{\max}(T) = \mu_{\max}(20 \circ C) \cdot \exp\{(towards(T - 20)\} \quad (3)$$

where $\mu_{\max}(T)$ is the maximum growth rate at temperature T°;

$\mu_{\max}(20 \circ C)$ is the maximum growth rate at temperature of 20°C;

K is the temperature constant;

T is temperature (°C).

2. Impact of oxygen (O_2) on aerobic processes according to Monod equation:

$$\mu_{obs} = \mu_{\max} \frac{S_2}{S_2 + K_S} \cdot \frac{S_{O2.2}}{S_{O2.2} + K_{S,02}} \qquad (4)$$

where S_2 is the substrate concentration in reactor (mg/L);

K_S is the saturation constant for the substrate (mg/L);

$S_{O2.2}$ is the oxygen concentration in reactor; and

K_S, O_2 is the saturation constant for oxygen.

3. Many toxic substances have an adverse effect on the aerobic process, for example, phenol and cyanide show noncompetitive reversible inhibition of the kinetics of the microorganism growth:

$$\mu_{\max,I} = \mu_{\max} \frac{K_{S,I}}{K_{S,I} + C_I} \qquad (5)$$

where $\mu_{\max,I}$ is the maximum growth value during inhibition;

$\mu_{\max}$ is the maximum growth value without inhibition;

$K_{S,I}$ is the saturation constant during the inhibition;

K_S is the saturation constant without inhibition.

4. The amount of nitrogen and phosphor needed for biological treatment depends on biochemical oxygen consumption (BOC) of wastewaters – BOC_5:N:P. The optimal ratio is BOC_5:N:P = 100:5:1, what is the most favorable for biological treatment. Figure 3 shows the impact of the age of the activated silt on BOC_5:N:P ratio.

The above-described process of organic substances removal is obviously a very simplified description of the biochemical oxygen consumption (BOC) reduction with the following final products: ammonium nitrogen (without nitrification) and nitrate (by nitrification), which is accompanied by formation of ammonium nitrogen (NH_4^+) referred to as nitrogen ammonification or mineralization.

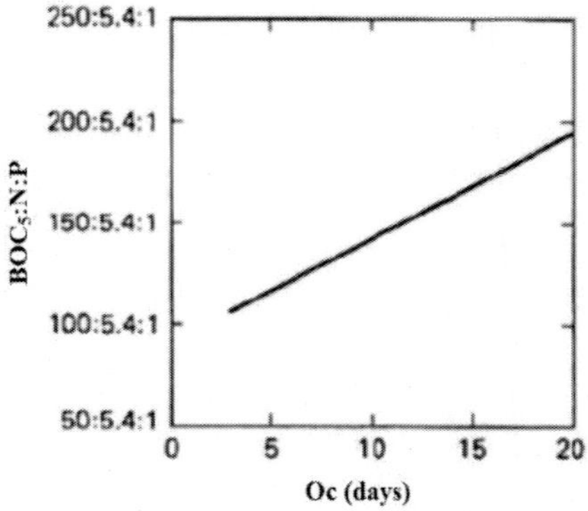

Figure 3. Impact of the Age of Activated Silt on $BOC_{5:}$ N: P ratio (Sherrad, 1975) [*Biological Process Design for Wastewater treatment*. Larry D. Benefield., Clifford W. Randall. 1980].

For instance, by heterotrophs of ammonitrifiers play a role in the biological transformation of organic nitrogen compounds by heterotrophic microorganisms (correspondingly) [47]:

Protein + nH_2O →peptones → polypeptides and olygopeptides → amino acids → ammonium nitrogen

Biological wastewater treatment methods rely on the natural action of heterotrophic and autotrophic microorganisms. Microorganisms have properties, three of which are commonly used for wastewater treatment:

- The ability to use a wide range of organic and inorganic compounds to generate energy and maintain the function;
- The ability to propagate quickly while retaining a certain number of bacteria in colonies;
- The ability to form colonies and groups that can be easily isolated from treated water after the wastewater treatment process is complete.

In a living microbial cell, two processes occur continuously and simultaneously: molecule disintegration (catabolism) and synthesis (anabolism), which combine to form the metabolic process. Carbohydrates, fats, proteins, spirits, and other nutrients can be disintegrated by heterotrophic microorganisms in both aerobic and anaerobic conditions. Some intermediate products form a food reserve to be used by the cell as the primary nutrients are depleted. Relevant ferments determine and regulate the entire cycle of a cell's relation with its environment during nutrient removal and transformation. The ferments are found in various cytoplasmic and cell membrane substructures, from which they are released on the cell surface or into the environment [26, 38].

In addition to removal of the major organic pollutants from the wastewaters during the treatment, no less important is the removal of nitrogen and phosphor compounds (biogenic elements). The biological treatment of nitrogen compounds in an air tank entails the processes of ammonization, nitrification, and denitrification.

Ammonium nitrogen, produced as a result of ammonization of nitrogen-containing compounds, in natural conditions, may be used by vegetative organisms for construction of cells or in the process of nitrification, for oxidation to nitrites and nitrates by bacteria. Two groups of microorganisms always participate in ammonium oxidation: some oxidize ammonium by forming nitrite, others oxidize nitrites to nitrates [7, 10, 30, 36].

Certain groups of microorganisms can isolate nitrogen from nitrates for the synthesis with nitrogen-containing cell components (reduction of such assimilative nitrates is possible both, under aerobic and anaerobic conditions), as well as for dissimilative reduction of nitrates, i.e., nitrate "respiration". Besides, in anaerobic conditions, nitrate is the final electron receiver. The latter process is referred to as "true denitrification".

Each stage is catalyzed by the relevant enzyme reductase. In both cases, nitrates first recover to nitrites by nitrate reductase enzyme. Then nitrites may recover to ammonia by assimilation or to N_2 and N_2O by dissimilation.

In addition to ammonia, household wastewaters contain significant amounts of organic nitrogen in the form of proteins, peptides, and amino acids. In the case of biological treatment using a traditional technological plan, ammonium nitrogen oxidizes while the organic nitrogen content remains unchanged or decreases insignificantly. When such wastewaters are discharged into water reservoirs, they create conditions for secondary pollutions due to the protein component of total nitrogen, which degrades over time under the influence of proteolytic ferments, resulting in the formation of nitrogen ammonia salts and causing secondary pollution of water reservoirs. To avoid secondary pollution, the amount of organic nitrogen must be reduced during biological treatment at treatment plants.

Nitrification Process [7, 13, 14, 19, 22]

Let us take a close look at the nitrification process. Nitrification is accomplished by bacteria, which are autotrophs and require inorganic carbon dioxide (carbon dioxide, carbonates, and bicarbonates). Nitrification bacteria (nitrifiers) are a homogeneous group of autotrophic bacteria that have a low growth rate due to the low energy coefficient of the ammonium and nitrate nitrogen oxidation process. The main issue with the nitrification process during wastewater treatment at treatment plants with a traditional biological plan is the slow growth rate of nitrifying bacteria. Nitrification takes place in two stages:

1. The first stage is ammonia (NH_4^+) oxidation to nitrites (NO_2^-). It is carried out by so-called "Nitroso" group bacteria: Nitrosomonas, Nitrosococcus, Nitrosolobus, Nitrosospira and Nitrosovibrio.
2. The second stage of nitrification takes place at the expense of oxidation of nitrous acids (nitrites) to nitric acids (nitrates). The nitrifiers of the second stage are "Nitro" group bacteria: Nitrobacter, Nitrospira, Nitrospina, Nitrococcus, Nitrocystis, Nitrobacter.

The nitrification processes take place in the presence of dissolved oxygen (O_2) in the system.

$$NH_4^+ \rightarrow NH_2 \rightarrow X \rightarrow NO_2 \rightarrow NO_3^- \qquad (6)$$

The reactions are related to energetic processes of ammonia oxidation (NH_4^+):

$$NH_4^+ + 2O_2 + 2HCO_2 \rightarrow NO_3^- + 2H_2CO_3 + H_2O \qquad (7)$$

and cell substance synthesis:

$$14NH_4^+ + 24HCO_3^- \rightarrow 4H_2CO_3 + 10NO_3^- + 2H_2CO_3 + 22H_2O + \\ +4C_5H_7O_2N \qquad (8)$$

This means that the oxidation of ammonium salt is accompanied by the consumption of substances defining the alkalinity of water (see 8).

The total reaction required for synthesis and energy, taking into account the amount of ammonia, can be represented as follows:

$$NH_4^+ + 1.76O_2 + 1.98HCO_3^- \rightarrow 0.98NO_3^- + 0.02C_5H_7O_2N + \\ +1.04H_2O + 1.88H_2CO_3 \quad (9)$$

According to the last balance equation (9), the output of ashless silt substance for oxidation of 1 mg/L nitrogen is (0.02×113)/0.98 × 14 = 0.16 mg/L N. This is due to Nitrosomonas having a much faster growth rate than Nitrobacter. The kinetics of the nitrification process in the design practice of wastewater treatment plants in the United States is justified by the belief that total reaction speed is determined by the development of Nitrosomonas. The following factors influence the nitrification processes: (a) substrate concentration; (b) temperature; (c) dissolved oxygen concentration; and (d) pH and toxic components.

a. It is known that nitrite (NO_2^-) and nitrate (NO_3^-) concentrations influence the maximum growth rate of *Nitrosomonas* and *Nitrobacter* and, consequently, the efficiency of nitrification processes. Monod equation can be used to describe the action of each component:

$$\mu = \mu_{max} \frac{S}{K_S + S}, \quad (10)$$

Where μ is the growth rate of nitrifiers (day^{-1});

μ_{Max} is the maximum growth rate of nitrifiers (day^{-1});

S is the substrate concentration (mg/L);

K_S is the substrate saturation constant (mg/L).

b. The effect of temperature on the nitrification process is defined by formula (3) in the 10–20°C range. Nitrifiers develop rapidly and reach their maximum growth rate at temperatures ranging from 30 to 35°C. The growth rate of nitrification agents decreases between 35 and 40°C, and no nitrification process takes place at thermophilic temperature (50-60°C).

c. Nitrifying bacteria are very sensitive to dissolved oxygen levels, whose impact kinetics can be expressed by Monod equation (4). Nitrification can occur at high oxygen concentrations, e.g., at wastewater treatment plants, where pure technical oxygen (oxygen tanks, etc.) is used, a concentration of 60 g O_2/m^3 does not hamper the nitrification process.

In practice, when designing aeration reservoirs, min. 2 g/L oxygen concentration is recommended. Figure 4 shows the impact of concentration of dissolved oxygen on nitrification speed.

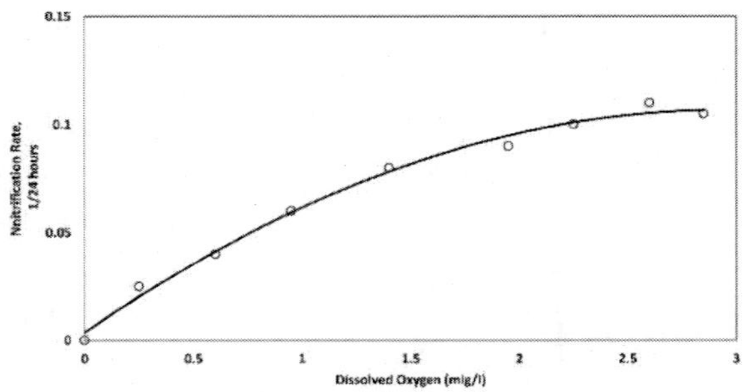

Figure 4. Impact of concentration of dissolved oxygen on the speed of nitrification.

d. In order to optimize the nitrification process, the pH value should be in the range of 7.2-8.5. The formula below describes the reduction of biochemical oxygen consumption and the impact of pH on the growth rate of nitrification agents throughout the entire nitrification process:

$$\mu' = \mu[1 - 0.833(7.2 - pH) \quad (11)$$

The dependence of the nitrification process efficiency on pH value is given in Figure 5.

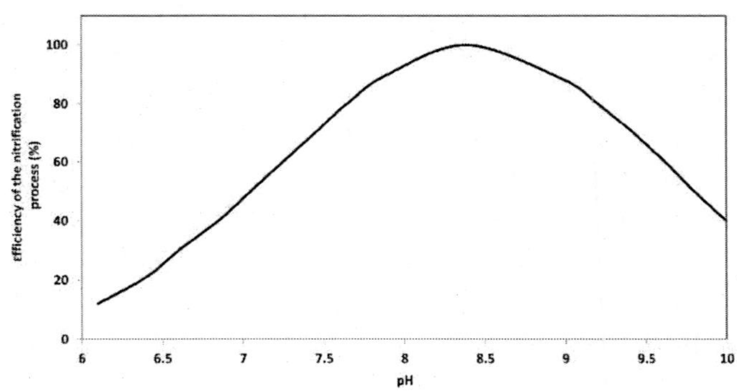

Figure 5. Dependence of the nitrification process efficiency on pH value (at +20°C temperature).

e. As compared to other types of bacteria, nitrifiers are not sensitive to toxic components, but such toxic components as heavy metals (*Cu, Ni, Cr, Zn, Co* and so on) and some organic compounds (sulfur-aniline-, phenol- and cyanide-based) may hamper the nitrification processes.

Kinetic parameters of nitrification are given in Table 4.

Table 4. Kinetic parameters of nitrifiers

Kinetic constants of the nitrification process (at +20°C)	Symbol	Unit	Value		
			Nitrosomonas	*Nitrobacter*	Total
Maximum specific growth rate	$\mu_{max\ A}$	(day^{-1})	0.6-0.8	0.6-1.0	0.6-0.8
NH_4^+ saturation constant	$K_{S,NH4,\ A}$	g(NH_4^+)/m^3	0.3-0.7	0.8-1.2	0.3-0.7
O_2 saturation constant	$K_{S,\ O_2,\ A}$	g(O_2) /m^3	0.5-1.0	0.5-1.5	0.5-1.0
Economic coefficient	$Y_{max,\ A}$	g biomass/ g Nitrate	0.1-0.12	0.05-0.07	0.15-0.2

Denitrification Process (Nitrate Respiration) [7, 22, 30, 43]

Denitrification is the nitrogen recovery process by denitrifying bacteria during their anaerobic respiration. As denitrifying bacteria are heterotrophic microorganisms, they require organic compounds, as the source of carbon. The can grow both in aerobic and anaerobic environments. Furthermore, denitrification is more intense in low-oxygen environments.

Denitrifying bacteria use two sources of energy. Each of them can oxidize organic substance using atmospheric oxygen, and in case of absence of oxygen, they can oxidize substances by the merging recovery of nitrates to form N_2.

Denitrifying bacteria, as previously stated, are heterotrophic organisms and a type of facultative anaerobe; that is, they use organic substances as a source of carbon during denitrification. Certain wastewater bacteria, such as denitrification: *Achromobater, Aerobater, Alkaligenes, Balicus, Flavobacterium, Micrococcus, Proteus, Psedomonas,* and others, are capable of denitrification. The following factors influence the denitrification process:

substrate (carbon source), temperature, dissolved oxygen concentration, and environmental pH; recovery of the oxidation forms of nitrogen by denitrification to (NO_3). Denitrification reactions may proceed by nitrate dissimilation (nitrate respiration) in this case, causing the substance to disintegrate. As a byproduct, gaseous nitrogen is produced.

$$NO_3^- \rightarrow NO_2^- \rightarrow NO \rightarrow N_2O \rightarrow N_2 \tag{12}$$

Another method of denitrification is nitrate assimilation, in which nitrogen does not leave water but remains as an organic compound.

$$NO_3^- \rightarrow NO_2^- \rightarrow X \rightarrow NH_2O \rightarrow N_{org,} \tag{13}$$

Nitrate respiration recovers nitrates to nitrites:

$$(NO_3^- \rightarrow NO_2^-)$$

Nitrate may be used as a final oxygen receiver by facultative anaerobic bacteria (Enterobacter, *Escherichia coli*, etc.) in the process of transporting electrons that supply energy. This type of nitrogen "respiration" differs from denitrification in that only the first step of nitrate formation (NO_3^-, NO_2^-) occurs, during which nitrites may accumulate in a cultural area and no N_2 is formed. Nitrites can also be converted to ammonia via assimilative nitroreduction, resulting in the release of NH_4^+ in the area. In this case, we talk about nitrate ammonification.

The main factors influencing the denitrification process are:

a. Substrate (carbon source),
b. Temperature,
c. Concentration of dissolved oxygen,
d. Environmental pH.

a. Substrate (carbon source). Denitrifying bacteria use different types of substrates; they may use inorganic sources, while organic substrates for denitrification may be the organic substances existing in the wastewaters and activated silt, the so-called internal sources. The rate of denitrification is influenced by the substrate sources (Figure 6).

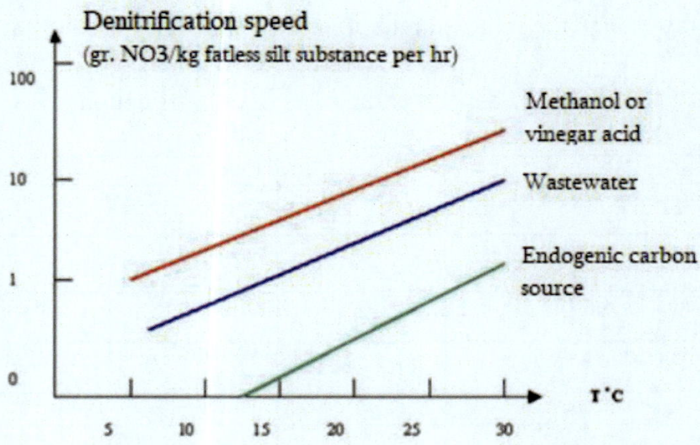

Figure 6. Relationship between temperature, substrate sources and denitrification frequency.

The speed of substrate (carbon) consumption (or utilization) can be calculated by formula:

$$r_{V,S} = \frac{\mu_{\max}}{Y_{\max}} \cdot \frac{S_{NO_3}}{S_{NO_3} + K_{S,NO_3}} \cdot \frac{S}{S + K_S} \cdot X_B, \tag{14}$$

Where $\mu_{\max}$ is the maximum growth rate, day-1;

$Y_{\max}$ is the maximum economic coefficient;

K_{S,NO_3} is the nitrate saturation constant, g/m^3;

S is the substrate concentration (e.g., concentration of organic substances in wastewater), g/m^3;

K_S is the substrate saturation constant, g/m;

X_B is the biomass concentration, g/m;

$r_{V,S}$ is the substrate consumption rate, kg/m^3 per day.

b. The dependence of heterotrophic denitrification process on temperature is expressed by formula (3.5). Denitrification may occur in a thermophilic regime (50-60°C), but experimental data about the operation of bioreactors in this mode are not sufficient to demonstrate this. The removal rate of thermophilic nitrates is approximately 50% faster than the removal rate of nitrates at 35°C.

Table 5. Kinetic parameters of denitrification

Parameters	Symbol	Unit	Value
Maximum specific growth rate*	μ_{max}	day^{-1}	3-6
Maximum specific growth rate for methanol	μ_{max}	day^{-1}	5-10
Nitrate saturation constant	K_S, NO_3	gr. (N)/m^3	0.2-0.5
Substrate saturation constant	K_S, BOC	g. BOD/m^3	10-20
Methanol saturation constant	$K_{S, MeOH}$	g. BOD/m^3	5-10
Maximum econ. coefficient*	Y_{max}	kg BOD/kg BOD	0.4-0.6
Maximum econ. coefficient*	Y_{max}	kg BOD/kg NO_3	1.6-1.8
Maximum econ. coefficient of methanol*	Y_{max}	kg BOD/kg BOD	0.5-0.65

* For organic substances in wastewaters

c. Denitrification is hampered by dissolved oxygen. According to various observations, in the system of attached microorganisms (e.g., biofilters), oxygen concentrations up to 2.5 mg/L in water, in some experiments, even concentrations up to 5 mg/L, and in the systems of weighted activated silt (aeration reservoirs), concentrations up to 0.5% mg/L have no effect on denitrification. According to formula 2.22, the denitrification rate in a weighted activated silt system approaches zero, while the dissolved oxygen concentration rises to 1 mg/L.

d. The optimal pH value for nitrification is 7-9. The final products of the denitrification process are influenced by a low pH (7). The amount of nitrogen oxide, particularly N_2O , increases as pH decreases. Table 5 shows some kinetic parameters of denitrifiers.

Anaerobic Oxidation of Nitrogen (ANAMMOX) [7, 9, 10, 21, 30, 41]

The first experiment evidencing anaerobic oxidation of ammonium was described by Mulder in 1992 and patented in 1995 (Mulder et al. 1995, 1992). The process of anaerobic nitrogen oxidation was called "ANAMMOX". Only in the late 1990s was the microbiological effect of anaerobic oxidation of ammonium salt (see equation 15) studied (Jetten et al. 1999, 2001).

$$NH_4^+ + NO_2^- \rightarrow N_2 + 2H_2O \qquad (15)$$

It is experimentally proven that anaerobic ammonia oxidation (ANAMMOX) process can by reached by various lithotrophic groups: 1. planctomycete: Cadidatus "Brodia anammoxidans", briefed to B.anammoxidans, as well as Kuenenia stuttgartiesis, briefed to K. Stuttgartiesis and 2. Nitrosomonas (e.g., N. Eutropha) [18, 22, 23].

Besides, as Nitrosomonas group demonstrated (Schmidt et al. 2001) in nitrogen oxide (NO_x) cycle, during aerobic and anaerobic oxidation of ammonium salt, ammonium salt (ANAMMOX) N_2O_4 is used in nitrogen dioxide (NO_2), as an oxidation agent and for converting into hydroxylamine. The latter is a significant intermediate compound of ANAMMOX process of B. anammoxidans bacteria (Figure 8).

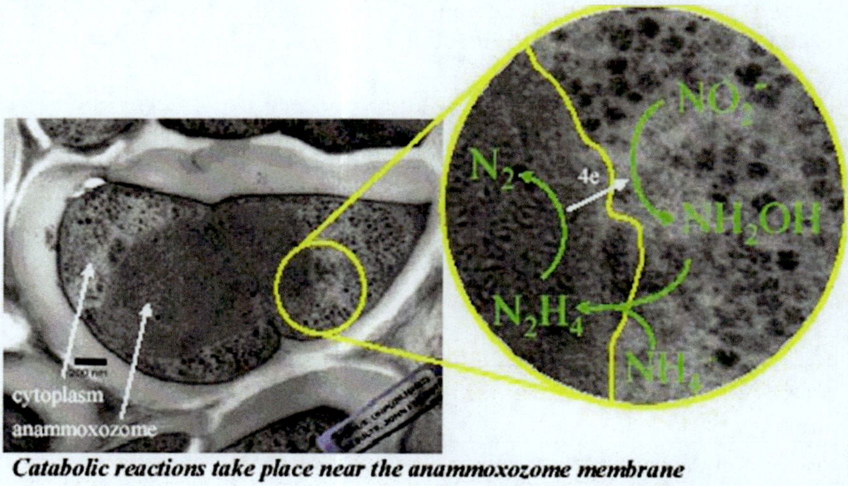

Figure 7. Catabolic reaction ANAMMOX (B.anammoxidans) (ongoing metabolic process in a cell membrane).

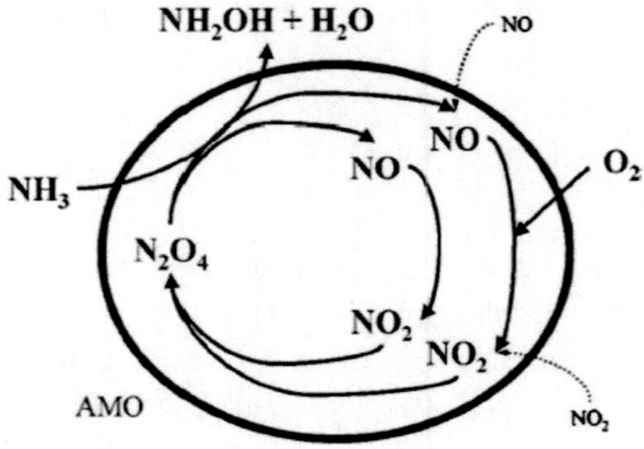

Figure 8. Cycle (NOx) during aerobic and anaerobic oxidation of ammonia by Nitrosomonas bacteria group (Schmidt et al. 2001).

In practice, ANAMMOX process of wastewaters is used in CANON and SHARON-ANAMMOX processes. The biological process of oxidation of ammoniacal nitrogen (NH_3, NH_4^+) to nitrate (NO2) is referred to as nitritation, and partial nitritation occurs ($NH_4^+ + 1.5O_2 \rightarrow NO_2^- + + H_2O + 2H^+$) in a combined system of SHARON-ANAMMOX process. Sharon and other reactor of ANAMMOX reaction ($NH_4^+ + 1NO_2^- \rightarrow N_2 + 2H_2O$) use ANAMMOX process.

Table 6. Main characteristics of the ANAMMOX process

Parameters	Symbol	Unit	Value
NH_4^+ maximum removal specific rate		g (NH_4^+)/g (protein). day	2-4
Economic coefficient	Y	g (protein)/kg (NH_4^+)	0.07
Inhibition of NH_4^+ removal by nitrates	K_i	g NH_4^+/l	0.8
Inhibition of NO_2^- ($\alpha = 0.7$) removal by nitrates	K_i	g NO_2^-/l	1
Content of proteins in biomass	-	g (protein)/g (total dry mass of biomass)	0.6
Protein density	-	g (protein)/(liter of biomass)	50

Like any biological process, the following external factors influence the ANAMMOX process: temperature, environmental pH, substrates (NO_2^-), etc. Temperature range of 20–43°C and pH 6.7-8.3 are ideal conditions for the ANAMMOX process. Table 6 shows the main characteristics of the ANAMMOX process.

Chapter 2

Biological Methods to Remove Biological Elements from Wastewaters

2.1. Deep Treatment of Wastewaters from Nitrogen Compounds

All biological methods of wastewater treatment from nitrogen compounds are based, as indicated in the previous chapter, on biological processes of oxidation of nitrogen compounds to nitrites and nitrates with subsequent reduction of oxidized nitrogen forms to free nitrogen. The main advantage of nitrification and nitri-denitrification technology is the possibility of its implementation in traditional biological treatment facilities. The processes of nitrification and nitri-denitrification have been investigated for a long time and are sufficiently studied.

The process of biological nitrification, i.e., removal of ammonia nitrogen (NH_4^+) from wastewater can be carried out in two ways:

- A separate or staged process of removal of organic pollutants (by BOD) and ammonia nitrogen (NH_4^+); and
- A combined process of removal of organic compounds (by BOD) and ammonia nitrogen (NH_4^+).

According to the principle of the treatment plant in the biological nitrification can be used suspended (in an aeration tank) or attached (in biofilter) activated sludge.

In addition, when considering biological methods, a distinction is made between those using a suspended sludge culture and those using an attached sludge culture. Within each group, nitrification and denitrification systems can be distinguished, combined and separate. Combined systems involve nitrification and denitrification in the same facility, while split systems involve nitrification or denitrification only.

Let us consider the biological methods using suspended sludge culture.

In separate systems using suspended culture, the organic treatment, nitrification and denitrification of the wastewater are carried out by specific sludge and each stage has its own secondary sedimentation tank. The sequence of the individual stages of the treatment process can be very diverse. The sequence of the individual stages of the treatment process can be very diverse. The most common schemes of separate nitrification and denitrification systems are shown in technical plan below (Figure 9).

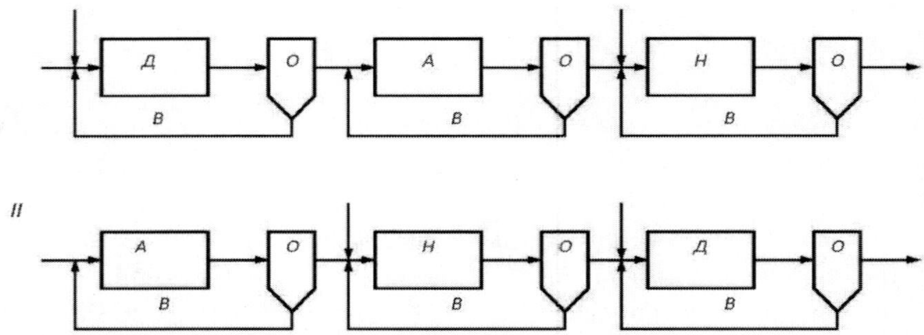

Figure 9. Technical plans of separate nitrification and denitrification systems. I – with a denitrifier at the beginning of the process; II – with a denitrifier at the end of the process.

The wastewater treatment process depicted in the technical plans above is characterized by high speed, ease of control, and stability at each stage. The disadvantage of the split systems is the need of additional secondary sedimentation tanks, requiring the construction of pumping stations for pumping circulating sludge and elevation differences. Individual stages of the processes may be carried out in reactors-mixers, displacers or in intermediate reactors, with or without separate regenerators, with or without supply of individual streams of nitrogen-containing water to the regenerators. The sludge separation unit can be designed as a conventional secondary sedimentation tank or a thin-layer two-stage sedimentation tank with a suspended sludge layer, a flotation sludge separator or a microfilter.

In combined systems using a suspended culture the processes of wastewater treatment from organic compounds, nitrification and denitrification are carried out in one facility by a mixed population of microorganisms. Activated sludge is separated from the treated liquid in a separate sludge separator or the one combined with a biochemical reactor. In certain cases, especially in the treatment of concentrated carbon- and nitrogen-containing wastewater, the combined system is divided into two treatment stages.

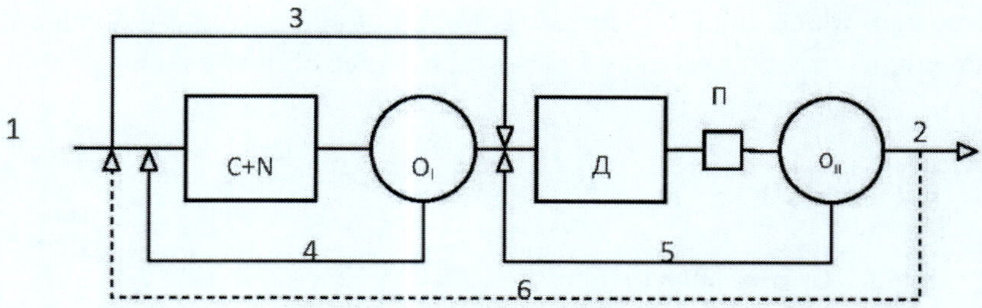

Figure 10. Combined system of nitri-denitrification.
C + N – aerotank-nitrifier; Д - denitrifier; O - sedimentation tanks; П - postaerator; 1 - source water; 2 - treated water; 3 - bypass of source water; 4 - return sludge of nitrifier; 5 - return sludge of denitrifier; 6 – transfer of flow from denitrifier for re-treatment.

The classical technical plan of nitri-denitrification developed by I. N. Churbanova and L. V. Yagolenko [48], using wastewater as a carbon source, is shown in Figure 11. The process occurring under this treatment scheme is characterized by stability in both nitrification and denitrification stages and ease of control. The ratio BOD_5: *N* total for denitrification can be of the order of (4-5): 1.

The rate of denitrification *RD* is determined by the reaction equation of zero order relative to the concentration of nitrate nitrogen, but depends on the concentration of pollutants in the wastewater by BOD_5. The equation is as follows:

$$RR_{DD} = aa \cdot (FF / MM)_{DD} + bb \qquad (16)$$

where (F/M)D is the load on the denitrifier sludge according to BOD without considering the residual BOD of the nitrified stream; a = 0.2 kg BOD_5/g; $b = 0.3$ g $N - NO_3$ per 1 kg of ashless sludge matter. Values of a and b are given for a temperature of 20°C.

The maximum value of RD = 9.5 mg N per 1 g of ashless sludge substance in 1 hour. Increasing the load on the denitrifier sludge reduces the efficiency of nitrogen removal, because a significant part of it enters the as ammonia nitrogen. If the BOD load far exceeds the organic carbon demand, the water leaving the denitrifier will have a high residual BOD. The excess of BOD over the amount of chemically bound nitrate oxygen should not be more than 20%, otherwise the leaving water will not be of satisfactory quality. In the described scheme the amount of return sludge can reach 300-400% of the water discharge, which naturally increases the cost of pumping and the volume of the sedimentation tank, but provides a high degree of nitrate removal.

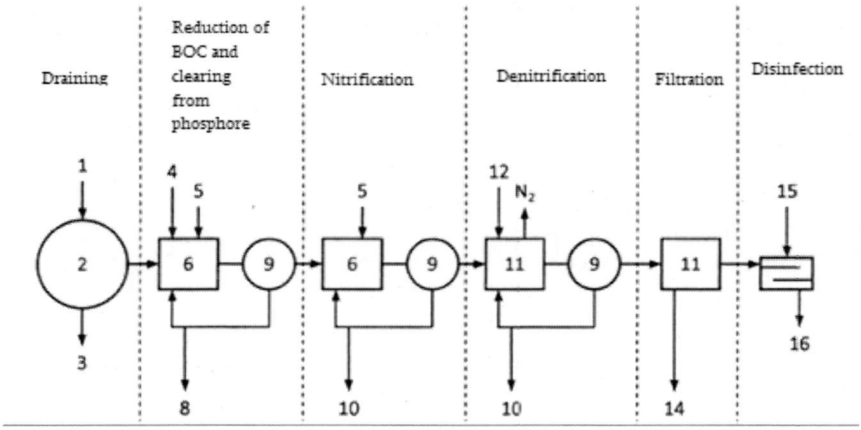

Figure 11. Nitri-denitrification plan.
1 – wastewater; 2 – primary sedimentation tank; 3 – organic matter precipitated; 4 – alum; 5 – air; 6 – aeration tank; 7 – return sludge; 8 – excess sludge; 9 – sedimentation tank; 10 – excess sludge of denitrification system; 11 – mixer; 12 – methanol; 13 – filters; 14 – rinsing water; 15 – chlorine; 16 – outlet.

Equally interesting is the nitrification – denitrification scheme, in which the treatment process allows for reduction of inorganic nitrogen by 90% and total nitrogen by 80-95% at the design wastewater flow rates. Such a system can be used in the reconstruction of sewage treatment plants as an addition to the existing biological treatment system. This nitrogen denitrification system consists of an agitator basin providing a displacement type flow followed by a sedimentation tank for separation and return of sludge. Agitation must be sufficient to keep the activated sludge in suspension, but without causing unnecessary aeration. Denitrification can also be achieved in a submerged biofilter; however, there are too few production tests available to serve as the foundation for the design of such a device (Figure 11) [49].

Three different patterns are currently used to treat low-concentration wastewater (Figure 12).

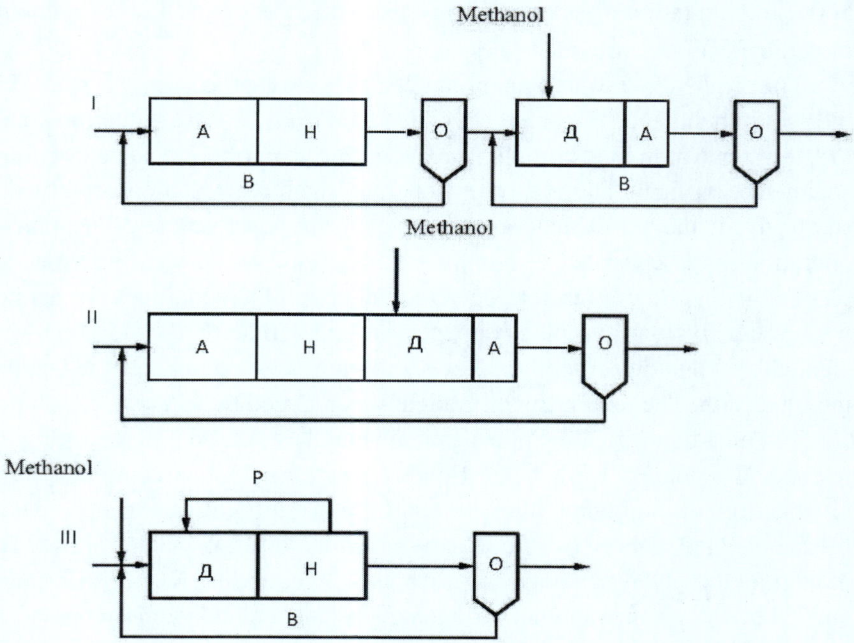

Figure 12. Plans of low-concentration wastewater treatment.
I – double-sludge; II – single-sludge; III – single-sludge plan with circulation.

Under the first plan, the wastewater, after the primary sedimentation tanks, is routed to aeration tanks with extended aeration, where deep nitrification is performed, and then the sludge mixture is separated in the secondary sedimentation tank. The settled sludge is directed to the beginning of the aerotank, and the clarified liquid containing nitrates moves to the denitrifier, where nitrate nitrogen is reduced to nitrogen gas without oxygen access under slow stirring of the sludge mixture. After the denitrification, the sludge mixture is aerated. Aeration enables nitrogen blowing from the sludge mixture, water oxygenation and prevention of further nitrogen formation, sludge stabilization, and removal of excessive carbon. The duration of the following aeration is 0.5-2 hours. Then the sludge mixture is fed into the tertiary sedimentation tank. The settled sludge returns to the top of the denitrifier, and the clarified liquid is discharged into the reservoir. The second plan differs from the first in the absence of a secondary sedimentation tank. Under the third plan, denitrification takes place as the treatment process starts. To reduce the residual content of nitrate nitrogen a considerable (up to 300-

500%) recirculation of sludge mixture from the reactor end to the beginning of denitrification is provided [50].

The efficiency of wastewater nitri-denitrification processes was studied in the equipment that included two reactors and a sedimentation tank. Wastewater was routed through the anaerobic reactor, aerobic reactor, and sedimentation tank. The equipment operated with recirculation of activated sludge from the sedimentation tank to the anaerobic reactor. The reactor operation mode consisted of four phases; phases 2 and 4 were intermediate phases, in which both reactors operated under aerobic conditions for aerated wastewater to flow into the sedimentation tank. Anaerobic conditions were created by reducing aeration to a level sufficient to maintain activated sludge in suspension. The total nitrogen content was reduced by 90% [51].

The nitri-denitrification plan using methanol as a carbon source is of great interest. The entire wastewater flow is treated in an aeration tank with nitrification of ammonia nitrogen, and flows into the denitrifier, where methanol is fed. Otherwise, the scheme is similar to that presented above. The oxidation of *C* and *N* can be divided, which will reduce the volume of aeration tanks, but will require another sedimentation tank and an additional pumping system. The peculiarity of using methanol is that this compound is easily oxidized, the oxidation products do not add contaminants to the treated wastewater, and the complete split of the processes provides optimal conditions to grow specialized sludge cultures [48].

Experimentally found values of the rate of nitrification with methanol range from 1 to 25 mg *N* per 1 g of ash-free sludge matter in 1 h. Other pure organic substances can be used instead of methanol.

In Germany, a method has been developed that allows for biological nitrogen removal to reduce the reaction volume at the nitrification stage by increasing the synthesis rate and growth rate of nitrifying bacteria as well as stabilize the process. Biological nitrification is accomplished by adding carbon dioxide or carbonic acid salts [52].

Johnson and Schroefer (USA) perform the denitrification process using raw sewage organics. According to the plan proposed by these authors, part of the raw sewage is aerated before conversion of ammonia nitrogen into nitrates, and part is fed directly to the denitrifier, where it is mixed with nitrified effluent. Depending on the concentration of effluent by BOD and nitrogen, the optimal ratio of flows into the aerotank and denitrificator can be calculated [33].

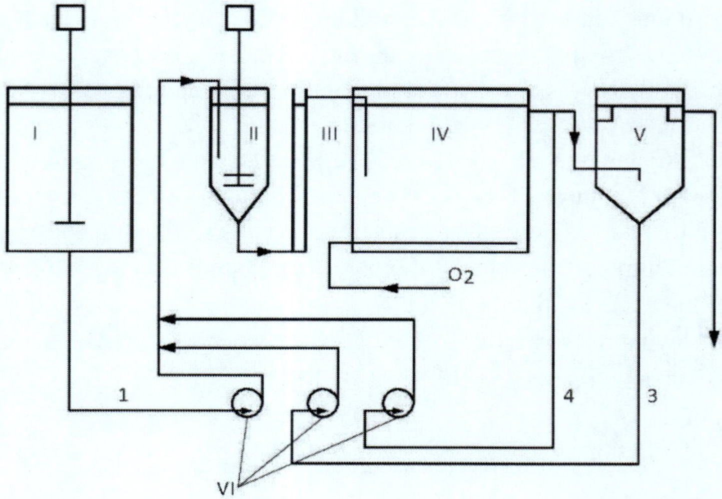

Figure 13. Treatment plan of wastewater with high nitrogen concentration.
I – equalizing tank; II – oxygen-free zone with an agitator; III – pressure regulator; IV – aerotank; V – sedimentation tank; VI – pumps; 1 – source wastewater; 2 – treated water; 3 – return sludge; 4 – return of water and sludge mixture.

In order to treat wastewater with the nitrogen content ranging from 100 to 500 mg/L, the treatment plan reducing the ammonia nitrogen content to 25 and the nitrate nitrogen content to 5 mg/L can be used (Figure 13) [6].

The advancement of pre-denitrification technology can be thought of a staged plan with multiple alternations of oxygen-free and aerated zones (Figure 16) [29].

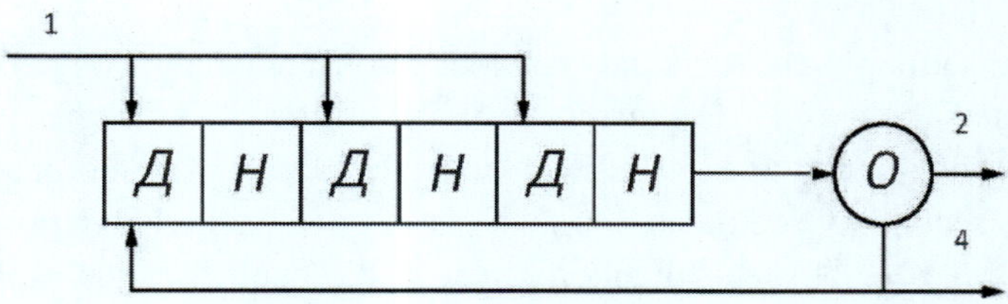

Figure 14. Plan of preliminary denitrification.
1 – supply of wastewater; 2 – treated water; 3 – return sludge; 4 – removal of excess sludge.

The following results were obtained when determining the possibility of removing nitrogen compounds in a two-corridor aeration tank: At a BOD_5 load of about 100 mg per 1 g of ashless sludge substance, without using additional carbon source, alternating aerobic and anaerobic conditions in each corridor allows for a 75-84% removal of nitrogen from wastewater. When air was supplied and the dissolved oxygen content was maintained at 2-3 mg/L, nitrification occurred in the aeration tank, which was replaced by denitrification if the air supply was terminated and the dissolved oxygen content was less than 0.5 mg/L. When air supply was stopped, the content of the aeration tank was stirred by mechanical agitators. Simultaneously with the removal of nitrogen the content of organic compounds decreased by more than 85% of the COD [42].

The layout proposed by Ekenfelder of the so-called "contact-stabilization process" is quite interesting (Figure 15) [33].

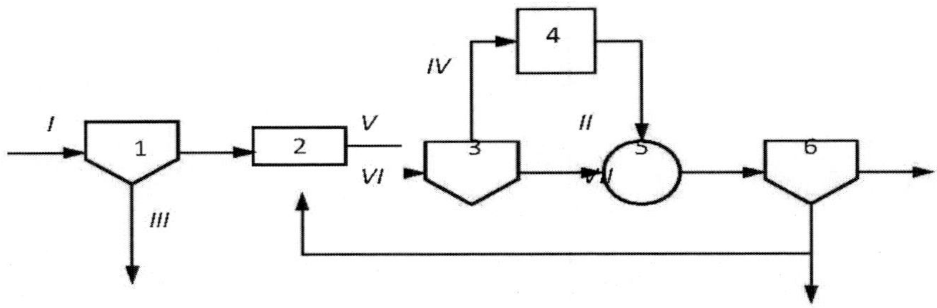

Figure 15. Contact-stabilization process diagram.
1 – primary sedimentation tank; 2 – aeration tank; 3 – secondary sedimentation tank; 4 – nitrification biofilter; 5 – denitrification reservoir; 6 – tertiary sedimentation tank; I – received wastewaters; II – treated water; III – row sludge; IV – wastewater from secondary sedimentation tank; V – activated sludge; VI – circulating activated sludge; VII – excess activated sludge.

After settling in the secondary sedimentation tank, the biologically treated water enters the biofilter for nitrification. The nitrified effluent then enters the denitrification tank, which is fed with activated sludge rich in organic matter from the secondary sedimentation tank. The activated sludge rich in organic matter is fed to the denitrification tank. In the denitrification tank, in the presence of anaerobic microorganisms, in addition to the denitrification process, stabilization of organic matter takes place. The sludge mixture from the denitrifiers goes to the tertiary sedimentation tank, from which the sludge returns to the aerotank and the treated water returns to the reservoir. This method allows the removal of up to 80-90% of nitrogen [33].

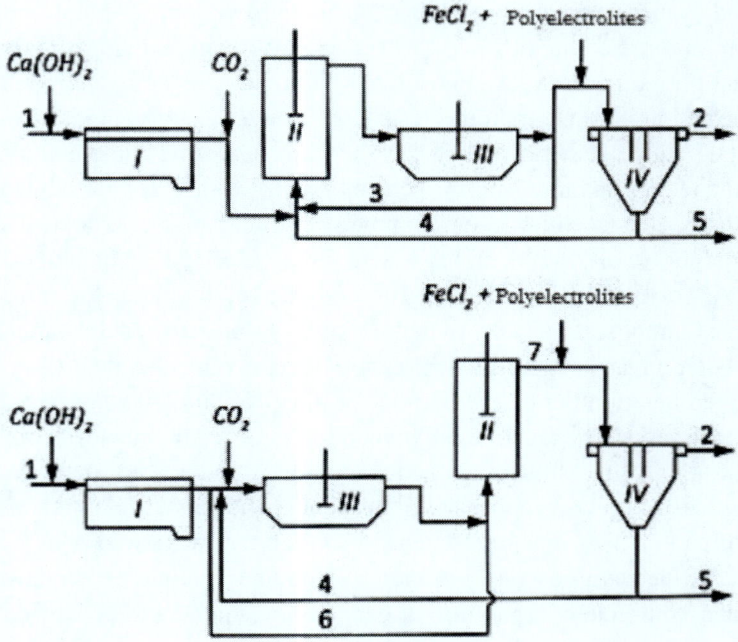

Figure 16. Nitri-denitrification diagrams with preliminary chemical treatment. a – for denitrification of total raw water flow with recycling of large amounts of nitrified effluent; b – for division of raw effluent into nitrification and denitrification; I – primary sedimentation tank; II – denitrifier; III – biological nitrification pond; IV – secondary sedimentation tank; 1 – raw sewage; 2 – treated water; 3 – nitrified sewage return; 4 – return sludge; 5 – excess sludge discharge; 6 – water clarified in the primary sedimentation tank.

Another method is that a closed nitrification tank is fed with gas containing more than 50% oxygen. From this tank, the water flows to the secondary deasotization tank and then to the spinning centrifuge.

The separated liquid is fed to the secondary sedimentation tank and part of the separated sludge is recirculated to the primary de-nitrification tank [38].

The denitrification effect can be increased by a combination of chemical pretreatment of wastewater with lime followed by biological denitrification and final sedimentation with the addition of chlorine iron and polyelectrolytes [33]. Water treatment diagrams are given in Figure 16.

The scheme shown in Figure 16 is featured by the return of a large amount of mixture (up to 400%) from the pond to the denitrifier and the use of part of the raw sewage in the denitrifier. The experiment found that 8-11 hrs. is sufficient for deep denitrification and COD reduction (chemical oxygen demand), and 6 hrs. is sufficient for denitrification to nitrate nitrogen concentration less than 10 mg/L. Less energy is required for diagram “b”, needing no recarbonization. Phosphorus in this case is completely removed, and the residual concentration is less than 0.2 mg/L.

The nitri-denitrification process can also be implemented by “simultaneous sedimentation” scheme, i.e., with the introduction of coagulants (ferric chloride or aluminum chloride) in aeration tanks, with aeration period of 2 hours and at a working dose of activated sludge 1.3 g/L (0.8 g/L for ashless substance). The complex of facilities for removal of nitrogen compounds should include a reactor for nitrification, appropriate sedimentation tanks, and denitrification reactor with sedimentation tanks. Estimated aeration period in reactors for nitrification of wastewater is taken equal to 4 hours. The reaction of the medium is corrected by introducing lime. The duration of the subsequent sedimentation is about 4 hours. To intensify the process, it is proposed to introduce methanol into reactors for denitrification. This reactor is intended for delay of wastewaters in it for 3-9 hours. To release gaseous nitrogen, 21-minute mixing of wastewater is provided. Subsequent separation of denitrifying sludge will be carried out in sedimentation tanks for 3.8 h.

Nitrifying and denitrifying sludge must be forwarded to the corresponding reactors, i.e., they must be in circulation all the time. Their excessive amounts are to be discharged and further treated with other plant sludge [50].

One of the possible biological methods of wastewater treatment from nitrogen is treatment in biological ponds with mass production of algae. Algae activity in the ponds results in direct consumption of nitrogen compounds from wastewater, as well as a significant reduction in concentrations of other residual pollutants Temperature, light, carbon, and nutrient concentrations have all been shown to have a significant impact on algae growth. At 21-28°C, the best conditions for algae growth and, as a result, the most complete removal of nitrogen compounds are achieved. Given the high light absorption of wastewater, particularly in the development of algae, effective phytoplankton development is only possible at a shallow depth. In most cases, complete nitrogen consumption necessitates the addition of carbon, which can be obtained through aeration with air at the expense of carbon dioxide in it. The depth of the pond should be no more than 1 m to reduce the nitrogen content in the water by 80-90% with a residence time of 3 to 5 days. The algae concentration in this case is 100-150 mg/L. It should be noted, however, that the cleaning effect is practically non-existent for weather conditions in the middle climatic zone during the autumn, winter, and spring seasons. Based on the results of the research described above, a process flow diagram of wastewater treatment in a three-section aerated biological pond was proposed. In the first two sections, wastewaters are purified using algae. In the third section, zooplankton organisms can be cultivated using algae, and algae can be utilized. Centrifugation can be used to remove excess algae biomass after it has been concentrated in the flotator.

Introduction of artificial aeration in biological ponds allows not only improving the productivity of these structures significantly, but also ensuring the stable high quality of treated water throughout the year and practically excluding the influence of climatic factors on the processes of treatment. Since artificial aeration provides a constant supply of oxygen to the pond sludge and mixing of all pond contents, it is possible to consider the pond sludge as active. Advantages of introduction of artificial aeration in ponds can be briefly stated as follows: increase in the depth of ponds up to 4 m and more, which leads to a 2-5 times reduction in the area of aerated ponds; increase in the rate of oxidation of impurities by 1.5-2 times compared with the non-aerated; possibility to significantly increase the dose of silt in ponds and, therefore, increase oxidation capacity of the structure. Studies of Moscow State University of Civil Engineering (MGSU) (former Moscow Institute of Civil Engineering named after V.V. Kuybyshev (MISI)) recommend using ponds consisting of three sections, two of which are aerated and the third is a settling pond. The duration of wastewater in the aerated zone of the pond depends on BOD, the concentration of microorganisms and the allowable load on the sludge according to BOD. The volume of the sedimentation section of the pond is appointed according to the conditions of water detention in it for 10 hours [5]. To increase the rate of nitrogen removal in bioponds, the fixation of nitrifiers on PVC sheets, nylon fishing net, car tires is proposed. The material is packaged in cassettes and placed in the pond. Wastewater pretreatment processes can also be carried out with symbiotic sludge composed of algae and bacteria (algobacterial sludge). The Scientific Research Institute "Vodgeo" conducted all the necessary tests proving that at an average specific oxidation rate of 36-37 mg/(g·h) and other equal conditions in the symbiotank, the efficiency of nitrogen removal was 87%, that of phosphorus was 88%, and 4.5 mg/L for oxygen concentration. These indicators were much lower in an aeration tank: 40%, 60% and 2 mlg/L, correspondingly. At the same time there were good sedimentation properties of the sludge, which did not bloat and the index did not exceed 42 cm^3/g. Additional treatment of wastewaters in symbioreservoirs is also possible in several stages [4].

To treat wastewater from nitrogen compounds using attached sludge culture, filters with water movement relative to the fixed loading material as well as with movement of loading relative to water are used. Wastewater, methanol, and other organic matters are used as carbon sources. The water movement can be from top to bottom and vice versa.

Nitrogen removal rates of 70 to 80% are achieved when wastewater is used as a carbon source, and over 90% with methanol.

The ratio of methanol to nitrogen quantities should be more than three. To purify wastewater from nitrogen compounds, studies were carried out in the models of non-flooded biofilters. The following processes were studied: joint oxidation of carbon and ammonia nitrogen; nitrification process in biofilter with natural aeration; and nitrification process in aerofilter.

Table 7. Parameters of operation of biofilters in a nitrification

A separate nitrification stage						
Biofilter with natural aeration			Aerofilter			
q	*C* *N-NH*	*OM*	*q*	*Q* air	*C* *N-NH*	*OM*
$m^3/m^2/day$	Mlg/L	$gr/m^3/day$	$m^3/m^2/day$	m^3/m^3	mlg/L.	$gr/m^3/day$
4.0	20.0	70.6	10.0	8.0	20.0	176.0
2.0	50.0	94.8	7.0	8.0	50.0	329.0
1.0	100.0	96.0	5.0	8.0	100.0	480.0

The ratio of methanol to nitrogen quantities should be more than three. To purify wastewater from nitrogen compounds, studies were carried out in the models of non-flooded biofilters. The following processes were studied: joint oxidation of carbon and ammonia nitrogen; nitrification process in biofilter with natural aeration; and nitrification process in aerofilter. Table 7 shows values of oxidative capacity of biofilters, determined by the amount of ammonia nitrogen removed in them. The highest values were obtained for aerofilters. At ammonia nitrogen concentrations above 100 mg/L, nitrification processes in biofilters are inhibited. At pH = 7-8 the provision of alkaline reserve by adding free carbon dioxide is required for biofilters-nitrifiers. Nitrification processes under the load have a buffering capacity. Biofilter-nitrifiers provide 80-90% removal of ammonia nitrogen even at lower temperatures and quickly restore oxidative capacity after various stress conditions. Biofilm on the biofilter load is a thin film that takes a long time to dry and does not wash off well. The removal of substances from the nitrification biofilters does not exceed 10 mg/L. So, there is no need to install sedimentation tanks after them.

The transformations of nitrogen compounds during filtration through a sand load were investigated in semi-production settings. The installation consisted of a sand filter and two columns, one of which had a load similar to the filter load, the second was loaded in several layers with mineral wool with a pore volume of 90%. In a part of loading of both columns air was fed. During this filtration process, nitrifying and denitrifying flora develop in the load. It was found that the division of the filtration process into stages in a single column, by separating zones of nitrification and denitrification by feeding air into the loading section, allows removing nitrogen compounds by 50-60% [53].

In studies of biochemical nitri-denitrification in biofilters with plastic loading, the best results were obtained for the loading material with a specific surface of 600, 250, 160 m^2/m^3 at 25-30°C with a 1 m layer, when the efficiency of nitrogen removal was 97-99% [54]

Submerged biofilters (VNII VODGEO) are of certain interest – where water moves from bottom to top. Such biofilters with a suspended layer of loading are highly efficient, allowing the reduction of the size of the loading material, which reduces the duration of water treatment. The nitrification processes were stable at temperatures up to 1°C above the ambient temperature. At a concentration of ammonium nitrogen of 20 mg/L, 90% oxidation of the input wastewater was achieved within 30 min at 25°C; 60 min at 10°C; and 90-120 min at 5°C [3].

If it is necessary to reduce the nitrogen concentration below 1 mg/L, it takes a very long time to oxidize wastewater. In this case, a more economical treatment can be nitrification in a submerged biofilter followed by chlorination.

J. Iida and A. Teranishi propose a way to remove nitrogen from municipal wastewater using a submerged filter. The filter is constructed as a column of sheet steel. For uniform dispersion of wastewater through the filter, a dispersing plate with 1 cm diameter holes was placed at a distance of 70 cm above the bottom of the filter. A mesh plastic material was placed in the column. The porosity of the material was about 0.94. The aeration fixture was created from porous stones and placed below the effluent inlet. Air was supplied periodically to create aerobic or anoxic conditions in the filter. Experiments have shown that successful co-oxidation of carbon, and nitrification and denitrification can be achieved in the primary effluent stream without external carbon sources in a single submerged filter with periodic aeration conditioning for aerobic or anoxic conditions. Efficient nitrogen removal is achieved at the expense of the ratio of on-cycle aeration to off-cycle aeration in a periodic aeration operation cycle, to the delay time, to the ratio of outgoing flow re-cycle, and to temperatures [55].

The process of denitrification in a frame-and-fill filter with downstream water flow was also studied. The system of a frame-and-fill filter and denitrifier is loaded with 40-60 mm-diameter gravel on the entire loading height. A 0.8-1 mm-diameter sand filler is placed in the lower part of the gravel cage, at a height of 90 cm. The purpose of the sand during filtration is to detain fine suspension, and to destroy the sediment formed on the grains of the fixed framework during washing.

In order to ensure that part of the biofilm is kept on the filter loading grains, filter partial washing has been proposed. Keeping a part of the biofilm on the load allows for a quicker start-up of the filter. Time of contact of the treated water with the film on the load should not be more than 2 hours. The maximum concentration of nitrate nitrogen in the initial water must not exceed 100 mg/L, otherwise the accumulation of gas in the load that leads to the increase of loading resistance and the necessity of washing practically clean filtrate is possible. The required dosage ratio of added substrate to $N\text{-}NO_3$ concentration should be taken as 4:1, with a nitrate removal of about 80%. G. Bringmann and R. Kühn suggested filling the denitrifier with coke. Denitrifying microflora forms a developed film on the coke load. Denitrifier operates in the turbulent mode of wastewater flow. This mode of operation provides intensive exchange between biofilm and wastewater. In 20 minutes, 72% of nitrogen is removed [49]. Particular attention is paid to the use of activated carbon as a loading material, combining the functionality of a biofilm carrier and sorbent. Nitrogen removal rate in this case reaches 6.7 kg/(m^3·day). Hydraulic load amounts to 20-50 m/h, which corresponds to water retention time of only 3-10 minutes. A similar result was obtained when using sand as a loading material. At holding in the biofilter for 6.5 minutes and water load of 37 m/h, the nitrogen removal was 99%. Operation of such filters is complicated by the need to control the biomass of the film. Denitrification generates a sludge increment of approximately 0.5 mg of dry matter per 1 mg of removed BOD_5 in combined systems and 0.5 mg of dry matter per 1 mg of removed nitrate nitrogen in split systems, i.e., less than in oxygen-oxidation systems. The sludge index is 50-100 mg/L of ash-free sludge matter with an ash content of about 70%. The nitrogen content in the sludge is 5-7 mg N/mg of dry matter.

Wastewater treatment of nitrogen compounds is also possible with a disc biofilter operating in the nitrification mode. The stability of the nitrate nitrogen concentration in the system is provided by the partial addition of fresh water and the corresponding discharge of contaminated water. The filter cleaning effect for ammonium nitrogen was 33-40%.

Following the denitrification in a biofilter, postaeration is also necessary, which provides nitrogen removal from liquid (otherwise, flotation of sludge in the sedimentation tank is expected), water oxygenation and prevention of further nitrogen formation, sludge stabilization, removal of excessive carbon, especially methanol. Depending on the action of each factor, the duration of postaeration varies from a few minutes to several hours, but most commonly, it is 30 to 50 minutes.

Studies conducted by A. Penaud and I. J. Mildbrooks on ammonia nitrogen removal on disc biofilters showed that ammonia nitrogen removal is affected by temperature and organic contamination load. Total ammonia removal ranged from 87 to 98% at 15°C and 91 to 99% at 20°C. No ammonia nitrogen is removed at 5°C. The total amount of ammoniacal nitrogen removed decreases as the organic pollution load of the wastewater entering the treatment plant increases.

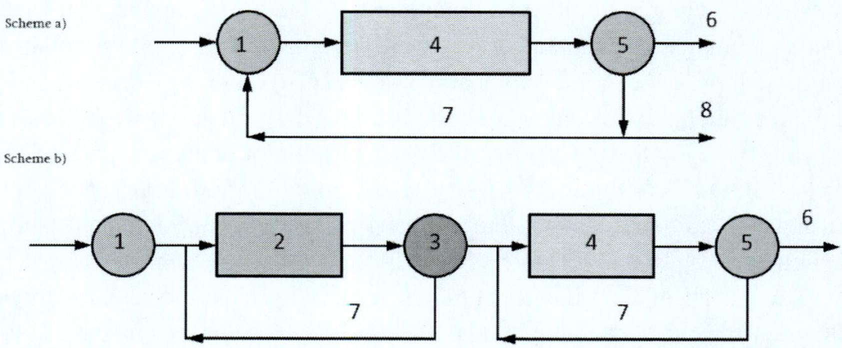

Figure 17. Diagrams of combined (a) and separate (b) nitrification.
1 – primary sedimentation tank; 2 – BOD removal facility; 3 – intermediate sedimentation tank; 4 – nitrification facilities; 5 – secondary sedimentation tank; 6 – treated wastewater; 7 – recirculation; 8 – excess sludge for utilization.

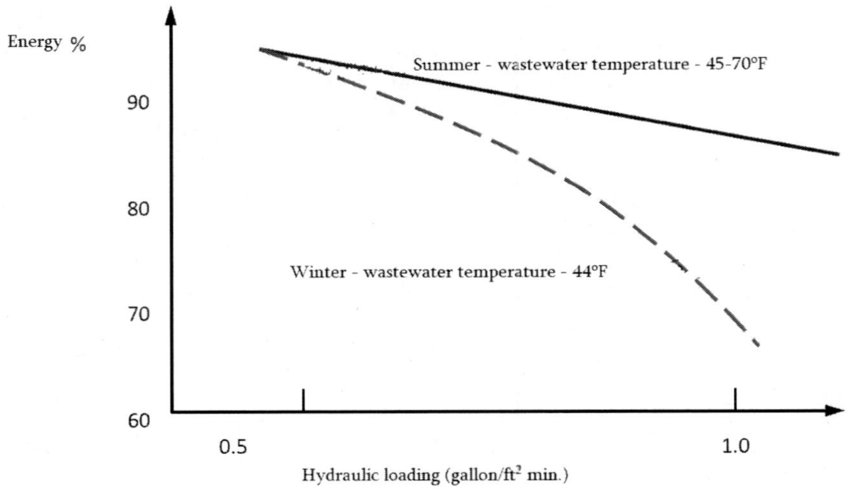

Figure 18. Impact of hydraulic loading on nitrification in biofilter; gal/ft2.min x 40.74 l/m^2 min.

Joint removal of organic compounds (according to BOD_5) and ammonium nitrogen ($NH_4 - N$) that occurs in a single-oil nitrification system is a process in which oxidation of organic compounds (BOD) and nitrification occur simultaneously in one bioreactor (Figure 19a). Nitrification is performed in all traditional processes of biological wastewater treatment (with suspended activated sludge, with attached active biomass). The degree of nitrification depends on many factors, such as the concentration of ammonia nitrogen and nitrite, BOD_5/TKN ratio, dissolved oxygen concentration, temperature, pH, wastewater residence time in the bioreactor, the degree of activated sludge recirculation.

Almost all of the above-mentioned technological wastewater treatment schemes for nitrogen compounds are used in a complex manner today. Therefore, tentatively we can say that most of the above described schemes of nitri-denitrification use a split process of BOD and ammonia nitrogen removal. The process is carried out in two stages. The first stage is designed to remove organic matter (according to BOD), and the second is designed for the removal of ammonia nitrogen. Schematic diagrams of joint and separate nitrification are shown in Figure 19. Both processes (with attached or suspended activated sludge) are used to maximize the effect of nitrification processes in separate structures, while providing more reliable and stable removal of organic pollutants (according to BOD_5) and ammonia nitrogen. At the same time, toxic substances and their bulk flow into the biological treatment plant, which may affect the processes of nitrification, will be localized in the first stage at a lower concentration of organic pollutants. However, the effectiveness of reducing BOD_5 in the first stage has an effect on the nitrification processes in the second stage, and the use of a bioreactor in the second stage with attached active biomass may be the cause of biomass imbalance in the bioreactor-nitrifier with suspended activated sludge.

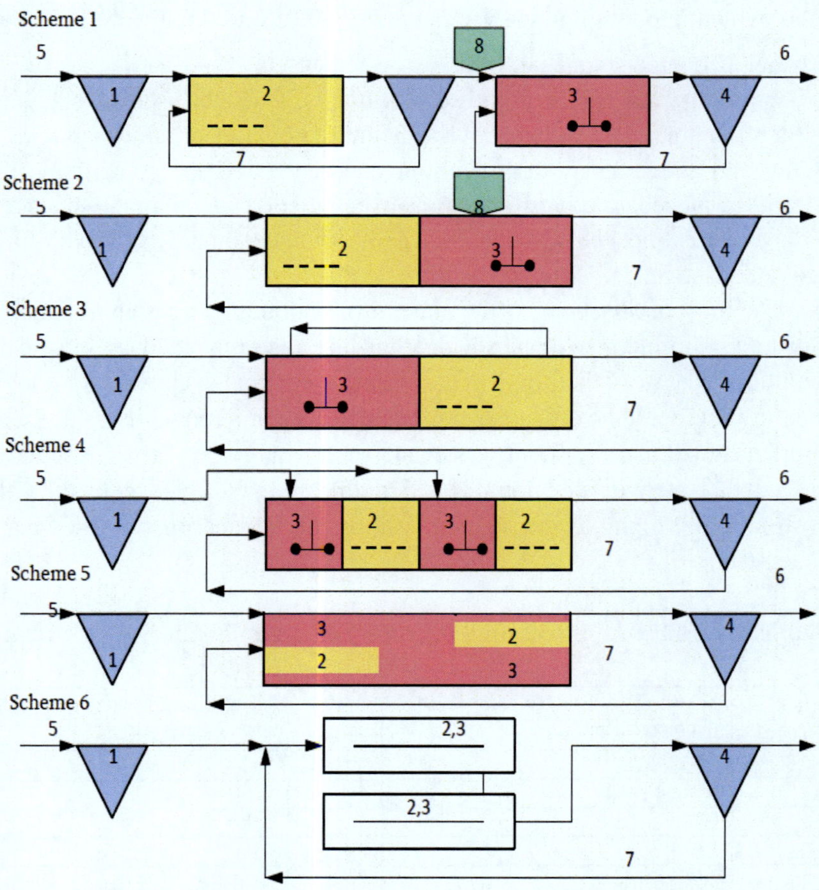

Figure 19. Technological diagrams of biological treatment from nitrogen compounds (nitri-denitrification technology).
1 – primary sedimentation tank; 2 – nitrifier; 3-denitrifier; 4 – secondary sedimentation tank; 5 – input wastewaters; 6 – treated wastewaters;
7 – recirculation of activated sludge.

To determine the intensity of the separate nitrification process, the term nitrification rate is used, which is determined experimentally and is measured in mg of oxidizable NH_4 per 1 g of ash-free activated sludge per unit time (hour or day). The nitrification rate increases with increasing temperature. The BOD_5/TKN (total Kjeldahl nitrogen) ratio is an important characteristic of the nitrification process. Depending on the temperature and wastewater characteristics, the nitrification rate increases with decreasing BOD5/TKN ratio, which in optimal mode varies between 0.05 and 0.6 g NH_4 per 1 g of ash-free activated sludge per day.

Biofilters and submerged disc biofilters are widely used in practice of wastewater treatment to carry out separate removal of organic pollutants by BOD_5 and ammonia nitrogen with attached activated sludge (Figure 19 b). Biofilters in separate nitrification can be applied after the first stage of biological treatment by suspended (in aeration tanks) or attached (in biofilters) activated sludge.

The most used scheme of separate nitrification is a two-step treatment on biofilters. Biofilters with plastic loading are recommended as nitrification facilities because of their high specific surface area (see above). As it can be seen in Figure 20, the effect of ammonium nitrogen removal decreases as the hydraulic load increases and wastewater temperature increases. Practice has proved that at hydraulic load of 0.5 gal/ft^2.min, which is equal to 20.37 l/(m^2·min), a high degree of nitrification in all seasons of the year is guaranteed.

Table 8. Number of nitrification microorganisms at BOC5/ TKN correlation

BOC_5/ TKN	Share of nitrification of microorganisms	BOC_5/ TKN	Share of nitrification of microorganisms
0.5	0.35	5	0.054
1	0.21	6	0.043
2	0.12	7	0.037
3	0.083	8	0.033
4	0.064	9	0.029

Nitrifying microorganisms are present in almost all aerobic biological wastewater treatment processes, but usually their number is limited. The ability of activated sludge microorganisms to the nitrification process is characterized by the BOD_5/TKN (total Kjeldahl nitrogen) ratio. When the BOD_5/TKN ratio is between 1 and 3, the biological wastewater treatment process corresponds to the process in a separate nitrification system. The proportion of nitrifying microorganisms in this case varies from 0.21 (BOD_5/TKN = 1) to 0.083 (BOD_5/TKN = 3) (see Table 8). The classical process flow diagram of biological wastewater treatment fixes the proportion of nitrifying microorganisms less than 0.083. When the BOD_5/TKN ratio is more than 5, joint removal of BOD and ammonia nitrogen is observed, at values less than 3 the process occurs in the mode of separate nitrification [56].

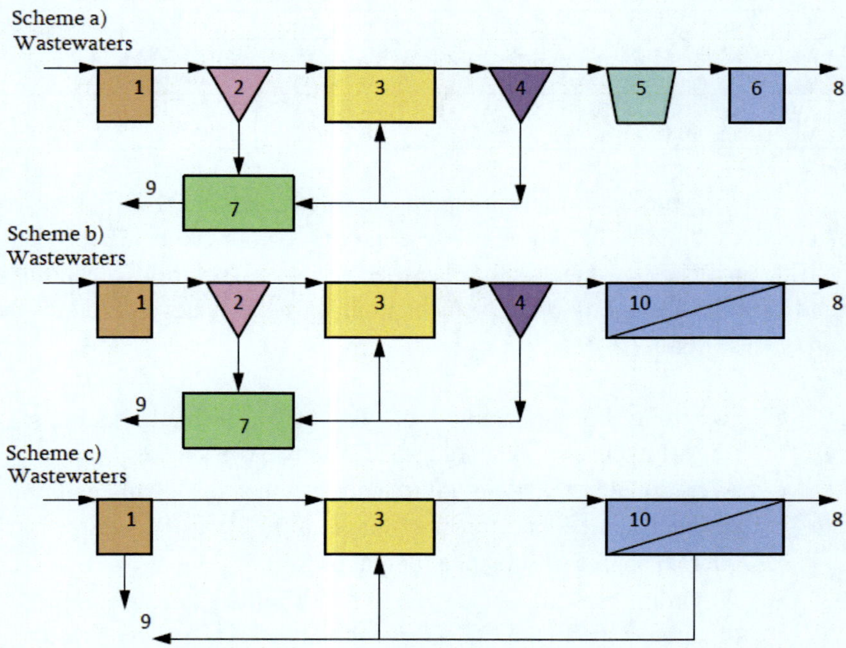

Figure 20. Technological diagrams of deep treatment of wastewaters.
a. traditional; b. traditional, with a final cleaning block of the filtration membrane; c. with membrane reactor; 1 – preliminary purification; 2 – primary sedimentation tank; 3 – aeration tank; 4 – secondary sedimentation tank; 5 – sand filter; 6 – disinfection of wastewaters; 7 – treatment of activated sludge; 8 – treated wastewaters; 9 – utilization of sediment; 10 – membrane reactor.

Biofilters (including submerged) refer to biological treatment facilities using attached microorganisms. The degree of nitrification in biofilters is determined by organic load by BOD_5. Table 9 shows data on the dependence of the efficiency of nitrification processes in different biofilter designs on the organic load of BOD5. At present, in the UK, where biofilters are used at almost 70% of biological wastewater treatment plants, an intense process of their reconstruction and modernization is underway to ensure the normative requirements for the treated wastewater on the content of ammonia nitrogen. The recommended minimum hydraulic load was accepted for biofilters with loading height of 1.7-2.0 (m) 2 $m^3/(m^2 \cdot day)$ [57].

Table 9. BOD5 load values for nitrification in a structure with attached microorganisms

Type of structure	Nitrification treatment effect	Loading according to BOD_5
Biofilters (gravel, rubble)	75-85 85-95	0.160-0.096 0.096-0.048
Tower biofilters, biofilters with plastics loads	75-85 85-95	0.288-0.192 0.192-0.096

Thus, the processes of nitrification and denitrification are sufficiently well studied. A number of process flow diagrams of the biological process of nitridenitrification, which can be classified according to various technological and technical methods of implementation, have been developed for these processes (Figure 19):

- According to the amount of the sludge formed: double-sludge (diagram-1) and single-sludge (diagrams 2-6);
- According to the types of the used substrates: with addition of external source of substrate (diagram 1, 2), using wastewater as internal source of substrate (diagrams 3-6);
- According to the stages of wastewater treatment: single-stage (diagrams 1-3), double-stage (diagram 4) and circulating (with repeated passage of aerobic and anaerobic zones in bioreactor, during purification) (diagram 5);
- Diagram of the wastewater treatment in an intermittent mode, with a regular alternation of aerobic and anaerobic processes in some zones of the structure (diagram 6).

Technically, the scheme of aerobic-anaerobic modes of wastewater treatment is carried out either by flowing sludge mixture through the anaerobic and aerobic zones of biological treatment facility, equipped with appropriate devices for mixing and aeration (diagrams 1-5), or by automatic change of aeration and mixing modes by mechanical means in the facility (diagram 6, Figure 21).

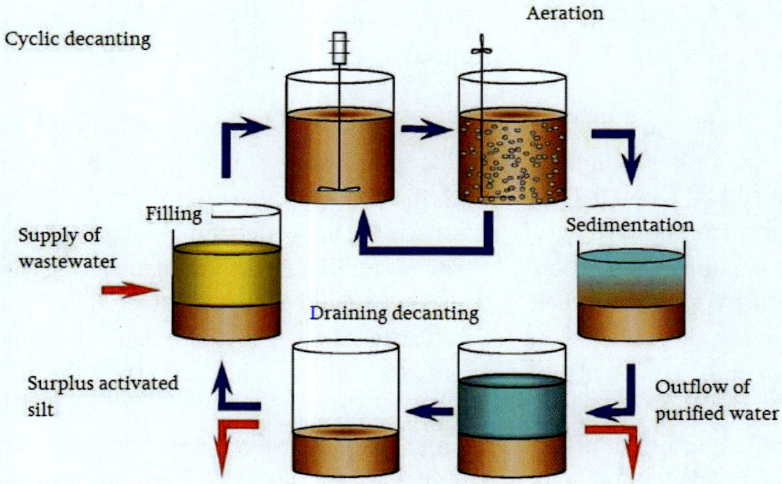

Figure 21. Diagram of wastewater treatment processes during one SBR cycle.

One promising way to intensify the nitrification-denitrification process is the use of attached microorganisms. Attached microflora can be used both in aeration tanks and in classical biofilters. At present, various systems of wastewater treatment from nitrogen compounds using attached biomass, which differ from each other by the principles of operation, have been developed and applied. These are biofilters with water movement relative to the fixed loading material, with the movement of the loading relative to water. Water movement can be from top to bottom and vice versa.

A new generation of submerged biofilters (filters B2a) has been developed in Europe. Submerged biofilter with fixed loading has been successfully used for the 2nd and 3rd stages of wastewater treatment. It should be noted that all submerged biofilters of the old generation are single-layer. The new generation of the submerged biofilter with aeration (B2a) is multilayer, the biofilter is equipped with a system of aeration washing and can be used in technology of pretreatment and wastewater treatment to remove nitrogen, phosphorus and organic compounds (BOC_5) [58, 59].

There are many options for bioreactor designs using different carriers:

- Volumetric rigid plastic cellular elements;
- Sheet and mesh blocks [42];
- Frame structures with a ruff carrier coiled on them [12, 41];

- Biodiscs in aeration tanks or submerged biofilters and rotary drums as independent structures [27, 42].

Another method of creating attached microflora in the aeration basin is the use of bulk synthetic materials, the density of which is close to one [42]. In order to retain the media, the elements of which float freely in the volume of the aeration basin, grids are installed at the outlet of the sludge mixture from the aeration basin. Another technical solution is the placement of the elements in the mesh boxes, such as expanded clay or polyurethane foam. The use in aeration tanks of elements of the carrier, the density of which is less than one (floating), is one of the most simple and structurally available methods of solving the considered problem.

The use of attached microorganisms allows accelerating the removal of organic matter and increasing removal of nitrogen compounds. This modern direction of biotechnology is intensively developed in different countries of the world in joint works of scientists of different specializations – microbiologists, ecologists and engineers [60].

Another new direction for the removal of nutrients is the use of membrane technology in wastewater treatment. The principle of the membrane bioreactor (Figure 20) is that the membrane filtration system prevents the loss of activated sludge from the system and thus maintains a high dose of it in the reactor.

The disadvantage of membrane technology is high capital investment and significant operating costs.

In the world practice of biological treatment of both municipal and industrial wastewater containing nitrogen, biological reactors (aerotanks) of cyclic filling type (SBR – Sequencing Batch Reactor) are widely used. Wastewater treatment by SBR-technology is carried out in cycles and is one of the alternatives to conventional cleaning in the flow-type reactors (aeration tanks) [61].

In the following years, several municipal wastewater treatment plants were built using this technology in England and the United States, but already by 1920. SBR technology was replaced and the cyclic reactors were converted to flow-type reactors. The reason for the rejection of SBR was due to a number of technical problems that arose due to the lack of process automation capability and the mechanical aeration used at the time.

For the next three decades, SBR technology was only rarely used and exclusively for the treatment of industrial effluents.

New era of development and improvement of SBR technology starts with the cyclic decanted reactor, designed by Dutch scientists Pasveer in 1959. Its example is intermittently decanted reactor with prolonged aeration (IDEA - Intermittently Decanted Extended Aeration), developed by Australian scientists in 1990. American scientists Irwin and Davis (1979) studied the impacts of sequence and duration of different phases on biological treatment processes (Wilderer et al, 2001).

With the need to remove nutrients in the 1990s, the SBR was improved with an anaerobic phase device for biological phosphorus removal. The SBR with Granula Sequencing Biofilm Batch Reactor (GSBR) (Rohricht, 2007) and the Sequencing Biofilm Batch Reactor (SBBR) (Podedworna, 2003) are currently being investigated.

The working principle of the SBR is based on the cyclic alternation of wastewater treatment processes occurring in a single reactor. Each cycle consists of certain phases, the duration and sequence of which is set depending on the desired effect of biological treatment. Figure 21 shows one typical diagram of the SBR cycle.

The phases of the SBR cycle are as follows:

- Filling phase: during this phase, wastewater is fed and the substrate is accumulated in the reactor. Wastewater supply can be carried out by several schemes: "fast filling" – when the supply is turned off before the start of the subsequent mixing phase; "slow filling" – water supply is also done during the mixing and aeration phases, the so-called reaction phase.
- Mixing phase: denitrification occurs as a result of the mixing of wastewater and activated sludge.
- Aeration phase: by means of aeration, the activated sludge mixture is saturated with dissolved oxygen (recommended concentration of O_2 is 2-3 mlg/L), under favorable conditions (environmental pH, temperature, etc.) autotrophic bacteria carry out the nitrification process.
- Sedimentation phase: when aeration and mixing are switched off, the activated sludge sedimentation starts. The pace and duration of the sedimentation process depend on the value of the sludge index.
- Decanting phase: upon the expiration of time set for the sedimentation of the activated sludge, the treated water is removed from the reactor.

- Settling phase: to synchronize the operation of several reactors, as well as to maintain the necessary discharge capacity, it is advisable to use the sedimentation phase. During this phase, it is possible to remove the excess activated sludge from the system (removal of excess sludge can be done during the other phases of the cycle).

The main advantage of SBR is that all biological treatment processes (oxidation of organic and biogenic substances, as well as sedimentation) are carried out in one reactor, which allows adjusting the duration and sequence of treatment phases depending on the concentration of wastewater subject to the treatment process using automated control systems.

In a process flow diagram with two or more reactors, with low loads, one of the reactors can be turned off. In this case, the sludge activity of the disabled reactor is preserved subject to its constant aeration (regeneration effect of activated sludge).

Another advantage is the provision of absolute mixing conditions in the SBR, which due to insufficient aeration diffusion cannot be achieved in a flow-type reactor.

The process of sedimentation of activated sludge is the cause of many problems in sewage treatment plants designed to remove nutrients. In the SBR, the sedimentation process is carried out under ideal hydraulic conditions because there is no inflow of wastewater and the resulting turbulence in the flow during the sedimentation as well as the decanting of the treated water. If the sludge index is increased, it is possible to extend the sedimentation phase and prevent the active sludge from being removed from the system.

The simplicity of the SBR design allows the reactor to be manufactured as standard modules, which speeds up the expansion of the treatment plant without large financial expenses.

Despite all of these advantages, it is worth noting that the efficiency of the SBR depends to a large extent on the reliability of the automatic control systems.

An increase in the volume of wastewater inflow into a flow reactor leads to a simultaneous increase in the volume of discharge. To regulate the wastewater flow in SBR technology, it is necessary to provide balance tanks or regulating reservoirs shall be considered.

The disadvantages also include a complex aeration system operated in cyclic mode and requiring the supply of oxygen depending on the concentration of the substrate in the reactor.

Creation of additional loading on a water reservoir receiving the treated wastewaters is also possible what may be caused by non-synchronous decanting of separate SBRs [47, 62-67].

The development of SBR technology has made it possible to use oxidizing channels at wastewater treatment plants. At some plants, two reactors may be the system, which, in principle, may be considered as one reactor performing several functions. Usually, in this type of system, it is impossible to determine the volume and concentration of the return sludge. The system, with these two functions, partially separated in a physical sense, makes it possible to delimit even the areas, where these two processes – aeration and sedimentation – occur [31]. The above-described processes occur in the same reactor, but at different times. The same is true with the SBR system, when aeration stops for some time and the reactor performs the function of sedimentation tank.

Another direction is the development of anaerobic wastewater treatment. In the field of wastewater treatment, the anaerobic process is traditionally used for the treatment of sludge coming from wastewater treatment plants, such as digester or highly concentrated industrial effluent. Using only anaerobic treatment for domestic wastewater treatment does not provide the standard values of treated wastewater to be released into water bodies, so the so-called combined ANANOX system was developed in Ital (ANaerobicANoxicOxic. Garuti et al., 1992) (Figure 24). ANANOX system is a two-stage scheme. The first stage is anaerobic baffled reactor (ABR), which consists of two anaerobic sections, one anoxic section, and one activated sludge trap section.

The second stage is aerobic followed by sedimentation.

In the first stage (ABR) processes of ammonification of the organic form of nitrogen, partial degradation of organic compounds through the combined action of acid-forming and methane-forming microorganisms, sulfate reduction (to sulfite) with sulfate-lowering microorganisms. The lower the BOD_5 concentrations and the BOD_5-sulfate ratio, the greater the impact on sulfate removal (Choi and Rim, 1991).

New discoveries and advances in microbiology and biochemistry over the last decade have supported the development of new generations of biological wastewater treatment facilities to remove nutrients. This is the process of anaerobic oxidation of ammonia nitrogen – ANAMMOX. Although the ANAMMOX process has not been fully investigated, it has been experimentally tested (Strous et al., 1997; Dijkman and Strous., 1999) and successfully applied by come wastewater treatment plants (Hippen et al., 1997; Siegrist et al., 1998; Helmer and Kunst, 1998; Helmer et al., 1999).

Another process, CANON (completely autotrophic N-removal over nitrite), is a one-step biological process of ammonium nitrogen removal in a bioreactor with attached microorganisms (Van Loosdrecht and Jetten, 1997), in which the two processes of nitrification and ANAMMOX (anaerobic ammonium oxidation) occur simultaneously. The CANON process has already found its application in practice (Figure 22) (Strous et al., 1997, 2000; Dijkman and Strous, 1999).

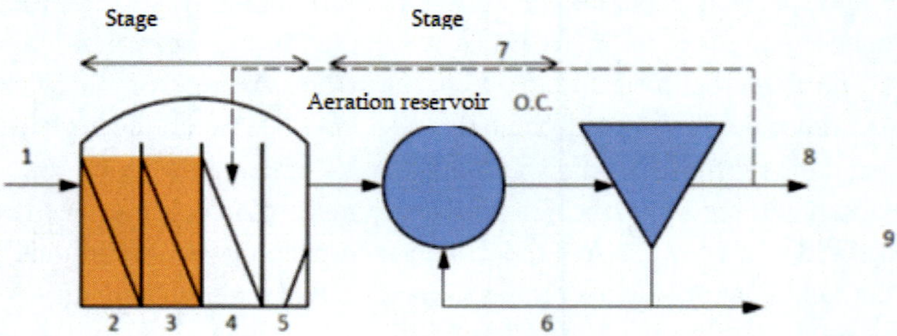

Figure 22. ANANOX diagram.
1 – Inlet flow; 2 – first anaerobic zone; 3 – second anaerobic zone; 4 – anoxic zone; 5 – activated sludge retainer; 6 – return of activated sludge; 7 – recirculation flow; 8 – treated water; 9 – excess activated sludge being treated [20].

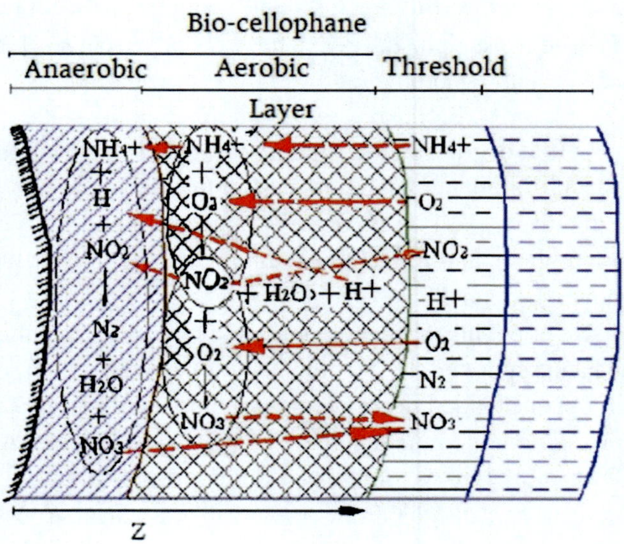

Figure 23. Biological treatment processes in a CANON bioreactor.

Both processes, nitrification and ANAMMOX, take place in the bioreactor biofilm and are carried out mainly by three groups of autotrophic microorganisms: ammonia, nitrite oxidizers and ANAMMOX. These microorganisms compete with each other for oxygen, ammonium nitrogen and nitrite.

Due to the different kinetic constants of oxygen demand between the ammonium and nitrite oxidizer groups and the limitation of mass exchange reactions, the accumulation of nitrite becomes possible, provided that the ANAMMOX process takes place.

Another application of ANAMMOX is the combined Sharon-ANAMMOX process for nitrogen removal from nitrogen-concentrated wastewater nitrogen (Van Loosdrecht and Jetten, 1997). Unlike the CANON process, in which both processes (nitrification and ANAMMOX) occur simultaneously in one reactor with attached microorganisms, in the combined Sharon-ANAMMOX process, they occur separately in different reactors (Figure 24).

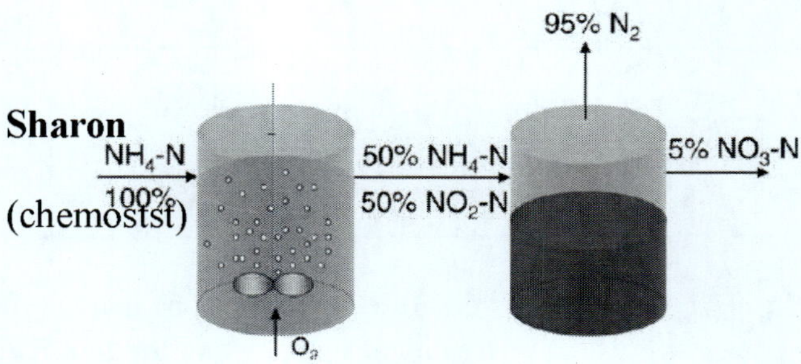

ANAMMOX
(IC reactor)

Figure 24. Fundamental Sharon-Anammox process [3, 54].

Thus, it should be noted that in the last decade, in Europe, thanks to new advances in microbiology, a completely new direction for removing nitrogen from wastewater has been developed, which has obvious advantages over conventional technologies of nitri-denitrification (see Table 10).

It is known that the issues of biological deep wastewater treatment in Russia were studied and investigated quite long ago (in the 1960s). Russian scientists and specialists such as A.A. Bondarev, T.A. Karyukhina, S.V. Yakovlev, I.V. Skirdov, Y.V. Voronov, N.A. Zaletova and others made significant contributions to study this field.

Table 10. Comparative technological characteristics of ANAMMOX and conventional nitri-denitrification processes [68-71]

System	Sharon	Anammox	Cannon	Traditional nitri-denitrification
Number of reactors	1	1	1	2
Content of nitrogen compounds at the outlet	NH_4^+, NO_2^-	N_2, NO_3^-	N_2, NO_3^-	NO_3^-, N_2O, N_2
Operation environment	Aerobic	Anaerobic	With little oxygen	Aerobic and anaerobic
Oxygen demand	Low	No	Low	High
pH-control	No	No	No	Yes
Biomass retention	No	Yes	Yes	No
Consumption of organic matters (BOC)	Yes/No	Yes/No	Yes/No	Yes
Volume of the activated excess sludge	Low	Low	Low	More than in previous 3 processes
Oxidizing power	1 (kg N/m^3 a day)	6-12 (kg N/m^3 a day)	1-3 (kg N/m^3 a day)	0.05-4 (kg N/m^3 a day)
Bacteria	Aerobic ammonium- (NH^+) oxidizer	Planktomycetes	Aerobic ammonium- (NH^+) oxidizer and planktomycetes	Nitrification and various heterotrophic processes

In the last ten years, scientific research on intensifying treatment processes at existing sewage treatment plants using modern technologies for deep nutrient removal (nitri-denitrification, deep biological nitrogen and phosphorus removal) has advanced rapidly in the Russian Federation, as has practical development of technologies for deep nutrient removal. The following leading Russian organizations in wastewater treatment technology play an important role in this direction: State Scientific Center "Scientific Research Institute Vodgeo", Moscow State University of Civil Engineering, JSC "Scientific-Research Institute KVOV", Scientific-Research Institute "IMPROEKT" of JSC Mosvodokanal, Moscow State Unitary Enterprise "Mosvodkanal".

The experience of introduction of foreign technological solutions in Russian environment evidences the need for their adaptation and modification.

The first large-scale facility with biogenic elements removal was a unit of Novo-Lubertsy wastewater treatment plants of Moscow with capacity of 500 thousand m^3/day, where the technology of stage denitrinitrification, developed by Scientific-Research Institute "Improekt" of Mosvodokanal. In the late 1990s, the specialists of Scientific-Research Institute "Improekt" of Mosvodokanal used pilot lines with a total capacity of about 300 thousand m^3/day, created at Kuryanovo and Lyuberetsky treatment plants both in cooperation with Danish and German colleagues and according to their own developments, to test a number of technologies, including AA/O with "carousel" zone, with simultaneous nitri-denitrification, UCT process. It was established that UCT process and its modifications provide the best results in Russia.

Since 2007, a line of biological nitrogen and phosphorus removal, designed on the basis of UCT process, has been also launched at the Lyubertsy wastewater treatment plant. In the aeration basin denitrification processes were organized in the anoxic part of the "carousel" zone, which was fed with return activated sludge. Denitrified sludge mixture was fed to the anaerobic zone, where it was mixed with influent wastewater. Nitrification processes were performed further in the aerobic "carousel" zone and the second aerobic zone. After the startup, which required the implementation of technical solutions to increase the content of volatile fatty acids in the influent clarified water, the quality of treated wastewater at the outlet of the facility by nitrogen compounds complies with the discharge standard into water bodies with the function of fisheries, and the phosphorus phosphate concentration of less than 0.9 mg/L is reached [16].

In recent years, in order to meet HELCOM Guidelines, St. Petersburg Vodokanal carries out intensive re-equipment of treatment facilities with their transfer to the removal of biogenic elements. Achievement of the requirements for phosphorus phosphate content of 0.5 mg/L is ensured by using a reagent (ferrous sulfate (III)).

Scientific-Research Laboratory "Reconstruction and Modernization of Water Drainage Systems" (Patent №212197436 of the Russian Federation "The Method of Deep Biological Purification of Wastewaters from Nitrogen Ammonium Salts") of the Chair of Water Drainage of Moscow State University of Civil Engineering developed a technology for wastewater treatment with simultaneous deep removal of organic pollutants, nitrogen compounds and partially phosphates [20].

Biological oxidizer – aeration reservoir includes for alternating anaerobic and aerobic zones. A successful treatment process needs to divide the inlet wastewater supply into two streams and supply them to the first and third zones in the appropriate percentage ratio. Essential condition for the intensification of the treatment process is a large percentage (up to 100%) of the recirculation sludge mixture and the separation of the recirculation flows.

Domestic wastewater contains a fairly large amount of organic nitrogen, represented by proteins, peptides, amino acids, in addition to ammonia nitrogen. In the process of biological treatment according to the traditional process flow diagram, ammonia nitrogen is oxidized, and the value of organic nitrogen remains unchanged or slightly decreases. Wastewater, entering further into the pond, creates conditions of secondary pollution due to the protein component of total nitrogen, which after some time is destroyed under the action of proteolytic enzymes to produce nitrogen of ammonium salts, creating favorable conditions for secondary pollution of water bodies. Consequently, in order to prevent secondary pollution, it is necessary to reduce the amount of organic nitrogen during the biological treatment at wastewater treatment plants. The action of oxidizer, based on single-sludge denitrification-nitrification method of Moscow State University of Civil Engineering, allows treating the wastewaters from organic nitrogen by 80-100%.

Thus, in a single-sludge scheme of biological treatment of wastewaters, with insufficient supply of carbon and ammonium to aeration reservoirs, the nitrifiers – the heterotrophes, can produce proteolytic ferments to disintegrate proteins, peptides and other complex organic substances. As a result, the aeration tank acquires the ability of deep treatment of wastewaters from organic compounds and various compounds of ammonia nitrogen.

According to the studies of "The Reconstruction and Modernization of Water Drainage Systems and Facilities" conducted by the Scientific-Research Laboratory of the Water Drainage Chair of Moscow State University of Civil Engineering, optimal treatment time for household wastewaters using the described technology is 8-10 hours, and sludge regeneration, for the household and industrial wastewaters with a similar content is not done.

As a result, a stable, sustainable and self-regulating (in case of unstable indicators of wastewater composition) biological system with its own specific biocoenosis is obtained, capable of treating wastewater from nitrogen compounds to the indicators required for its discharge into the reservoirs used as fisheries, and partially (to 50%) of treating from phosphor compounds [20]. Another trend of developing deep wastewater treatment technology is based on the results of research of a number of universities and institutes of the Russian Federation. The most significant are the scientific works performed at State Scientific Center "Scientific-Research Institute Vodgeo", Moscow State University of Civil Engineering, JSC Scientific-Research Institute

KVOV, Scientific-Research Institute “Improekt” of JSC “Mosvodkanal”, and Moscow State Unitary Enterprise “Mosvodkanal”.

A number of scientific researches for municipal sewage waters were carried out at JSC “Scientific Research Institute KVOV”, where schemes using treated wastewater as a substrate on laboratory and pilot plants were considered. The results of studies of one- and two-stage nitridenitrification schemes proved that the latter is preferable due to the high and stable effect of treatment of nitrogen compounds. N.A. Zaletova developed an effective nitrogen removal scheme using a “dry biofilter”, which is a fast unsubmerged filter, in which biologically treated water is sprayed over the surface of the loading material, similar to the sewage treatment in biofilters. The advantage of “dry” filters comes from the large amount of air that is introduced into the filter bed along with the treated water passing through the filter. By design, “dry” filters are two-layer, as loading materials are used porous and non-porous materials, such as anthracite, basalt, quartz, various types of coke, synthetic materials, etc. One of the main directions in Russia for deep biological wastewater treatment is the development and application of submerged biofilters [29].

In the 1980-1990s, new methods that combined the advantages of filters were introduced in wastewater pretreatment systems. They provide the possibility of biological degradation of residual organic contaminants after full biological treatment of wastewater by means of attached biomass. Polymeric elements such as “Contour “, “Algae” and some other materials are used as loading materials, on which the processes of deep removal of pollutants take place [11, 26].

2.2. Deep Treatment of Wastewaters from Phosphor Compounds

It is commonly known that during traditional wastewater treatment, the efficiency of phosphorus removal is 20-40%, but this fails to meet modern requirements for the content of phosphorus in the treated wastewater.

The scientific literature of the 1960s had the first reports on the successful method of phosphorus removal by biological treatment without the use of chemical reagents at a number of sewage treatment plants in the United States [56, 72]. It was noted that the phosphorus removal effect was observed where aeration tanks operated at high loads without nitrate formation. By design, these were displacer aeration tanks with a low-pressure large-bubble aeration system. These facilities effectively reduced phosphate concentrations to 1 mg/L.

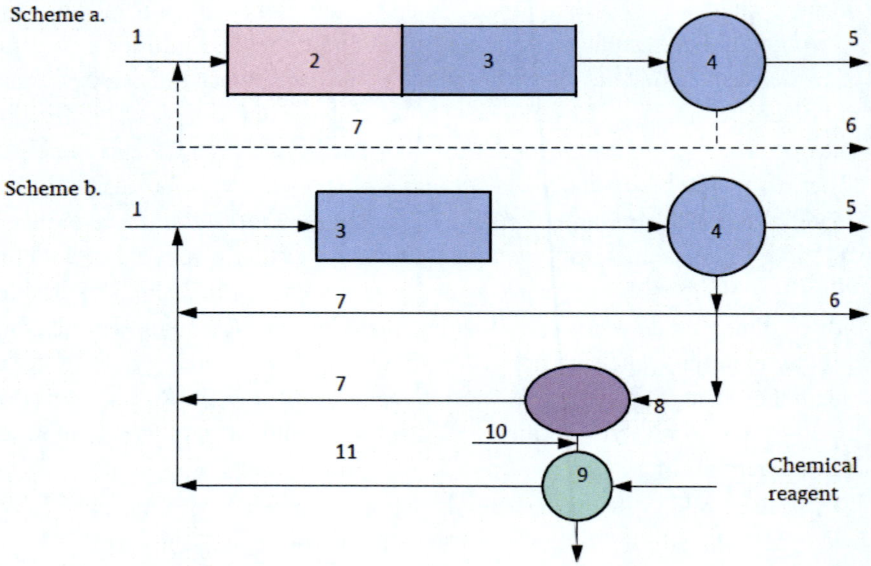

Figure 25. Diagram of biological removal of phosphates.
a. A/O process; b. Phostrip process; 1 – influent wastewater; 2 – anaerobic reactor; 3 – aerobic reactor; 4 – settling tank; 5 – treated wastewater; 6 – excess activated sludge; 7 – return activated sludge; 8 – anaerobic reactor; 9 – chemical settling reactor; 10 – mixture containing concentrated phosphorous; 11 – return flow; 12 – mixture of activated sludge and chemical sediment for disposal [56].

One of the original phosphorus removal processes that used a combined chemical-biological mechanism to remove phosphorus was called the Phostrip Process (Figure 25).

At present, a number of process flow diagrams of biological treatment of wastewater from phosphorus have been developed: A/O (Anaerobic-Oxic) technology, "Phostrip" technology, periodic bioreactor, EASC (Extended Anaerobic Sludge Contact Process) technology, MUCT technology. The Phostrip technology was already in use at 14 wastewater treatment plants in the United States by 1985, as well as at 9 wastewater treatment plants in Japan. The analysis of the available literary data on the quality of wastewater treatment from phosphorus showed that the most profound treatment from phosphorus is provided by the scheme "Phostrip" with anaerobic treatment of return activated sludge, which can remove phosphates by 85-90% and provide residual total phosphorus content in treated water less than 1.5 mg/L. The A/O process removes only 60-70% of the phosphorus, while the MUCT process improves the treatment effect by 10-20%.

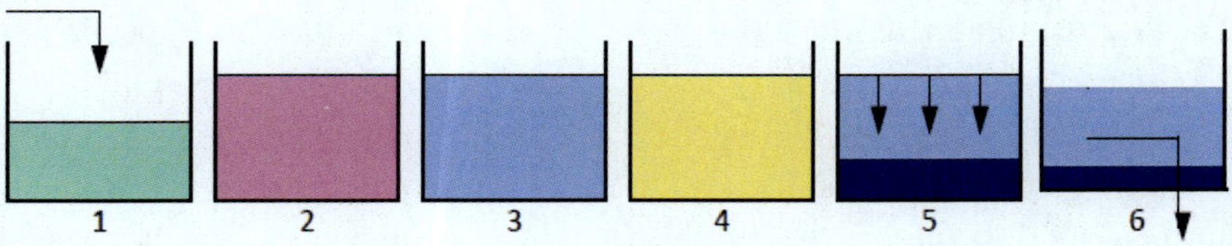

Figure 26. Operating principle of the Sequencing Batch Reactor (SBR) for phosphorus removal.
1 – filling; 2 – anaerobic phase; 3 – aerobic phase; 4 – anoxic phase; 5 – sedimentation; 6 – dumping [56].

A/O process is a single-sludge system with alternating anaerobic and aerobic zones (Figure 25a). The concentration of phosphorus in the treated water depends on the ratio of BOD_5/P (to phosphorus). When this ratio is greater than 10:1, the phosphorus concentration at the output can be less than 1 mg/L, when this ratio is less than 10:1, the use of reagents is recommended.

In the "Phostrip" process, the activated sludge must go through a fairly long anaerobic treatment, then the phosphorus-rich mixture of activated sludge is treated chemically (usually with lime) to remove phosphorus (Figure 25b).

Table 11. Technological parameters of biological processes of phosphorus removal

No.	Technological parameters	Process		
		A/O	Phostrip	SBR
1	Loading (BOC_5/g. ashless substance/day)	0.2-0.7	0.1-0.5	0.15-0.5
2	Age of activated sludge (daily)	2-25	10-30	–
3	Concentration of activated sludge (g/L)	2-4	0.6-5	2-3
4	Time of delay in the zone (h): anaerobic/aerobic	0.5-0.15 1-3	8-12 4-10	1.8-3 1.0-4
5	Age of sludge (%Q)	25-40	20-50	–
6	Internal recirculation (%Q)	–	10-20	–

The principle of operation of the Sequencing Batch Reactor (SBR) is shown in Figure 28. The SBR can remove simultaneously BOD, phosphates and partly nitrogen compounds, and can be operated with or without chemical reagents. The total cycle time varies from 3 to 24 hours. Feeding is necessary to intensify the denitrification process in the anoxic phase. Technological parameters of the above processes are given in Table 11.

Particular attention should be paid to the biological corrosion or biogalvanic method of phosphate removal from wastewater, which can also be attributed to biological methods of phosphate removal from wastewater, because the treatment process is based on biochemical processes occurring in the bioreactor's microflora.

Back in the 70s of the twentieth century, Japanese scientists discovered the influence of iron ions on the activity of activated sludge. It was found that iron ionFe_3^+ strongly excites the reproduction of bacteria in the activated sludge. The effect of remained constant, regardless of changes in its concentration, varies from 0.1 to 5 mg/L [68].

The first reports on the study and application of the method using iron-containing material for intensification of biological treatment and phosphorus removal from wastewater appeared in 1986 and was developed by Japanese scientists. Further research in this area was conducted by scientists in Russia, the Czech Republic, Poland, and the USA [33, 54, 68-70, 73].

The Japanese scientist T. Nishiguchi was the first to note the possibility of phosphorus removal from wastewater by this method. In his works, T. Nishiguchi showed the possibility of highly effective phosphorus removal by means of metal rotating discs or contacting material and developed a method of combined phosphorus and nitrogen removal with periodic aeration when iron filler was used. From his point of view, phosphate removal was achieved by "washing" iron ions out of the iron material. The characteristic features of this method are as follows:

- There is no need to use a reagent;
- It is easy to combine with the method of nitrogen removal (biological nitrification);
- The release of phosphorus from the excess sludge during storage and further processing is insignificant;
- The increased rate of sedimentation of activated sludge is significant.

Two hardly soluble compounds were identified as phosphorus and iron compounds in this method: basic iron phosphate (II and III) and iron (II) orthophosphate octahydrate [69].

Japanese scientists conducted studies on laboratory and pilot plants. Having received a positive result, this technology was introduced at the real wastewater treatment plants [66].

The research involved a batch plant consisting of a reactor equipped with a diffuser pipe, an agitator and a level gauge, by means of which aeration, mixing, feeding and discharge of wastewater were accomplished. Steel rods with a diameter of 16 mm were installed in the reactor as material for phosphorus removal. Different amounts of iron filler were used at different stages of the experiment. The experiment took into account the fact that in case of intensive aeration, a solid film of iron oxide and iron phosphate is formed on the iron material [31, 73], due to which the degree of phosphorus removal decreases over time. Taking this into account, the amount of supplied air was regulated so that the maximum value of dissolved oxygen in the aeration tank did not exceed 2 mg/L.

Depending on the phosphorus load on the surface of the iron filler, the effect of phosphate removal varied, but was not less than 70%.

The concentration of total phosphorus decreased from 4.3 mg/L to 0.8 mgP/L, and that of BOD concentration decreased from 166 mg/L to 5 mg/L. The concentration of dissolved iron in the reactor was almost the same as in the inlet wastewater and did not exceed 0.4 mg/L.

Aerobic and anoxic conditions were alternately created in the reactor. The authors noted that this method made practically no impact on the concentration of phosphor and iron, dissolved in the reactor. Based on this, the researchers supposed that the purification from phosphor was mainly conditioned by flocculation of metals and cell synthesis of microorganisms.

It was found that this method produced an insignificant amount of inorganic sludge, while using aluminum sulfate produced inorganic sludge in an amount approximately four times greater than the amount of added aluminum [40]. It was found that the wear of the iron sheets under these operating conditions was on the order of 0.25 mm/year. However, in the upper part of the reactor, where the water-air flow is most intense, the wear more than doubled. Iron sheets during the period of operation grew a biological film with thickness of 0.5-4.0 mm, which periodically grew and peeled off. The biological film in this case has a high content of inorganic components.

It should be noted that during this process it is necessary to maintain the concentration of dissolved oxygen less than 2.0 mg/L for the entire period of operation. Therefore, additional agitators were installed to ensure mixing of activated sludge, which led to an increase in energy costs. In addition, high consumption of iron material was noted.

American scientists have patented a method that provides a 95% degree of phosphate removal and reduction of the sludge index. The essence of this method is the use of electrochemical corrosion in aerobic conditions and biological corrosion in anaerobic conditions with the use of sulfate-reducing bacteria. In order to ensure that the process is carried out correctly, the concentration of dissolved oxygen should not exceed 3.2 mg/L in order to create optimal conditions for iron corrosion. Under anaerobic conditions, in order to achieve biological corrosion, it is necessary to observe conditions of complete absence of oxygen with the obligatory presence of sulfate-reducing microorganisms in the range of 10^5-10^6 cells per millimeter [54]. However, this method is difficult to apply when the concentration of dissolved oxygen is higher than 3.2 mg/L and the positive redox potential, typical for urban municipal wastewater. In addition, using this method of treatment does not provide an increase in specific oxidation rates of organic compounds and requires constant monitoring of the treated water flow rate to prevent fouling of iron contactors with biofilm.

Russian scientists (Y.F. El, A.S. Shelomkov, N.V. Zakhvataeva) accomplished the studies aimed at simplifying this method, reducing operating costs by reducing the number of stages and the need to regulate the redox potential and oxygen concentration, intensifying the process of biological treatment by increasing the specific oxidation rates of organic compounds while maintaining a high degree of treatment [65, 74]. In this case, during their life activity the activated sludge microorganisms, oxidizing organic substances, produce acidic products into the external environment. Consequently, at the boundary of contact of biofilm and wastewater a local zone is formed in which an acidic reaction of the environment is created. When placed in the microsphere of the metal biofilm due to the potential difference between the metal and the solution the process of electrochemical corrosion occurs, where metal ions pass into the solution and form insoluble salts with orthophosphoric acid ions.

Studies on the effect of corrosion current on the efficiency of phosphate removal from wastewater and on the activity of active sludge micro-organisms were conducted during the contact experiments.

The activated sludge from the aeration tank was placed in columns equipped with iron-reinforced loading material and aerated for 24 hours. The activated sludge was taken away and oxidation kinetics was studied. Studies have shown that the corrosive current resulting from the electrochemical reaction at the "biofilm-metal" boundary has a positive effect on the microorganisms of activated sludge, so that the specific rate of biological oxidation of wastewater contaminants increases significantly. Thus, the maximum specific rate of oxidation of pollutants without the use of biogalvanic element is 11.76 mg/(g·h), with the use of biogalvanic element – 41.7 and 58.8 mg/(g·h) depending on the amount of iron used in the experiments. The researchers noted that in the aeration basin with reinforced loading organic impurities were oxidized faster than in the aeration basin with unreinforced loading. The concentration of phosphate in the experimental aeration tank after one day decreased to 0.24 mg/L and after two days to zero, while in the control aeration tank there was a decrease in phosphate to 1.0 mg/L only after 5 days. In addition, the rate of oxidation of organic matter in the control aeration tank was significantly lower than in the experimental one. Decrease in sludge index was recorded as well.

A process flow diagram of wastewater treatment from phosphates with the use of aeration bioreactor with iron-containing charging material was developed by Moscow State University of Civil Engineering. This method of biogalvanic removal of phosphate provides the concentration of phosphorus compounds at the outlet of the treatment plant of 0.25 mg/L, which corresponds to the standards for discharging treated wastewater into waters of fish industry [75].

2.3. Process Flow Diagrams of Biological Treatment of Wastewaters, Combined Purification from Biogenic Elements

The free-floating activated sludge treatment method is mainly used for the combined biological removal of nitrogen and phosphorus from domestic wastewaters.

The main difficulty of joint, or simultaneous, removal of nitrogen and phosphorus compounds from wastewater is that different conditions are required for their removal. Thus, the main condition for the processes of nitrification and denitrification is the presence of activated sludge, the age of which is at least 20 days. Removal of phosphorus compounds is optimal when the age of the activated sludge is smaller.

In Europe, researchers have developed single-sludge system, in which all biochemical reactions occur simultaneously. The single-sludge system is characterized by alternating anoxic-aerobic zones. According to the researchers, biological phosphorus removal is determined by the ability of activated sludge microorganisms to remove more phosphorus than they need for their own metabolic process.

In the 1960s and early 1970s, the essence and mechanisms of biological phosphorus removal were defined. Most researchers (Alarcon (1961), Levin and Shaprio (1965), Wells (1969), Scalph (1969), Millbur (1970) et al.) paid considerable attention to the influence of aeration intensity in bioreactors and the degree of phosphorus accumulation by activated sludge in a displacer rather than an ideal mixer [56, 72].

In 1975, it was found that a group of Acinetobacter ssp. microorganisms was capable of accumulating more phosphate than they needed for their own cells in the presence of short-chain volatile fatty acids (e.g., acetate) [56, 72].

During the 1970s, the scientists from Princeton University (Barnard (1976), Davelaar and Davis (1978)) conducted a number of experiments to study the process of biological removal of phosphorus. Barnard, based on studies of 1974, concluded that there is a relationship between biological phosphorus removal and nitrate (NO_3) content. He described anaerobic zone as a zone with no oxygen (O_2) and nitrates (NO_3). These observations led to the development of the Phorendox and Bardenpho Proccess configuration biological phosphorus removal technology, which has been the basis of all biological phosphorus removal processes currently in use. Following the studies of 1979, Nicholls and Osborne suggested that "nitrate-free anaerobic" zone, recommended by Bernard, allows the Acinetobacter ssp. group to selectively consume acetate, using reserve polyphosphate as an energy source and releasing it into the liquid phase.

Later, researches (Renssink (Holland), Wentzel et al. (South Africa) and Comeau et al. (Canada)) refined the hypothesis of Nicholls and Osborne, developed this hypothesis and found out that the anaerobic zone serves for reproduction of semiphosphate-accumulating microorganisms, which is one of the most important points to develop bioreactors for joint removal of biogenic elements.

In the 1970s, several treatment plants were to remove biogenic elements from wastewaters were built in South Africa. The fundamentals of their design were provided by Bernard (in 1974-1975). All plants of simultaneous removal of nitrogen and phosphorus were single-sludge, with alternating anaerobic-anoxic-aerobic zones providing all necessary conditions for nitrification, denitrification, and phosphorus removal (dephosphotation). Various modifications of single-sludge system (Phorendox, Three-stage Bardenpho and Five-stage Bardenpho process) are given in Figure 27 and Figure 28.

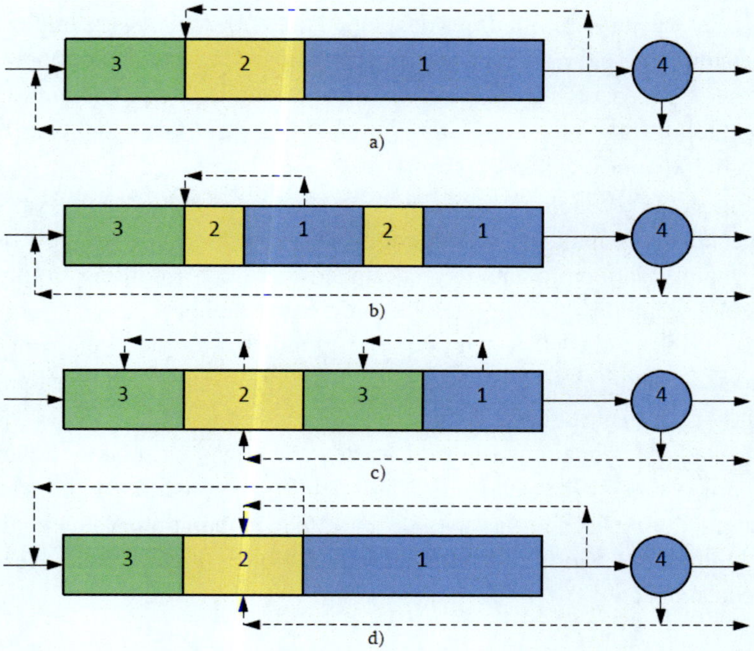

Figure 27. Schemes of combined biological nitrogen and phosphorus removal.
a – A2/O process; b – 5-step Barenpho; c – UCT process; d – VIP process [56].
1 – aerobic zone; 2- anoxic zone; 3 – anaerobic zone; 4 – sedimentation tank.

Researchers of Capetown University (Rabinovich, Marais and Sibritz (1980)) and the scientist of Johannesburg University (Pitmann (1992)) proposed modifications of the Bardenpho process, which were given the name of UCT (Capetown University) and modified UCT (Figures 29, 30).

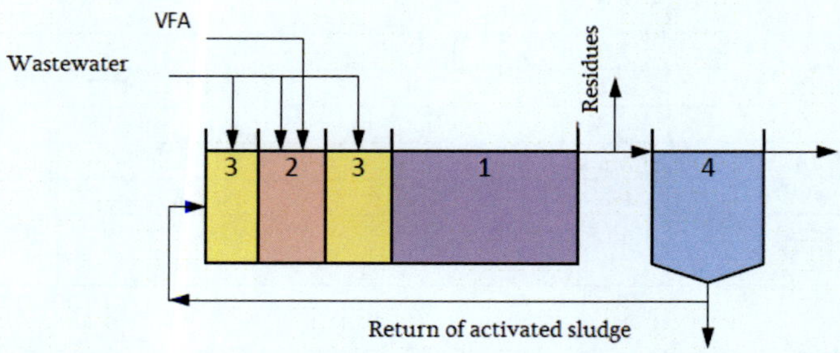

Figure 28. Canadian diagram of simultaneous removal of biogenic elements.
1 – aerobic zone, 2 – anaerobic zone, 3 – anoxic; 4 – secondary sedimentation tank [56]. (VFA-fermentation of activated sludge).

In the early 1970s, solutions developed in South Africa were implemented in Canada (where the average winter wastewater temperature is about -10°C) to remove phosphorus from Kelowna wastewater (Dew and Oldham, 1979 A second treatment plant, using a similar phosphorus removal plan, was built in the mid-1980s in Westbank (Okanagan Valley).

Later, the technological process of wastewater treatment was optimized taking into account the climatic conditions of Canada, where several new wastewater treatment plants were designed and built according to improved technology and the existing ones were reconstructed.

In 1989, in the USA (Noflock, Virginia), wastewater treatment plants were built using VIP process, and in 1993, a modified UCT process technology was introduced in the cities of Calispell and Mont [76].

Canadian companies designed wastewater treatment plants in Denmark (Frederiksvaerk (1988) and Grimstad (1995)); reconstructed the treatment plants in Portugal (Beirolas and Lisbon) and the aeration plants in the UK (Beckton and London); Australian cities Logan city, Noosa Head and Queensland, etc.

Table 12. Technological characteristics of the main processes of combined removal of biogenic elements from wastewater

Parameters	2/O		Bardenpho		IT		VIP	
Loading per g.l (g. BOC_5-/g ashless subst/ day)	0.15-0.25		0.1-0.2		0.1-0.2		0.1-0.2	
Age of sludge (days)	4-27		10-40		10-30		5-10	
Sludge dose (g/L)	2-4		2-5		2-5		1.5-3	
Zones	hr.	%	hr.	%	hr.	%	hr.	%
Aerobic	0.5-1.5	11-18	1-2	8-11	1-2	9-11	1-2	22-25
Anaerobic-1	0.5-1.0	11-15	2-4	17-21	2-4	18-22	1-2	22-25
Aerobic-1	3.5-6.0	70-80	4-12	42-52	-	-	2.5-4	50-60
Anaerobic-2	-	-	2-4	17-21	2-4	18-22	-	-
Aerobic-2	-	-	0.5-1	4-6	4-12	44-55	-	-
Total time (hr.)	4.5-8.5		9.5-23.0		9.0-22.0		4.5-8	
Sludge age (% Q)	20 -50		50-100		50-100		50-100	
Internal recirculation (% Q)	100-300		400		100-600		200-400	

In the last two decades, significant progress has been made in the field of nitrogen and phosphorus removal from wastewater, the main schemes and characteristics of which are presented in Table 12. However, apparatus design of the processes is imperfect, and all technological schemes of biological nitrogen and phosphorus removal need anaerobic and anoxic zones. It should be noted that all types of biological processes occur at low BOD load of less than 0.4 g BOD_5/(g·day).

It is established that single-sludge biological treatment schemes can ensure effective removal of nitrogen and phosphorus only at a certain ratio of pollutants in the wastewaters. The most important parameter of wastewater composition is COD/TKN ratio (to total nitrogen). For example, when the COD/TKN ratio is more than 14, it is possible to use any scheme of biological removal of biological elements; when the sane ratio is within the range of 7-14, the most effective is one of the options of UCT scheme, and when the ratio is less than 7, the technology of biological removal of either nitrogen or phosphorus must be selected.

In spite of significant effectiveness of biological treatment of wastewaters from nitrogen and phosphorus, the quality of treated water after single-sludge treatment stage in some cases, fails to meet the parameters, required by the legislation for wastewater treatment from nitrogen and phosphorus. When there are high regulatory requirements for discharging wastewater containing nitrogen and phosphorus into water bodies, a combined biological and chemical scheme for the removal of biogenic compounds is usually used. Most often a combination of biological nitrification-denitrification and chemical treatment of wastewater with iron salts or aluminum is most common during the reconstruction of sewage treatment plants.

All biological methods of wastewater treatment from nitrogen compounds are based, as indicated in the previous chapter, on biological processes of oxidation of nitrogen compounds to nitrites and nitrates with subsequent reduction of oxidized nitrogen forms to free nitrogen. The main advantage of nitrification and nitri-denitrification technology is the possibility of its implementation in traditional biological treatment facilities. The processes of nitrification and nitri-denitrification have been investigated for a long time and are sufficiently studied.

Chapter 3

Models of River Pollution

The global ongoing process of ground water pollution endangers human health and negatively impacts aquatic life. There are currently many sections of polluted rivers, banks of lakes and water reservoirs, and sea coastal zones.

Pollution and self-purification of waters are two processes that occur as a result of human economic activity and are caused by the natural or artificial penetration of pollutants into water systems and reservoirs. Industrial and household waters that enter rivers, lakes, reservoirs, and seas cause significant changes in the water environment and disrupt the normal viability of organisms.

The diversity of a set of factors and the insufficient study of pollution processes indicate that the aforementioned problem has not been thoroughly investigated. As a result, when studying the dynamics of surface and ground water pollution, special attention must be paid to the dissolution process, which reduces the concentration of pollutants in aquatic environment.

The sources of pollution caused by oil- or oil product pipeline accidents, in which the transported product ends up in the water environment, are a separate issue. Despite strict modern requirements for oil and oil product pipelines, preventing such events is nearly impossible. Predicting potential accidents is also difficult.

Pollution of surface and ground waters with oil and oil products caused by various accidents (e.g., oil pipeline or railway accidents while transporting oil tanks near the aquatic environment) has a negative impact on the performance of power plants. Polluted water in the flows from various units (turbines, pumps, etc.) of power plants (HPPs, hydro accumulation stations, TPPs, nuclear power stations) causes various irregularities that negatively affect the reliable performance and life cycle of these power plants.

This chapter discusses the findings of the author and other researchers regarding the mixture of pollutants and the aquatic environment. To solve the aforementioned problems, classical and modern approaches to hydrodynamics and hydrology are used. The research was carried out with the goal of minimizing ecological risk using the proposed methods and designing optimal environmental protection measures.

The global expansion of the main oil pipeline network raises the importance of operational safety, particularly in terms of environmental impact. Even small-scale oil spills have the potential to trigger a catastrophic, irreversible ecological process in the surrounding environment. The identification of risk factors in advance and their minimization during the design and operation stages is regarded as an important factor in the safe operation of oil pipelines.

Georgia has seen a surge in the construction of major oil pipelines in recent years. The main Baku-Supsa Pipeline (annual capacity: 7 million tons, length: 854 km, internal diameter: 500 mm) and Vale-Turkish Border Pipeline (length: 9 km, internal diameter: 300 mm) have been completed and put to operation; Baku-Tbilisi-Ceyhan Oil Pipeline has also been completed.

The main oil pipeline river overpasses operate under extremely difficult conditions. Thus, under-water passages of main oil pipelines with lengths greater than 20 meters are classified as first category sites ("Technical Regulations for Building and Installation of Main Pipelines"). Pipelines are made up of small diameter pipes. Physical control methods are used to inspect all welded joints (gamma-ray irradiation or magnetography). The hydraulic method shall be used to test the under-water passages for pressures that must exceed the operational pressure by 25%. Stronger pipe insulation is considered during construction to ensure the failure-free operation of under-water passages.

Damage to under-water passages, in any case, falls into the category of severe damages, the liquidation of which takes a long time and is costly.

Oil spills in the aquatic environment from bridges or near-coast roads, as practice shows, are frequently the result of accidents during the transportation of oil and oil products by railway or highway. According to 2022 data, 763 bridge accidents and 1034 near-coast road accidents occurred worldwide, resulting in 100000 t oil and oil products spilled into the aquatic environment.

As there is no scientifically grounded, complete, methodologically justified, theory- or experimentally based method to forecast and prevent the outcomes of a poor state or accidents of main oil pipelines, it is very timely to study the above-mentioned problem.

3.1. Continuous Flow Stirred Reactor Model of River Pollution (CFSTR)

Let us consider a section of the river channel pool, as a CFSTR process (CFSTR – Continuous Flow Stirred Reactor Model). Let us assume that a tracer or other pollutant (tracer is a pollutant, which either reacts or not) enters the starting point of the study river section quite slowly. Let us admit that the initial flow discharge is Q, and the concentration of tracer flow is C_1. According to the CFSTR model, the liquid flowing into the river section is well-stirred. It means that the concentration gradient in this river section equals to zero. Thus, flow discharge is Q, and initial concentration is C. Our goal is to identify the regularity of change of concentration C in time (i.e., to determine $C = C(t)$ function). Let us assume that at the initial moment of time, the tracer concentration in river tailrace is zero, and as it flows, it increases by certain regularity. The plan of the CFSTR system is given in Figure 29. Let us assume that at the initial moment of time, the flow concentration equals to the river concentration (implying that the pollutant is completely stirred). In this case:

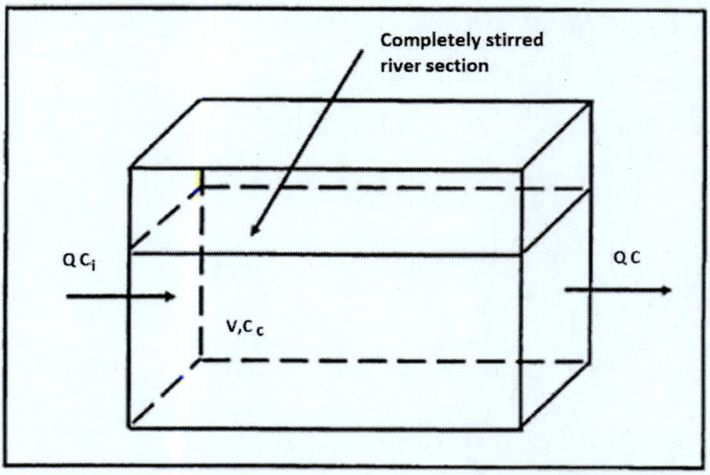

Figure 29. Plan of the CFSTR model.

$$QC_i - QC + rV = \frac{dC_V}{dt} \tag{17}$$

where, Q is the flow discharge (m^3/sec); C_i is the concentration of the tracer flow (mg/L or g/m^3); C is the concentration of outflowing tracer (mg/L or g/m^3); V is the volume of the river section.

Let us assume that at the initial point, there is a non-reactive tracer in the flow. Then, $r = 0$, and for the flow and volume concentration, C remains a variable value. As our goal is to identify the change of concentration C in time, then:

$$Q(C_i - C) = \frac{dC}{dt}V \tag{18}$$

Let us introduce a new value, the mean time of hydraulic delay $\Phi = V/Q$ (where V in the volume of the study river section). If we consider this value a constant, then:

$$\frac{dC}{C_i - C} = \frac{1}{\Phi}dt \tag{19}$$

The initial condition will be as follows: if $t = 0$, $C = C_0$, then:

$$\left[\begin{array}{c} \int_{C_0}^{C} \frac{dC}{C - C_i} = -\frac{1}{\Phi}\int_0^t dt; \\ \ln\left|C - C_i\right|\Big|_{C_0}^{C} = -\frac{1}{\Phi}\left|t\right|_0^t; \\ \ln\left(\frac{C - C_i}{C_0 - C_i}\right) = -\frac{t}{\Phi}. \end{array}\right] \tag{20}$$

Following simple transformations, we will obtain:

$$C = C_i + (C_0 - C_i)e^{-t/\Phi} = C_i\left(1 - e^{-t/\Phi}\right) + C_0 e^{-t/\Phi} \tag{21}$$

i.e., the concentration in river at any time moment t is the function of C_i, C_0 and V/Q values. If C_0 equals to zero (as it is mostly the case), then the equation (21) will be as follows:

$$C = C_i\left(1 - e^{t/\Phi}\right) \quad (22)$$

As an example, let us consider the regularity of the concentration change of the tracer flowing into the river section under the following conditions: the concentration of the discharged tracer: $C_i = 300$ mg/L; flow discharge: $Q =$ 700 m^3/day; initial river concentration: $C_0 = 50$ mg/L; the volume of the study river section: $V = 200$ m^3.

As $\Phi = V/Q = 200/700 = \frac{1}{3.5} days = 6.7\ hrs$, equation (21) in our case will be written down as follows:

$$C = 300\left(1 - e^{-3,5t}\right) + 50e^{-3,5t} \quad (23)$$

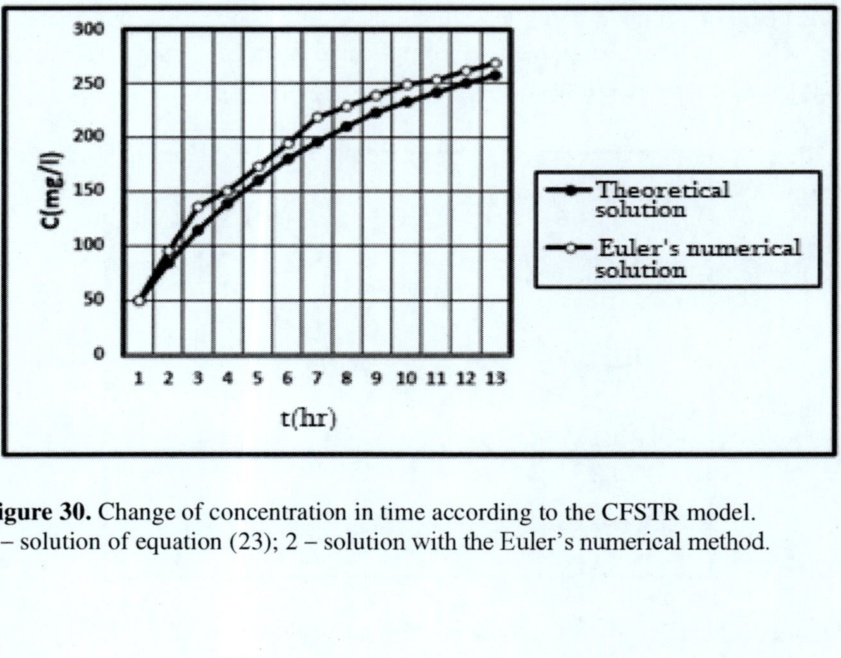

Figure 30. Change of concentration in time according to the CFSTR model.
1 – solution of equation (23); 2 – solution with the Euler's numerical method.

The graph of the exact solution of this equation is given in Figure 30. In this example, it is assumed that the tracer concentration at the initial moment was 4 mg/L. During a single period of hydraulic delay (≈ 6.7 hr.), the concentration increases from 5 to approximately over 250 mg/L and continues to increase. It is obvious that the limit concentration $(t \Rightarrow \infty)$ will be 300 mg/L. The same figure shows the solution obtained by numerical method (Euler's method in particular), which yields a bit higher concentration value.

When the process involves a bacterial reactant, e.g., the operating treatment plant, then, for the CFSTR model, equation (17), obtained previously and its solution (22) are only a part of the process history. In this case, to obtain an exact solution, it is necessary to solve two equations: one for the biomass, and another for the feeding substrate.

The CFSTR model can be used to evaluate the efficiency of a waste or sewage treatment plant, i.e., when there are several completely stirred basins, which could be modeled by the CFSTR series. Similarly, a preliminary analysis for each tracer (e.g., oil) discharged in river systems is possible, if the system is viewed as a system made of a discrete quantity of well-stirred sections. The CFSTR is also applicable when the flow containing the tracer is discharged into a lake that can be stirred well. In this case, it is possible to calculate the change of concentration levels of the lake pollution in time in advance.

The situation is much more complicated with an acting reactant and varying speed of reactions.

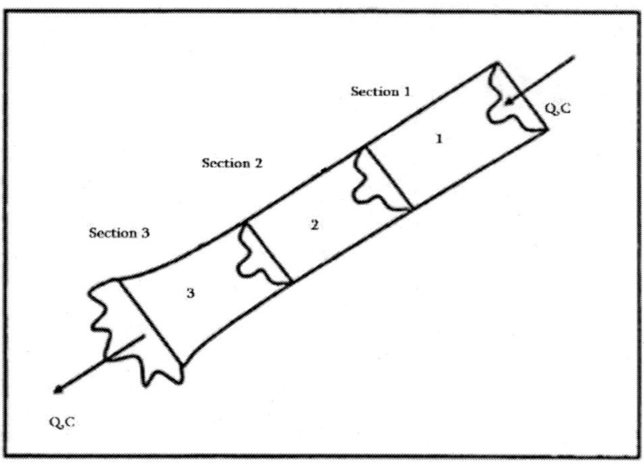

Figure 31. Modeling of the river sections using CFSTR series.

The outcome of the process along the river can be modeled quite simply, if a river is considered as the CFSTR series that can be stirred well. The example below will consider such a case:

Let us consider the model of certain river section divided into three CFSTR series, as shown in Figure 31. Let us assume that the concentrations of stationary state are 300, 600 and 900 mg/L. Let us also assume that pollution reached into the upper section of the first site along the river current, and the tracer concentration at the end of the current is 100 mg/L (or 100 g/m^3).

Let us assume that the tracer concentration reduces right along the first section during the reaction, i.e., $\tau = -kC$ and also let us assume by approximation that $k \approx -0.3$ days^{-1}. In this case, the mass balance for the first section will be:

Inflow – outflow + reaction product = accumulation:

$$QC_{in} - QC_1 + rV_1 = \frac{dC}{dt}V_1 \tag{24}$$

For a stationary state:

$$QC_{in} - QC_1 + rV_1 = 0 \tag{25}$$

The volumes of the study section will be: $V_1 = 1.8 \cdot 10^4 m^3$; $V_2 = 2.7 \cdot 10^4 m^3$; $V_3 = 3.6 \cdot 10^4 m^3$; $Q = 12\ m^3 / s$

For the times of hydraulic delay: $\Phi_1 = V_1 / Q = 0.018\ 24\ hrs$; $\Phi_2 = V_2 / Q = 0.027\ 24\ hrs$; $\Phi_3 = V_3 / Q = 0.035\ 24\ hrs$

Thus, the mass balance equations for the three study sections will be:

$$\begin{cases} \mathbf{QC_{in} - QC_1 - kC_1V_1 = 0} \\ \mathbf{QC_1 - QC_2 - kC_2V_2 = 0} \\ \mathbf{QC_2 - QC_3 - rC_3V_3 = 0} \end{cases} \tag{26}$$

where $\mathbf{C_1}$, $\mathbf{C_2}, \mathbf{C_3}$ are tracer concentrations at the final points of the sections, respectively, and $\mathbf{\Phi_1}, \mathbf{\Phi_2}, \mathbf{\Phi_3}$ are respective times of the hydraulic delay. If we solve the obtained linear algebraic equation system to C_1, C_2, C_3 we will obtain:

$$\begin{cases} C_1 = \dfrac{C_{in}}{1+k\Phi_1} = \dfrac{100}{1+0{,}3*0{,}018} \\ C_2 = \dfrac{C_{in}}{(1+k\Phi_1)(1+k\Phi_2)} \\ C_3 = \dfrac{C_{in}}{(1+k\Phi_1)(1+k\Phi_2)(1+k\Phi_3)} \end{cases} \tag{27}$$

After introducing numeric values, we will obtain:

$$C_1 = 9.5\,g/m^3;\ C_2 = 99.7\,g/m^3;\ C_3 = 97.6\,g/m^3$$

Thus, the variation of the tracer concentrations is obtained along the first kilometer of the current. Wit subsequent calculations for 3, 6 and 9 km long sections, we will obtain: $C_1 = 94.8\,g/m^3$; $C_2 = 87.6g/m^3$; $C_3 = 79.3\,g/m^3$, respectively.

This example, for the sake of clarity and simplicity, considered a stationary process and assumed that terms $\dfrac{\partial C}{\partial t}$ equal to zero. Surely, a non-stationary process can also be considered, in which case, if the number of equations is not great, they can be solved using Laplace transform [11], while many equations can be solved using numerical methods, such as Runge-Kutta or Kutta- Messner methods [2, 3]. However, it should be noted that following the physical aspect of the phenomenon, non-stationary solutions, when $t \to \infty$, approximate the previously obtained stationary solutions.

3.2. Plug Flow Reactor (PFR)

The Plug Flow Reactor (PFR) Model allows identifying linear gradient indicators of concentration. It is implied that in the horizontal direction along the reactor, the initial gradient of concentration equals to zero. When a reactor is used to treat activated biological material in a sewage system, the impact is mainly exerted at the end of the reactor section. The current, moving along the "plug" reactor, gets cleaned at the end of the flow of the reactor section (Figure 12). The "Plug" reactor is usually used for an activated tracer [4].

Now, let us consider the river section, when the reactor makes an impact on the flow. Let us use the "plug" model and determine the concentration balance of the inflowing and outflowing tracer mass. For the elementary volume, this balance will be as follows (let us consider that $\Delta V = A\Delta x$) (Figure 32):

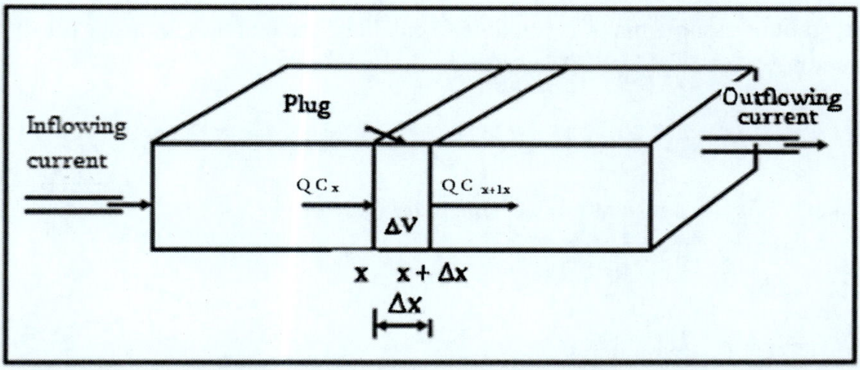

Figure 32. PFR Plan.

$$QC(x) - QC(x + \Delta x) + r\Delta V = \frac{\partial C(x)}{\partial t}\Delta V \tag{28}$$

$$QC(x) - Q\left[C(x) + \frac{\partial C}{\partial x}\Delta x\right] + rA\Delta x = \frac{\partial C(x)}{\partial t}A\Delta x \tag{29}$$

where $C(x)$ is the concentration for coordinate x (g/m^3); $C(x + \Delta x)$ is the concentration for coordinate $x + \Delta x$ (g/m^3); Q is the flow discharge (m^3/s); r is the intensity of tracer reaction (g/m^3); ΔV is the volume of an isolated element (m^3).

If we divide equation (26) by $A\Delta x$ and move to the limit, when $\Delta x \to 0$, we will obtain:

$$\frac{\partial C}{\partial t}=-\frac{Q}{A}\frac{\partial C}{\partial x}+r \tag{30}$$

It is clear that for the stationary state, when $\left(\frac{\partial C}{\partial t}\right)=0$, we will obtain:

$$\frac{Q}{A}\frac{dC}{dx}=r \tag{31}$$

Let us assume that it is possible to calculate the reaction intensity for PFR as follows:

$$r=-kC \tag{32}$$

where k is the constant reaction intensity ($k=const$, day^{-1}).

Thus,

$$\frac{Q}{A}\frac{dC}{dx}=-kC \tag{33}$$

Similar to the previous analysis, let us introduce the mean time of hydraulic delay: $\Phi=V/Q$, where V is the reactor's volume and let us integrate equation (32) within limits $\mathrm{C_i}=0-\mathrm{C};$, $\mathbf{\Phi_i}=\mathbf{0}-\mathbf{\Phi}$, where C_i is the concentration of the inflowing tracer (g/m^3), and $\mathbf{C}$ is the outflow concentration (g/m^3). Finally, we will obtain:

$$C=C_i e^{-k\Phi} \tag{34}$$

Equation (19) makes it clear that the tracer inflow concentration is the function of a flow concentration, and as shown in Figure 33, changes in time when $k \approx 0.25$ day^{-1} and $\Phi=\mathrm{V/Q}=200/700$, $\mathrm{C}=0.93\mathrm{C_i}$. Thus, if C_i is a constant value, C will be constant.

Let us consider a more complex case using “plug” model and determine, what kind of phenomenon occurs in the river (reactor). Let us consider the situation along the current, in x direction. We will obtain:

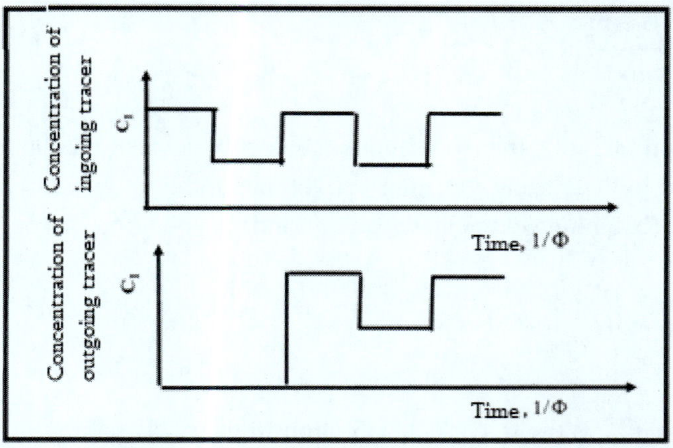

Figure 33. Relationship in case of step-wise function of tracer outflow from ideal PFR.

$$QC(x)-Q\left[C(x)+\frac{\partial C(x)}{\partial x}\Delta x\right]-DA\frac{\partial C(x)}{\partial x}+$$
$$+DA\left[\frac{\partial C(x)}{\partial x}+\frac{\partial}{\partial x}\frac{\partial C(x)}{\partial x}\Delta x\right]-k\,C(x)\,V=V\frac{\Delta C(x)}{\Delta t} \tag{35}$$

where D is the dispersion coefficient (m^3/day), k is the primary reduction coefficient (day^{-1}). A is the area of effective cross-section. As it is known, Fick's Law is as follows: $q=-D\frac{\partial C}{\partial x}$, where D is the turbulent stirring ratio, which moves the "plug" from the high concentration zone to the low concentration zone (i.e., from left to right in Figure 4). Within the limit, when $\Delta x \to 0$ and $\Delta t \to 0$, we will obtain:

$$\frac{\partial C}{\partial t}=D\frac{\partial^2 C}{\partial x^2}-U\frac{\partial C}{\partial x}-kC \tag{36}$$

where $U=Q/A$ is the mean velocity of water current along the river (reactor). This equation formally coincides with the advection-diffusion equation. In a stationery state, it transforms into the second order ordinary differential equation:

$$0 = D\frac{d^2C}{dx^2} - U\frac{dC}{dx} - kC \tag{37}$$

When time $t < 0$, the river section is filled with water, but the tracer is not introduced in the current yet. At $t = 0$ moment, the introduction of a tracer starts at the beginning of the upper section and the condition will be as follows:

$$QC_{in} - QC_0 = -DA\frac{dC_0}{dx} \tag{38}$$

Where C_{in} is the tracer concentration in the cross-section of the inflow into the reactor, and C_0 is the tracer concentration at the beginning of the upper section of the current, i.e., when $x = 0$.

Equation (37) can be solved with numerical methods. If introducing (37) in finite differences, then:

$$0 = D\frac{C_{i+1} - 2C_i + C_{i-1}}{\Delta x^2} - U\frac{C_{i+1} - C_{i-1}}{2\Delta x} - kC_i \tag{39}$$

where C_i is the concentration in node i, C_{i+1} is the concentration in node $i+1$, and C_{i-1} is the concentration in node $i-1$. If we multiply equation (39) by term $\Delta x / U$ and group it, we will obtain:

$$\begin{aligned} &-\left(\frac{D}{U\Delta x} + \frac{1}{2}\right)C_{i-1} + \left(\frac{2D}{U\Delta x} + \frac{k\Delta x}{U}\right)C_i - \\ &-\left(\frac{D}{U\Delta x} - \frac{1}{2}\right)C_{i+1} = 0 \end{aligned} \tag{40}$$

Equation (40) can be written for each node in x direction. In the initial cross-section of the current, it will be as follows:

$$-\left(\frac{D}{U\Delta x} + \frac{1}{2}\right)C_{-1} + \left(\frac{2D}{U\Delta x} + \frac{k\Delta x}{U}\right)C_0 - \left(\frac{D}{U\Delta x} - \frac{1}{2}\right)C_1 = 0 \tag{41}$$

where C_{-1} is obtained from the first boundary condition. For a narrow section:

$$QC_{in} = QC_0 - DA\frac{DC}{dx} \tag{42}$$

where C_0 is the concentration, when $x = 0$. It demonstrates that the concentration obtained by the reactant in the reactor through advection is the same as in case of its removal by advection and turbulent diffusion in the reactor [4]:

$$QC_{in} = QC_0 - DA\frac{C_1 - C_{-1}}{2\Delta x} \tag{43}$$

Equation (42) is used to determine C_{-1}. As $Q = UA$:

$$C_1 - C_{-1} = -\frac{2\Delta x}{D}\left(UC_{in} - UC_0\right) \tag{44}$$

By introducing (44) in (41) and ordering the terms, we will obtain:

$$\left(\frac{2D}{U\Delta x} + \frac{k\Delta x}{U} + \frac{U\Delta x}{D}\right)C_0 - \left(\frac{2D}{U\Delta x}\right)C_1 = \left(2 + \frac{U\Delta x}{D}\right)C_{in} \tag{45}$$

This equation corresponds to the final cross-section of the site of the current. Equation (40) for the tailrace will be as follows:

$$\begin{aligned}&\left(-\frac{D}{U\Delta x} + \frac{1}{2}\right)C_{n-1} + \left(\frac{2D}{U\Delta x} + \frac{k\Delta x}{U}\right)C_n - \\ &-\left(\frac{D}{U\Delta x} - \frac{1}{2}\right)C_{n+1} = 0\end{aligned} \tag{46}$$

where n corresponds to the nth node at the end of the tailrace. The boundary condition of the lower node will be as follows:

$$QC_n - DA\frac{dC_n}{dx} = QC_n \tag{47}$$

In finite differences, equation (47) will be as follows:

$$QC_n - DA\frac{C_{n+1} - C_{n-1}}{2\Delta x} = QC_n \tag{48}$$

Equation (48) implies that $C_{n+1} = C_{n-1}$ i.e., the concentration gradient at the exit equals to zero. If replacing C_{n-1} with C_{n+1}, we will obtain:

$$\left(\frac{2D}{U\Delta x}\right)C_{n-1} + \left(\frac{2D}{U\Delta x} + \frac{k\Delta x}{U}\right)C_n = 0 \tag{49}$$

Thus, equations (41), (45) and (48) must be solved. They form a system of n three-diagonal equations, where n is a sought value and san be solved if the parameters (i.e. D) and boundary conditions are known.

As an illustration, let us look at the following example. Let us assume that $D = 1.5\ m^2/day$; $U = 0.5\ m/s$; $\Delta x = 2.0\ m$; $C_{in} = 300\ mg/L$. Let us determine reaction of the PFR reactor in x direction.

Let us compile three diagonal matrixes. According to the above-described equations, we will obtain:

$$\begin{bmatrix} +4,66 & -3,0 & - & - & - \\ -1,5 & +3,33 & -1,0 & - & - \\ - & -1,5 & +3,33 & -1,0 & - \\ - & - & -1,5 & +3,33 & -1,0 \\ - & - & - & -3,0 & +3,33 \end{bmatrix} \begin{bmatrix} C_0 \\ C_1 \\ C_2 \\ C_3 \\ C_4 \end{bmatrix} = \begin{bmatrix} 300 \\ 0 \\ 0 \\ 0 \\ 0 \end{bmatrix} \tag{50}$$

By solving equation (50), we will obtain:

$C_0 = 263,2;$ $C_1 = 142,2$ $C_2 = 78,6;$ $C_3 = 48,6;$ $C_4 = 43,7$. The obtained equations, as linear equations, can be solved quite easily using Gaussian elimination, which can easily be computerized.

The graphical illustration of the obtained results is given in Figure 34, for two different values of a turbulent diffusion coefficient. As the figure shows, as the tracers move along the reactor, the concentration decreases due to reaction attenuation. If D decreases further, stirring will be less due to the reduced advection and attenuation.

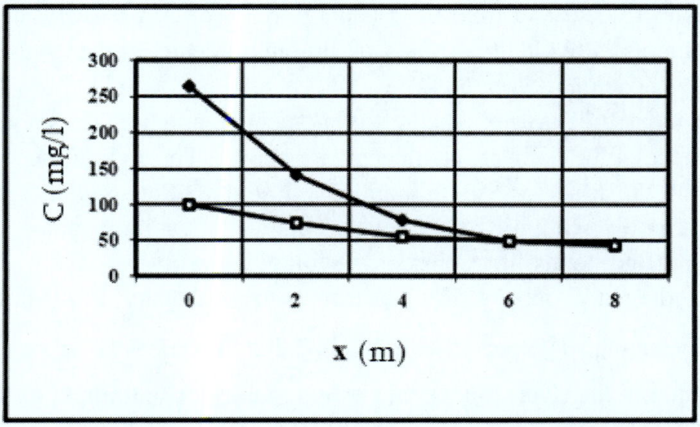

Figure 34. Graphs of the variation of tracer concentration along the reactor: 1. $D =$ 1.5 m^2/day; 2. $D =$ 6,0 m^2/day.

3.3. Determination of the Oil Stream Trajectory Spilled in the River as a Result of Accidents during the Transportation of Oil and Oil Products

Analytical Deduction of Evaluating Equations Determining the Oil Stream Trajectory Spilled in the River Due to Accidents

For the sake of simplicity, consider an oil stream spilling from a certain height into a river with H and constant velocity U_0 at all of its points for the sake of simplicity [8].

This may happen when a train of oil tanks on the railway bridge or a tank truck on the highway has an accident.

Every day, large quantities of hazardous materials (pollutants) (including oil and oil products) are transported on railways and highways, and spills in the event of road accidents are naturally expected. Spills pollute ground waters, rivers, drinking water, and soil. Accidents may occur during road reconstruction due to the explosion of toxic chemical substances or during the transportation of pollutants by roads; accidents may be caused by natural disasters (floods, fire, landslide, earthquake, etc.), which may change road ecology, making the road the main factor contributing to the accident. Pollutant transportation shall be regulated and supervised, including the limitation of route and time of transportation, so that passage near aquatic environments is avoided as much as possible. Vehicle types must also be carefully chosen.

Let us assume *apriori*, that at the moment of contact of a stream with a free surface of the river, its parameters are known. The goal of the study is to determine the trajectory of the spilled oil stream. Let us consider certain idealization, which will allow us to obtain evaluating equations [2]. In particular, first, let us first consider the following problem: say, granule with small D diameter, density of which equals to ρ density of oil, falls on the river surface with V_0 speed. Let us assume that the trajectory of movement of the granule in the river, to a certain extent, coincides with that of oil stream. Such idealization is, to a certain extent, fair, because when the stream falls from big height, its aeration and disintegration (fragmentation) into small particles occurs, form of which is nearly spherical. In addition to these data, composition of oil or oil products and their physical parameters shall be known.

Let us draw z axis vertically downwards, and x axis along the current. The movement equation along z axis will then be as follows:

$$mg - F_A - F_C = m\frac{dV_z}{dt}, \tag{51}$$

where granule mass $m = \rho W$; it is obvious that buoyant force $F_A = \rho_0 g W$; and resistive force [3]: $F_C = c\rho_0 V_z^2 \omega.$

Here, ρ and ρ_0, are the densities of the granule and the liquid, respectively ($\rho_0 > \rho$); W is the granule volume; ω is the area of the granule model; c is the resistance coefficient.

If we introduce the obtained values in (50), we will obtain:

$$\rho g W - \rho_0 g W - c\rho_0 V_z^{\,2}\omega = \rho W \frac{dV_z}{dt} \tag{52}$$

It is also obvious that $\omega = \frac{3W}{2D}$.

Equation (52) will be as follows:

$$W(\rho - \rho_0)g - c\rho_0 V_z^{\,2}\frac{3W}{2D} = \rho W \frac{dV_z}{dt} \tag{53}$$

hence:

$$\frac{dV_z}{dt} = \frac{\rho - \rho_0}{\rho} g - c\frac{\rho_0}{\rho}\frac{3}{2D}V_z^{\,2} \tag{54}$$

as $\frac{\rho - \rho_0}{\rho} g < 0$, so $\frac{\rho - \rho_0}{\rho} g = -A; \quad A > 0.$ $\frac{dV_z}{dt} = -A - \frac{c\rho_0}{\rho}\frac{3}{2D}V_z^{\,2}.$

hence, $\frac{dV_z}{dt} = -\left(A + \frac{3c\rho_0}{2\rho}V_z^{\,2}\right)$

Finally:

$$dt = -\frac{dV_z}{A + \frac{3c\rho_0}{2\rho}V_z^{\,2}} \tag{55}$$

Let us denote $B = \frac{3c\rho_0}{2\rho}$, then: $dt = -\frac{dV_z}{A + BV_z^{\,2}}$, or/and

$$dt = -\frac{1}{B}\frac{dV_z}{\frac{A}{B} + V_z^{\,2}} \tag{56}$$

Let us denote:

$$a = \sqrt{\frac{A}{B}} = \sqrt{\frac{(\rho_0 - \rho) g 2\rho}{\rho 3c\rho_0}} = \sqrt{\frac{(\rho_0 - \rho)2g}{3c\rho_0}} \tag{57}$$

It is clear that:

$$a^2 = \frac{(\rho_0 - \rho)2g}{3c\rho_0} \tag{58}$$

Let us integrate (56) from 0 to t. We will obtain:

$$t = -\frac{1}{B}\int \frac{dV_z}{a^2 + V_z^{\,2}} + C \tag{59}$$

As it is known:

$$\int \frac{dx}{a^2 + x^2} = \frac{1}{6a^2}\ln\frac{(a+x)^2}{a^2 - ax + x^2} + \frac{1}{a^2\sqrt{3}}\arg tg\frac{2x - a}{a\sqrt{3}} \tag{60}$$

Thus:

$$t = -\frac{1}{B}\left[\frac{1}{6a^2}\ln\frac{(a+V_z)^2}{a^2 - aV_z^{\,2} + V_z^{\,2}} + \frac{1}{a^2\sqrt{3}}\arg tg\frac{2V_z - a}{a\sqrt{3}}\right] + C \tag{61}$$

Integrating constant C is defined from the condition: when $t = 0$, then $V_z = V_0$. So:

$$-\frac{1}{B}\left[\frac{1}{6a^2}\ln\frac{a^2}{a^2} + \frac{1}{a^2\sqrt{3}}\arg tg\left(-\frac{1}{\sqrt{3}}\right)\right] + C = 0 \tag{62}$$

As $\arg tg\left(-\frac{1}{\sqrt{3}}\right) = \frac{5}{6}\pi$, then $C = \frac{1}{B}\frac{1}{a^2\sqrt{3}}\frac{5\pi}{6}$

Thus:

$$t = -\frac{1}{Ba^2\sqrt{3}}\left(\frac{5\pi}{6} - arctg\frac{2V_z - a}{a\sqrt{3}}\right) - \frac{1}{B}\frac{1}{6a^2}\ln\frac{\left(a + V_z\right)^2}{a^2 - aV_z + V_z^2} \tag{63}$$

as

$$\left[\begin{array}{c} \dfrac{1}{Ba^2\sqrt{3}} = \dfrac{2\rho 3c\rho_0}{3c\rho_0\left(\rho - \rho_0\right)2g}; \\ \dfrac{1}{6a^2 B} = \dfrac{3c\rho_0 2\rho}{6\left(\rho - \rho_0\right)2g3c\rho_0} = \dfrac{\rho}{6\left(\rho - \rho_0\right)} \end{array}\right] \tag{64}$$

Finally:

$$\begin{aligned} t = \frac{\rho}{\rho - \rho_0}&\left(\frac{5\pi}{6} - arctg\frac{2V_z - \sqrt{\dfrac{\left(\rho_0 - \rho\right)2g}{3c\rho_0}}}{\sqrt{\dfrac{\left(\rho_0 - \rho\right)2g}{2c\rho_0}}}\right) - \\ &- \frac{\rho}{6\left(\rho - \rho_0\right)}\ln\frac{\left(\sqrt{\dfrac{\left(\rho_0 - \rho\right)2g}{3c\rho_0}} + V_z\right)^2}{\dfrac{\left(\rho_0 - \rho\right)2g}{3c\rho_0} - \sqrt{\dfrac{\left(\rho_0 - \rho\right)2g}{3c\rho_0}}V_z + V_z^2} \end{aligned} \tag{65}$$

Let us start deducing the equation along x axis. First, for simplicity, let us assume that V_x, the local velocity, is the same at all points of the effective river cross-section local speed. In this case, the equation of motion along x axis will be as follows (Figure 35):

$$m\frac{dV_x}{dt} = c\rho V_x^2\omega \tag{66}$$

Using the previously introduced denotations, we will obtain:

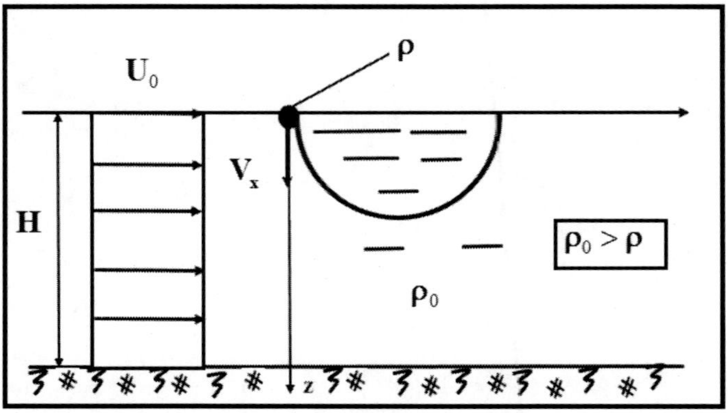

Figure 35. The Plan to determine stream trajectory in the river when local velocity is the same at all points of the effective cross-section of the river.

$$\rho W \frac{dV_x}{dt} = c\rho_0 V_x^2 \frac{3}{2}\frac{W}{D} \tag{67}$$

$$\frac{dV_x}{dt} = c\frac{\rho_0}{\rho}\frac{3}{2D}V_x^2 \tag{68}$$

Hence:

$$dt = \frac{1}{c}\frac{\rho}{\rho_0}\frac{2D}{3}\frac{dV_x}{V_x^2} \tag{69}$$

Let us integrate equation (68). We will obtain:

$$t = \frac{1}{c}\frac{\rho}{\rho_0}\frac{2D}{3}\int \frac{dV_x}{V_x^2} + C = \frac{1}{c}\frac{\rho}{\rho_0}\frac{2D}{3}\frac{V_x^{-1}}{(-1)} + C = -\frac{1}{c}\frac{\rho}{\rho_0}\frac{2D}{3}\frac{1}{V_x} + C \tag{70}$$

Integration constant C shall be defined under the following condition: when $t = 0$, then $V_x = U_0$:

$$C = \frac{1}{c}\frac{\rho}{\rho_0}\frac{2D}{3}\frac{1}{U_0} \tag{71}$$

Let us introduce (70) in (69). We will obtain:

$$t = -\frac{1}{c}\frac{\rho}{\rho_0}\frac{2D}{3}\frac{1}{V_x} + \frac{1}{c}\frac{\rho}{\rho_0}\frac{2D}{3}\frac{1}{U_0} \tag{72}$$

Finally:

$$t = -\frac{1}{c}\frac{\rho}{\rho_0}\frac{2D}{3}\left(\frac{1}{U_0} - \frac{1}{V_x}\right) \tag{73}$$

Thus, dependences (65) and (73) provide stream trajectory as a parameter. To build the stream trajectory, several numerical approaches, following the results above, may be used. The procedure of the first approach is as follows:

1. It is clear that the starting point of the trajectory is $x = 0; \quad z = 0$;
2. a certain small-time interval Δt will be assigned;
3. V_x and V_z will be determined for fixed time value Δt;
4. The coordinates of the corresponding trajectory point by time moment Δt will be: $x_1 = V_x \Delta t$ and $z_1 = V_z \Delta t$;
5. The procedure will be repeated with Δt span to the moment, until the point with ordinate $z_N = 0$ is reached.

This is followed by the oil propagation all over the surface and the diffusion theory is applied.

The second approach: the first three clauses of the first approach are used. Then, the speed vector will be calculated: $V = \sqrt{V_x^{\,2} + V_z^{\,2}}$. The angles of inclination towards the trajectory tangent axles ($\sin\alpha = \frac{V_x}{V}$ and $\cos\alpha = \frac{V_z}{V}$) will be calculated, the tangent and, accordingly, stream trajectory will be drawn.

The third approach: a flow line equation is given:

$$\frac{dx}{V_x} = \frac{dz}{V_z} \tag{74}$$

where V_x and V_y values are taken from relations (64) and (72). By integrating the obtained equation, a flow line equation will be obtained. It should be noted that this approach is quite complex and numerical methods must be used.

Thus, the obtained results allow evaluating the trajectory of the spilled oil currents in the river.

It should be noted that the obtained equations contain resistance coefficient c, which depends on the speed both, in vertical and horizontal directions. It is clear that this fact must be given in numerical calculations. In particular, classical results can be calculated [4].

Based on the obtained results, it is quite easy to solve some consequent problems, e.g., reverse problem to calculate the initial stream velocity V_z, with which the stream will reach the riverbed and pollute the bed ground; or to calculate the distance between where the stream enters and exits the river surface, etc.

3.4. Solution of Evaluating Equations Determining the Trajectory of Oil Stream Spilled in the River Using Numerical Methods

The obtained equations were numerically solved using the mathematical software *Maple 9.5.* The numerical experiment was carried out for three different scenarios: 1. the considered scenario from the previous study, when local velocity is the same at all points of the stream's horizontal; 2. local velocity is distributed linearly on the horizontal; and 3. local velocity on the horizontal is distributed according to the logarithmic or qualitative law.

A distribution diagram of the local velocity distributed linearly on the horizontal will be as follows (Figure 36):

$$V_x = U_0\left(1+\frac{z}{H}\right) \tag{75}$$

where U_0 is the surface velocity.

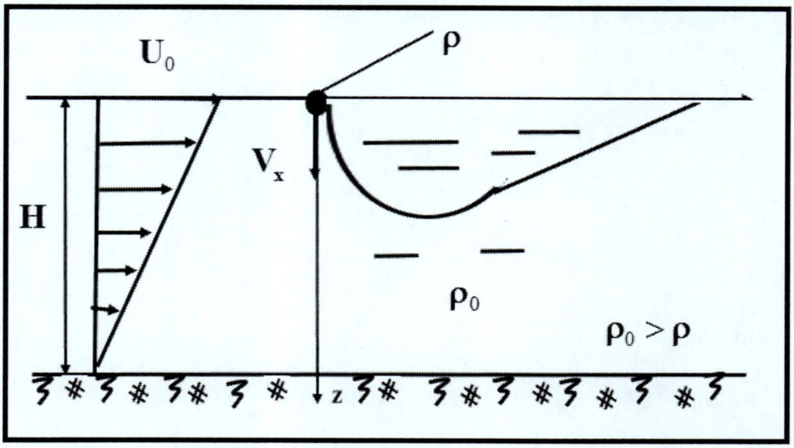

Figure 36. The plan to determine stream trajectory in the river for the linearly distributed velocity in the effective cross-section of the river.

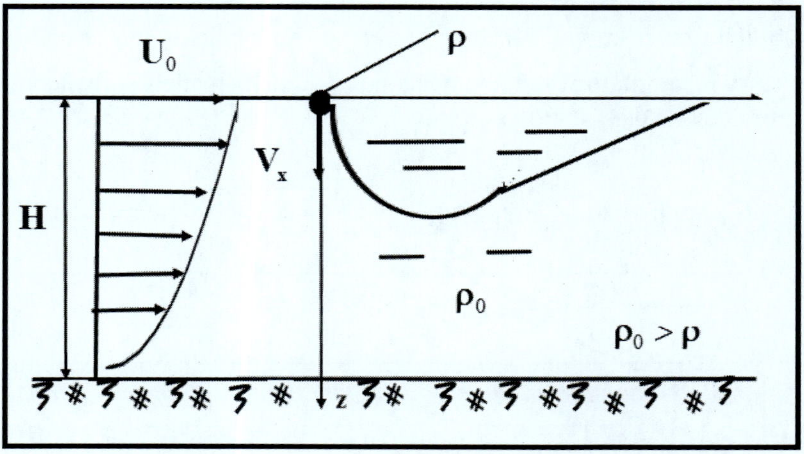

Figure 37. The plan to determine stream trajectory in the river for the logarithmic distribution of the velocity in the effective cross-section of the river.

For the local velocity distributed on the horizontal according to the logarithmic law (Figure 37), the following procedure is appropriate:

Let us consider the riverbed of a rectangular cross-section with the depth of H, and width of B. Let us denote the height of the projections of the bed roughness by Δ_D, and that of the walls – by Δ_C. Let us denote the mean stream velocity by V. According to the result obtained in the previous chapter, the field of local velocities can be described by the following equation [12]:

$$V_x = V\frac{\lg\dfrac{y}{0,06\Delta_c}}{\lg\dfrac{B}{0,1\Delta_c}\lg\dfrac{H}{0,16\Delta_D}}\lg\frac{x}{0,06\Delta_c} = A(y)\lg\frac{x}{M} \qquad (76)$$

The following values were selected as initial parameters: initial acceleration: $a = \dfrac{\rho - \rho_0}{\rho}g = 2\ m/s^2$, as $\rho = 800\ kg/m^3$ is taken as oil density; the speed of falling on the surface: $V_0 = 5\ m/s$; local velocity on the surface: $V_z = 2\ m/s$; river depth: $H = 10\ m$; surface velocity for linear and logarithmic distribution: $U_0 = 4\ m/s$.

In the first case, function $x = f(z)$ is given explicitly, constructing the trajectory is straightforward. In the second case, mathematical software *Maple 9.5* provides a clear solution as follows:

$$z = \frac{\left[\left(8b^3d - 36abdcx + 108cx^2 + 12\sqrt{3}xc\sqrt{\dfrac{a^2b^2cd^2x + 4b^3d - 18abcdx + 27cx^2}{c}}\right)d^2\right]^{1/3}}{6cd} - \frac{2\left(-b^2 + 3acx\right)d}{3c\left[\left(\begin{array}{l}8b^3d - 36abcdx + 108cx^2 + \\ +12c\sqrt{3}x\sqrt{\dfrac{-a^2b^2cd^2 + 4a^3c^2d^2x + 4b^3d - 18abcdx + 27cx^2}{c}}\end{array}\right)d^2\right]^{1/3}} - \frac{2b}{3c} \qquad (77)$$

where a, b, c and d parameters depend on the hydraulic and geometric parameters of the stream and granule.

Figure 38 shows stream trajectories for (1) constant and (2) linearly distributed local velocities on the horizontal.

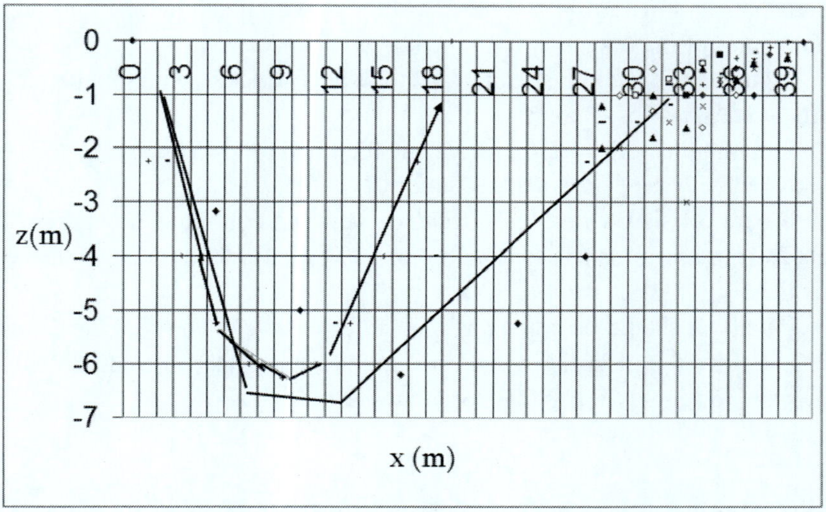

Figure 38. Stream trajectories for (1) constant and (2) linearly distributed local velocities on the horizontal.

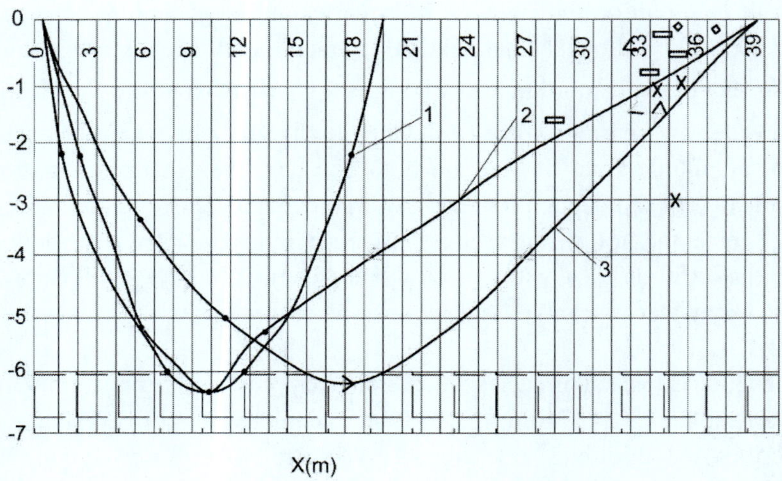

Figure 39. Stream trajectories for (1) constant, (2) linearly distributed and (3) logarithmically distributed local velocity on the horizontal, and Harlman's experimental data.

As for the equation to calculate stream trajectory, when the local velocity on the horizontal is distributed according to logarithmic or qualitative law, mathematical software *Maple 9.5* does not give an explicit solution, but the coordinates of the trajectory with the numerical solution.

Figure 39 shows the stream trajectories constructed using mathematical software *Maple 9.5*.

Stream trajectories were experimentally tested by Harleman et al. [53] and compared with the experimental data of [53].

Figure 39 shows that the difference between Harleman's experimental data and our assessments (approximately 20%) is sufficient for an engineering practice.

Finally, it should be noted that it is quite possible to consider the distance of the point of spill in the river from the river bank to construct the stream trajectory, as expression (75) incorporates $\mathbf{y}$ coordinate [1, 10, 20].

3.5. Calculation of the Trajectory of an Oil Stream Spilled in an Estuary

The case when there is more dense liquid on the left of the origin of coordinates than on the right, as in estuaries, is interesting. Such a case is typical of salinization (salt penetration) in an estuary, with its seashore located in the section with coordinate $x = 0$. Speed U_r corresponds to the stationary freshwater river current. If the freshwater discharge in the estuary and the tide wave amplitude from the sea are both constant, then there is a stationary distribution of salinization for an observer moving at the speed of a periodical tide. Thus, the following factors influence the stationary distribution of salinization in an ideal estuary: turbulence intensity in the salinization area [21], freshwater discharge, and the difference in densities of fresh and sea waters.

Figure 20 is an image of two boundary cases of salinization in the estuaries. The first (Figure 40, A) is a "completely stratified estuary" and describes the minimum tide impact. The stream profile is conditionally divided into two parts in this case. The lower part of the current has nearly the same salinity as the sea, while the upper freshwater section barely mixes with sea water. This is known as density stratification, and the layer beneath the dividing surface is known as salinity stratification. A wedge acts as a long spillway that transports fresh water into the sea. The large density gradients between fresh and salt waters reduce the intensity of turbulent mixing [20].

If the tide is strong, the turbulence caused by wave impact, a weak river stream, and wind-created currents can create powerful mixing. This type of estuary is known as a “completely mixed estuary” (Figure 20, *B*). In this case, the salinization zone has no clearly defined border [10].

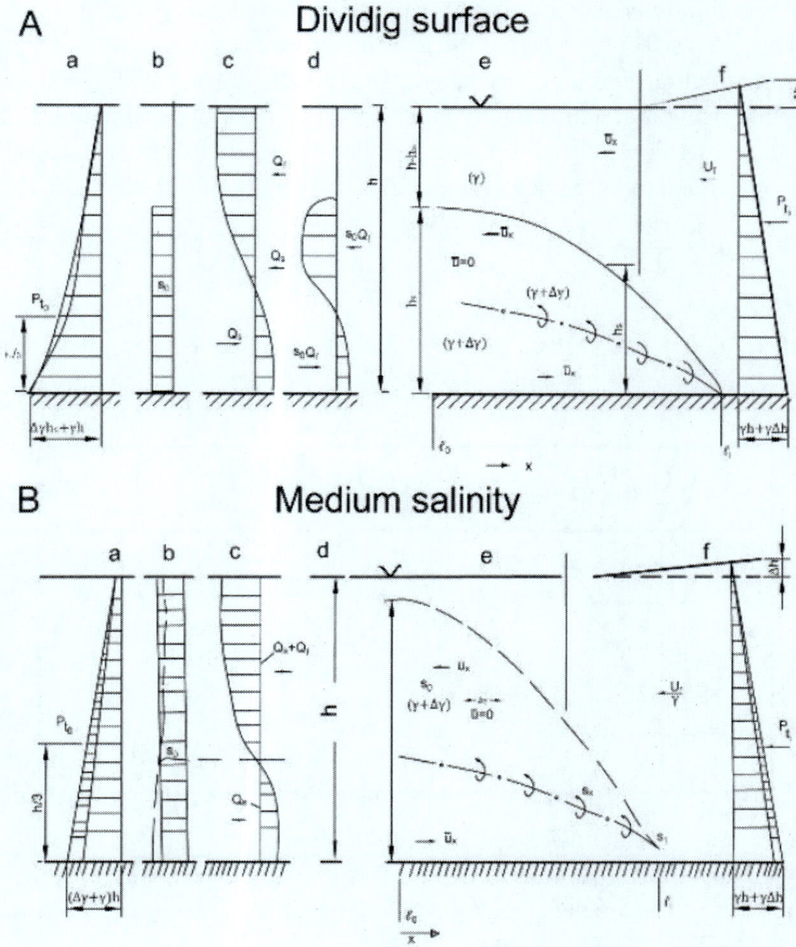

Figure 40. Salinization in estuaries.
A is the completely stratified estuary; *B* is the completely mixed estuary; *a* is the pressure in the lower course of the estuary; *b* is the distribution of salinity; *c* is the velocity distribution; *d* is the salt transportation; *e* is the average level; *f* is the pressure in the upper course of the estuary.

Historically, a man always tried to make the following three types of changes to a river regime: 1. changing the riverbed cross-section and depth for better economy; 2. using estuaries to remove industrial and household wastes; and 3. controlling and changing freshwater runoff in tidal estuaries.

There has been still another change identified recently: the problem of general pollution of estuaries possibly caused by accidental oil spills.

Despite the fact that each of the aforementioned actions can be viewed as a separate cause of a regime change, their effects are not isolated and are evaluated using a systemic approach. Let us use linear approximation in the first stage of calculating an oil stream trajectory spilled in the estuary. The following equation expresses the vertical distribution of local velocity:

$$V_x = u_1 + \frac{z}{H}(u_1 + u_2) \tag{78}$$

where u_1 and u_2 are surface ($V_z = 0$) and bed local velocities, respectively (Figure 41).

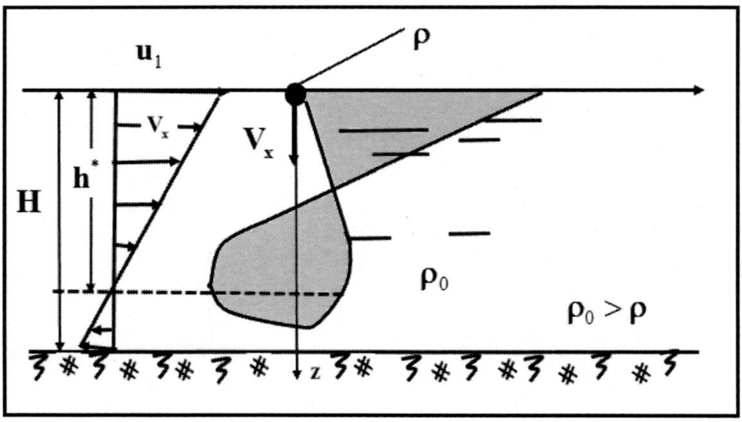

Figure 41. The plan to determine stream trajectory spilled in the estuary for the linearly distributed velocity.

It is obvious that depth z^*, at which the stream direction changes, can be calculated from the following condition as follows:

$$z^* = -\frac{u_1 H}{u_1 + u_2} \tag{79}$$

The mean velocity in estuary can be obtained from the following condition:

$$\frac{z^* u_1}{2} - \frac{\left(H - z^*\right) u_2}{2} = VH \tag{80}$$

where V is the mean stream velocity. Thus, equation (78) will yield:

$$V = \frac{u_1^{\ 2}}{2\left(u_1 + u_2\right)} + \frac{u_1 - u_2}{2} \tag{81}$$

It is obvious that in this case, the shape of the stream trajectory is complex: first, the stream moves downwards; once it reaches the point where the current direction changes, the stream curve radius changes and the stream loops; and only then, does it ascend onto the surface of the current.

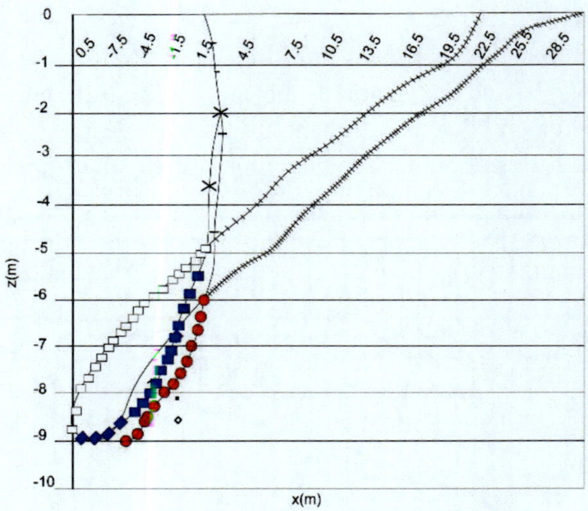

Figure 42. Trajectories of a stream spilled in the estuary generated by the mathematical software Maple 9.5 for: (1) $\mathbf{u}_1 = 2$ m/s; $\mathbf{u}_2 = 6$ m/s; (2) $\mathbf{u}_1 = 6$ m/s; $\mathbf{u}_2 = 2$ m/s.

The stream trajectory in the estuary is determined in the same order as a single-directional stream. In this case, there arise challenges, which we did not face in the previous case, specifically: 1. the mathematical software *Maple 9.5* does not produce an explicit mathematical solution; 2. the loop creates some uncertainties (the solution, is obviously, monotonous following the dynamics of the event, but not explicit). The loop is invisible to *Maple 9.5,* which interprets its solutions as complex numbers. Consequently, sub-software for calculating stream coordinates by area was created. As the stream trajectory changes, the software stops calculations and starts a new calculation.

Two tests were carried out with the help of the modified mathematical 42software *Maple 9.5.* Both trajectories are plotted in Figure 42 for comparison.

The next stage of the research involved applying the findings to a real estuary with real natural data. The case described in [10] was considered. The following are the baseline data in the given case: $\rho = 857\ kg/m^3$; $V_0 = 12\ m/s$; $H = 9\ m$; $u_1 = 0.6\ m/s$; $u_2 = 0.4\ m/s$. As a real distribution diagram of local velocities quite differs from a linear one, and its analytical description is complicated, it was fed as a numerical row into mathematical software *Maple 9.5.* The depth-dependent distribution of liquid density was also fed as a numerical row.

Figure 43 depicts the stream trajectory generated by the mathematical software *Maple 9.5* and the natural data from [1]. The difference between our results and the natural data is less than 20%. S, it is clear that the method we have proposed for a preliminary engineering assessment is quite acceptable.

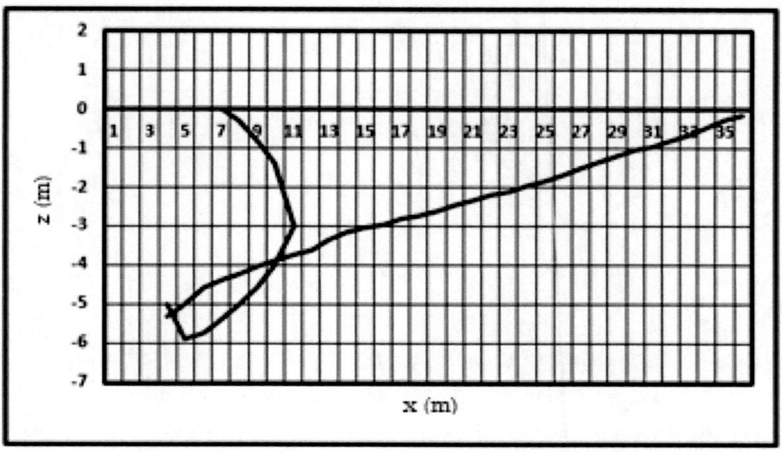

Figure 43. Trajectories of a stream spilled in the estuary generated by the mathematical software Maple 9.5 for: $\mathbf{u}_1 = 0.6$ m/s; $\mathbf{u}_2 = 0.4$ m/s, and the natural data.

3.6. Studying Oil Filtration Phenomena in the Ground

Physical Principles of Liquid Filtration in the Ground

A flow in both unsaturated areas and water-bearing grounds is, at a certain extent, three-dimensional. If a hydraulic gradient is more or less non-oriented, the flow will be practically one-dimensional (81). If coefficients $K = K_x = K_y = K_z$ are equal, the water-bearing ground will be considered "isotropic", which is the simplest case for movement analysis. If K does not depend on ground orientation, it is considered homogeneous. As the practice and the analysis show, the movement is either mostly isotropic, or homogeneous. Darcy's law for the liquid flow in the ground is as follows:

$$Q = -KA\frac{dh}{dx} = KA\frac{h_2 - h}{l_2 - l_1}. \tag{82}$$

where, Q is the liquid discharge along a horizontal carrier (m^3/s). K is the hydraulic coefficient of filtration (m/s), A is the cross-section area (m^2); $h_2 - h_1$ is the pressure differential (m); $l_2 - l_1$ is the distance along the horizontal direction between h_2 and h_1 (m).

In addition:

$$q = \frac{Q}{A} = K\frac{dh}{dl};\ q_x = K_x\frac{\partial h}{\partial x};\quad q_y = K_y\frac{\partial h}{\partial y};\quad q_z = K_z\frac{\partial h}{\partial z}, \tag{83}$$

where, q is the specific discharge per unit area.

Figure 44 shows the elementary volume of ground saturated with liquid. Let us use the mass balance principle to deduce the movement equation. The mass balance equation along x axis will be as follows (for simplicity, movement in y and z directions is not given):

$$\rho q_x \Delta y \Delta z - \left[\rho q_x + \frac{\partial(\rho q_x)\Delta x}{\partial x}\right]\Delta y \Delta z = \frac{\partial(\rho n)}{\partial t}\Delta x \Delta y \Delta z \tag{84}$$

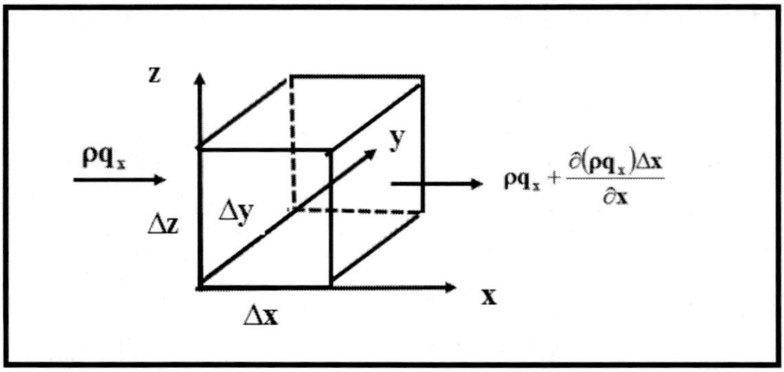

Figure 44. Saturated ground element without free surface.

where, n is effective porosity, is the elementary volume mass, q_x is the specific discharge per $\Delta_y \Delta_z$ elementary area. Thus, (84) will be written as follows:

$$\begin{bmatrix} -\dfrac{\partial q_x}{\partial x} = \dfrac{\partial n_x}{\partial t}; \\ -\left(\dfrac{\partial q_x}{\partial x} + \dfrac{\partial q_y}{\partial y} + \dfrac{\partial q_z}{\partial z}\right) = \dfrac{\partial n}{\partial t}. \end{bmatrix} \tag{85}$$

Let us consider S_0 as the volume of liquid, which is separated from the volume unit of the liquid-bearing environment. As it is known from hydrostatistics, $P = \rho g\left(h - Z_0\right)$, where h is the piesometric pressure, and Z_0 is the geodesic height. Therefore:

$$-\left(\frac{\partial q_x}{\partial x} + \frac{\partial q_y}{\partial y} + \frac{\partial q_z}{\partial z}\right). = -S_0 \frac{\partial h}{\partial t} \tag{86}$$

In a stationary case:

$$-\left(\frac{\partial q_x}{\partial x} + \frac{\partial q_y}{\partial y} + \frac{\partial q_z}{\partial z}\right). = 0 \tag{87}$$

If we use Darcy's law, then:

$$\frac{\partial}{\partial x}\left(K_x \frac{\partial h}{\partial x}\right)+\frac{\partial}{\partial y}\left(K_y \frac{\partial h}{\partial y}\right)+\frac{\partial}{\partial z}\left(K_z \frac{\partial h}{\partial z}\right)=0 \qquad (88)$$

If we consider that the ground is isotropic, i.e., $K_x = K_y = K_z = K$, we will obtain the Laplace equation:

$$\left[\begin{array}{c} \dfrac{\partial^2 h}{\partial x^2}+\dfrac{\partial^2 h}{\partial y^2}+\dfrac{\partial^2 h}{\partial z^2}=0; \\ \nabla^2 h = 0. \end{array}\right] \qquad (89)$$

There are various methods available to solve Equation (89), including analytical and graphical methods, electronic hydraulic analogy, and numerical methods, as described in papers by Show (1994), Brass (1990), and Ewing and Anderson (1982). The analytical solutions described in the papers are based on the Dupuit-Forchheimer's simplified assumptions for unconfined flow. One of the main conclusions reached as a result of these assumptions is that hydraulic gradient dh/dx approximates water table and free surface gradient.

The Laplace equation (88) is used to solve aquifer filtration movement problems.

The characteristics of the water-bearing ground are critical and are affected by a variety of factors. Ground porosity must be mentioned first, which physically equals the amount of water contained in the ground, expressed as a percentage and subject to gravity's influence. It is less than the absolute porosity, according to the definition, because a certain amount of water is not subject to gravity due to surface tension.

1. Storage coefficient S : this shows the volume of water stored by the unit volume of ground. For confined grounds, $10^{-5} < S < 10^{-3}$, and for unconfined grounds, $10^{-2} < S < 0{,}35$ (Davis and Cornwall, 1991). In fact, this is the volume of water (m^3) divided by the volume of ground (m^3).
2. Hydraulic gradient dh/dx: this causes the movement of ground waters at a specific speed.

3. Hydraulic coefficient K: in an unsaturated area, is included in Darcy's law. K is a parameter of both environments of ground and liquid. It is a dynamic value and changes depending on the moisture content. K may be within the following limits: for gravel and lime: approximately 10^{-2} to 10^{-8}, and for magmatic and metamorphic rock and clays: $10^{-8} \div 10^{-14}$.

3.7. Methodology for Building Depression Curves and Calculating the Amount of Oil Spilled in Rivers during the Accidental Breakage of Oil Pipeline Mains

Oil Flow between Two Rivers with No Accidental Leakages

Figure 45 shows the ground waters flow between two rivers with different water tables.

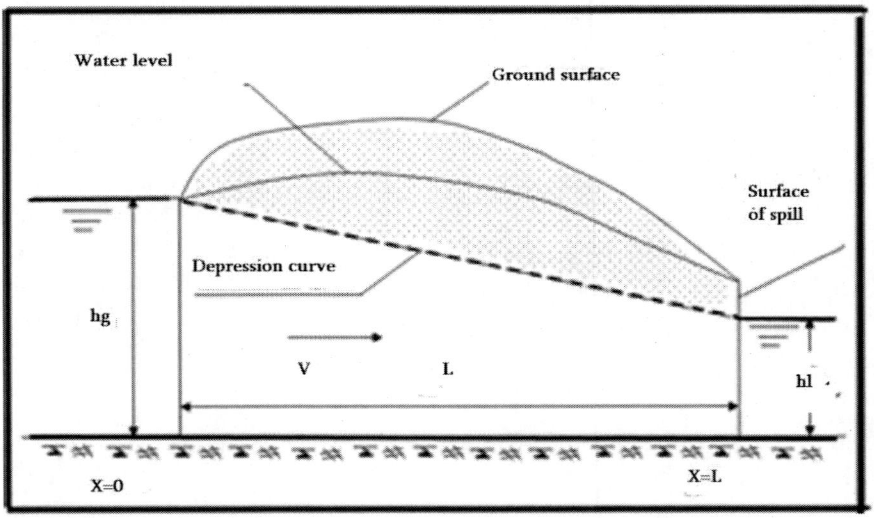

Figure 45. Flow between two rivers without accidental leakage.

Assuming that the flow is one-dimensional and has an established regime with K hydraulic coefficient, the Laplace equation will be as follows:

$$\frac{d^2h^2}{dx^2}=0 \tag{90}$$

By integrating equation (90), we will obtain:

$$h^2 = ax + b \tag{91}$$

Let us denote the depths of the right and the left rivers by h_R and h_L respectively, and by L the distance between the rivers. Following the first boundary condition, $h = h_L$, when $\mathbf{x} = 0$. Consequently:

$$b = h_L{}^2 \tag{92}$$

By differentiating equation (91), we will obtain the following equation: $2h\dfrac{dh}{dx} = a.$

From Darcy's equation, we will obtain:

$$q = -Kh\frac{dh}{dx} \tag{93}$$

Equation (83) will be as follows:

$$h^2 = 2h\frac{dh}{dx}x + h_L{}^2 = h_L{}^2 - \frac{2q}{K}x \tag{94}$$

From the second boundary condition: $h = h_R$, if $x = L$. So:

$$h_R{}^2 = h_L{}^2 - \frac{2q}{K}L \tag{95}$$

Wherefrom:

$$q = \frac{K}{2L}\left(h_L^{\ 2} - h_R^{\ 2}\right) \tag{96}$$

Equation (94) will be as follows:

$$h^2 = h_L^{\ 2} - \frac{x}{L}\left(h_L^{\ 2} - h_R^{\ 2}\right) \tag{97}$$

Equation (96) is known as the Dupuit parabola.

Flow between Two Rivers in Case of Accidental Oil Leakages

The equation obtained in the preceding paragraph is only applicable in the absence of any accidental leakage scenarios. Let us give the name "loading" to the portion of oil leakage, which finds its way to the saturated aquifer and causes an increase in the liquid level. If R is loading (Figure 46) (in case of full loading, i.e., when the total area between the rivers is damaged), we will obtain:

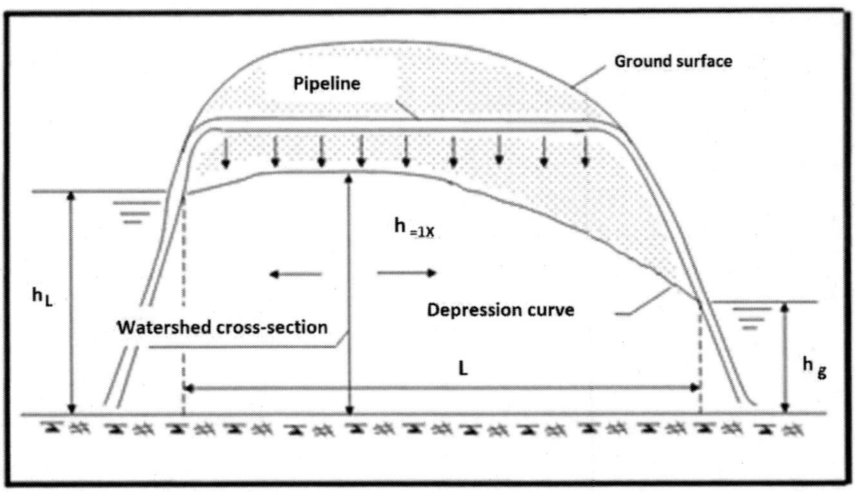

Figure 46. Flow between two rivers in case of full loading.

$$\frac{dq}{dx} = R \tag{98}$$

According to Darcy's law:

$$q = -Kh\frac{dh}{dx} \tag{99}$$

Wherefrom:

$$\frac{dq}{dx} = -\frac{K}{2}\frac{d^2h^2}{dx^2} = R \tag{100}$$

By double integration of equation (99), we will obtain:

$$h^2 = -\frac{Rx^2}{K} + ax + b \tag{101}$$

In case of full loading, the boundary conditions will be the same, so:

$$\begin{cases} b = h_L^{\ 2}; \\ a = \dfrac{h_R^{\ 2} - h_L^{\ 2}}{L} + \dfrac{RL}{K} \end{cases} \tag{102}$$

If we introduce these values, we will obtain:

$$h^2 = h_L^{\ 2} - \frac{x}{L}\left(h_L^{\ 2} - h_R^{\ 2}\right) + \frac{Rx}{K}\left(L - x\right) \tag{103}$$

This equation gives the contour line of liquid level, which is a parabola. Now, the level of flow along the aquifer can be determined as follows:

By differentiating equation (103), we will obtain:

$$2h\frac{dh}{dx} = \frac{h_L^{\ 2} - h_R^{\ 2}}{L} + \frac{R}{K}\left(L - 2x\right) \tag{104}$$

Now, equation (104) will be as follows:

$$q = \frac{K}{2L}\left(h_R^{\,2} - h_L^{\,2}\right) - \frac{R}{2}(L - 2x) \tag{105}$$

Equation (104) is a modified Dupuit equation for the flow with a loading effect.

Equation (103) yields a curve, which may have maximum within the range of $(0 - L)$. Let us find value x, for which the given maximum is valid. From (104), we will have:

$$h = \sqrt{h_L^{\,2} - \frac{x}{L}\left(h_L^{\,2} - h_R^{\,2}\right) + \frac{Rx}{L}(L - x)} \tag{106}$$

Therefore:

$$\frac{dh}{dx} = \frac{\dfrac{h_R^{\,2} - h_L^{\,2}}{L} + \dfrac{RL}{K} - \dfrac{2Rx}{K}}{2\sqrt{h_L^{\,2} - \dfrac{x}{L}\left(h_L^{\,2} - h_R^{\,2}\right) + \dfrac{Rx}{L}(L - x)}} = 0 \tag{107}$$

As the denominator of the fraction does not equal to zero, then:

$$\frac{h_R^{\,2} - h_L^{\,2}}{L} + \frac{RL}{K} - \frac{2}{K}Rx = 0 \tag{108}$$

$$x = \frac{K}{2R}\frac{h_R^{\,2} - h_L^{\,2}}{L} + \frac{L}{2} \tag{109}$$

Consider an example that is very similar to the case of the Baku-Supsa main pipeline, in particular, with an annual capacity of 5 million tons. Assume in our case, $h_R = 18$ m; $h_L = 10$ m; $L = 10$ km; and $K = 10$ m/s. Several loading scenarios are considered, ranging from 2% to 10% of total discharge. The depression lines are depicted in Figure 47.

It should be noted that the maximum height may exceed the level of a deeper river.

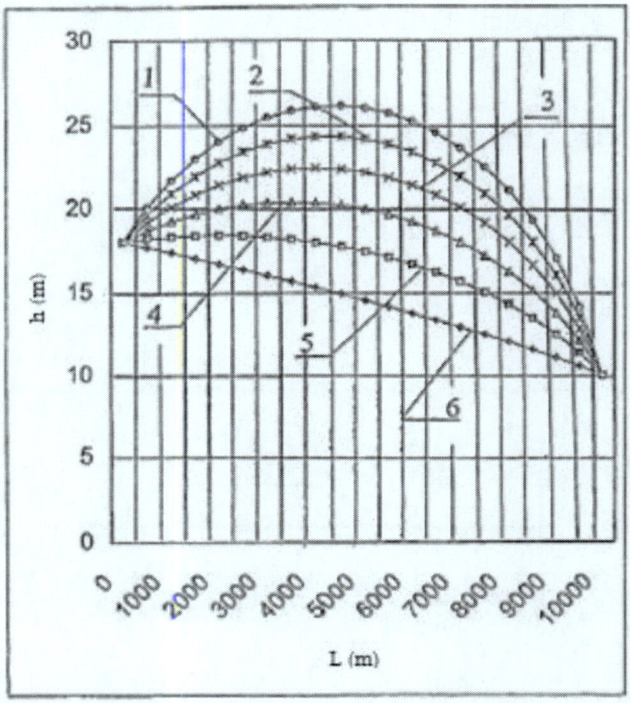

Figure 47. Flow between two rivers for a full loading scenario.
1. R= 0.0000186 m/s (10% of total discharge); 2. R= 0.00001488 m/s (8% of total discharge); 3. R = 0.00001116 m/s (6% of total discharge); 4. R = 0.00000744 m/s (4% of total discharge); 5. R = 0.00000372 m/s (2% of total discharge); 6. R = 0.

Flow between Two Rivers in Case of Partial Loading

Consider the section of a main pipeline that runs along the bed of one river, then continues through the ground and crosses another river. The layout is given in Figure 48. Suppose there is a leakage of a pipeline buried in the ground from intersection with a coordinate x_1 to intersection with a coordinate x_2. This process can be described by Heaviside unit step function, which is as follows:

$$\sigma(x) = \begin{cases} 1; x > 0; \\ 0; x < 0 \end{cases} \tag{110}$$

Similarly, the following function can be introduced (Figure 49):

$$\sigma\left(x-x_0\right)=\begin{cases}1; x>x_0;\\ 0' x<x_0\end{cases} \tag{111}$$

We will also consider a new function (Figure 49):

$$f\left(x\right)=\sigma\left(x-x_2\right)-\sigma\left(x-x_1\right) \tag{112}$$

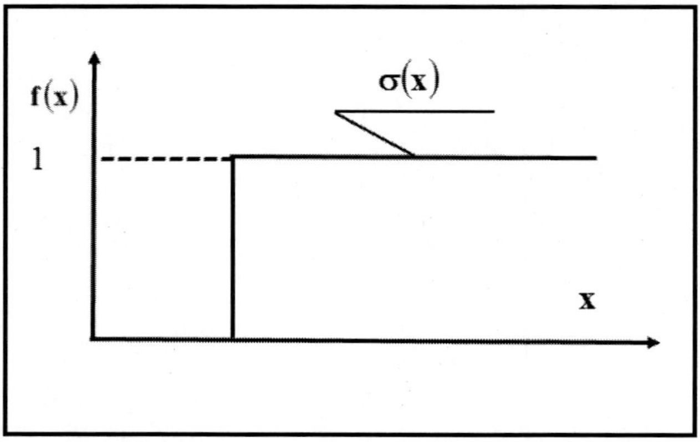

Figure 48. Flow between two rivers in case of partial loading.

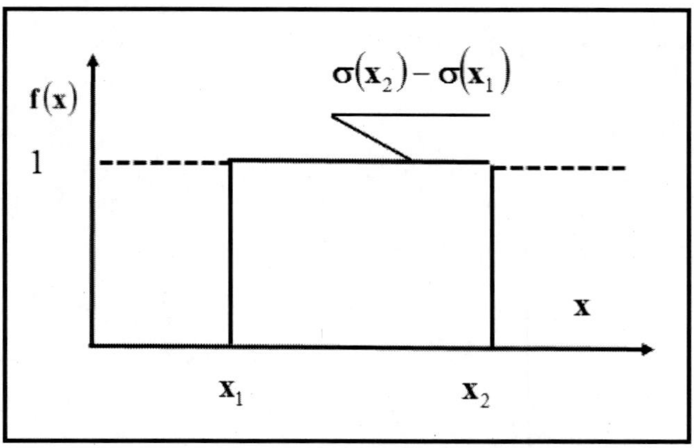

Figure 49. Unit step function graph.

So, this time, analogous to the preceding case, we will have:

$$\frac{dq}{dx} = R_{\cdot 0}\left|\sigma(x - x_2) - \sigma(x - x_1)\right| \tag{113}$$

or

$$-\frac{K}{2}\frac{d^2h^2}{dx^2} = R_0\left|\sigma(x - x_2) - \sigma(x - x_1)\right| \tag{114}$$

where R_0 is the spilled discharge from the oil pipeline per unit area.

By integrating equation (114), we will obtain:

$$\frac{dh^2}{dx} = -\frac{2R_0}{K}\int\left|\sigma(x - x_2) - \sigma(x - x_1)\right|dx + a =$$
$$= -\frac{2R_0}{K}\left[\sigma(x - x_2) - \sigma(x - x_1)\right] + a \tag{115}$$

After the second integration, we will obtain:

$$h^2 = -\frac{R_0}{K}\left[\sigma(x - x_2) - \sigma(x - x_1)\right]x^2 + ax + b \tag{116}$$

Let us find integration constants following the boundary conditions. The first boundary condition $(x = 0;\ h = h_L)$ will yield:

$$b = h_L{}^2. \tag{117}$$

while the second will yield: $(x = L; h = h_R)$:

$$h_R{}^2 = -\frac{R_0}{K}\left[\sigma(x - x_2) - \sigma(x - x_1)\right]L^2 + aL + h_L{}^2 \tag{118}$$

Considering (117):

$$h_R^{\ 2} = -\frac{R_0}{K}\left[\sigma(x-x_2)-\sigma(x-x_1)\right]L^2 + aL + h_L^{\ 2} \tag{119}$$

By introducing (117) and (115) into (116), we will obtain:

$$h^2 = -\frac{R_0}{K}\left[\sigma(x-x_2)-\sigma(x-x_1)\right]x^2 +$$

$$+\left\{\frac{h_R^{\ 2}-h_L^{\ 2}}{L}+\frac{R_0 L}{K}\left[\sigma(x-x_2)-\sigma(x-x_1)\right]\right\}x + h_L^{\ 2}$$

$$= h_L^{\ 2} + \frac{x}{L}\left(h_L^{\ 2}-h_R^{\ 2}\right) + \frac{R_0 x}{K}(L-x)\left[\sigma(x-x_2)-\sigma(x-x_1)\right] \tag{120}$$

Following the differentiation of equation (120), we will have:

$$2h\frac{dh}{dx} = \frac{h_l^{\ 2}-h_R^{\ 2}}{L} + \frac{R_0 L}{K}\left[\sigma(x-x_2)-\sigma(x-x_1)\right] -$$

$$-\frac{2R_0 x}{K}\left[\sigma(x-x_2)-\sigma(x-x_1)\right] \tag{121}$$

or

$$-\frac{2q}{K} = \frac{h_L^{\ 2}-h_R^{\ 2}}{L} + \frac{R_0(L-2x)}{K}\left[\sigma(x-x_2)-\sigma(x-x_1)\right] \tag{122}$$

0.00000372 m/s (2% of total discharge, damaged length: 2 km); 6. $R = 0$.

Finally, for specific discharge:

$$q = \frac{R_0}{K}\left[\sigma(x-x_2)-\sigma(x-x_1)\right] +$$

$$+\left\{\frac{h_R^{\ 2}-h_L^{\ 2}}{L}+\frac{R_0L}{K}\left[\sigma(x-x_2)-\sigma(x-x_1)\right]\right\} \qquad (123)$$

If $x_1 = 0;\ x_2 = L,$ (122) describes the previous scenario (i.e., when whole pipeline section from one river to another is damaged).

If $x_1 = x_2 = 0,$ (123) describes the scenario with no damage and with only natural filtration.

Figure 50 shows depression curves in the case similar to the previous one. The length of the damaged section varies from 2 to 6 km.

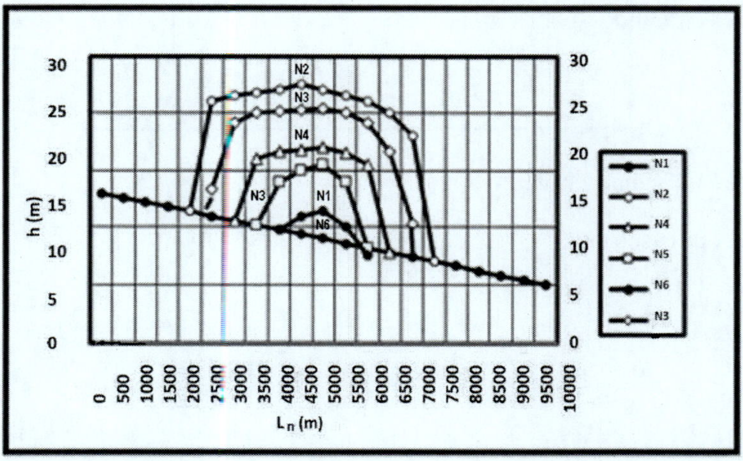

Figure 50. Flow between two rivers in case of partial loading.
№1. R = 0.0000186 m/sec (10% of total discharge, length of damage: 6 km);
№2. R = 0.00001488 m/s (8% of total discharge, length of damage: 5 km);
№3. R = 0.00001116 m/s (6% of total discharge, length of damage: 4 km);
№4. R = 0.00000744 m/s (4% of total discharge, length of damage: 3 km).

Flow between Two Rivers in Case of Parabolic Loading

Consider an accidental break-up of an oil pipeline, which corresponds to parabolic loading, as shown in Figure 51.

It is obvious that function $R(x)$ can be approximated to $R(x) = ax^2 + bx + c.$ by a, b parabola, and three typical points A, B and C with the following coordinates can be used to find coefficient c :

$$\begin{cases} x_1 = 0; R(x_1) = R_2; \\ x_2 = L/2; R(x_2) = R_1; \\ x_3 = L; R(x_3) = R_2 \end{cases} \tag{124}$$

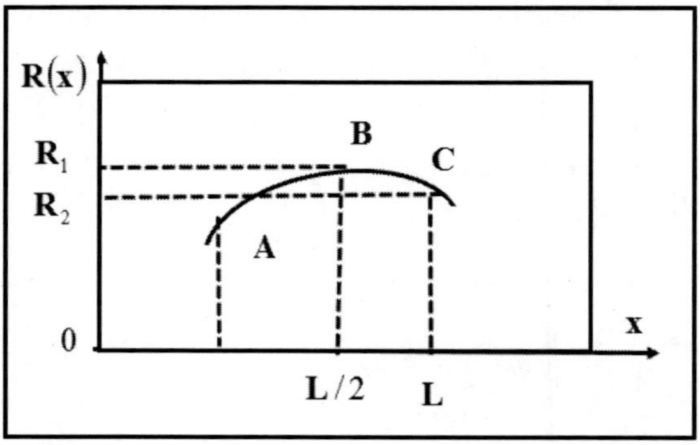

Figure 51. Parabolic loading.

In our case:

$$\begin{cases} R_2 = c; \\ R_1 = a\frac{L^2}{4} + \frac{bL}{2} + c; \\ R_2 = aL^2 + bL + c \end{cases} \tag{125}$$

As $c = R_2$, so:

$$\begin{cases} R_1 = \frac{aL^2}{4} + \frac{bL}{2} + R_2; \\ R_2 = aL^2 + bL + R_2 \end{cases} \tag{126}$$

The solution of system (125) will yield:

$$\begin{cases} a = -\dfrac{4(R_1 - R_2)}{L^2}; \\ b = \dfrac{4(R_1 - R_2)}{L} \end{cases} \tag{127}$$

So:

$$R(x) = -\frac{4}{L^2}(R_1 - R_2)x^2 + \frac{4}{L}(R_1 - R_2)x + R_2 \tag{128}$$

Now, let us solve the main problem. In our case, the above-given equation will be as follows:

$$-\frac{K}{2}\frac{d^2h^2}{dx^2} = -\frac{4}{L^2}(R_1 - R_2)x^2 + \frac{4}{L}(R_1 - R_2)x + R_2 \tag{129}$$

Or:

$$\frac{d^2h^2}{dx^2} = \frac{8}{KL^2}(R_1 - R_2)x^2 - \frac{8}{KL}(R_1 - R_2)x - \frac{2}{K}R_2 \tag{130}$$

The first and second integrations will yield:

$$h^2 = \frac{4}{3KL^2}(R_1 - R_2)x^4 - \frac{4}{3KL}(R_1 - R_2)x^3 - \frac{R_2}{K}x^2 + Ax + B \tag{131}$$

Using the first boundary condition $(x = 0; h = h_L)$, $B = h_L{}^2$ Thus, the equation will be as follows:

$$h^2 = \frac{4}{3KL^2}(R_1 - R_2)x^4 - \frac{4}{3KL}(R_1 - R_2)x^3 - \frac{R_2}{K}x^2 + Ax + h_L{}^2 \tag{132}$$

Using the second boundary condition: $x = L; h = h_R$:

$$h_R{}^2 = \frac{4}{3KL^2}(R_1 - R_2)L^4 - \frac{4}{3KL}(R_1 - R_2)L^3 - \frac{R_2}{K}L^2 + h_L{}^2 + AL \quad (133)$$

Wherefrom:

$$A = \frac{R_2}{K}L + \frac{h_R{}^2 - h_L{}^2}{L}. \quad (134)$$

Thus, finally:

$$h^2 = \frac{4}{3KL^2}(R_1 - R_2)x^4 - \frac{4}{3KL}(R_1 - R_2)x^3 -$$

$$-\frac{R_2}{K}x^2 + \left(\frac{R_2}{K}L + \frac{h_R{}^2 - h_L{}^2}{L}\right)x + h_L{}^2 \quad (135)$$

As an example, let us consider the following case: $h_L = 18$ m; $h_R = 10m$;

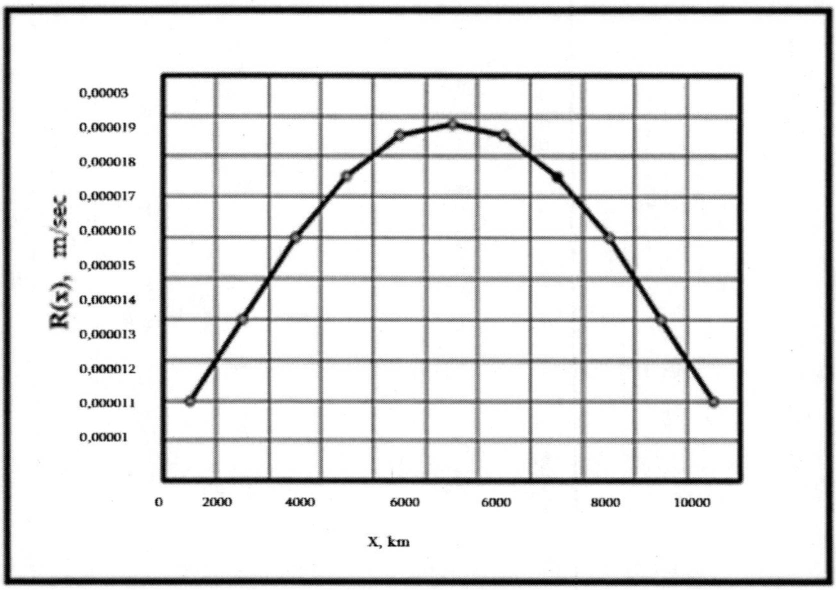

Figure 52. Real parabolic loading graph.

$R_1 = 0{,}00000372 m/s$; $R_2 = 0{,}00001116 m/s$; $K = 10\ m/s$ (R_1 and R_2 are selected to correspond to 2% and 6% of total discharge of Baku-Supsa Pipeline). The graph of parabolic loading, corresponding to R_1 and R_2 is given in Figure 52. For calculation purposes, it is better to write equation (135) as follows:

$$h^2 = \frac{4(R_1 - R_2)}{3K}\left(\frac{x}{L}\right)^2 x^2 - \frac{4(R_1 - R_2)}{3K}\left(\frac{x}{L}\right)x^2 +$$

$$+\frac{R_2 L^2}{K}\left(1-\frac{x}{L}\right)\frac{x}{L} + \left(h_R^{\ 2} - h_L^{\ 2}\right)\left(\frac{x}{L}\right) + h_L^{\ 2} \qquad (136)$$

Calculation results are given as a graph in Figure 53. The upper curve is constructed using equation (136), and the lower curve, describing the case of $R_1 = R_2 = 0$, i.e., the case with no accidental break-up, is given as an example.

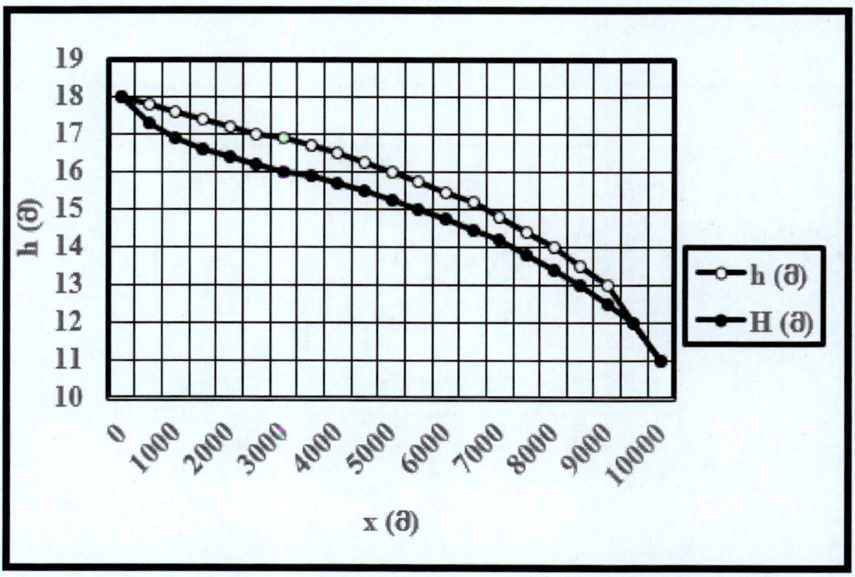

Figure 53. Flow between two rivers for real parabolic loading.
h (m): according to equation (135); HH (m): $R_1 = R_2 = 0$.

Flow between Two Rivers When Loading Changes over Time

Consider the case when following an accidental rupture of an oil pipeline, the damaged section is covered by sluices, and the volume of spilled oil decreases per unit time. As practice shows, the volume of spilled oil changes in time according to the exponential law:

$$R = R_0 e^{-Kt} \tag{137}$$

where, R_0 is the amount of oil spilled at the initial moment of the accident.

As in this case, R is the time function only, practically nothing will change in the judgment above, and the depression curve equation will be as follows:

$$\left[\begin{aligned} h^2 &= h_L^{\,2} - \frac{x}{L}\left(h_L^{\,2} - h_R^{\,2}\right) + \frac{R(t)x}{K}(L-x); \\ h^2 &= h_L^{\,2} - \frac{x}{L}\left(h_L^{\,2} - h_R^{\,2}\right) + \frac{R_0 e^{-Kt}x}{K}(L-x) \end{aligned}\right] \tag{138}$$

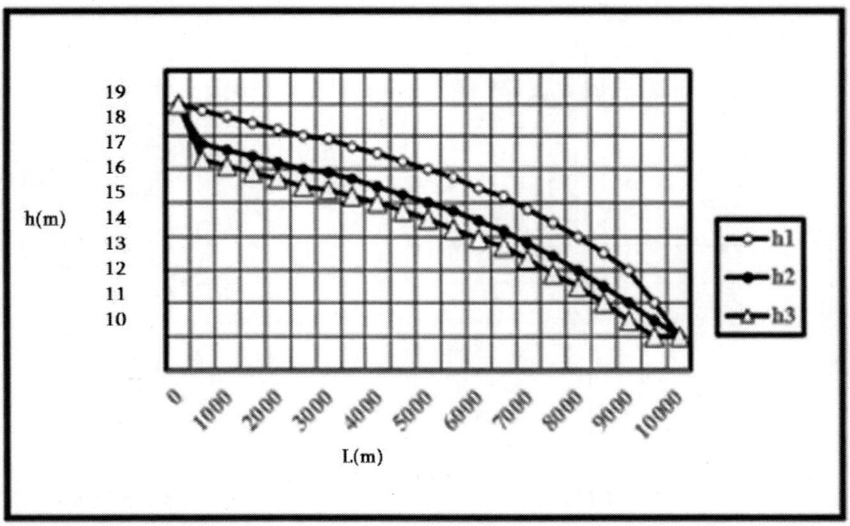

Figure 54. Diagrams of change of depression curves over time in case of covering the damaged section of the oil mains with sluices.
1 – Initial loading ($\mathbf{R}_0 = 0,0000186$ m/s); 2 – Loading after 1 hour; 3 – Zero loading

As an example, Figure 54 shows the diagrams of a depression curve change over time, describing the previous case. The discharge spilled during the accidental rupture of Baku-Supsa Pipeline is taken as an initial value, which is 10% of the total discharge. The law of change of R is: $R(t)=0{,}000018e^{-t/0{,}3364}$ (the diagram of this function is given in Figure 55).

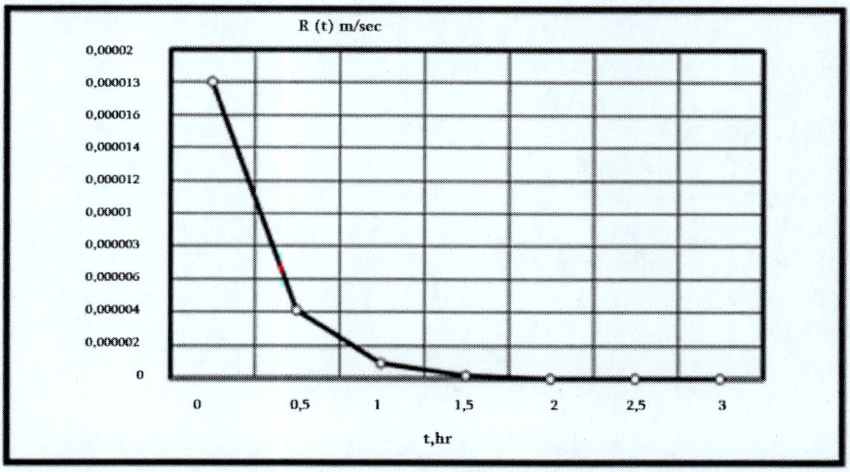

Figure 55. Diagram of loading $\mathbf{R(t)}=0{,}000018\mathbf{e}^{-t/0{,}3364}$ change over time.

Chapter 4

Efficiency of Measures to Protect Water Resources

4.1. Indices of Economic Efficiency of Hydroresources Protective Measures

During the construction of hydraulic structures, including high dams, special importance is attached to the efficiency of measures for the protection of hydraulic resources and indicators of their economic efficiency. Virtually, the reliability of such measures is correlated to the amount of capital investments made.

There are currently a large number of parameters to assess the efficiency of investment project measures. The absolute and relative efficiency criteria can be used to assess the effectiveness of environmental protection measures. The formula below calculates the absolute efficiency of capital investments in environmental protection measures:

$$E_p = \left[\sum_{j=1}^{n} \sum_{i=1}^{m} \left(Э_{ij} - C \right) \right] / K \tag{139}$$

where E_p is the indicator of total efficiency of capital investments in environmental protection measures; $Э_{ij}$ is the effect of environmental measures of the *i*-th type obtained by preventing losses at the *j*-th facility; C is the annual operating expenses for maintenance of fixed assets that caused the effect; K is the capital investments in the protection measures of water resources.

To assess the feasibility of implementing measures, it is proposed to compare E_p with the normative coefficient of efficiency E_H = 0.12. A measure is considered cost-effective provided $E_p \geq E_H$. Thus, the calculation is based on the normative investment payback period $T_H = 1/E_H$. At the same time it is offered to use the index of efficiency in the natural-value form which is named by the index of absolute ecological efficiency of capital investments that is not really accurate.

This indicator is proposed to calculate by the formula:

$$Э = \Delta B / K \tag{140}$$

where ΔB is the reduction of harmful substances in the atmosphere, soil and water.

$$\Delta B = \sum_j K_j \left(B_{0j} - B_{1j} \right) \tag{141}$$

where $B_{0j} (B_{1j})$ is the initial (resulting) emission volume of *j*-th ingredient; and *K* is the harmfulness factor of *i*-th ingredient.

The considered indicators do not reflect the dynamics of implementation of measures, do not give an idea about the prevented losses in the national economy, and do not show the value of the effect of the water resources protective measures. The program of measures is considered simply as the sum of measures without taking into account the sequence of their investment. The popular criterion of minimum present value does not eliminate these shortcomings either.

$$C + E_H K \rightarrow \min \tag{142}$$

To compare options for activities carried out in different terms, it is proposed to use the method of discounting, based on which one can calculate the relative economic effect criterion:

$$\sum_{t=1}^{T} \left(K_{П} + K_{Дt} + C_t \right) \left(1 + E_{НП} \right)^{-t} \rightarrow \min \tag{143}$$

where $K_{П}$ is the initial capital investments in environmental protection measures; $K_{Дt}$ is the additional capital investments necessary for normal operation of environmental facility in year t of operation; C_t is the current costs of year t for operation and maintenance of fixed assets.

Comparison of the annual present value of the cost of environmental measures Z with the achieved economic result P allows to determine the annual economic effect:

$$(P - Z) \rightarrow \max \tag{144}$$

The typical methodology developed in 1987 corresponds to the approach recommended in methods for evaluating the effectiveness of investment projects. In the vast majority of publications this criterion is called net discounted revenue (NDR), net discounted value (NDV) or net present value (NPV). In general, the formula used to calculate it is as follows:

$$NPR = \sum_{t=t_0}^{T} \left(P_t - K_t - C_t\right)\left(1 + r\right)^{t_0 - t} \rightarrow \max \tag{145}$$

where P_t is the economic effect received in year t; K_t is the investments in the protective measures of water resources in year t; C_t is the operational costs of the water resources protective facility in year t without deductions for renovation; T is the year of the end of operation; t_0 is the year of beginning of construction of the hydroresources protective facility; and r is the discount factor.

It is proposed to use the normative coefficient of reduction $E_{НП}$ as a discount factor, the value of which is taken in accordance with the sectoral methods for determining the economic efficiency of environmental protection costs (this value is temporarily proposed to take $E_{НП} = 0.08$).

It is often proposed to use a bank interest rate as a discount factor. Both state-funded and non-state projects employ these techniques.

Literary sources more often give the evaluation of the return on investment for non-governmental (commercial) projects. There are some peculiarities in how government-funded project effectiveness is evaluated:

1. A single discount factor is set for the project. Usually it is determined by the minimum internal rate of return, calculated for private sector investments with minimal risk. In most Western European countries, such a discount rate is 8-12%;
2. Not only economic, but also social effect is taken into account.

If denoting the measure by $i = 1, n$, the first year of its implementation by T_i^H and the year of its completion by T_i^K, we will obtain an option of calculation of NPR of the plan of hydroresources protective measures:

$$NPR = \sum_{t=t_0}^{T} \sum_{i \in G_t} \left(\sum_{j} Э_{ijt} - C_{it} \right) - \sum_{i \in J_t} K_{it} (1+r)^{t_0 - t} \to \max \tag{146}$$

where $Э_{ijt}$ is the result of implementation of the *i*-th hydroresources protective measure, expressed by the amount of prevented damage in the *j*-th economic or social field in year *t*; C_{it} is the operational measures, not related to the *i*-th measures in year t, without deductions for renovation; K_{it} is the investments of the *i*-th measures implemented in year t; and G_t is the set of measures implemented before year t and bringing the result (damage reduction):

$$\begin{aligned} G_t &= \{ i : T_i^k < t \} \\ J_t &= \{ i : T_t^k \leq t \leq T_i^H \} \end{aligned} \tag{147}$$

where J_t is the number of measures to be implemented in year t.

Besides NPR, there is one more indicator calculated by the same elements. This is revenue index (S_1):

$$S_1 = \sum_{t=t_0}^{T} \left[\sum_{i \in G_t} (P_{it} - З_{it})(1+r)^{t_0 - t} \right] \Bigg/ \left[\left(\sum_{i \in J_t} K_{it} \right) (1+r)^{t_0 - t} \right] \to \max \tag{148}$$

This indicator is the ratio of the discounted outcome and the discounted capital expenses and is similar to the profitability index, but takes time factor into account. If $S_1 < 1$, the plan does not pay off in time *T*, and if $S_1 > 1$, the plan pays off within the planned time.

Based on this indicator, a similar criterion called performance index (S_2) can be construed.

$$S_2 = \sum_{i=t_0}^{T} \left[\sum_{i \in G_t} W_i (1+r)^{t_0 - t} \right] \Bigg/ \left[\left(\sum_{i \in J_t} K_{it} \right) (1+r)^{t_0 - t} \right] \quad (149)$$

This criterion cannot serve as an indicator of the effectiveness of an environmental plan (if NPV > 0 and $S_1 > 1$, the plan is efficient, and if NPV < 0 and $S_1 < 1$, the plan is in inefficient). Rather, the following methods are more commonly used to assess the efficiency of environmental solutions: present value method, net profit method, profitability method, and payback period method.

The techniques to assess the efficiency of environmental investments without taking into account the time factor are simple enough, and therefore are widely used in practice to compare and choose the most appropriate option among alternative investment projects. However, these methods do not take into account the time factor, and therefore, have a number of drawbacks:

- They do not consider the changes in costs and benefits over time;
- They assume the availability of reliable information;
- Since these methods are designed to evaluate investments in a specific project, the calculations should highlight the part of the benefit that is due to this particular investment what significantly complicates the calculations.

The essence of the method to assess the return on investments in terms of profitability is to determine the profitability of the project and compare it with the target profitability, the amount of which is chosen by the investor.

It is also possible to compare several project alternatives, where the most effective alternative will have the highest profitability. Profitability can be calculated by the formula:

$$Profitability = \frac{Average\ profit}{Average\ used\ capital} \quad (150)$$

The method to assess the effectiveness of investments depending on the payback period, also called the method of return, or the method of pay-off, or payback of investment, describes the period of time during which the investment capital is returned (paid back) due to the profit from the sale of products. In this case, the payback period corresponds to the period when the amount of profit becomes equal to the amount of investment:

$$Time\ period = \frac{Invested\ capital}{Average\ profit},\ year \tag{151}$$

In foreign practice, there is no normative value of the payback period: any approach sooner or later will pay back the investment. The question to decide is whether the investor is satisfied with the estimated payback period or not. A project option is considered appropriate if the payback period is less than or equal to a predetermined term, which can be determined on the basis of experience or other considerations. The disadvantage of this method is that it does not take into account the dynamics of events that occur after the project has paid for itself, i.e., the method does not cover the entire period of operation of the project and, therefore, it is not affected by all the returns that lie beyond the payback period. In addition, the method is focused not on measuring the profitability of the project, but on determining its liquidity.

The basis for calculating the efficiency of investments, taking into account the time factor, is the flow of payments, which is the total of the income and expenditure parts of the balance.

4.2. Improving the Economic Efficiency of Water Resources Protection Plans

As the territorial environmental plan is developed, a set of measures allowing achieving the goal of stabilizing or improving the environmental conditions in the considered cities, regions or provinces, is designed. Analysis of the current practice of national and regional water resources management plans evidences that measures are selected without a special methodology, for individual industries and inter-sectoral complexes (for individual enterprises from different industries, including communications, healthcare, social welfare, etc.). At the same time, the fact that the goal of an environmental plan is broken down into subgoals, such as the reduction of pollution of some environmental elements, e.g., air, water, soil, etc.), is often ignored. As a result, the set of measures fails to satisfy the entire set of sub-goals, and, accordingly, their implementation does not give the opportunity to achieve the goal. Another drawback is that the measures are developed without considering the size of necessary investments, or the outcomes of those measures.

The functional-cost analysis (FCA), which includes the determination of target requirements and the development of solutions, is the most perfect, comprehensive approach to solving the problems under consideration. The FCA method has received worldwide recognition; in our country it has been developing since the 1940s as an economic analysis of design and technical solutions. In the 1960s, the field of application of FSA to reduce costs expanded to a fairly large number of machine-building and instrument-making enterprises. In the 1970s and 1980s, laboratories and centers for the application of FCA were created, and new methods of carrying out and using FCA and the use of computers in its implementation were developed.

FCA allows for essential reduction of costs for the establishment or operation of a facility. Using one of the many methods of FCA for a systemic study of expenses of the outcomes of such specific and complex object as the territorial environmental plan is, is impossible, as the application of FCA at some or other facility needs special methods, though the methodological essence of FCA does not change: it involves dividing an enterprise into components, identifying their functions, assessing the values of functions and components, and comparing them to the costs, what allows judging the appropriateness of expenses against the expected outcomes.

There are four stages in the implementation of the FCA: *informational, analytical, creative, and research.* The information stage usually includes the collection, preparation and systematization of data about the object.

An environmental protection plan may be viewed as a complex system, which must be the object of analysis and design. It would be more expedient to try and apply FCA methods to the development of environmental protection measures.

The measures are better to form based on the alternatives of the environmental projects (Figure 56). This shall occur at the research stage of FCA.

In Figure 56, the final objectives are correlated with the measures that ensure their accomplishment. For example, objective O.1.1 needs two measures, while objective O.1.2 needs only one measure. At the same time, one measure of Objective O.1.1 has three alternative options: $M^{1}_{1,1,1}$, $M^{2}_{1,1,1}$, $M^{3}_{1,1,1}$, and the other by two: $M^{1}_{1,1,2}$ and $M^{2}_{1,1,2}$, $M^{3}_{1,1,2}$. There are no alternatives of measures for Objectives O.2.1 and O.2.2.

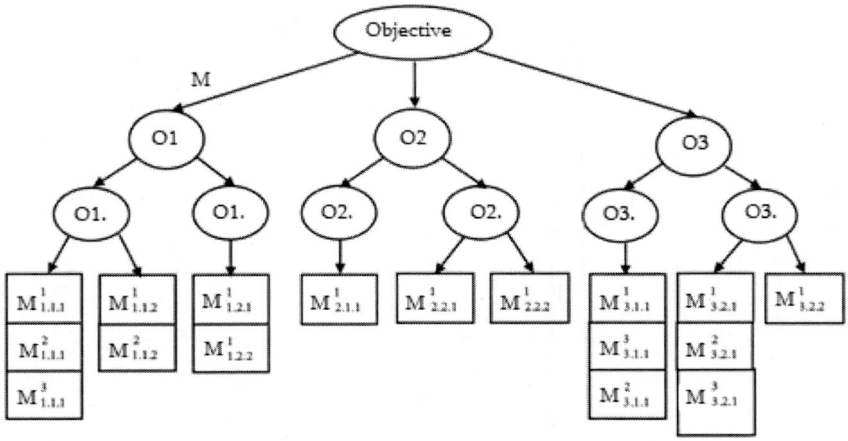

Figure 56. Tree of objectives (goal tree) with alternatives of measures.

The solutions from alternatives in FCA and ideologically similar approaches are chosen as follows: either a solution is selected from the set of alternatives by one or more criteria, or an economic-mathematical model is used to form the best set of solutions by selecting from alternatives. Both approaches are legitimate, but the second one is more logical because it takes into account the entire set of complementary solutions when solving the optimization problem.

When selecting protective measures for hydroresources, it is necessary to adjust the above approaches. So, in the first case, it is advisable to be based on the maximum information about the measure: the value of significance of the measure ($\bar{\omega}_i$); the value of the prospects of the measure (ρ_i); and the cost of realization of the measure (K_i).

Selection of the best measure among alternatives should be carried out by the maximum integral evaluation of the measure:

$$\eta_i = \lambda_1\bar{\omega}_i + \lambda_2\rho_i + \lambda_3 K_i \qquad (152)$$

where λ_1, λ_2, λ_3 are the weighting coefficients of relevant indicators obtained through expertise ($\lambda_1 + \lambda_2 + \lambda_3 = 1$).

When selecting the protective measure for water resources based on optimization approach for every final objective, which has alternative measures, it is possible to generate the following economic-mathematical model:

$$\sum_{i=1}^{n_j} K_i X_i \to \min$$
$$\sum_{i=1}^{n_j} \omega_i X_i \geq 1$$
$$\sum_{i \in J_{ij}} X_i = 1, I = 1, L_j \qquad (153)$$
$$X_i = \begin{Bmatrix} 0 \\ 1, i=1, n_j \end{Bmatrix}$$

where n_j is the number of measures providing the *j*-th final objective, including alternatives; L_j is the number of options of alternative measures for the *j*-th objective; J_{ij} is the set of alternative measures in option *i* for the *j*-th objective.

By solving this problem, a choice of measures is made ensuring the minimum cost of full satisfaction of the *j*-th objective. If the set of measures does not ensure the full satisfaction of the corresponding objective, then this problem will have no solutions. For a solution to be found, it is necessary to relax the first constraint:

$$\sum_{i=1}^{n} \varpi_i X_i \geq \varepsilon_j \qquad (154)$$

where ε_j is the sufficient value to satisfy the *j*-th objective ($\varepsilon_j > 0$).

The set of measures formed in this way may need an excessively large amount of investment. In this case, it is necessary to allocate the most important measures from the set. The boundary of allocation is determined either by the value of the presented financial resources, or the degree of achieving the goal (or its individual subgoals).

Let us consider the option of selecting measures in the plan from their broader range in such a way that the cost of their implementation is minimal. This problem is commonly discussed in special literature, and its solution consists directly in minimization of the costs of implementation of measures. In other words, it is proposed to solve the problem:

$$\sum_{i=1}^{m} Z_i U_i \to \min$$
$$\sum_{i=1}^{m} e_{ij} U_i \ge E_j, j = \overline{1,n} \qquad (155)$$
$$X_i = \begin{Bmatrix} 0 \\ 1, i = \overline{1,m} \end{Bmatrix}$$

where i in the number of alternative measures ($i = \overline{1,m}$); Z_i is the cost of implementing the i-th measure; U_i is the sought Boolean variable with the following meaning: if U_i = 1, the i-th measure is included in the plan, and if U_i = 0, the i-th measure is rejected. ε_{ij} is the improvement of the j-th indicator due to the implementation of the i-th measure; E_j is the value of improvement of the jth indicator, which is to be achieved.

Sometimes, when selecting measures, a reciprocal model is proposed to use:

$$\sum_{i=1}^{m} e_{ij} U_i \to \max$$
$$\sum_{i=1}^{m} Z_j U_i \le \Phi \qquad (156)$$
$$X_i = \begin{Bmatrix} 0 \\ 1, i = \overline{1,m} \end{Bmatrix}$$

where Φ is the volume of investments allocated for implementation of the environmental plan.

Use of such models is justified, for example, for a choice of a variant of technological process or a complex of measures of struggle against atmospheric pollution at the industrial enterprise. To solve this problem, it is necessary to use the hierarchical representation of the criteria in the form of a tree, the end tops of which are specific indicators. In this case:

$$x_i = \sum_{i \in J_j} a_{ij} X_j \tag{157}$$

where J_j is the set of the i-th criteria, which form criterion j; a_{ij} is the constant of the impact of the j-th criterion on criterion i; x_i (X_j) is the value of the i-th (j-th) criterion.

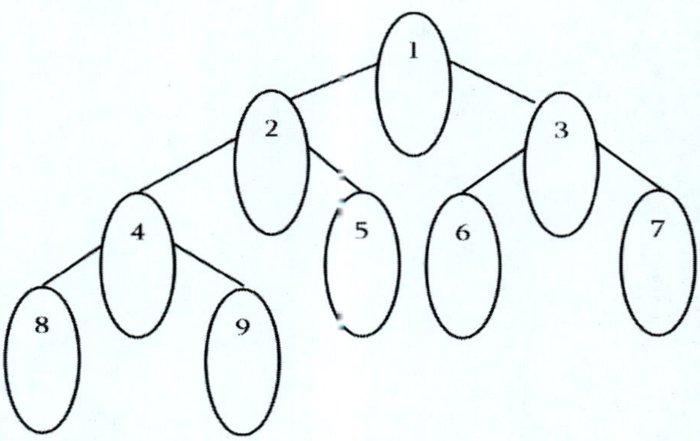

$$x_1 = a_{12}x_2 + a_{13}x_3$$
$$x_2 = a_{24}x_4 + a_{25}x_5$$
$$x_3 = a_{36}x_6 + a_{37}x_7$$
$$x_4 = a_{48}x_8 + a_{49}x_9$$

Figure 57. Sample criterion-indicator tree.

We can write the set of relations given in Figure 57 for the tree of criteria in the same figure. In order to improve common criterion of condition of a social-ecological-economic system by one, there is a wide range of options to improve x_1 and x_2 available, and the number of options increases when moving from the upper to the lower level. The indicators on the treetops can be changed by the set of alternative measures, $l = \overline{1,m}$. We may like to improve the criteria not generally, but some of them at a $i \in J^{k^*}$ k^* level.

To find the optimistic set of measures giving the value of x_i^* ($i \in J^{k^*}$) criteria, the following problem must be solved:

$$\sum_{i=1}^{m} Z_i U_i \to \min;$$
$$x_j = x_j^0 + \sum_{i=1}^{m} d_{ij} U_i, i \in J^k; \quad (158)$$
$$x_i = \sum_{j \in k+1} a_{ij} x_j, i \in J^k, k = k^*, k-1$$

where x_j^0 is the base value of indicator j; J^k is a set of indicators (hanging treetops) at the final level k.

To solve the inverse problem, i.e., to find the best in a certain sense option to change the system criteria at the expense of the allocated investments, it is necessary to modify the model:

$$\min_{i \in J^k} \left\{ \alpha_j \left(x_j - x_j^0 \right) / x_j^0 \right\} \to \max;$$
$$x_j = \sum_{j \in J^{k+1}} a_{ij} x_j, i \in J^k, k = k^*, k-1; \quad (159)$$
$$\sum_{i=1}^{m} Z_i U_i \le \Phi$$

where α_j is the value (priority) of the j-th criterion: $\sum_{i \in J^{k^*}} \alpha_j = 1$; Φ is the volume of investments allocated for the project implementation.

The proposed model maximizes the value of relative improvement of criteria $\left(x_j - x_j^0 \right) / x_j^0$ becomes maximal. Since in a general case, the number of improved criteria is more than one, it is necessary to solve the multi-criterial problem of simultaneous improvement of all $i \in J^{k^*}$ criteria. For this purpose, it is reasonable to use a maximizing criterion, which implements the Chebyshev principle of equal concession:

$$\min_{i \in J^k} \left\{ a_j \left(x_j - x_j^0 \right) / x_j^0 \right\} \to \max \quad (160)$$

Since criteria $i \in J^{k^*}$ can have different significance, it is necessary to take into account the importance (priority) of criteria with the help of coefficient α_j. The importance of criteria is established by expert method. When defining the importance of criteria, the contribution of each criterion to the overall criterion must be taken into account. For this purpose, the PERT tool must be used. For the individual branches of the criteria tree, the values of individual criteria must be assessed.

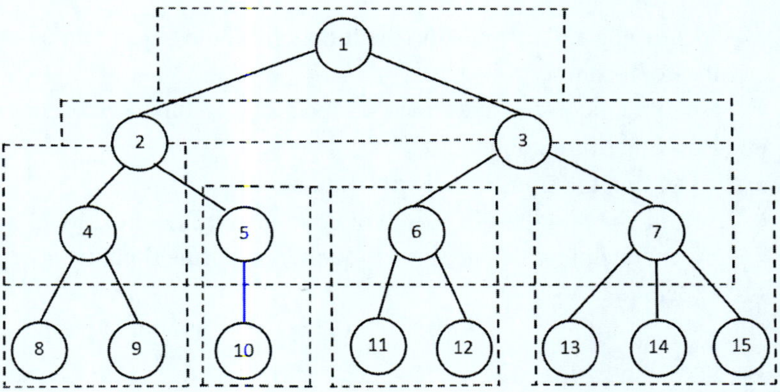

Figure 58. Sample criteria tree.

So, for the criterion tree in Figure 58, the following branches are marked with a dotted line:

For each branch, an expert evaluation is necessary to establish the importance of the hanging criteria of the branches in achieving the criterion – the top of the branches v_j, $j \in J^k$, It is assumed that values v_j are normalized within a branch, i.e.: $\sum_{j \in R} v_j = 1$.

Based on the calculations, it is not difficult to determine the importance of the criteria of level k^*, which are included in the target function of the multicriteria problem formulated above:

$$\alpha_i = \prod_{j \in L_i} v_j, i \in J^k \tag{161}$$

where L_j is the set of criteria on the path from criterion i to the general criterion.

The direct and inverse problems of forming a set of measures of the territorial environmental program presented above belong to the class of discrete mathematical programming problems with Boolean variables. A random search method can be used to solve this kind of problems.

For such specific object of the analysis, as measures of nature protection program, the following most important works require a special toolkit:

- Identifying and formulating the functions of the object as a whole and the composition of its parts;
- Isolating the expensive zones, and identifying functional reserves;
- Building of functional model;
- Assessing the significance of the function;
- Setting the problems of search of options to realize functional models by maintaining the necessary quality and functionally acceptable expenses.

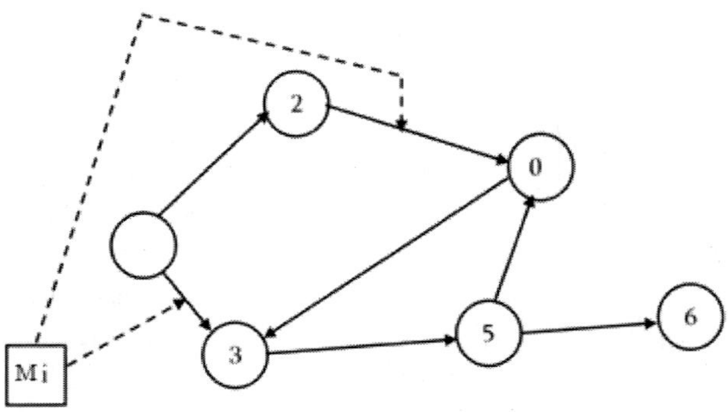

Figure 59. An example of impact of measure M on several directed lines.

The FCA methodology has the main, auxiliary and unnecessary functions. With regard to the analysis of the measures of environmental management plans, the functions of the measures can be determined by analyzing the socio-eco-economic model of the region's functioning. It was demonstrated above that the systematic study of the region's functioning can be effectively performed by modeling with orgraphs. To identify the functions of measures, it is necessary to link them to the directed lines of the orgraph. Then, the functions will be formulated in accordance with the action of these lines. Note that one measure can be linked to several others (Figure 59).

To assess the development of the socio-eco-economic system, it is necessary that the goals of one of the levels of the structural-target model should be present as vertices of the orgraph. As a result, it is possible to specify the impact of the primary pollutants on these vertices and ensure the comparability of structural-target and functional models.

The total effect of the influence of factor *j* on factor *l*, which is one of the objectives of the socio-eco-economic system, is calculated by the formula:

$$T_{(jl)} = \left\{ \left(\sum_{t=1}^{R} E^{t}_{(jl)} \prod_{s=1}^{S} (1 - L_s) \right) \Big/ \prod_{s=1}^{S} (1 - L_s) \right\}^{*} \tag{162}$$

where $E^{t}_{(jl)}$ is a separate open path effect from *j* to *l*; L_s is the inverse effect of loop *S*, providing relevant feedback; R is the number of open paths from *j* to *l*; S is the number of *S* loops, providing relevant feedback; $\{\ \}^{*}$ is the operator, which means that first the numerator and the denominator are multiplied, then the terms equal to the products of the relevant paths are subtracted, and only then the division is done.

If calculating the total effect of factor *j* on factor *l* before ($T^{0}_{(jl)}$) and after ($T^{I}_{(jl)}$) the measure is realized, the change in effect will be as follows:

$$\Delta T_{(il)} = T^{I}_{(jl)} - T^{0}_{(jl)} \tag{163}$$

To detail the effect variation, $T_{(il)}$ can be expressed as the function of directed line coefficients: $T_{(jl)} = f\left(a_m, m = 1, M\right)$. The change in effect caused by impact of the measures on directed line m is calculated by the formula:

$$b_m = \frac{dT_{(jl)}}{da_m} \tag{164}$$

where b_m is the magnitude of change of coefficient m. The sum of changes in the effects of the individual directed lines equals the change in the total effect:

$$\Delta T_{(jI)} = \sum_{m=1}^{M} b_m \frac{dT_{(ij)}}{da_m} \tag{165}$$

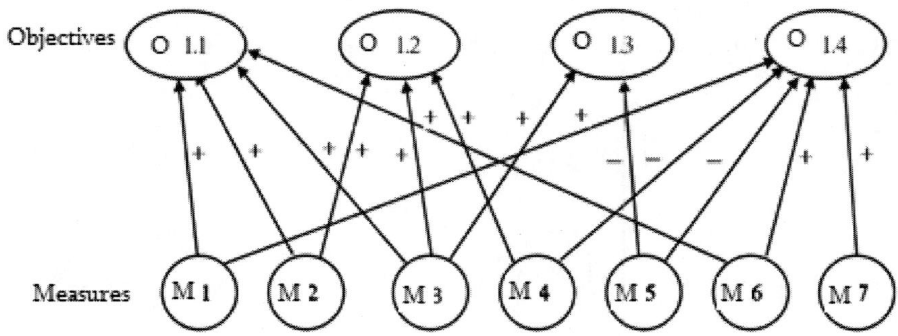

Figure 60. Functional model of realization of objectives on the basis of measures.

As a result, based on the analysis of the orgraph, we can build the following functional model (Figure 60).

The model has two levels: the level of objectives and the level of measures. Directed lines from *j* measure are drawn to the objective, if $\Delta T_{(jI)}$ = 0. In Figure 40, one part of the lines is denoted by „+" and another part is denoted by "-". This is because on the basis of $\Delta T_{(jI)}$, it is possible to identify a useful effect (improving the system indicators and contributing to the objective, or sign "+") and a harmful effect of the measure (worsening the system indicators and opposing the achievement of the objective, i.e., sign "-").

The functional model can be given as a table for a more in-depth presentation (see Table 13).

A structural-functional model provides a comprehensive assessment of each measure, a whole set of them, with their blocks focusing the structural objective. A structural model allows evaluating the completeness of achievement of the immediate structural objective. As for the functional model, it gives the "useful" and "harmful" effects of measures and their blocks. All evaluations are summarized in the evaluations of achieving the main objective of the plan.

Table 13. A functional model of impact of the set of measures on social- ecological-economic system

Impact of measure	Effect of measures on the objective			
	Objective 1.1	Objective 1.2	Objective 1.3	Objective 1.4
Measure 1	+0.3			
Useful	-0.1	+0.2	+0.8	–
Harmful	+0.6	–	-0.3	–
Total		+0.2	+0.5	–
Measure 2				
Useful	–	+0.3	+0.4	+0.6
Harmful	–	-0.1	-0.3	-0.1
Total	–	+0.2	+0.4	+0.5

The analytical stage of the systemic study of the measures of the plan involves the analysis of the costs of implementation of measures and their compliance with the obtained outcomes.

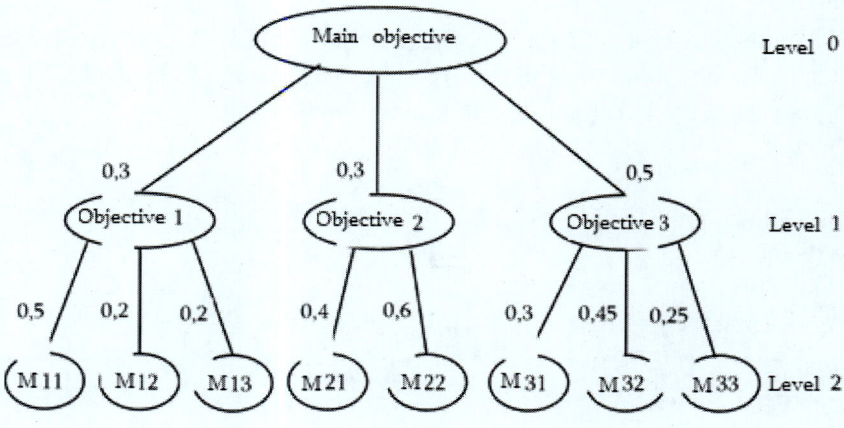

Figure 61. Sample tree of objectives.

The method to compare the costs of the functions with the numerical scores of the significance of the function is based on the fact that the condition normalizing the distribution of costs is the significance of the function. When applied to the system analysis of measures, this method should be modified and called the method of comparing the cost of the measures with the evaluation of the outcomes. The outcome of the measure can be evaluated based on the priority indicator of the measure. In this case, the word "function" disappears from the definition of the method, and since we consider a set of measures, the method can be called "complex-value analysis". For its implementation, one should use the structural-cost diagram and priority assessments on the objectives tree (Figure 61, Table 14).

Table 14. Quantitative parameters of objectives and measures

Objectives	Assessment, point	Expenses, mln. GEL, %	Cost-benefit ratio
Objective 1	0.3	23/36.5	1.22
M11	0.15	10/15.9	1.06
M12	0.6	5/8.3	1.38
M13	0.09	8/12.7	1.41
Objective 2	0.2	10/15.9	0.79
M21	0.08	4/6.0	0.75
M22	0.12	6/9.5	0.79
Objective 3	0.5	30/47.6	0.95
M31	0.15	8/12.7	0.85
M32	0.225	12/19.0	0.84
M33	0.125	10/15.9	0.27

A complex-cost analysis can be carried out with any level of detalization in the hierarchy of levels of the tree of objectives, starting from level 1. To do this, a cost-benefit diagram should be built (Figure 62).

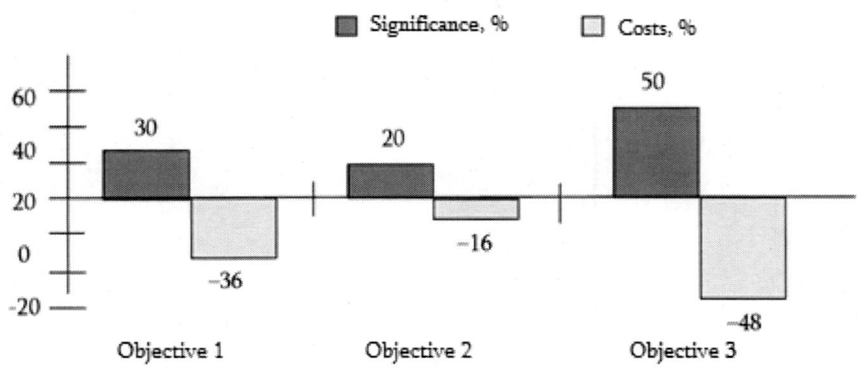

Figure 62. "Cost-benefit" diagram for level 1.

The cost-benefit ratio of less than one seems natural and no more exact specification of measures or costs seems necessary. If the ratio exceeds one, then it is worth trying to clarify the source information and to improve the set of measures.

Thus, a functional model for implementation of the analytical stage of FCA is built on the basis of the orgraph of the socio-ecological-economic system. The impact of the environmental measures is evaluated by calculating the full effect and breaking it down by individual directed lines. Among the various methods for analyzing the cost of implementation of activities and compliance with the results obtained, the method of comparing the cost of functions with numerical scores of the importance of functions was selected.

4.3. Development of Complex Environmental Management Programs

Territorial Approach to Solve Environmental Issues

Today, the need for a territorial orientation in environmental management is dictated by at least four considerations:

- Deep political changes caused by the collapse of the USSR into sovereign states, the formation of the CIS and the separation of a number of former Soviet republics.
- The increasing value of the social aspect in the development of the economy. A man is the main productive force, and he lives in a certain territory. To qualitatively meet his needs for food, housing, recreation, medical treatment and partly education, it is necessary to keep in view the entire territory as a whole.
- Increasing value of integrated development of territories instead of their frequently one-sided specialization. Different regions have different supplies of natural resources and different environmental conditions, socio-historical features of development, national and social structure and population density. All this necessitates a harmonious, integrated development of the territory.
- Effective solution to the problems of environmental management only with a territorial approach. The specific nature of environmental protection measures requires their territorial anchoring.

The experience accumulated in solving regional environmental problems allows identifying three main groups of development:

- Sectoral working programs of environmental protection measures by regions;

- Plans of measures to protect a particular natural resource or component of the natural environment;
- Territorial-complex environmental protection plans.

As an example of the first group of developments we can cite the Work Plan for the implementation of environmental protection measures at metallurgical plants in 25 areas of the former USSR. The Work Plan comprised measures aimed at dissipation of harmful substances through exhaust flues, trapping them through gas filters, creation of special services for operation of gas treatment plants and environmental protection at the enterprises in the industry, etc.

Obviously, such Work Plans can not solve the problem of environmental protection in the region as a whole, as they cover only certain measures, poorly linked in an interdisciplinary context.

The second group of developments is also characterized by a lack of comprehensiveness, since measures are considered from the perspective of only a single natural resource or component of the natural environment. For example, in order to protect soils from water and wind erosion, work was done to realize the general plans of anti-erosion measures on the territory of nine economic regions, covering 3/4 of the total area of agricultural lands.

The plans provided for the application of organizational and economic, agro-technical, forest-reclamation, and hydrotechnical measures, provided for the elimination, prevention or significant reduction of erosion processes and restoration of fertility of eroded lands.

The coordinator of this program was the Scientific Research Institute of Hydrotechnics and Land Reclamation of Georgia, presently the Ts. Mirtskhulava Water Management Institute of Georgia of Georgian Technical University.

In methodological terms, plans and drafts of district planning are more perfect. In their development, they are guided by the plans of development of individual sectors of national economy, plans of development and distribution of productive forces, other documents on the development of national economy, as well as planned and forecasted data on the development of the area under consideration. District planning projects are developed for individual parts of the territory of regions, providing territorial-production complexes or including groups of administrative districts with common economic ties and identical problems.

Plans and projects of regional planning are essentially intended for the territorial and economic organization of the projected area in accordance with the direction of its development, which is laid down in the General Plan of development and distribution of productive forces and in industry-specific plans.

Thus, regional planning is a tool for detailing decisions made primarily in the interests of the development of individual industries. However, it is obvious that such decisions, as a rule, are not consistent with the interests of the development of the projected area, especially in the field of environmental protection. Guided by purely economic criteria of production efficiency, sectoral ministries and departments determine such development options that lead to unacceptably high loads on the region's environment. For example, they prefer to locate energy-intensive productions (aluminum production, electric steelmaking, etc.) that are especially harmful to the environment and human health in densely populated areas with a developed industrial and social infrastructure characterized by relatively low costs of fuel production and power generation. Such cases are quite typical, because the schemes of development of national economy branches are built according to the production purposes and do not take into account the total environmental load on the environment of the projected area of location.

Finally, the third group of developments provides for the preparation of the environmental protection territorial complex plans (EPTCP) for regions, cities and major industrial hubs.

Pre-plan documents include the EPTCP, as well as the Comprehensive Program of the scientific-technical progress (STP); General plans of development and distribution of productive forces; General plans of settlement; plans and projects of STP; plans and projects of regional planning; general plans of cities and settlements, groups of enterprises, agro-industrial formations, etc. Since all these documents have special sections related to environmental protection and rational use of natural resources, the main objective of the EPTCP is given as the linkage, coordination and integration of the relevant sections of these documents.

The extreme difficulty and complexity of nature management problems, the great influence of the environment on indicators of the quality of life of the population require a fundamentally different – normative approach to the development of EPTCP, which should provide a link between environmental quality standards that determine the standard of living of the population, in a system of specific environmental protection measures. In this case, the territorial integrated nature protection scheme is a reasonable long-term concept of environmental management in the region, which is an alternative to the sectoral options of pre-planning justification.

Normative, or target, forecasts are based on the need to achieve a certain desired state of the natural environment while linking with other final goals of socio-economic development.

If extrapolation forecasts allow identifying the problems caused by the anticipated state of the natural environment, the normative forecasts act as a goal – the requirements. Therefore, a quality normative forecast allows focusing the entire planning and management system on the goals and needs of the socio-economic system, and not only on the available resources.

It is possible to identify at least two methodological approaches that allow solving such problems:

- Preliminary calculation of economic and some types of social damage related to the environmental pollution in a certain area. Comparing expenses on environmental protection measures with value of prevented damage, it is possible to receive data about the level of economic efficiency of expenses for environmental protection, which can be used during planning and design calculations at the stage of preparation and substantiation of decisions in environmental protection.
- Assertion that in case of justification of the environmental decisions, it is necessary to take into account the economic and social, as well as the environmental efficiency of the measures considered to the extent possible. Meanwhile, there is no single criterion for socio-environmental and economic efficiency caused not only by a number of undeveloped, and sometimes incomparable indicators that describe the economic, but mainly social and environmental effects of the environmental protection measures. For example, the moral, ethical, and psychological damage caused to humans by the destruction of natural landscapes cannot be a subject of economic evaluation at all, while similar effects of anthropogenic activities are necessary to consider.

Each approach certainly has its merits and drawbacks. However, the second approach seems preferable when it comes to solving very difficult and complicated regional problems of environmental management. Mathematical models, on the predominant use of which the first approach is oriented, oversimplify reality. They do not completely describe the behavior of the real system and can never answer all the questions that arise. The disadvantage of mathematical models is their non-uniqueness. The use of different models to solve the same problem yields different results.

Their greatest drawback must be sought in the normative base. At the same time, in practice, the situation is typical when decisions are made in terms of incompleteness or lack of necessary information. Models usually ignore the probabilistic nature of many environmental, social, and economic characteristics of the considered systems. All this makes it necessary to involve highly qualified experts at all levels of the decision-making process in the field of environmental management.

Although the accuracy of expert evaluations is intrinsically subject to some uncertainty, and the use of at first glance rigidly formalized methods of managerial decision-making is also ultimately based on the use of experience and intuition of decision-makers, the optimal solutions of economic and mathematical models require serious expert fine-tuning for their practical use in managerial decision-making. To carry out such a fine-tuning in practice is often very difficult, and in most situations – even impossible.

The methodology for solving the above territorial socio-ecological-economic problems should be based on the approach by ranking the goals by considering the strategic and milestone objectives. At the same time, social objectives and environmental safety requirements should be highly prioritized, and maximization of economic efficiency should be of the least priority.

4.4. Structuring and System Analysis of Regional Environmental Problems

Despite the difference between the system representations in different areas of specific application of system analysis, common in them is the desire to recreate a holistic picture of the phenomena under study. This means, first of all, to consider the object of research as a system, and its components – not as such, but only taking into account their place in the system assuming that the properties of the system as a whole are not the sum of the properties of its individual components, but are generated by the interaction of the components.

System analysis is based on two fundamental ideas:

- The principle of separation of sub-systems; and
- The cybernetical principle of feedback.

One of the types of systemic analysis is the program-targeted approach – a method aimed exclusively at solving socio-economic and scientific and technical problems.

The program-targeted approach objectively contributes to the completeness of forecasting and management.

How important the integrated treatment of the problem is demonstrated, for instance, by the experience of car industry. Related capital investments, including non-production construction costs including the related costs of building garages, gas stations and service stations, roads and road infrastructure, exceeded the amount of direct capital investments by more than tenfold. Narrow-branch approaches to such complex problems can dramatically slow down or make it impossible to implement them.

Problems to be solved can be divided into three categories: quantitative, qualitative, and combined.

Quantitative problems are those that can be solved using strictly formal (mathematical) procedures. Such problems in the area of management of interest to us are solved by methods of the investigation of operations.

Qualitative problems are those whose properties and characteristics are not subject to formal, and often even logical description. The existence of such problems is often associated with their insufficient study. Qualitative problems should also include those for which no adequate mathematical apparatus has yet been devised. For the most part, heuristic methods based on expert estimates of the problem's precise quantitative characteristics rather than strict formal-mathematical methods are used to solve these problems.

Combined problems are those described with both, qualitative and quantitative characteristics.

System analysis is most valuable exactly for solving combined, quantitative and qualitative problems, envisaging the use of both strict mathematical methods to study the operations (insofar as optimization of separate processes or subsystems does not harm, but helps to achieve the goal of the whole system in question), and intuitive expert evaluations and heuristic procedures used within a fairly rigorous methodology of system analysis.

The quantitative and qualitative problems have a number of common features: sizable, perspective, and capital-intensive.

The large size and complexity of the links between the components of the problem, and the rational use of natural resources should be considered in conjunction. For example, land resources should be considered together with water resources, since their fertility directly depends on the water regime of soils. Water resources cannot be considered separately from forest resources, since the degree of afforestation of the territory strongly affects the hydrological regime. When solving nature management problems, one should always keep in mind that connections in natural systems are much more complicated than in man-made ones. In addition, due to the increasing scale of production, more and more natural resources are brought into economic circulation and the environment is polluted. All this make it clear how large-scale and complex the problems of natural resource management are.

- *Prospectivity.* The solution of such problems of nature management as afforestation of big territories, development and introduction of effective systems of treatment of industrial emissions, creation of national parks, nature reserves, etc., requires consideration of these problems in the long term
- *High capital intensity.* The solution of certain nature management tasks, such as the rebuilding of centralized treatment facilities, sewerage and irrigation systems, etc., requires multi-million dollar capital investments.
- *A wide range of alternatives to achieve the goals.* Many alternatives can be proposed to solve any major environmental management problem. For example, the problem of protection from pollution of surface waters of a certain section of a river or basin can be solved by introducing waterless technologies or technological schemes at the polluting enterprises allowing treating and reusing water, or construction of a collector of polluted sewage from the whole industrial zone for the subsequent consolidated treatment. One or another combination of the listed options can be recommended, which differ in requirements to resources, terms of implementation, efficiency in achieving the set goal, etc.
- *Imperfection of modern scientific ideas and technical achievements, providing a solution to the problem.* Many important problems of natural resource management cannot be solved without the results of preliminary, often quite complicated, scientific research. For example, in order to prevent pollution of groundwater sources in some river basins, it is necessary to conduct research and find out the trends and extent of already existing groundwater pollution
- *Uncertainty of cost and time requirements.* The large-scale, complex, prospective nature management problems do not allow a priori determination of the resources and time needed to solve the entire problem. To clarify these characteristics, it is necessary to consider

the problems systematically, and then to coordinate and link the individual parts of the solution.

The final product of the normative, program-targeted approach to solving the problem is a program, which is a set of comprehensively coordinated economic, social, industrial-technical, organizational and research activities aimed at achieving a clearly delineated goal. In other words, the program serves as a tool for translating social development goals into the goals and objectives of specific localities, businesses, and organizations.

The procedure of shaping programs is largely informal; it is essentially an expertise. In order to make the formation of the program successful, it is necessary to make greater use of formalization methods and technical means, i.e., it is necessary to create a complex system, which includes many expert procedures and a variety of supporting tools.

It is possible to identify several basic stages in the preparation of a regional program:

1. Baseline analysis and formulation of the program goal. At this stage, environmental problems in the region are analyzed both retrospectively and prospectively in order to localize the boundaries of the program to be developed for its clear orientation and to prepare the initial assignment for its development.

At this stage, a series of extrapolations and target (normative) forecasts are usually performed, the synthesis of which makes it possible to outline the boundaries of the studied problems, various aspects of socio-ecological and economic development of the region that are essential for their solution and formulate the final goal of the program.

2. Formulation of the set of program objectives. At this stage the final goal is structured, i.e., broken down into a set of subgoals related to the solution of the problem.

Construction of the tree of program objectives, using the logical property of conjunctive notions, serves as a method of such a breakdown.

This allows constructing a complete set of goals and subgoals, reflecting the desired functions of future real-world objects, which in total should satisfy the needs of the overall objective. At this stage, target standards are set, i.e., quantitative characteristics of levels of achievement of the regional program goals

Obviously, it is difficult to allocate resources between the functional goals of the program considered within the whole region, because consideration of sufficiently large functional goals masks territorial differences in terms of the relative importance of their achievement. This creates the necessity of additional territorial binding to these sub-areas.

Note that at the lower level of the tree, the objectives and resources must be matched. Obviously, the more fractional are the lower level goals, the more accurate can be the characteristics of time and resources required for their implementation.

Knowing these characteristics is necessary for the best allocation of resources. Thus, the allocation of local goals – a necessary point in the construction of the goal tree – allows allocating resources between the elements of the lower level of the goal tree in turn according to the values of the coefficients of relative importance of their contribution to the global goal of the program. In this case, the order of achieving the local objectives of the tree will not violate the simultaneity in the implementation of major functional objectives, and thus will provide the necessary comprehensiveness in solving the problem.

Compilation of the tree of real and ultimate objectives is a complex task and may be implemented only by highly qualified experts, having necessary information about their completeness and reality.

3. Formulating program options and selecting the most effective of them. Several levels of alternatives emerge in the construction of the program, highlighted according to the sequence of problem solving: first – due to the fact that the levels of target standards may be unattainable under the constraints acceptable to the national economy on the resources allocated for the implementation of the program, second – the level of alternativeness is the formation of objectively expressed systems that implement one or another functional goal of the program, and the third is the formation of ways to create these systems, characterized by different technologies, a set of resources and the time required to implement the program.

The goal tree serves as a framework for the formation of alternative sets of goal-implementing systems, as well as alternative sets of objectives, which are understood as technological ways of creating these systems.

In further detailing, individual objectives can be broken down into specific activities that potentially ensure the fulfillment of the program with the specified end indicators. Here another level of alternativeness emerges. Combination of alternatives selected by various criteria to implement a system of conjunctive functional objectives forms the option of the program.

The existence of several levels of alternativeness dramatically complicates the problem of choosing the best option for the program and makes it multi-level.

4. Detailing of the selected option. Since the program is designed for specific implementation, its measures are detailed in accordance with the requirements of the management system, which brings specific tasks to specific performers (the program measures are bound to certain intermediate and final implementation timelines).

5. As a separate stage in the development of *a regional environmental management program*, the formation of the organizational structure of the program management should be singled out. It can be carried out on the basis of classification algorithms based on the division of the whole set of objectives of the program into relatively independent groups, within which the objectives are closely interrelated.

Let us consider the problem of building a tree of goals of the environmental program on the example of the basin of the Mtkvari, the only trans-boundary river in South Caucasus. The economy of this vast region (Turkey, Georgia, Azerbaijan, and Armenia) is characterized by a complex multi-sectoral structure and dense population. So, the load on the environment is rather high. This region has acute nature management problems. The ultimate goal of the integrated hydroresources protection program in the river Mtkvari catch basin is the improvement of the natural environment.

According to hydrological zoning, the study area—which includes Turkey, Georgia, Azerbaijan, and Armenia—covers the basins of the Mtkvari and Araksi rivers. However, since the program encompasses on all major components of the natural environment, not just the water basin, it is necessary to clarify the originally established boundaries of the region. The conditions of protection, reproduction and rational use of land and forest funds of the region should be taken into account for this purpose.

The target stage of development of the complex program for the protection of regional hydroresources includes two phases:

- *The first phase* includes the analysis of the initial state of the natural environment, and identification of environmental problems in the region.
- *The second phase* includes the construction of the tree of goals, objectives and measures of the program.

In the first phase, the existing and anticipated problems of the nature management are identified. The object of analysis is the ecological-economic system of the region, including the economy of the region and its natural environment.

The state of the natural environment is evaluated according to such components, as air, water basin, as well as land and forest funds.

The rational use of mineral resources is a separate problem, which is mainly sectoral (for single-purpose resources) or cross-sectoral (for multi-purpose resources) and is not considered in the development of this regional program.

The analysis showed that the ultimate goal was the preservation and improvement of the state of the natural environment in the study region.

The consistent structuring of the final goal of the program is carried out by constructing a conjunctive tree of goals. For this purpose, it is necessary to have specific information about regional problems of nature management. All goals of the constructed tree have real content and reflect the main directions of nature protection activity in the region.

The final goal of the program – the preservation and improvement of the state of the environment in the study region was initially divided into eight functional subgoals of the first level. Four of them correspond to the components of the natural environment highlighted in the analysis. The remaining subgoals are of national economic importance and are given in the tree of goals of the regional program only in general – at the first level, without further subdivision.

The allocation of two groups of subgoals at the first level and further expansion of the goal tree only for one of them forms a well-defined structure of the regional program. It includes only those objectives and activities that ensure the implementation of the highlighted final goal and are solved within the region.

The division of subgoals forms the second level of the goal tree, reflecting the problems of water protection activities in the region.

The process of constructing the conjunctive functional tree of goals is completed by the territorial division of the goals and the formation of local goals of the program, which are the goals assigned for relevant administrative areas.

The problems of natural resource management are diverse, but they are mostly classified in different parts of the region. As a rule, forestry and land use problems are differentiated by regions. The problems of water basin protection and rational use of water resources are territorially "tied" to water management areas, which can also be correlated with regional boundaries.

Expert Evaluations at the Target Stage of Program Development

Expert evaluations refer to quantitative or ordinal assessments by competent specialists of factors that are not directly measurable. Methods of expert evaluations based on the use of professional experience and intuition of specialists are a useful tool for studying complex, multi-criteria problems, the analysis of which does not quite lend itself to formalization. Such is the nature of the problems of natural resource management that make up the content of the goal tree discussed above.

Experience and intuition help a specialist solve many problems that arise in terms of uncertainty, but at the same time, it is obvious that when solving complex, multi-criteria problems, the participation of a group of erudite specialists is necessary for qualitative expertise, which allows a comprehensive analysis of the quantitative and qualitative aspects of the study problems.

The problem of group quantification of goals as coefficients of relative importance was first set and solved in the U.S. during the development of the well-known PATTERN system. Coefficients of relative importance in this system are obtained by the method of expert evaluations and multiple balloting of coefficient values. The results of the first balloting are announced to the group members, and everyone has an opportunity to challenge them and bring new arguments. Then a second ballot is carried out; the results are averaged, and so on.

There is another method of expert evaluation – an individual expert evaluation followed by averaging. This simplest and most widespread method of obtaining a group expert evaluation makes it possible to eliminate the features of subjective uncertainty inherent in individual evaluations.

It is possible to distinguish the following main stages of the expertise: formation of a group of experts; interviewing of experts; and processing of expert evaluations.

The goal tree allows us to reveal the hierarchy of goals by levels of the hierarchy and to determine the place of the program activities in the achievement of a given goal (Figure 63). For large-scale programs, it is advisable to introduce a division into smaller territorial sections.

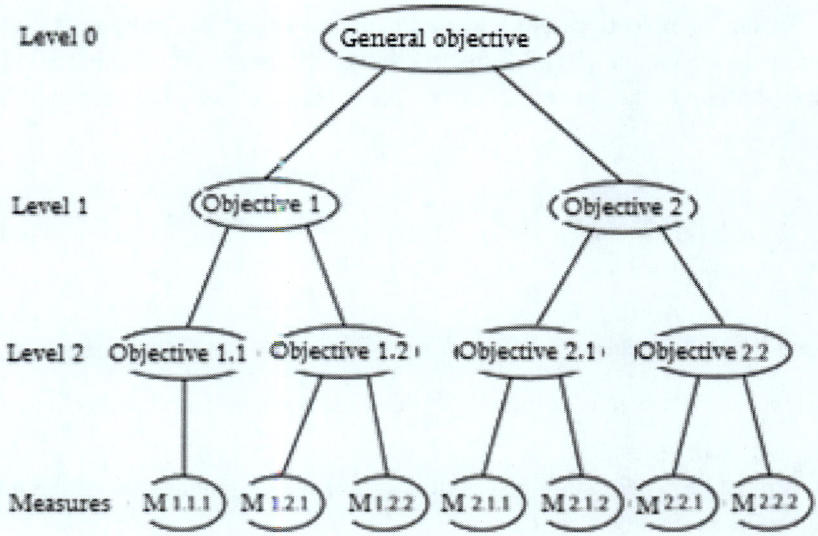

Figure 63. Structure of the tree of objectives.

No formalized structure can be recommended for constructing the goal tree, since the definition of goals of different hierarchical levels and their subordination are determined by the skills of the researcher. Let us list the main requirements for the construction of such a tree of objectives:

- The formulation of goals must be clear leaving no room for ambiguous interpretation;
- The goals of one level of the hierarchy must be comparable in their scale and importance;
- The formulation of objectives must allow for quantitative or ordinal evaluation of the degree of their achievement;
- The completeness of the goal tree: each goal at any level must be represented as a conjunction of all possible lower level goals;
- The continuity of the goal tree: between two consecutive levels of the tree there must not be intermediate goals;
- There must not be cycles in the tree of objectives;
- There must not be isolated peaks in the tree of objectives.

Values of objectives are assessed using an expert evaluation. The idea behind the calculation is that the priority coefficients of the final results, corresponding to the general objective, are calculated based on the priority of each objective $\eta_i \ (i \in D)$:

$$\omega_j = \prod_{i \in L_j} \eta_i \ (j \in M) \tag{166}$$

where ω_j is the priority coefficient to the general objective of measure j; L_j is the set of objectives from objective j to the general objective; and M is the set of final results.

It must be noted that the sum of coefficients within each set of the goal tree branches shall be 1. In this case,

$$\sum_{j \in M} \omega_j = 1 \tag{167}$$

This approach suggests averaging expert assessments to calculate the coefficients, which are determined by the experts' intuition based on their professional experience. Expert evaluations are used to investigate complex issues that, in whole or in part, cannot be formalized; structurization issues and program measure evaluation are two examples of such issues. The collective selection of dimensions and the multi-criteria nature of the program objectives are two peculiarities of these problems that share characteristics of two classes of different tasks. To solve this issue, it is first necessary to evaluate the importance of each criterion, which can vary and correspond to various goals.

Experts must evaluate each criterion's objectives on an individual basis.

The presented information is sufficient for full assessment of the priority levels of objectives, from the viewpoint of achievement of general objective. For this purpose, it is recommended to use the following formula:

$$\omega_j = \sum_{i \in Lj} \sum_{K} \left(n_{ik} y_k \right) \Big/ \left(\sum_{K} K \right) \sum_{K} \left[a_{ik} y_k \Big/ \left(\sum_{i} aik \sum_{K} 4k \right) \right] \tag{168}$$

i.e., additive summation of criteria is used. However, from the perspective of one criterion, the considered objective is too significant, while on the other hand, an addivite sum does not allow making am accurate assessment of the value of the objectives. To eliminate this gap, it is advisable to consider the priorities of the assessment of the objectives; then, formula (168) will be clarified as follows:

$$\omega_{jk} = \prod_{\ell \in Lj} \sum_{j} \left[n_{\ell k} y_k \Big/ \left(\sum_{\ell} n_{\ell k} \sum_{k} Y_k \right) \right] \left[a_{\ell k} y_k \Big/ \left(\sum_{\ell} n_{\ell k} \sum_{k} Y_k \right) \right] \qquad (169)$$

Besides, each program objective shall be assessed by the vector of coefficients ($\omega_1, \omega_2, ... \omega_k$), whose dimension equals to the number of criteria and is used during the expertise. The priority of the objectives can be evaluated by one of the given options:

1. Adaptive – $\sum_k \omega_{jk}$
2. Multiplication – $\prod_K \omega_{jk}$
3. Threshold value – $\max_k \{\omega_{jk}\}$ or $\min_k \{\omega_{jk}\}$

They allow considering the differences in the values of the criteria. The Pareto[1] optimality principles can be used to solve the problem. In the case of two criteria, Pareto set finds solutions when one criterion improves while the other deteriorates. For instance, moving from objective 1 to objective 2 can simultaneously improve the values of the criteria used to evaluate objective 1. This indicates that objective 1 is not a part of Pareto set. At the same time, moving from objective 2 to objective 3 can simultaneously increase the value of the second criterion, but in this case the value of the first criterion will decline. Therefore, it can be said that of a set of objectives, 2 and 3 are Pareto-optimal. Prioritizing any of them is impossible. Consequently, it makes sense to give them rank 1.

After these objectives are ignored, Pareto-optimal solutions can be selected among the remaining ones and assigned rank 2. In this example, such

---

[1] Wilfredo Pareto, an economist and social scientist, was born on July 15, 1848, anddied on August 20, 1923.

objectives will be 1 and 7. The results of the evaluation of calculations based on the sequential selection of pareto-optimal solutions are as follows:

Objectives: 1 2 3 4 5 6 7
Ranks: 2 1 1 3 4 4 2

Priority coefficients are calculated in such a way that expert errors are not taken into account. Decision-making that is based on expert opinions must envisage a certain degree of reliability. The proposed ranking method is based on the idea that depending on the distance to the center of coordinates in the space of criteria, the ranks can be assigned from the point that corresponds to some or other objective. This distance shall be calculated by the formula:

$$R_\ell = \sqrt{\sum_K \omega_{\ell k}^2} \tag{170}$$

The greatest distance can also be calculated as follows:

$$R^* = \max_\ell \{R_\ell\} \tag{171}$$

If it is necessary to divide all objectives in L ranks, then objective rank i in $\Delta R(\ell-1) \le R_i \le R_\ell$ interval will be defined by the formula:

$$\ell_i = (L+1-\ell) \tag{172}$$

Step ΔR takes an expert error into account, as the deviation limit during the assessment of priorities is admissible within the above-given interval.

The value of the step ΔR depends on the obtained scale (i.e., the number of ranks) and shall be calculated by the formula:

$$\Delta R = R^*/L \tag{173}$$

If objectives 2 and 3 are between the spheres radii $\Delta R^* 3$ and $\Delta R^* 4$, then $\ell_2 = 4+1-4=1$ and $\ell_3 = 4+1-4=1$. Objective 1 is assigned rank $\ell_1 = 4+1-3=2$, and so on.

However, the criteria have different priorities. In this case, the spheres are transformed (are stretched to an ellipse) in accordance with the following formula:

$$R_{\ell} = \sqrt{\sum_{k} a_k \omega_{ik}} \tag{174}$$

where a_k is importance of the k -th criterion.

Another important problem emerging during the structurization of objectives, is the assessment of degree of the objectives achievement.

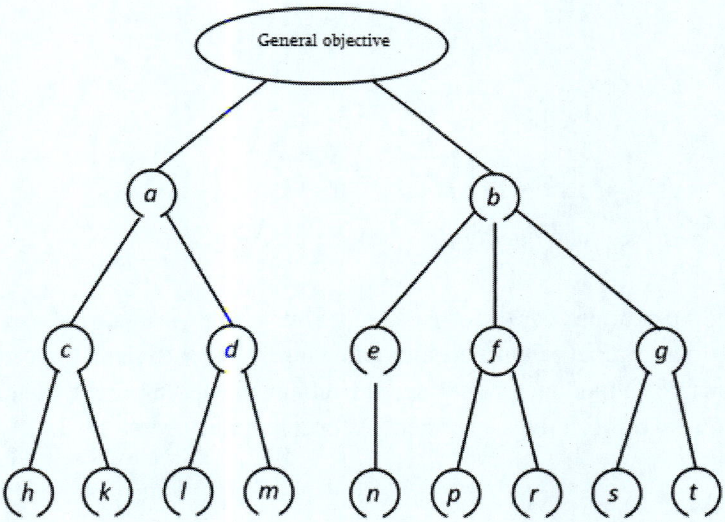

Figure 64. Completeness of achievement of objectives.

This problem is solved based on the measures attached to the lower level of the structural-objective tree. In this case, it is necessary to correct the priority coefficients and measures, by taking the completeness of achievement of objectives into account (Figure 64).

The following formulas will be used to determine the priority with respect to the upper level objectives, without taking the extent of achievement of the objectives into account:

$$h^* = hca;\ k^* = kca;\ \ell^* = \ell da;\ m^* = mda;\ldots\ t^* = tgb \tag{175}$$

Let us assume that the completeness of achievement of the lower level objectives is described by values: ℓ_n, ℓ_k, ℓ_i, ℓ_m,... ℓ_t.

By considering the completeness of achievement of objectives, the assessment of values shall be re-calculated for the entire structural-objective model:

$$h^{**} = \lambda_n h / [\lambda_n h + \lambda_k K];$$
$$C^{**} = [(\lambda_n h + \lambda_k k)c] / [(\lambda_n h + \lambda_k k)c + (\lambda_i I + \lambda_m m)d];$$
$$a^{**} = [(\lambda_h h + \lambda_k k)c + (\lambda_i \ell + \lambda_m m)d]a / \{[(\lambda_n n + \lambda_k k)c + (\lambda_i \ell + \lambda_m m)d]a +$$
$$+ [\lambda_n ne + (\lambda_p P + \lambda_r r)f + (\lambda_s s + \lambda_t t)g]b...\}$$

So:

$$h^{**} + K^{**} = 1;\ t^{**} + m^{**} = 1;...$$
$$c^{**} + d^{**} = 1;\ e^{**} + f^{**} + g^{**} = 1;\ a^{**} + b^{**} = 1 \qquad (176)$$

The performed transformations prove that instead of extended calculations of coefficients on the entire tree, it is sufficient to correct the coefficient of importance of measured from the viewpoint of completeness of achievement of objectives, and then perform ranking.

4.5. Management of Investment Projects of Measures to Protect Water Resources. Plan Adjustment for Regional Environmental Management Projects

The success of the implementation of the environmental program depends on the environment, which is a source of resources, energy, personnel, as well as the development of production factors in the specified area, scientific and technological progress, the development of the needs of society in relation to the environment. Although the program realization opportunities strongly depends on the program management, the managerial staff must identify the environment factors significant to the program, determining the appropriate management decisions, allow to predetermine the further development of environmental factors and their impact on the environmental program. Environmental factors can be divided into two subgroups:

- External factors of direct impact;
- External factors of indirect impact.

The classification of environmental factors is given in Figure 65.

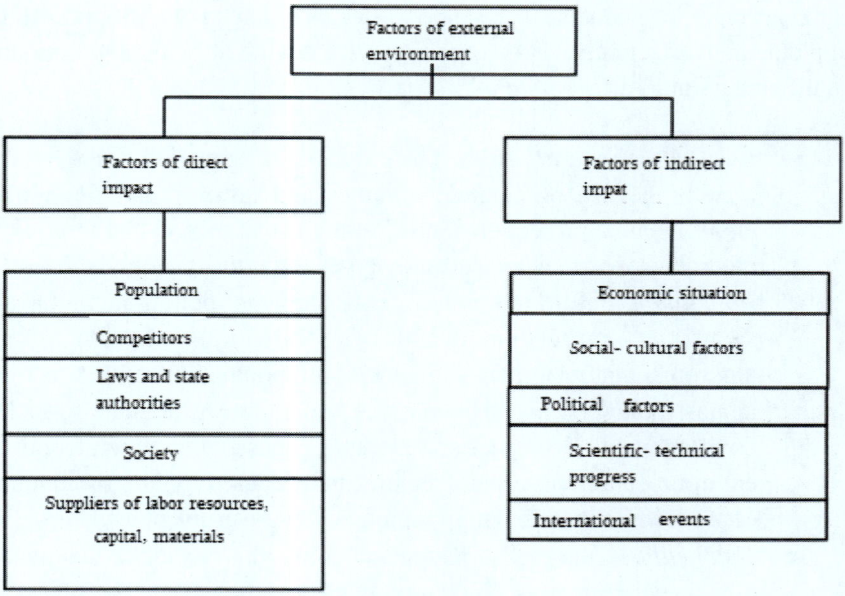

Figure 65. Classification of environmental factors.

The environment of direct influence includes the factors directly affecting the implementation of the program activities, as well as those under their influence. Indirect environmental factors do not have a direct and direct influence on the implementation of program activities, but will affect them in the future or through a chain of other factors.

Let us consider these factors in detail:

Suppliers. Suppliers are one of the main factors. From them the organization receives material, labor and financial resources. Material resources include materials, equipment, and energy. The relationship between the supplier network and program management is an example of the direct influence of the environment on the implementation of program activities. Threats of environmental change, fluctuating exchange resources, political instability, etc. can be expected. In addition, it can also prevent the development of entrepreneurs, as well as the creation of additional jobs for the population of the country.

Disruptions in supply, under-delivery of the proper amount of material resources can lead to serious losses: the suspension or delay, and in some cases even the refusal to implement measures. Suppliers of financial resources are banks, private individuals, shareholders, etc. In order for the program to be implemented effectively, it is necessary to provide it with appropriately qualified personnel.

- *Laws and state authorities.* The government agencies use the laws to control the use of natural resources and develop and implement environmental protection plans. Programs that protect and restore the natural environment are currently given top priority around the world.
- *Population.* Public reactions to environmental pollution can have a significant impact on the design and implementation of an environmental program. Sometimes, the population refuses to fight against polluters, and their passive actions push the state to tackle environmental issues. For example, mass migration from an environmentally hazardous region can be caused by major economic consequences that do not go unnoticed by government agencies.
- *Competitors.* In a perfect market economy, this is a factor that makes a business operate as efficiently as a competing firm. The objective of competition can be to reduce the burden on the environment, but this requires appropriate economic leverage – taxes and tax incentives, disposal of hazardous substances, trading licenses, and so on.
- *Society.* The activities of various environmental societies and foundations are becoming increasingly relevant. Public associations such as the Greens bring together people of different professions, who are able to identify and investigate the causes and sources of pollution, and report on environmental problems in the media, which has a significant impact on the process of creating and implementing an environmental protection program.
- *Scientific-technical progress.* As the program is implemented, technological innovations in the field of nature conservation may evolve; as the measures become obsolete, they are replaced with more

advanced ones to increase the effectiveness of the program. The conservation program keeps pace with the latest scientific and technological advances.

- *Economic situation.* Economic program management needs to assess the prospective impact of general changes on the progress of an environmental protection program. The global economy affects the cost of all imported resources. Program management should try to manage activities in light of expected changes. For example, if inflation is expected, a decision may be made to borrow funds on the assumption that interest on the money will be low when it becomes due, thereby partially offsetting the loss of interest payments. If an economic downturn is predicted, management may prioritize the release of finished goods from the warehouse, the reduction in the number of workers, etc. The state of the economy is mirrored in the real incomes of the population, which is immediately reflected in how they view the challenges of improving the environment.
- *Sociocultural activities.* The sociocultural environment varies across the world's regions and nations and is presented by a variety of rules, moral principles, cultural norms, and religious practices. The population of America, for instance, differs significantly from that of European nations, where traditions are highly valued. Orthodoxy-based Georgian cultural traditions that date back hundreds of years take into account the harmonious coexistence of humans and the natural world. Because of this, it is essential to adapt environmental concerns to the preservation of Georgia's historical, material, and cultural heritage. The program's management should have a close relationship with the Georgian community and take into account its unique needs and traditions.
- *International events.* Predicting international events can be very useful for program management, as it will allow additional funding by foreign investors.
- *Political factors.* The connection between local political factors and international ones is apparent, and it should be considered in the context of influence on the government's activities to protect the hydro resources of one's own country.

The following features of the external environment factors must be taken into account when analyzing and forecasting them:

1. *Correlation of Factors.* A brief discussion of the environmental factors leads us to the conclusion that they are interrelated. There is a particularly close relationship between international, economic, and political factors.
2. *Complexity of the environment.* The complexity of the environment refers to the number of factors to which program management must respond, as well as the level of variability of each factor. It should be noted that factors based on different technologies are in a more complex environment, and technologies change rapidly.
3. *Flexibility of the environment.* The flexibility of the environmental refers to the rate, at which changes occur in an organization's environment. Many economists have noted that the environment is changing at an increasing pace. At the same time, the environment for the water resources protection program in different industries changes at different paces. For instance, the pace of technological advancement is greater in the chemical, electrical, and pharmaceutical sectors than in those of mechanical engineering, auto parts, aerospace, and other sectors.
4. *Uncertainty of the external environment* is a feature of the quality of information available to the enterprise about a particular factor, as well as the reliability of this information. When the amount and accuracy of information decreases, the ambiguity of the analysis and description of the environment increases.

Environmental analysis is necessary to develop a specific strategy for the implementation of environmental programs on the basis of increasing the reliability of the program. Both external positive factors and external threats must be taken into account.

The environment has the factors (elements) affecting environmental protection programs. After assessing these factors, a complete analysis of the environment can be performed. Since some of the environmental factors are directly influenced by the environmental program, an environmental impact analysis is not possible without considering the impact of the program on these factors.

When analyzing an environmental program, the following activities can be emphasized:

- Identification of external factors;
- Assessment of external factors;

- Analysis of important external factors (assessment of changes, identification of factors threatening the implementation of program goals, definition of desirable factors).

The above-listed activities, as well as the whole process of strategic planning, are characterized by complexity and dynamism. The depth, accuracy, and frequency of each activity can ensure the effectiveness of a conservation program analysis.

The analysis of the environment helps the management of the program to obtain the necessary information for forecasting the implementation; in contingency planning (with contingency plans); in developing an appropriate system to timely prevent possible threats to the program implementation; in developing a strategy that can turn this threat into an opportunity. The environmental analysis in strategic planning allows identifying the following:

- The actual state of the environmental program;
- The target state of the environmental program; and
- The managerial actions to achieve the desired goal.

The specific list of factors having direct or indirect impact depends on the nature of the environmental program and the territory where it is implemented. A fairly complete list of the factors is given in Table 15.

It is quite possible that in a particular situation most of the factors listed will not be used at all, and some factors will need to be thoroughly changed.

Among the main parameters of the environmental program, it is advisable to use such things as *flexibility* and *reliability*. *Flexibility* refers to the level of achievement of the ultimate goal by avoiding harm to the natural environment as the terms of the goal change, and *reliability* of an environmental program refers to the ability to accomplish the program activities at certain costs in the specified time.

The most important way to manage the reliability and flexibility of a program is the levers of market economy and financial maneuvers. Contingency plans also contribute to an improved reliability of the environmental protection programs.

Along with external factors, the program's implementation is also influenced by the variable internal conditions of realization.

Table 15. External factors

Group of factors	Name of factor	Impact: Direct: 1 Indirect: 2
Economic	Inflation and deflation Monetary market Credit policy Fiscal policy Occupation level International tax balance	2 2 2 2 2 2
Political	Laws on the regulation of water resources protection measures State of control over compliance with the law Investment policy Political situation	2 2 2 2
Market	Capital market Suppliers Brokers	1 1 1
Technological	Level of technology	2
Competitive	Competitor types Competitor objectives	1 2
International	Activities of foreign entrepreneurs International economic activities International political situation	2 2 2
Socio-cultural	Attitude of society towards water resources protection measures Demographic factors Cultural level of population Level of religious consciousness Psychological traits of consumer behavior	1 2 2 2 2
Natural- geographic	Shortage of certain resources Energy supply Climatic peculiarities Ecological state of the natural environment	2 2 2 2

4.6. Reliability Indicators of Implementation of Programs to Protect Water Resources

The options for navigating the environmental protection program have become much more limited since the governmental decree on the adoption and implementation of the environmental protection program: the program becomes *inert.* The problem of determining the allowable maneuvering range can be reduced to limiting the allowable differences in program performance, i.e., if considering the loss prevention dynamics during the program realization, the dynamics may deteriorate a lot, with an already existing deviation from the mean annual value of program funding. Figure 66 shows estimate curves of the expected losses during the implementation of the environmental protection program and annual funding.

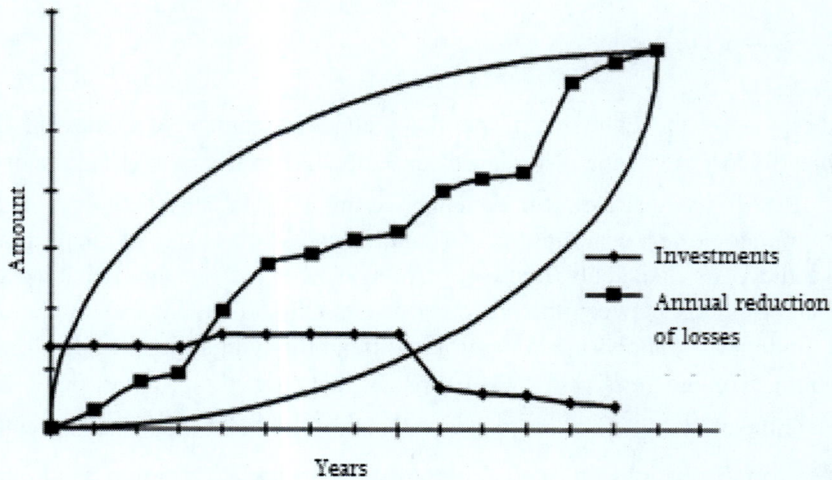

Figure 66. Dynamics of decrease in investments and losses during the implementation of the environmental protection program (example).

The data above show that since the curve for achieving the goal of the program (economic result) is damped as the cost curve goes down at the end of the program implementation period, in the developed program, more effective and efficient measures are carried out at the beginning, and less effective – at the end of the calendar period. The closer the goal achievement curve is to the upper smooth curve, the more efficient the program execution schedule. The more the curve approaches the bottom smooth curve, the less efficiency of the program realization.

The task of maneuvering envisages the development of an option when the curve of achieving the objective does not go beyond the specified limits and gets maximally close to the upper curve.

Besides, it is possible to change the timing of the events or replace them with new ones:

$$\sqrt{\left(\sum_{t=1}^{T}\left[\left(\sum_{i\in G}P_i\right)\Big/T-\sum_{i\in G'_\tau}P_i\right]^2\right)\Big/T} \le \sqrt{\left(\sum_{t=1}^{T}\left[\left(\sum_{i\in G}P_i\right)\Big/T-\sum_{i\in G'_\tau}P_i\right]^2\right)\Big/T} \quad (177)$$

where $i \in G'_{\tau}$ is the timeline of realization of measures obtained based on maneuverability.

The level of maneuverability of the environmental protection program can be determined as follows:

$$M = \psi\left(\delta/\xi\right) \tag{178}$$

where δ is the diversion from, the planned dynamics of achieving the objective; and ξ is the disturbance caused by the impact of external factors.

Flexibility is also related to maneuvering as well. The flexibility of the program to protect water resources is understood as the ability of the program to achieve the final goals in case of certain changes without significant losses. The correlation between the prevented losses (Y) and the change (reduction) in funding (F) allows attaining program flexibility with ratio "avoided loss – funding volume", $f(\Delta Y/Y, \Delta\Phi/\Phi) = 0$; in this case, the program flexibility $e = (\Delta\Phi/\Phi)/(\Delta Y/Y)$ is viewed at each point of the flexibility function, while the inverse relationship $g = e^{-1}$ describes the lack of program flexibility. *Program inertia* is the source of flexibility. The management of program flexibility can be internal or external. External management includes an increase in program reserves at the expense of mutual exchange of measures, the possibility of reducing the costs of several measures, etc. Internal management implies an increase in maneuverability, the number of interchangeable measures, opportunities of financial maneuverability, etc.

As flexibility is related to program inertia, which decreases as the planning horizon increases, the management of flexibility is topical in the near future.

The reliability of realization of water resources protection programs is a potential opportunity for the implementation of measures of the program according to the value of prevented losses and timelines. Program reliability may be determined based on the value of prevented losses H^Y or volume of received funds H^F.

$$H^Y = 1-(E(\Delta Y)/Y) \text{ ან } H^F = 1-(E(\Delta F)/F) \tag{179}$$

where $E(\Delta Y)$ is the mathematical expectation of reduction of prevented loss; $E(\Delta F)$ is the mathematical expectation of reduction of incompletely received funds.

The adapted quality of the program can be evaluated by using index *cost momentum*, which is commonly used in the analysis of a number of possible options within the zone of economic uncertainty, as additional criterion for the choice of options of calendar plans (contingency plans). If little knowledge of the effects of environmental factors is expected to obtain when implementing an environmental program, the later the costs are incurred (all other things being equal), the more the plan will be adapted:

$$\sum_{t=t_0}^{T_{ox}} \sum_{i \in J_t} K_i (1+r)^{t_0-t} (1+\Theta)^{t-t_0} \quad (180)$$

where Θ is the average annual growth rate of uncertain future opportunities to implement the plan; the value of Θ is determined based on the notion of program reliability. If the reliability of the program is determined for each year of the planning period, decreasing values $H_1 > H_2 > ... > H_T$ are obtained. They can be used to calculate the average rate without knowing the probability of the plan fulfillment:

$$\Theta = (1 - H_t)/(1 - H_{t-1})$$

Prevented losses are not taken into account when cost momentum is used. Characterization of dynamics of the program realization will be more complete prevented losses are included in this indicator:

$$\sum_{t=t_0}^{T_{ox}} \left[\sum_{i \in G_t} (Y_{it} - C_{it}) - \sum_{i \in J_t} K_{it} (1+\Theta)^{t-t_0} \right] (1+r)^{t_0-t} \quad (181)$$

4.7. Financial Indices of Implementation of Water Resource Programs

Freedom of maneuver is determined by the structure of the plan, which is a set of measures of different values related to different areas and territories of the region, as well as the sources and conditions of funding.

The main sources of funding for hydro-resource protection programs are: the state budget, the municipal budget, the state environmental fund, and the environmental funds of enterprises and organizations. Some other sources are insurance funds, target contributions, donations, and bank loans. The most important of them are local environmental funds.

The main sources of incomes of the environmental funds are: depreciations on hydro-resource conservation facilities, pollution taxes, fines for violations of pollution standards, and rental taxes for the use of natural resources.

4.8. Engineering-Innovative Structure to Protect Hydroresources and Calculate Their Technical and Economic Efficiency

Engineering-Innovative Structure to Protect Water Resources

The purpose of the novel open-end anti-mudflow springboard-type innovative structures is to reduce the impact force of the flow, especially with catastrophic parameters, as well as to simplify and reduce the cost of the structures.

Below are the advantages of the new structures as compared with the existing ones:

a) Reliability and durability;
b) Efficient stabilization of mountain rivers; and
c) Great economic effect – the given structures are made of reinforced concrete and second-hand materials (written-off metal rails, depreciated metal cables, etc.) making 50÷80% of the total construction materials.

The anti-mudflow structure in the step-arch shape [copyright certificate #1191515, authors: Eduard Kukhalashvili, Givi Gavardashvili, David Pruidze] is the frame of iron rails, which are either welded or riveted together. The iron frame is fixed to the riverbed by reinforced concrete (Figure 67).

The rectangular openings of the structure enable effective energy quenching while preventing the current's maximum force impact on the structure. During a mudflow passage, the main (initial) powerful impact is received by the first step of the structure breaking down the first current; then the current flows over the cylindrical steps of the structure, where the mudflow energy is quenched evenly.

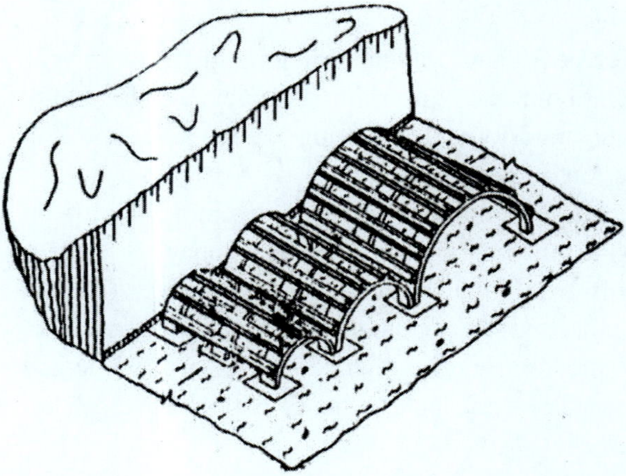

Figure 67. The stepped-arch structure.

The structure [copyright certificate #1242570. Author: Givi Gavardashvili] in Figure 68 is a trapezoidal channeled flow guiding structure with reinforced concrete walls; the slopes of the structure are connected with the sides of the riverbed (gorge), with their angles varying between 110 and 160°.

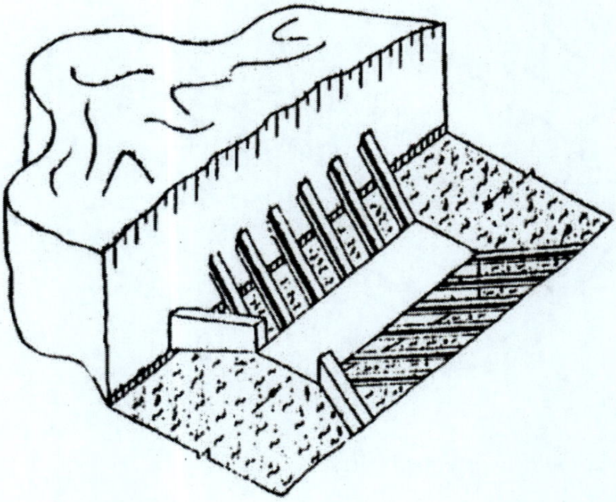

Figure 68. Trapezoidal structure.

The slopes of the structure are made of iron rails forming rectangular openings in between. There is a reinforced concrete foundation in the center of the structure, which has a springboard-like shape and along which the mudflow moves.

The trapezoidal shape of the structure, with its current guiding walls, allows reducing both, the current impact force and the gravitational (weight) pressure of the mudflow mass acting on the structure what guarantees a reliable operation of the structure.

The stepped anti-mudflow barrage (inventor's certificate No. 1596006. Authors: Givi Gavardashvili and Elarion Khegay) is made up of reinforced concrete beams positioned horizontally, with the iron beams fixed to them in the vertical plane, and with another end fixed to the riverbed (See Figure 69). The ends of the reinforced concrete beams are connected with ellipsoid concrete caps, which contribute to better performance and increased stability of the structure.

As the mudflow moves, the horizontally located reinforced concrete beams reduce the stream power in the vertical plane, while the ellipsoid concrete caps distribute the stream in the horizontal plane across the whole width of the bed.

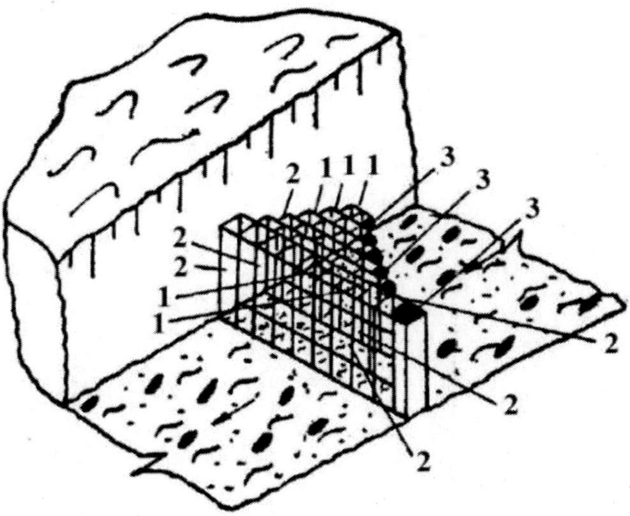

Figure 69. Anti-mudflow stepped barrage.

Assessment of Economic Efficiency of Using Natural Resources

Calculating the annual economic impact is necessary when planning the use of natural resources (soil, water, forests, etc.).

If the use of natural resources involves the introduction of new equipment or technology, the annual economic effect shall be calculated by the formula:

$$E = [(C_c PK_c) - (C_n + E_n K_n)] \cdot A_n \qquad (182)$$

where A_n is the annual economic effect (GEL); C_c and C_n are the prime cost of a unit production or expenses before and after the introduction of new technology in production (GEL); K_c, K_n are the specific capital expenses before and after the introduction of new equipment (GEL); and A_n is the annual production volume (GEL); $E_n = 0{,}12$.

As the deadlines of building construction facilities or major repair works are cut, the economic effect is calculated by the following expression:

$$E_d = E_n K(T_n - T_f) \qquad (183)$$

where K is the cost of fixed assets of production (GEL); T_n and T_F are the estimated and actual construction deadlines (year), respectively. The payback period of additional capital investments will be:

$$T = \frac{(K_z - K_\tau)}{(C_\tau - C_n)} \qquad (184)$$

The annual economic impact as the engineering-innovative structures to protect hydroresources are used in practice is:

E = (K1 – K2) x En (185)

Where K1 and K2 are capital investments for building, respectively, the engineering-innovative structure to protect water resources and the basic hydrotechnical facility; En is the coefficient of normative efficiency, equal to 0.15.

Figure 70. Anti-mudflow structure in the Telavis Khevi riverbed.

An open-end anti-mudflow hydrotechnical structure has been selected as a basic facility. The structure is known in practice as Professor Irakli Kherkheulidze's structure and is presently used in the Telavis Khevi riverbed to protect the city of Telavi against mudflow currents (Figure 70).

As per the project estimates, the construction cost of 1 linear meter of Kherkheulidze's anti-mudflow structure is 1811 USD. Since the innovative anti-mudflow structures are made of secondary raw materials, e.g., written-off metal rails, its annual economic effect, as per the preliminary calculations, is as follows:

- For an anti-mudflow stepped structure:
  E = (K1 – K2) x En = (1811,0 – 252,17) x 0.15 = 233, 82 USD/ lin.m;
- For an anti-mudflow rapezoidal structure:
  E = (K1 – K2) x En = (1811,0 – 768,26) x 0.15 = 156, 41 USD/ lin.m;
- For an anti-mudflow stepped barrage:
  E = (K1 – K2) x En = (1811,0 – 326,77)x0.15=222, 63 USD/lin.m.

Thus, based on our calculations it can be concluded, that the technical-economic parameters of most innovative anti-mudflow structures to introduce are better than those of the existing ones. In particular, the annual economic effect is 233,82 USD, 156, 41 USD and 222, 63 USD per linear meter for an anti-mudflow stepped structure, trapezoidal anti-mudflow structure and stepped anti-mudflow barrage, respectively.

Chapter 5

The State and the Market for Environmental Protection

5.1. Macroeconomic Policy and Ecological Factors

The state can facilitate the shift of the environmental economy to market economy by ecology-balancing economic reforms and the creation of an appropriate economic environment at a macro-level. Let us consider the impact of ecology on the macroeconomical policy. An effective implementation of the environmental policy requires the awareness of the level and subordination of the measures carried out, as well as the scales and limits of their impact. Two major groups of measures can be identified:

- The macroeconomic measures, and
- The environmental measures.

The first group includes measures that are implemented throughout the economy or at the level of sectors of the national economic complex. They may not have clear environmental goals. Such measures include: structural changes, changes in the national currency exchange rate, reduction of the state budget deficit, credit and financial policy, liberalization of foreign trade, strengthening the role of the private sector, institutional changes (privatization policy, demonopolization, etc.), subsidization or taxation in major economic sectors, reforming plans and prices (in energetics, agriculture, industry), creating conditions for foreign investment, etc. All these measures, inevitable mechanisms and reforms affect the environment in one way or another.

The second group of measures includes measures of pronounced ecological orientation: introduction of "ecological" and other types of taxes and fines for polluted environment, adoption of environmental standards and norms, implementation of regional or sectoral environmental programs, etc. These measures essentially lead to environmental protection and improvement of the use of natural resources.

In the present-day economy, the priority of macroeconomic measures that determine economic development, economic growth rates, and the growth of well-being of the population is obvious to decision-makers. Meanwhile, the environmental consequences of the macroeconomic policies are usually ignored or given the least priority.

For instance, the existing problems may lead to the implementation of necessary and effective measures, such as reducing the state budget deficit what will improve the macroeconomical balance. With maximum fiscal stringency, environmental expenditures are often among the first victimized. Exchange rate changes can stimulate extra exploitation and export of natural resources (some of these decisions are justified by the poorly understood relationship between macroeconomic measures and their environmental consequences in the world).

Unlike the first macroeconomic group of measures, the second group includes measures with a convincing environmental focus and expected environmental effects. In this regard, it can be noted that these measures in most cases have an auxiliary, compensatory and local character in relation to macroeconomic measures. If a negative environmental effect appears as a result of a "big" economic policy, the state is forced to implement additional environmental programs or measures necessary to stabilize the deteriorating environmental situation.

Among the main causes of the negative impact of macroeconomic measures on the environment are three: public policy inefficiency, market failure, and as a separate cause, institutional inefficiency.

For example, special measures of environmental compensation are needed in the case of ineffective public policy in the agricultural sector. Positive solutions will ease the situation of agricultural enterprises and increase agricultural production. It is important to note that subsidizing the purchase of pesticides, applying a low tax on water or not paying it at all in agriculture will lead to significant pollution of water resources, up to their disappearance. This requires special environmental programs, as well as economic and legal measures.

Likewise, during economic growth caused by economic reforms, one may see an increase in environmental damage. The reason may be the stalling of the market mechanism. If we know the exact external obstacles, the external effects of the activities of the polluting enterprises, we will not need various environmental protection measures, and the implementation of the principle – "polluter pays" will cause additional costs for the subjects of pollution. It is worth noting that practical complexity of "touching", internalization of externalities, and calculation of external obstacles leads to the need to introduce various additional economic instruments (pollution taxes, "green" taxes, etc.) or general environmental protection measures (cleaning polluted water by municipal services, etc.).

Let us take a closer look at the environmental effect of institutional reforms. Legal reform of property is of great importance for environmental protection. In many cases, accurate definition of property rights allows to solve problems of common, "no-one's" ownership of natural resources, problems of "granted" natural goods, problems of free access to natural resources (e.g., forest resources). A clear definition of property rights is necessary to solve environmental problems in a market economy. The need for this problem in economic theory was discussed by the American scientist and economist R. Coase. He noted the superiority of the market over the state regulation (through taxes, subsidies, established norms, etc.) in achieving socially optimal levels of pollution. The market economy operates primarily through a system of property rights, which guarantees legal ownership of natural resources.

According to R. Coase's theory, the polluter and the victim of pollution may find themselves in an unregulated situation. If the property right belongs to the victim of the pollution, the polluter must compensate for the damage. This reduces production and pollution to a level at which the marginal net profit of the producer does not exceed the amount of loss it compensates. Otherwise, the appropriate payment is made by the victim of the pollution who compensated the owner-producer for reducing production and pollution to the public optimum.

The provisions of R. Coase's theory are often criticized. In particular, the impossibility of ingenuous competition, high transaction costs, and the difficulty of identifying polluters and victims of pollution are noted. It is also impossible to determine the ownership of the ozone layer, the lower layers of the atmosphere, etc.

For example, for the economy of some countries, the issues of property rights are very acute. The need for a clear decision on the division of ownership of natural resources between the regional and municipal levels should be underlined. This problem is related to the protection of resources and obtaining the benefits and effects of a clean environment. In a transitional economy, the lack of resources of regional and municipal bodies leads to intensified exploitation of natural resources in the regions in an effort to receive quick profits. This often leads to predatory use of natural resources, exploitation and sale of resources without regard for environmental consequences. Regions strive to privatize as many natural resources as possible for their further exploitation and profit. It is justified to retain state ownership of many natural objects of this kind.

Monopoly is a complex problem for macroeconomic regulation. In the absence of competition, the largest monopolies, lobbied by legislative and executive structures, give minimal consideration to environmental factors. The monopolistic position is especially characteristic of the mining industries, especially the gas and oil industries. Environmental degradation, huge losses of natural resources due to backward production and transportation technologies, and numerous accidents have a great impact on the state of these industrial giants. Monopoly causes another socio-economic problem – the appropriation of natural rent by the monopoly itself, when a significant part of the rent should belong to the whole society. This is caused by the acquisition and purchase of natural resources and their sale at world prices. The resulting superprofits belong to a small group of people what makes them rich. In these cases, state intervention is necessary to realize the social, economic, and ecological interests of society.

Among examples of the positive impact of macroeconomic measures on the environment is price reform – more adequate accounting of natural resources at real costs. A change in prices in one sector of the economy causes a general change in their structure and affects the entire social economy. For example, a reasonable increase in the price of energy resources contributes to their rational use in all sectors of the economy and the population.

The "purely" negative and positive examples of the environmental impact of macroeconomic policies were given above. In economic reality, measures often produce mixed environmental effects, for example, measures aimed at macroeconomic stabilization produce a certain environmental gain. Unstable economic development is caused by an increase in the exploitation of natural resources, saving at the expense of nature conservation. Economic projects will be realized through stability. However, the process of macroeconomic stabilization can contribute to negative impacts on the environment. For example, reductions in government spending to balance the budget often lead to a reduction in funding for environmental protection measures.

Thus, the implementation of macroeconomic measures can theoretically have a positive environmental effect (or be environmentally neutral). What is needed is an environmentally consistent macroeconomic coordinated policy, in which "Double Gains" are economic and ecological. Unfortunately, this is not always the case in practice, and the environmental and economic measures are produced more by coercion than basic economic measures. One of the goals of environmental economics is to examine the relationship between macroeconomic policies and environmental impacts, to undertake general economic measures, and to determine which ones produce economic effects and environmental benefits. The design of economic programs must take into account their possible environmental impacts and a set of appropriate programs of preventive and compensatory environmental measures.

5.2. Types of Economic Mechanisms of Natural Management

The formation of an effective economic mechanism of nature use is a priority.

We will consider this mechanism in a unified system, rather than at a macroeconomic level. Below, we highlight the perspective directions in formation of the nature management mechanism.

Within the framework of this approach, we can distinguish two types:

1. Inter-dependent nature of economic mechanisms and tools, sectoral and branch coverage;
2. Mechanisms and tools operate at a macro-level in the whole economy, sectors and branches.

Specific mechanisms and tools are related to environmental protection and exploitation of natural resources.

Presently, it is possible to develop an effective concept of the economic mechanism of nature management based on the following principles:

- By developing an effective concept of rationalization of nature management and environmental and economic mechanisms in environmental management branches. Only the concept of branches, complexes and the whole economy can be developed and implemented in complexes;
- The economic mechanism must be an organic part of the global economy, it cannot be local and limited to complexes and industries using natural resources. This mechanism must be coordinated with other economic mechanisms. Thus, the economic mechanism of nature management must become a part of a single mechanism, the vertical of natural products of individual enterprises with regulating functioning and be oriented on the final outcome;

- The economic mechanism in branches and complexes of nature management must be formed on industry-wide, industry-wide and region-wide principles. For example, the nature of the development of the agro-industrial complex and thermal energy complex are environmental problems in an alternative solution. In this case, effective economic mechanisms of nature management can be created only with an integrated approach.

For the development of the economic mechanism of nature management, the development of these sectors and the entire economy is observed in different sectors and complexes. The answer to the question implies that it is necessary to develop the concept of economic mechanism of nature use. This mechanism cannot form on its own, separately from the ongoing core processes.

Great importance is attached to environmental goals in industries and complexes. They can be ecologically balanced in terms of adaptation and natural environmental destabilizers. A simple example is the choice between extensive or intensive mode of development. In the first case, the use of nature under the economic mechanism is slightly restrictive and includes the trajectory of development of a much broader economic framework.

It is possible to distinguish three types of economic mechanisms of nature management:

Soft "catch-up" mechanisms are liberal in environmental terms. It puts the most general restrictive ecological frames for economic development of sectors and branches, practically not inhibiting it. This type of economic mechanism is mainly aimed at eliminating negative ecological consequences, rather than at the causes of ecological deformations, with little influence on the pace and scale of development. This type of mechanism for the use of natural resources is typical of the technogenic type of economic development.

The basis of functioning of the *mechanisms of nature management stimulating the development of environmentally balanced and friendly industries and activities* is market tools. It promotes an increase in production on the basis of new technologies, makes it possible to improve the use and protection of natural resources. An example of such a mechanism could be the creation of a favorable economic environment for the development of biological agriculture. In theoretical terms, this type is characteristic of weak sustainability.

Rigid, "suppressive" mechanism uses administrative and market tools and through a strict tax, credit, and punitive policy, practically suppresses, pressurizes the development of certain industries and complexes in the expansion of their natural base, in general contributing to the economic use of natural resources. This type of mechanism is typical of strong sustainability.

In reality, these types of environmental management mechanisms do not exist in a pure state. Rather, they must be combined. Much depends on specific technologies, industries, and activities. For example, in the near future, from the perspective of ecologization of economic development, a combination of incentive and hard mechanisms is advisable. For the agrarian sector, this will be the already mentioned stimulation of biological agriculture in combination with the economic tools inherent in the rigid mechanism of nature management and aimed at "suppressing" the technogenic type of agriculture.

To choose, let us consider the problem of forming an economic mechanism for the development of industries and complexes on the example of the heat and power complex of nature management. At present, it is fundamentally important to develop further ways for it. It is possible to distinguish two concepts of development of heat power engineering for the whole economy – increase in energy production or energy saving. The economic mechanism of use of natural resources in this complex must be chosen carefully. In this regard, transition to energy supply and fundamental structural transformation of the economy require its own mechanism of implementation and, consequently, the mechanism of natural resources use. This can be the development of organic legislation on tax and credit issues, the creation of favorable conditions for the development of energy production, heavy fines for environmental pollution and violations of the norms of the use of deposits.

With extensive orientation, the growth of the economic mechanism of the heat and power complex is necessary taking into account the low land prices. A low price is acceptable to the investor in the use of natural resources, e.g., preferential conditions for the construction of new power plants (clear examples of Namakhvani and Khudoni HPPs).

It should be noted that the situation is similar in other sectors. In the agro-industrial complex, the level of agricultural production is also critical, if we assume that this production is sufficient, and the shortage of production is due to the quality of infrastructure and processing industry. This concept of the economic mechanism of production of natural resources will take the following format: limiting the use of new lands by setting high prices on them, with a large tax for the additional use of land, and a large fine for the unsustainable use of land. It is about stabilizing agriculture and reducing the natural base, increasing its protection. This ensures the establishment of a favorable market climate for the development of infrastructure facilities and processing industries.

If the postulate underlies the concept of agro-industrial development, then there is a shortage of agricultural products. Therefore, the economic mechanism of natural resources use should be soft enough and not contradict the introduction of new land and water resources into agriculture, as well as additional use of chemicals in production. Agrarian policy should be aimed at sustainable scenario of agro-industrial complex development, economic mechanism in the production of natural resources – stabilization and reduced production of wooden items.

Regional peculiarities of formation of economic mechanism of nature management are important. So, fundamental questions of development of economic mechanism of nature use are focusing on rationalization, nature use and environment protection; application of the scale effect to economy of natural resources; or focusing on stabilization and reduction of scale at the expense of the nature use. This dilemma may not be formulated in such an obvious way and may be the result of a choice in the environmental context of economic or social goals. Given the above, it is impossible to create a logical economic mechanism for the nature use with a highly logical second principle, which in the first stage acts along the vertical of natural products. The regulated processes of the future processing of natural substances and the production of finished products are separated from the mechanism. A single logical formation of the economic mechanism throughout the vertical of natural products, which will link the primary products derived from these resources with the final products or services, is necessary.

In this case, the mechanism of nature resources management must become part of the overall mechanism. The regulated functioning of individual enterprises along the natural production vertical must be oriented to the end result. The formative economic mechanism of nature management in the thermal power complex can currently be characterized as a soft mechanism. However, given the reality, the development of the agro-industrial complex allows this mechanism to become much more rigid and suppressive.

By changing the export policy, it is possible to significantly reduce the environmental burden in the regions extracting energy resources. Reducing the ecological burden and increasing the economic benefit more effectively eliminates production losses than increasing production, which would increase all costs and cause severe eco-deformation.

It is necessary to reconsider significant changes in the general economic mechanism, both in and between individual complexes, mostly through market instruments, state regulation and establishment of certain stabilization in the thermal energy complex, while stimulating the infrastructure of the agricultural sector and the development of processing industries, which gives the opportunity to sharply reduce production losses. With such changes in the structure of the economy, it is possible to reduce the volume of exports of heat and energy resources. In the heat and energy complex of nature management, the economic mechanism can become more rigid with regard to ecology. A rigid mechanism in the agro-industrial complex of nature management focuses on the reduction of land and water resource use. From the foregoing, it is clear that the development of infrastructure and processing plants gives us, on the one hand, a large internal economic and environmental effect in the agro-industrial complex, and on the other hand, a significantly positive external effect.

In such conditions, less effective attempts to create strictly regional programs – redistribution of financial and material resources to individual territories – are made to overcome the ecological crisis. Overcoming the ecological crisis requires changes in the development of individual complexes and industries, coordinated environmental and economic programs aimed at environmental stabilization and sustainable development, as well as combined economic mechanisms linked to each other with a common mechanism of nature management. The whole natural-production vertical, its agreement on the final result of mechanisms and orientation of natural resource use can be established on the natural-production vertical of the tax system, on the rigid mechanism of natural resource use. The primary stages contained in the natural-productive vertical are located on the time axis.

The amounts of taxes are determined at the first stage according to the natural-productive vertical, which depends on the use of natural resources. At the next stage, these tax amounts are reduced owing to the increase in products obtained from reprocessing the natural resources. This stimulates the development of types of work in non-natural productions, allows the rational and economical use of resources, and increases the quality of their processing what results in the reduced burden on nature.

For example, such a rigid mechanism of nature management can develop the agro-industrial and forestry complexes to a certain level. The nature-production vertical combines land resources with the end agricultural product what causes the reduction of lands in the agrarian sector. By themselves, preferential taxes, infrastructure and processing subsidies reduce the loss of agricultural production. Thus, an increased use of land resources in agriculture is mirrored in the final output of agricultural production.

5.3. Trends in Formation of the Economic Mechanism of Nature Management

Let us consider special mechanisms and means directly related to environmental protection and the use of natural resources, namely economic mechanisms of environmental management. For greater efficiency, economic tools must be used in the areas of economy, where their use will be less costly compared to direct regulation employed to solve the same environmental problems.

The following elements can be distinguished as the forming economic mechanism of natural resource use shifts to the market mechanism:

- Tax on the use of natural resources;
- Economic incentives for environmental protection activities;
- Pollution tax;
- Establishment of a natural resource market;
- Improvement of pricing by considering the environmental factor, especially for products using natural resources;
- Environmental funds;
- Environmental programs;
- Selling a pollution right;
- Collateral-refund principle;
- Environmental insurance.

The introduction of a tax on the use of natural resources should facilitate more adequate consideration of the environmental factor for the rational use of natural resources. In a certain respect, a tax on natural resources is similar to the environmental tax. The following taxes can be identified among the taxes on natural resources:

- The tax on the right to use natural resources, and
- The tax on the protection and restoration of natural resources.

The natural resource tax focuses on the owner of that natural resource, regardless of whether it is the state or an individual. It is associated with a full rent exemption. The natural resources tax in Georgia was introduced in 1999 after the adoption of the laws "Land Tax", "Natural Minerals Tax", and others. Taxes for protection and restoration of natural resources compensate for the natural resources used for production. Special importance in the system of natural resources tax is given to fines, various types of sanctions for irrational use of natural resources and environmental pollution. A special importance in the system of taxes on natural resources is given to fines, various types of sanctions for irrational use of natural resources and pollution of the environment. In case of land depletion, their irrational use (unauthorized accumulation of waste, pollution with heavy metals and radioactive elements, exhaustive soil treatment, etc.), or in case of exceeding the standards of air and water pollution, strict sanctions that provide for economic and legal responsibility should be in place. In particular, the amount of the fine must be such as to have a significant impact on the activities of the entrepreneur.

In some cases, the tax on the use of natural resources defines the types of measures and systems of economic incentives for nature protection to reduce the level of environmental pollution.

This system should contribute to the formation of "eco-balanced" behavior of producer and consumer, and for this purpose, the supply and demand mechanism should be used.

The system of economic incentives may cover the following areas: taxation, subsidies, preferential loans for environmental protection activities, accelerated depreciation of environmental funds, etc.

Most of these directions have already shown their environmental effectiveness in many countries around the world. Taxes are considered a particularly widely used and effective tool. Environmental (often called "green") taxes are designed to solve at least two problems:

1. To make the product price more adequate to the expenses, including natural resources;
2. To help compensate for environmental damage by the polluter himself, rather than the entire society (to promote the "polluter pays" principle).

"Green taxes can play a stimulating role for the development of environmentally balanced industries and activities, as well as a "suppressive" role for nature-intensive activities. In this case, the state provides only an initial impetus, influencing prices through taxes, and everything else should be done by market mechanisms – to influence the behavior of producers and consumers, the demand and supply of products depending on the degree of their environmental friendliness, etc.

In general, tax incentives for producers should be established taking into account the degree of implementation of environmental protection measures, and environmental friendliness of the given type of activity. When carrying out effective environmental protection activities, it is advisable to reduce taxable profit. An example could be the reduction of taxable profit by the amount that the enterprise has reinvested for environmental purposes.

In some cases, taxes may not be levied at all. For example, environmental funds are exempt from taxation. Such a policy is also advisable for corporate income received from the disposal of various kinds of secondary resources and waste, for voluntary contributions from organizations and the public, as well as Russian and foreign grants for environmental purposes, etc.

Four aspects can be distinguished in the ecologically-oriented tax system: sectoral, technological, regional and product.

From the point of view of the economy's transition to a sustainable type of development, its ecologization and structural reorganization, the tax system should provide for higher taxes on nature-exploiting industries and sectors located at the beginning of the natural-product vertical, which will reduce the efficiency of investment in their development. In this case, taxes can play a role in suppressing nature-intensive activities or switch these activities to ecologically balanced ones.

In turn, the processing, service, and infrastructure industries, which are closer to the end of the natural-product vertical, should be subject to lower taxes that stimulate their development. Reduced taxes shall be used for rational use of natural resources and low-waste technologies, while technogenic enterprises shall be subject to higher taxes.

The regional aspect of taxation is also essential. In regions with a tense ecological situation, the taxation system should be "milder" compared to environmentally favorable areas for all activities associated with the rehabilitation of the territory or increased costs due to additional environmental costs.

Tax exemptions should be granted to public and private enterprises and organizations that produce environmental and ecological equipment, materials, and environmental services (construction and reconstruction of environmental facilities, etc.). Higher taxes should be used when taxing environmentally dangerous products – ozone-depleting substances, lead gasoline, pesticides, energy-intensive machinery, etc.

Much attention is paid to the introduction of "green" taxes in the United States. In 1989, in order to reduce the production of ozone-depleting CFCs, a sales tax on them was introduced. In order to give the industry time to shift to the production replacing commonly used CFCs, they the tax progressing in time was introduced: first, the tax for one kg of Freon was 3.02 USD; in 1995, it was 6.83 USD, and 10.8 USD in. As statistics show, the introduction of even a limited number of "green" taxes would generate an additional $100 billion annually in federal revenues.

The most realistic in the near future is the extensive introduction of a carbon tax – a tax on carbon emissions from the burning of fossil fuels by many world countries. The threat of global warming, international agreements signed on the obligations of states to reduce carbon emissions make the introduction of this tax necessary. It is already in force in Finland and the Netherlands. Even at the minimum rates of the carbon tax for atmospheric emissions in the amount of $10 per one ton in the developed countries it will be possible to receive an additional $25 billion a year. A presumable carbon dioxide tax in the US will be 100 USD per ton what generate an additional $140 billion USD annually in the budget. The tax should be considerably differentiated depending on the source of carbon emission into the atmosphere. Thus, when taxing different types of fuel and energy resources, the highest tax should be imposed on coal, the combustion of which is one of the main sources of carbon emissions. Under these conditions, the tax on natural gas should be substantially lower. In the long term, the widespread introduction of a carbon tax in the world will reduce the extraction of primary energy resources, encourage greater use of alternative energy sources, plant carbon-binding forests, etc.

Speaking in general about the improvement of the entire tax system, we can point out the direction of a significant increase in the natural-resource share of taxes. Modern tax systems in the world are focused primarily on levying taxes on the population, on profits, on added value, etc. Payments for the use of natural resources constitute, at best, only few percent of the revenue part of the budget. While maintaining the total amount of taxes, it is advisable to drastically change the proportions in favor of increasing the share of taxes associated with the use of natural resources, primarily payments for the right to use natural resources and "green" taxes. This share should increase to reach 30-50% of the total state budget revenues. This will make it possible to more adequately account for the impact on the environment and the degradation of natural resources and will create an incentive to reduce the nature-intensity of the economy.

In Georgia, this will also give an opportunity to sharply increase the withdrawal of enormous natural rent, which belongs to the whole society, and is now largely monopolized by nature-exploiting sectors, primarily the fuel and energy complex. Special improvement in required by the system of state allocations in economy. These monetary revenues shall be mainly used for stimulation of eco-balanced activities in the national economy.

The system of state subsidies for the economy needs significant improvement. These monetary subsidies should be granted primarily to stimulate ecologically balanced activity in the national economy. At present, subsidies play rather the opposite, anti-environmental role. This is especially evident in the two largest economic complexes – the fuel and energy complex and the agro-industrial complex. Until very recently, state subsidies actually contributed to the destruction of the natural environment by stimulating the development of new fields, the use of energy-intensive technologies in the economy and utilities, the use of pesticides, mineral fertilizers, heavy agricultural machinery, global and irrational measures for irrigation and land drainage, etc.

For example, the purchase of chemical products for agriculture costs about half as much as the actual cost of their production. Tractors, combines, and reclamation equipment manufactured by agricultural machinery and engineering plants would be much cheaper for agricultural facilities. Land reclamation activities were almost entirely paid for by the state, which deprived agricultural producers of the opportunity to determine the real costs and influence the quality of work.

Accelerated depreciation of fixed assets is a well-established measure in the world to stimulate priority activities and scientific and technological progress.

The enterprise, by overstating depreciation deductions, thereby reduces the amount of profit subject to taxation, resulting in an increase in its net profit.

Charges for environmental pollution are an important element of the economic mechanism of nature management. However, it compensates only a minor part of losses. Environmental pollution tax is deemed a method of punishment of the entrepreneurs who pollute environment. Thus, the the "polluter pays" principle is realized.

In Georgia, the environmental pollution tax was introduced in 1999.

Depending on the degree of impact on the environment, two types of payment standards are established: for maximum permissible emissions (discharges, waste disposal) of pollutants into the environment (within the established standards) and for exceeding these rates. In the latter case, payments increase several times. The essential point is also the mechanism of formation of payment sources. Payments within the limits of standards of pollution can be included in the cost of production and thus paid by the consumer. Supernormative payments are generated at the expense of the profit of enterprises, which reduces their profitability.

Such a system of payments in case of sufficiently high standards, stimulates a polluter to minimize the pollution. Modern standards are quite low, but their very existence plays an important role in the birth of a new situation in which the economy needs to adapt to environmental constraints and change the behavior of producers. Another incentive is the possibility of accounting payments in the amount and thereby reducing them at the expense of the costs made by the enterprise for environmental protection purposes (construction of various types of treatment facilities, filters, land protection measures, etc.).

Establishing a market of natural resources is expedient in case of their scarcity and the possibility of receiving significant funds from their sale. This is especially topical in the context of enormous natural wealth and the shortage of funds for its rational use and protection.

A civilized market for resources could allow the active mobilization of foreign capital in natural resource industries. The establishment of natural resource exchanges, and the holding of auctions, where local and foreign entrepreneurs could buy natural resources on a competitive basis, the right to develop or lease them, with strict environmental control and comprehensive environmental expertise, would significantly increase state and regional revenues from natural resource use.

The market of natural resources (primarily land) should provide for the creation of a mortgage system, which will allow owners of resources to mortgage them in order to obtain investment in the development of production.

The problem of improving pricing in the economy and, above all, in the nature-exploiting industries is important for improving the use of natural resources. Two aspects of this problem can be singled out:

First, many of the problems of using the achievements of scientific and technological progress and the introduction of low-waste technologies run up against the inefficiency of resource conservation at low prices for natural resources. It turns out to be much more profitable to pursue a *resource-depleting policy* and compensate for the backwardness of technology by overconsumption of resources. In such circumstances, a reasonable increase in the price of natural resources and a fuller consideration of the environmental factor in the price of the products of nature-exploiting industries would encourage producers in the economy to switch to a resource-saving regime.

Secondly, the price should more fully take into account the level of ecology of products. Products that are environmentally friendly should have a lower price and be more preferable to the consumer than products whose production is associated with a negative impact on the environment, or which themselves pose a risk to human health and nature in the process of consumption or in the form of waste. Again, it is necessary to use the mechanism of taxes on environmentally hazardous products, markups, subsidies and benefits for producers and consumers of clean products. For example, in agriculture, it should be more profitable for producers to use biological plant protection agents compared to pesticides, and organic fertilizers compared to mineral fertilizers.

Extrabudgetary environmental funds play an important role in financing nature conservation measures. The main goal of forming such funds is to create a centralized source of funding for environmental needs, independent of the state budget. These funds were created as a supporting financial structure to supplement state expenditures on environmental purposes.

Some of the main tasks of environmental funds are:

- Financing and crediting various programs and scientific and technical projects aimed at improving the quality of the environment and ensuring the environmental safety of the population;
- Mobilizing financial resources for environmental activities and programs;
- Providing economic incentives for rational nature management and introducing environmentally friendly technologies;
- Facilitating the development of environmental training and education.

The sources of formation of environmental funds are mainly payments by enterprises for emissions, discharges of pollutants and waste disposal; fines for accidental pollution; funds for compensation of environmental damage in case of violation of environmental legislation by enterprises; voluntary contributions. As practice shows, the largest contribution to the funds is made by payments for environmental pollution (80-85%).

The formation of environmental programs is of great importance for the realization of the most important environmental goals of society. Depending on the goal, they can be implemented at the international, country, or regional level. The program is a coordinated set of measures coordinated by resources, actors and timing, aimed at effectively solving environmental problems. Examples include the grandiose environmental programs in the United States for the revival of the Great Lakes, Japanese environmental programs, etc.

The state plays a significant role in the implementation of programs, as the need for rapid concentration of significant resources, the complexity of the problem and the uncertainty of economic efficiency make it advisable to use direct regulation with the market tools playing a supporting role. Targeted environmental programs are needed to solve the following problems:

- Fulfillment of international obligations (protection of the ozone layer, greenhouse gases, conservation of biodiversity);
- Protection and rational use of a particular type of natural resource;
- Protection of particularly valuable natural objects (Lake Baikal, river systems, sea basins);
- Rehabilitation of ecological disaster areas (Chernobyl zone); and
- Targeted environmental scientific and technical programs.

The development of market mechanisms for the sale of pollution rights is very promising. This market is now actively being formed in the United States. One of the most important principles of such a market is the right to sell various kinds of emissions and discharges. A simplified pattern of such trading is as follows. Within a limited territory, a limit is imposed on a certain amount of emissions (discharges) of pollutants. This limit amount of pollution cannot be exceeded for a new construction. This system of pollution regulation is eloquently called "bubble principal".

In these circumstances, a newly built or reconstructed enterprise wishing to expand its operations finds itself under strict environmental constraints regarding increased pollution in the region. Therefore, the enterprise is facing a choice: to create a reliable treatment system in-house or to buy the right to additional pollution from another enterprise. The choice mainly depends on the value of treatment costs at the enterprise and other production facilities in this region. If the cost of limiting one's own pollution is greater than that of the neighboring enterprise, it is profitable to pay the neighbor to improve its treatment system and reduce its pollution load. As a result, the total amount of pollution does not increase, and the amount of environmental costs is minimized.

A mechanism for the sale of pollution rights is also possible to create at the global level. For example, the introduction of a "carbon" tax creates a lot of problems for industry in developed countries, which has already practically exhausted "cheap" ways of reducing emissions. In this regard, the proposal of German parliamentarians to allow Russia to take over part of Germany's carbon sequestration obligations is illustrative. This is achieved by planting forests in Russia at the expense of Germany. The cost of the entire program is 100 billion euros. The key point here is that afforestation in Russia will cost Germany 10 times less than attempts to solve the problem of carbon reduction through technical measures on the German territory. At first glance, this rather exotic project seems to have a solid economic basis and a cost-benefit assessment. According to calculations, to absorb one billion tons of "German" carbon dioxide, it is necessary to plant forests on an area of one million square kilometers, which is 6% of the area of Russia.

If strict pollution taxes are introduced, one can expect widespread use of such purchases of pollution rights between different countries around the world, which will be beneficial for global environmental protection and the fight against poverty, since such a mechanism will allow additional financial resources to flow from developed to developing countries, where the fight against pollution is much less capital-intensive.

Perhaps the oldest and most proven economic tool in environmental protection is a well-known "collateral-refund" system meaning that when we buy a product, we also pay an additional cost, which is then returned to us, e.g., returning empty bottles, or used electric batteries that is increasingly common in various countries. Despite its simplicity, this mechanism allows us to reduce the amount of waste entering the environment, including toxic waste.

The problem of eliminating environmental pollution as a result of accidents and disasters is increasingly pressing every year. Their enormous ecological and economic harm is evidenced by the statistics of numerous oil pipeline accidents alone. A possible economic mechanism to prevent or mitigate the consequences of accidents is environmental insurance – liability insurance of enterprises, which are sources of increased risk for losses caused by an accident, a technological failure or a natural disaster that leads to environmental pollution.

Establishing insurance companies allows solving a number of economic problems: to compensate the losses incurred by the insured enterprise and third parties as a result of environmental pollution; to economically stimulate the prevention of accidents by increasing the accident-prevention costs of the insurance company while reducing the costs of the insured himself; to increase the efficiency of the use of funds concentrated in the insurance funds, etc.

References

[1] *Achievements of Science Related to Corrosion and Technology of Protection against it.* Moscow: "Metallurgia", 1990.

[2] Bespamyatkov G.P., Krotov Y.A. *Maximum Permitted Concentrations of Chemical Substances in Environment.* "Khimia", 1985.

[3] Bondarev A.A., Ilyinskaya N.M. "Impact of Oxidation-Reduction Potential on the Effectiveness of Nitrification and Denitrification Processes." *Collection of Scientific Papers of VNII VODGEO. Methods of Raising the Effectiveness of Performance of Treatment Facilities of Sewage*, 1989: 66-69.

[4] Bondarev A.A., Sokolova A.A., Sokolova E.V., Ponomaryov A.V. "Denitrification in Reactors with Weighted Layer of Active Sludge during Wastewater Treatment." *Perfection of Methods of Biological and Physical-Mechanical Purification PSV VNII VODGEO*, 1990: 3-7.

[5] *Collection of Papers MISI.* 1975.

[6] Lukinih N.A. *Methods of Final Purification of Wastewaters.* Moscow: "Stroiizdat", 1978.

[7] "Study of Chemical and Biological Removal of Phosphor in Urban Treatment Plants." *Korrespond. Abwasser*, 1991: 163-169.

[8] Vladimirov V.C. *Physical Nature of Disintegration of Metals.* Moscow: "Metallurgia", 1984.

[9] "Influence of Additives on Removal of Phosphor from Wastewaters in Biological Reactor of Periodical Operation." *Water Science and Technology*, 1997: 75-80.

[10] Dobrovolskyi V.V. *Fundamentals of Biogeochemistry.* Moscow: "Vysshaia Shkola", 1998.

[11] Abramov A.V., Kulikov N.I. "Biological Biosorptional Final Purification of Wastewaters on Granular and Fiber Loadings." *Collection of Scientific Papers VNII VODGEO*, 1991: 4-29.

[12] Voronov Y.V., Salomeev V.P. *Examples of Calcuation of Biological Filters and Biofiltation Stations.* Moscow: "Kuibyshev MISI", 1983.

[13] *Microbiology of Polluted Waters.* "Meditsina", 1976.

[14] "*Multi-step Process for Biological Removal of Nitrogen and Phosphor from Wastewaters.*" n.d.

[15] SniP. "SniP 2.04.03-85 Sewage. *External Networks and Facilities.*" n.d.

[16] Moscow State Enterprise Mosvodkanal. "Development of Moscow Sewage." *Collection of Scientific Papers*, 2003.

[17] Esavkin E.V. "Purification of Wastewaters from Phosphates." *VNII VODGEO*, 1991.

[18] Nigusiti T. "Method of Purification with Periodical Aeration Using Iron Filler." *Kange Gidzyutsu*, 1986: 39-47.

[19] Eroshenko V.B. *Chemistry and Technology of Water Use of Magnetic-Gypsum Composition for Purification of Urban Wastewaters from Phosphates.* 1986.

[20] Gogina E.S. *Optimization of the Process of Removal of Nitrogen Compounds from Household Wastewaters.* Moscow, 2000.

[21] *Extraction of Phosphates from Wastewaters in Magnetic Chambers.* 1991.

[22] Kaneku M., Nambu T. "Toxicity of the Impact of Metals on Active Sludge. Impact of Ions of Various Metals on Bacteria." *Gesuido Kekai Sience*, 1983.

[23] "Experience of Use of Two-Step Sedimentation of Phosphor." *WLB: Wasser, Luft und Boden*, 1990 : 34-35.

[24] Phosphorelimination durch geregelte Fallung. Kommunalwirtschaft. "Removal of Phosphor by Regulation of the Process of Sedimentation." *Phosphorelimination durch geregelte Fallung. Kommunalwirtschaft*, 1990.

[25] "Separation of Phosphor Using Magnetic Separation." *Entsorg. Prax.*, 1991: 174-176.

[26] "*Method of Reduction of Phosphor Concentration during Purification of Urban Wastewaters.*" n.d.

[27] Sokolova E.V., Polezayeva T.V. "Biochemical Nitrification of Wastewaters in Sunk Biofiter." *Collection of Scientific Papers of VNII VODGEO*, 1991: 104-107.

[28] Yamori Y., Sudon R. "Modern Technologies of Treatment of Household and Industrial Wastewaters for the Purpose of Nitrogen and Phosphor Remova." *Kogai To Taisaku. Environ Pollution Control*, 1991: 823-831.

[29] Zaletova N.A. *Purification of Urban Wastewaters from Biogenic Substances.* (Nitrogen and Phosphor Compounds). Moscow, 1999.

[30] "*Removal of Nitrogen and Phosphor Compounds from Wastewaters without Use of Reagents*. Patent 134048 PNR." 1986.

[31] Mogens H., Harremoes P., Arvin E. *Wastewater treatment: Biological and Chemical Processes.* Verlag: Springer, 1995.

[32] Resolution of the Council of Ministers of Ukraine. "*Procedures of Protection of Surface Waters against Pollution with Wastewaters*." Bereznya, 1999.

[33] Hammer M. *Technology of treatment of Natural and Wastewaters.* Moscow: "Stroiizdat", 1979.

[34] Committee of Russian Federation on Fishing. *List of Maximum Permitted Concentrations and Approximately Safe Levels of the Impact of Harmful Substances For the Water of Fishery Reservoirs.* Moscow: "Medinor", 1995.

[35] State Committee of USSR for Nature Protection. "*Regulations of Protection of Surface Waters (Typical Provisions).*" 1991.

[36] Zaletova N.A. "Removal of Biogenic Substances from Urban Wastewaters." *Water Supply and Sanitary Equipment*, 1992: 16-17.

[37] All-Union Sanitary-Hygienic and Sanitary-Anti-epidemic Rules and Norms. *Sanitary Rules and Norms of Protection of Surface Waters from Pollution SanPiN 4630-88.* 1989.

[38] *"Method of Biological Purification from Nitrogen.* Application 63-22200 CO2F 3/30,3/34.11.05.88.N2-555." Japan, 1988.

[39] Ruzhitskaya O.A. *Optimization of the Process of Removal of Phosphates from Wastewater.* MGSU, 2002.

[40] Masakhiro I. "Removal of Nitrogen and Phosphor from Wastewaters by Anaerobic-Aerobic Biological Treatment." *Environmental Pollution Control*, 1991 : 877-882.

[41] Voronov Y.V., Salomeev V.P., Ivchatov A.L. *Reconstruction and Intensification of Operation of Sewage Facilities.* Moscow: "Stroiizdat", 1989.

[42] Voronov Y.V. *Drainage and Purification of Wastewaters.* Moscow: ASV, 2009.

[43] *Magnetic Removal of Phosphor. Water and Waste Treat.* 1992.

[44] "Use of Light Expandable Clay for Purification of Wastewaters from Phosphor Compounds." *Water Science and Technology*, 1997: 87-93.

[45] Environmental Protection against Pollution with Industrial Wastes. *"Removal of Biogenic Substances from Urban Wastewaters."* 1999.

[46] "Purification of Wastewaters from Ammonia Nitrogen Using Zeolites." *Express Information. Series: Water Supply and Sewage*, 1986.

[47] Hopkins L.N., Lant P.A., Newell R.B. "Using the Flexibility Index to compare Batch and continuous activated sludge process." *Proceedings of 2nd International simposium on Sequencing Batch Reactor Technology.* Narbonne, 2000. 57-66.

[48] Yakovlev S.V., Karyukhina T.A. *Biochemical Processes in Wastewater Purification.* Moscow: "Stroiizdat", 1980.

[49] *"Process for biological wastewater treatment.* Application 3833185 FRG MKI5 CO 2 F 3/30. N P3833185 9/30/88 – 4/12/90." 1990.

[50] Dombrovski T., Lamre D., Wiesmann U. "Biological nitrogen elimination from wastewater." *Bioengineering*, 1986: 22-27.

[51] Bohnke B. "Eliminate nutrients in one or two stages. The cleaning performance of most sewage treatment plants needs to be improved." *Energie*, 1989: 48-52.

[52] Nigel H. "Nutrient removal from wastewaters." *Water and Waste treatment*, 1992 : 16-17.

[53] Brum H.S., Hoizey D. "Elimination of nitrogen compounds contained in water effluents." *Misan Ses*, 1991: 69-70.

[54] Wutscher L. "Test results for extended nutrient elimination in the two-stage system." *Korrespondenz Abwasser*, 1992: 57-63.

[55] Yoshishige K. "Research of Extraction of Phosphor from Wastewaters Using Addition of Dolomite." *Natural Institute Resource and Environment*, 1992: 1-87.

[56] Metcalf and Eddy Incorporation. *Wastewater engineering. Treatment, Disposal and Reuse.* McGraw-Hill, 1991.

[57] Grau P., Doh M., Chudova J. *Kinetics of Chemical Technology.* Prague: "Prague Institute of Chemical Technology", 1974.

[58] Bigot B. "A new Generation of Biological Aerated Filters." *Journal CIWEM*, 1999: 363-368.

[59] Brenner A., Argaman Ye. "Effect of feed composition, aerobic volume fraction and recycle rate on nitrogen removal in the single-sludge system." *War. Res.*, 1990 : 8.

[60] Yuger Zh., Sazhyus L. *Kinetic Methods of Study of Chemical Processes.* "Khimia", 1972.

[61] Wilderer P.A., Irvine R.L., Goronsky M.C. "*Sequencing Batch Reactor Technology, Scientific and Technical Report N.10.*" 2001.

[62] Dockhorn. *COD elimination depending on the type of activated sludge reactor.* Braunschweig, 1999.

[63] German Water Association. *Design of single-stage activated sludge systems.* Hennef, 2000.

[64] German Water Association. *Activation plants with accumulation operation.* Hennef, 1997.

[65] Podedworna J., Zubrowska-Sudot M. *Experiences in nitrogen and phosphorus elimination in a sequencing batch reactor with a fluidized bed.* 2003.

[66] Röhricht M., Keller J. *Granulated activated sludge – an alternative to conventional activated sludge?* 2007.

[67] Weber W.G., DiGiano F.A. *Process dynamics and environmental system.* New York, 1995.

[68] Benefild L.D. *Biological Process design for Wastewater treatment.* Englewood Cliffs: "Prentice Hall Inc", 1980.

[69] Strous M. "Effects of Aerobic and Microaerobic Conditions on Anaerobic Ammonium-Oxidizing (ANAMMOX) Sludge." *Applied and environmental microbiology*, 1997: 2446-2448.

[70] Strous M. "Key Philosophy of Ananerobic Ammonium Oxidation." *Applied and environmental microbiology*, 1999: 3248-3250.

[71] Pynaert K., Barth F.S., Wyffels S., Beheydt D., Siciliano S.D., Verstraete W. "Characterization of an Autotrophic Nitrogen-Removing Biofilm from a Highly Loaded Lab-Scale Rotating Biological Contactor." *Applied and environmental microbiology*, 2003: 3626–3635.

[72] Oldham W.K., Rabinowtz B. "Development of biological nutrient removal technology in western Canada." *Civil Engineering*, 2001: 92-101.

[73] Strous M. "Improved nitrogen removal by application of new nitrogen-cycle bacteria." *Re-Views in Environmental Science and Bio/Technology*, 2002: 51–63.

[74] Kazuhiro N., Atsuhiro H. "Effective Removal of Nitrogenn and Phosphor I the System of High-quality Biological Treatment of Wastewaters." *Water and Liquid Wastes Treat*, 1989: 69-73.

[75] Yamamoto Ya., Kavanisi S. *Removal of Nitrogen and Phosphor from Wastewaters Using Iron Filler.* "Kanke Godzyutsu", 1988.

[76] Chemical Protection Environment. "*Chemical Sedimentation of Phosphates by Little Doses of Lime.*" 1987.

Index

E

F

H

I

L

M

S

T

W

Author's Contact Information

David Gurgenidze
Professor, Rector
Georgian Technical University
Tbilisi, Georgia
Email: d_gurgenidze@gtu.ge